Decoding Digital Assets

"A CBDC reference book for decision makers who want to understand technological trade-offs and their socio-economic implications."

—Prof. Christian Grothoff, *Bern University of Applied Sciences*

"Decoding Digital Assets takes you on a deep dive into the world of the digital money and asset (r-)evolution. This book doesn't just explore; it unpacks the complexities with a keen eye for detail. Offering a comprehensive high-level overview, the book seamlessly navigates the intricate landscape of digital assets while delving deep into crucial discussions. Always with a balanced and open-minded approach, the author addresses pivotal benefits as well as challenges surrounding digital money, with a particular emphasis on the paramount importance of privacy. This book uniquely blends theoretical insights with practical applications, weaving together the realms of technology, cryptography, economics, business and political considerations. A must-read for those intrigued by the digital monetary landscape, Decoding Digital Assets serves as both a guide for the curious and a practical handbook for individuals in the private and public sectors. Whether you're seeking a broad understanding of the evolving digital currency ecosystem or practical insights for implementation, this book offers a compelling and insightful journey into the heart of the financial (r-)evolution."

—Dr. Jonas Gross, *Chairman Digital Euro Association*

"Leon provides a deep insight into the future of money, focusing more on stablecoins and CBDCs, providing clarity and understanding in a new area that needs many more books like this one. The reader will learn, among many other things, about how CBDCs are designed from a technical perspective, their risks and benefits, the main ongoing projects... This is a comprehensive study that I recommend to anyone willing to get introduced to the fascinating world of CBDCs."

—Dr. Oriol Caudevilla, *FinTech Expert, Board Director at the Global Impact FinTech Forum (GIFT)*

"Decoding Digital Assets is an essential read that will revolutionize your understanding of the topic. It's the most comprehensive book I've encountered, presented in an unbiased and accessible manner. The author's technical expertise shines through, accompanied by a wealth of graphs and pictures to keep you engaged and informed about the latest advancements."

—Richard Turrin, *bestselling author of Cashless and Innovation Lab Excellence, and Consultant & Speaker*

"Leon Schumacher has produced a marvellous and very comprehensive overview of the current debate on the future of money. It is a must read for anyone looking for a place to start as well as those in need of a go-to reference. It clearly covers both economic and technological aspects and is a treasure trove of interesting facts and figures."

—Morten Bech, *Head of the Bank of International Settlements - Innovation Hub Switzerland*

"In Decoding Digital Assets, Leon Schumacher skillfully navigates the complex landscape of the digital financial revolution, offering readers a comprehensive understanding of key concepts like stablecoins, tokenized deposits, and central bank digital currencies (CBDCs). This book stands out for its clarity, making complex topics accessible to a wide audience. It is a must read for anyone seeking to grasp the future of finance."

—John Ho, *Head Legal & Financial Markets at Standard Chartered Bank*

"With Decoding Digital Assets, Leon Schumacher decrypts the new frontiers of Central Bank Digital Currencies (CBDCs). With a pragmatic and easy to understand approach, the book takes us from key foundation considerations around money through relevant concepts to practical use cases. A reference to whoever, from starter to advanced, wants to grasp (or revisit) CDBC in all its dimensions."

—Gilles Coccoli, *Executive Committee member at Edenred*

Leon V. Schumacher

Decoding Digital Assets

Distinguishing the Dream from the Dystopia in Stablecoins, Tokenized Deposits, and Central Bank Digital Currencies

palgrave
macmillan

Leon V. Schumacher
Erpeldange, Luxembourg

ISBN 978-3-031-54600-6 ISBN 978-3-031-54601-3 (eBook)
https://doi.org/10.1007/978-3-031-54601-3

Cover illustration: eStudioCalamar

This Palgrave Macmillan imprint is published by the registered company Springer Nature Switzerland AG
The registered company address is: Gewerbestrasse 11, 6330 Cham, Switzerland

Paper in this product is recyclable.

Preface

In an age where technology is interwoven into the very fabric of our daily lives, the landscape of currency and payments is undergoing a revolutionary transformation. New terms like Central Bank Digital Currencies (CBDCs) and payment tokens (the technology that allows for "digital" cash) have emerged at the forefront of this transformation and many people still ignore their meaning. However, as these novelties continue to evolve, there is a pressing need for clarity and understanding, and hence the reason for this book is to share the knowledge that I have assembled over the past years on these subjects.

My journey into the realm of CBDCs and payment tokens has been both immersive and insightful. After having spent a decade protecting company assets for large international enterprises, I have dedicated the next decade to protecting privacy. I hence have a clear bias for privacy protecting solutions, a strong aversion to mass surveillance and you will realize that when reading this book. Having actively contributed to the architecture and development of three CBDC solutions, I found myself delving into an ocean of information and white papers. In parallel, my thirst for knowledge led me to extensively explore publications from different sources. It was through this process that I recognized a concerning pattern; a myriad of knowledge gaps and misunderstandings marred the papers I encountered. Some of the analyses I came across lacked depth or understanding of specific topics, and too often, culminated in incomplete propositions or misguided conclusions.

This revelation acted as a catalyst, inspiring me to piece together the fragmented information into a comprehensive and coherent guide. My aspiration was to weave the complex themes and dimensions of CBDCs and payment tokens into an accessible and flowing narrative.

One of the core objectives of this book is to provide readers with practical examples that ground the often abstract theories into real-world contexts. These examples serve as the connective tissue between theory and practice, allowing for a more enriching and relatable understanding.

To ensure a structured and thorough coverage of the topic, I employed the methodology and framework I developed through my involvement in past CBDC projects. I rely upon the same methodology in my advisory work. This framework acted as a compass, guiding me through the multifaceted terrain of CBDCs and ensuring that all pertinent aspects were addressed comprehensively.

Whether you are a policy maker, a financial enthusiast, or someone with a curiosity for the future of money, this book is meant to serve as your gateway to understanding, supporting, or opposing the revolution that is upon us. At the end of the book, you will be able to assess proposed CBDC projects on their merits, decide for yourself if these tools are "a solution waiting for problem" or if they will benefit society as a whole. You will have a good knowledge of the characteristics necessary in a CBDC solution and understand the full scope of options available for each feature or characteristic, including their potential impact on our lives.

Embark on this journey with me and let us explore the potential and the intricacies of what may well be the future of money.

Erpeldange, Luxembourg — Leon V. Schumacher

Acknowledgments

To Berna, my guiding star and first reader, whose feedback is always honest, straight to the point, and who has gifted me endless evenings typing away, and to Athena and Kayleigh, who have patiently waited many evenings for 'just one more paragraph.' Your belief in me has been my strength. Here's our shared journey, bound and printed.

Additional thanks go to Prof. Christian Grothoff and Chantal Schumacher for their input and feedback, the European Union for their support (in part) under Project 101135475—TALER, the ECB, BIS, IMF which have contributed data, graphs, and tables that can all be accessed for free on their respective websites, as well as thanks to anyone else who has contributed to the final result of this printed book.

Views and opinions expressed are only those of the author and do not necessarily reflect those of the European Union, the BIS, or other organizations. Neither the European Union nor the granting authority can be held responsible for them.

Contents

About the Author

Leon V. Schumacher is a seasoned technology leader and entrepreneur with an impressive academic background. He holds a master's in electrical engineering with a specialization in communications technology from the Swiss Federal Institute of Technology (ETH) Zurich, a master's in management from HEC Paris, and a Post-MBA from the Kellogg School of Business at Northwestern. Schumacher is a veteran in the global corporate sector, having served as Group Chief Information Officer for prominent multinational corporations such as Novartis and ArcelorMittal. His entrepreneurial spirit is demonstrated by his successful launch of various startups in cybersecurity, privacy, payments, custody, and Central Bank Digital Currency (CBDC) spheres.

His profound expertise in the CBDC and digital payments domain is further manifested through his pivotal role as co-founder and chairman of Taler Systems. Under his guidance, the firm entered the market with a privacy-preserving CBDC with unique one-sided anonymity characteristics. Furthermore, as head of SICPA's CBDC activities and Joint Venture, he has devised a second pseudonymous solution for retail CBDC and one for wholesale CBDC.

Schumacher's wealth of practical experience, deep technical expertise, and strong business acumen position him as a credible and authoritative voice in the digital currency and payments industry. His insights draw from his experiences at the intersection of technology, finance, and business, offering a unique perspective on the transformational potential of CBDCs, stablecoins, and digital payments.

Abbreviations

2PC	2 Phase Commit architecture
AE	Advanced Economy
AFI	Authorized Financial Institutions
AML	Anti-Money Laundering
API	Application Programming Interface
BIS	Bank for International Settlements
BISIH	Bank for International Settlements—Innovation Hub
BoE	Bank of England
BoJ	Bank of Japan
BOJA	Bank of Jamaica
BVN	Bank Verification Number (Nigeria)
CBDC	Central Bank Digital Currency
CBN	Central Bank of Nigeria
CBOB	Central Bank of the Bahamas
CCPA	California Consumer Privacy Act
CFA	Communauté Financière Africaine (African Financial Community)
CFT	Combatting the Financing of Terrorism
CHAPS	Clearing House Automated Payment Systems (UK)
CLS	Continuous Linked Settlement for FX transactions
DAG	Directed Acyclic Graph (for a DLT)
dApps	Decentralized Applications
DB	Database
DCash	ECCB Central Bank Digital Currency
DCEP	Digital Currency Electronic Payment (China)
DDoS	Distributed Denial of Service Attack

DEX	Decentralized Crypto Exchanges
DLT	Distributed Ledger Technology
DPOS	Decentralized Proof of Stake consensus
DXCD	ECCB Central Bank Digital Currency
EBICS	Electronic Banking Internet Communication Standard
ECB	European Central Bank
ECCB	Eastern Caribbean Central Bank
ECCU	Eastern Caribbean Currency Union
ECDSA	Elliptic Curve Digital Signature Algorithm
e-CNY	Electronic Chinese Yuan (Chinese CBDC)
EDPB	European Data Protection Board
ELA	Emergency Liquidity Assistance
EMDE	Emerging Market and Developing Economy
EU	European Union
EULA	End User License Agreement
Eurosystem	Monetary Authority of the Euro Area
FATF	Financial Action Task Force
FDIC	Federal Deposit Insurance Company
FHE	Fully Homomorphic Encryption
FLOSS	Free/Libre Open-Source software
FSB	Financial Stability Board
FX	Foreign Exchange
G2B	Government to Business
G2P	Government to Person
GDP	Gross Domestic Product
GDPR	General Data Protection Regulation (EU)
HQLA	High-Quality Liquid Assets
HTTP	Hypertext Transfer Protocol
HTTPS	Hypertext Transfer Protocol Secure
IAAS	Infrastructure as a Service
ICSD	International Central Securities Depositories
ID	Identity
IETF	Internet Engineering Task Force
IMF	International Monetary Fund
JAM-DEX	Jamaican CBDC
KYB	Know-Your-Business
KYC	Know-Your-Customer
KYT	Know-Your-Transaction
LCR	Liquidity Coverage Ratio
LMU	Latin Monetary Union
LSM	Liquidity Saving Mechanism
MAGA	Make America Great Again (Trump slogan)
MAS	Monetary Authority of Singapore
MIT DCI	Massachusetts Institute of Technology's Digital Currency Initiative

MIT	Massachusetts Institute of Technology
MNO	Mobile Network Operator
MVP	Minimum Viable Product
NCB	National Commercial Bank (Jamaica)
NCB	National Central Banks (EU)
NFC	Nearfield Communication
NIST	National Institute of Standards and Technology (USA)
NYDFS	New York Department of Financial Services
OECD	Organization for Economic Cooperation and Development
OECS	Organization of Eastern Caribbean States
OTC	Over the Counter
P2B	Person to Business
P2G	Person to Government
P2P	Person to Person
PBOC	People's Bank of China
PCI-DSS	Payment Card Industry—Data Security Standard
PET	Privacy-Enhancing Technologies
PFS	Perfect Forward Secrecy
PHE	Partially Homomorphic Encryption
PII	Personal Identifiable Information
PIP	Payment Interface Provider
PKI	Public Key Infrastructure
POCA	Proceeds of Crime Act (Jamaica)
POH	Proof of History consensus
PoS	Point of Sale
POS	Proof of Stake Consensus
POW	Proof of Work Consensus
PSD2	Payment Services Directive 2 (EU)
PSP	Payment Service Provider
QR code	Quick Response Code
rCBDC	retail Central Bank Digital Currency
RSA	Rivest-Shamir-Adleman Public Key Encryption Scheme
RTGS	Real Time Gross Settlement
SaaS	Software as a Service
SCTInst	Single Euro Payments Area (SEPA) Instant Credit Transfer
SEPA	Single Euro Payments Area
SIM	Subscriber Identity Module
SSID	Self Sovereign Identity
TEE	Trusted Execution Environment
TLS	Transport Layer Security
TPS	Transactions Per Second
TTP	Trusted Third Party
UDHR	Universal Declaration of Human Rights
UEBL	Union économique Belgo-Luxembourgeoise (Belgian-Luxembourg Economic Union)

UN	United Nations
USP	Unique Sales Proposition
USSD	Unstructured Supplementary Service Data
UTXO	Unspent Transaction Output
wCBDC	wholesale Central Bank Digital Currency
WEF	World Economic Forum
ZKP	Zero-Knowledge Proof
ZKRP	Zero-Knowledge Range Proof
ZK-SNARK	Zero-Knowledge Succinct Non-Interactive Argument of Knowledge
ZK-STARK	Zero-Knowledge Scalable Transparent Argument of Knowledge

List of Figures

List of Tables

1 Introduction

1.1 Background

Today we live in times of recurring financial crisis and of growing financial disparity between people. Our global economy has endured two catastrophic financial crises in the span of less than twenty years. Both sent shockwaves through the global financial systems. The initial meltdown of 2008, triggered by the collapses of Bear Stearns and Lehman Brothers, was a stark reminder of the fragility of some of our established financial institutions. Fast forward to 2023, when we witnessed an eerie replay of the earlier crisis, with the collapses of Silicon Valley Bank (SVB), Signature Bank and First Republic Bank in the United States. The spill-over to Europe forced a Swiss government intervention to rescue the local Credit Suisse Bank, a prominent global financial institution in its jurisdiction.

SVB's downfall was a classic case of a bank run, a scenario where panic-driven depositors all attempt to withdraw their deposits simultaneously due to a perceived insolvency risk of the bank. Despite having safety nets in place such as the federal deposit insurance from the FDIC and liquidity coverage ratios (LCR) aimed at ensuring banks hold enough high-quality liquid assets to survive cash outflows for 30 days, these banks were unable to withstand the onslaught. These events exposed the fragility of the safeguarding measures for financial institutions worldwide and ultimately lead to the closures of all these banks by the regulators.

Apart from these high-profile financial shocks, perennial challenges like money laundering, black market activities, and tax evasion are increasing, draining global economies of trillions of dollars each year. Estimates suggest

L. V. Schumacher, *Decoding Digital Assets*, https://doi.org/10.1007/978-3-031-54601-3_1

between US$800 billion and US$2 trillion are laundered annually, with the US accounting for at least $300 billion. Moreover, the Tax Justice Network's 2021 report [74] indicates that international tax abuse leads to a global loss of over $483 billion a year. All these actions take a significant toll on our economies and indirectly on our lives.

Amid these difficulties, other trends are causing concerns as well. Physical cash, as the most inclusive and prevalent global means of payment for the last centuries, is experiencing a noticeable decline in use. This trend is spurred on by convenient digital alternatives and a concerted drive to thwart criminal undertakings. Countries like Sweden exemplify the ongoing shift toward a cashless society. However, this transition bears its own set of problems, particularly for segments of society like the poor and elderly who heavily rely on cash transactions.

In comparison, China has witnessed a surge in financial inclusion, especially within their rural populace. This progress is due to innovative private payment initiatives like AliPay, WeChat Pay, and public microfinance programs in rural areas. Indeed, private payment solutions are always launched with an expectation of positive financial returns by its owners and investors.

Hence, the downside of private payment solutions often is the high fees they come with. According to McKinsey's Global Payments reports [130, 207], global payment fees grew by 11% from 2020 to 2021 to reach US$2.1 trillion and these fees are projected to hit US$3.3 trillion by 2026. These amounts represent nearly 40% of global banking revenues (Graph 1.1).

1.2 Purpose of the Book

Against this backdrop of financial crises, persistent economic challenges, and the evolving paradigm of cash usage, the notion of digital currencies has steadily gained traction since the dawn of personal computers in the 1980s. The launch of Bitcoin in 2008 marked a pivotal moment in this journey, catalyzing a new era of research and development in the sphere of digital currencies.

In response to the surge of cryptocurrencies like Bitcoin, and further developments like Facebook's Libra, central banks worldwide began contemplating the issuance of their own digital currencies to safeguard their monetary sovereignty. The ensuing discourse around Central Bank Digital Currencies (CBDCs) has brought forth the potential for significant disruption in either direction within the financial landscape.

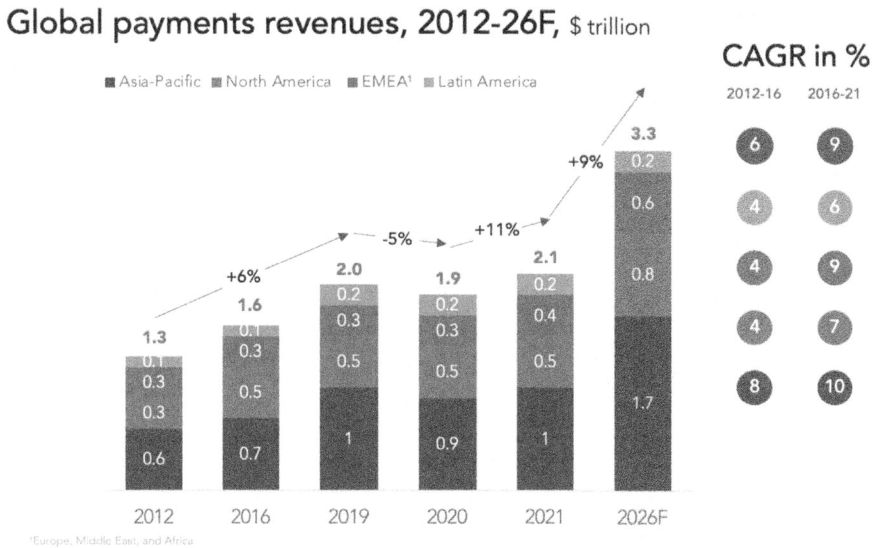

Graph 1.1 Global payment revenues (*Source* McKinsey's 2021/2022 Global Payments [207])

Numerous countries have embarked on CBDC projects, and this book aims to explore the concept of payment tokens and CBDCs. It is important to understand their relations to existing types of money and payments, their risks and benefits, and how they can address or mitigate some of the problems outlined earlier. Graph 1.2 splits the CBDC projects in 2 categories, one being wholesale (for banks) and one being retail (for people).

Many authors grapple with cryptography's complexities, the potential of emerging technologies, and nuanced notions like security, privacy, anonymity, and offline functionality, resulting too often in incomplete or misguided conclusions.

This book builds on the methodology I developed while creating 3 CBDC solutions and aims to pick up the narrative with the cryptocurrencies that started this whole movement in an attempt to fill these gaps. The goal of this book is to break down the complicated topics into easy and simple accessible underlying concepts, peeled out of the complexities surrounding them.

On our journey through the chapters of this book, we will explore first some basics in cryptography and IT architectures necessary for a good understanding. Then we will approach the concept of cryptocurrencies, leading us to payment tokens and CBDCs, their relation to existing forms of money and payments, their potential risks and benefits, and their capacity to address the problems we've outlined.

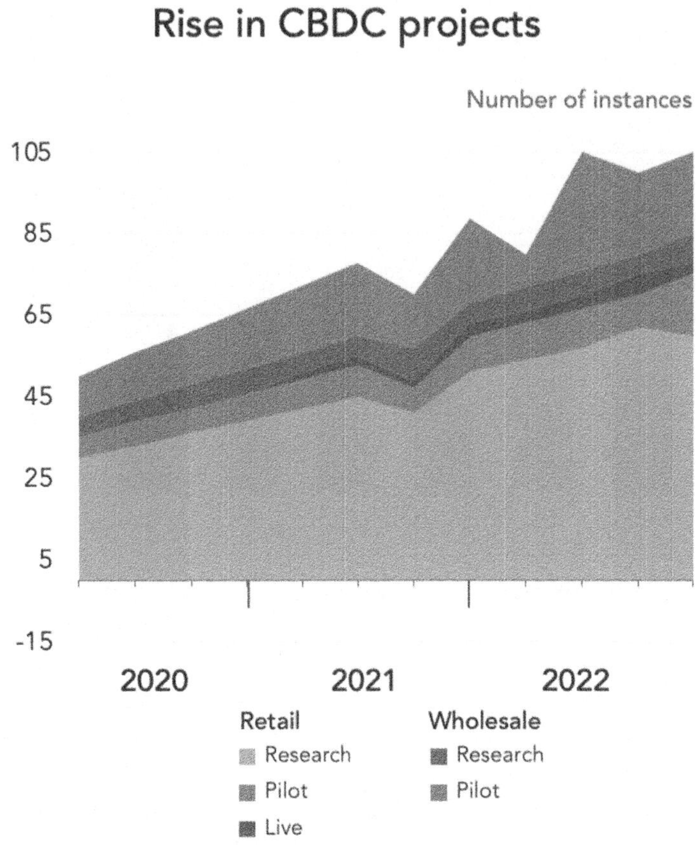

Graph 1.2 Global rise in CBDC projects (*Source* Data from BIS [203])

By demystifying these intricate subjects, by providing practical examples, and by grounding abstract theories in real-world contexts, this book seeks to deliver a more accurate, comprehensive, and nuanced insight into the exciting world of CBDCs. As we delve into the areas in which CBDCs might revolutionize our financial world and everyday lives, I invite you to join in exploring this new frontier in digital payments.

This book is designed to be particularly appealing to the selected audience of interested laymen, politicians, bankers, central bankers, and payment system designers. It is not an academic or specialized book. Instead, it integrates many dimensions in a comprehensible way and is written in a way that is understandable for all.

The book was written so that the complete material is accessible to all readers, pre-existing knowhow is not required. Those totally unfamiliar with these topics may nevertheless benefit from first reading through the glossary we have provided at the end of the book.

We divided the book into three parts and we would recommend everyone to read the entire book in order. But those already familiar with the cryptography used in cryptocurrencies and short of time could dive directly into Central Bank Digital Currencies starting in Part II. Part III goes one level deeper into the intricacies of technology and design for both retail and wholesale Central Bank Digital Currencies.

Part I

Decoding Digital Assets

2

An Introduction to Cryptography: Unlocking the Future of Money

The future of money is digital and will embrace both cryptocurrencies and Central Bank Digital Currencies. Securing this digital financial frontier involves understanding and applying the mathematical principles of cryptography. This book will help you gain a sufficient conceptual understanding of cryptography, vital to navigating the opportunities and potential pitfalls that lie ahead in the digital/crypto money landscape.

Do not worry because we will not delve into cryptographic equations. Neither will we introduce you to cryptographic sample scenarios involving Alice and Bob. Instead, we will focus on the fundamental concepts and objectives of information security, typically revolving around the **CIA triad** [131]:

- **Confidentiality (secrecy) means** ensuring data is accessible only to authorized users, thereby keeping it secure from unauthorized entities, even if transmitted through insecure channels.
- **Integrity (anti-tampering) means** verifying that received messages and related metadata, like the sender's identity, remain unaltered without authorized intervention.
- **Availability means** ensuring that information assets are accessible to authorized parties whenever required.

These objectives are primarily achieved through cryptographic tools, which we'll explore further in this context. Let us start at the beginning:

A **message** is a sequence of bits that can for example represent texts, payment transactions, or medical images. This message can have a signature

L. V. Schumacher, *Decoding Digital Assets*, https://doi.org/10.1007/978-3-031-54601-3_2

appended to it. The signature attests to the message's origin or approval by the signer, much like an ink signature on a physical contract. A digital signature, the digital counterpart of a handwritten one, should be unforgeable and protect the message's integrity, ensuring it hasn't been tampered with.

In order to use digital signatures, it is first necessary to create a key pair consisting of a private signing key and a public verification key. The signing algorithm uses the private key and the message to generate a signature. To verify the signed message, the verifier requires the signature and the public verification key.

We also encounter variations of digital signatures, such as blind signatures, which enable signing without knowledge of the message content, multi-signatures requiring joint creation by multiple signers, and ring or group signatures allowing multiple signers to sign for a group without disclosing the participating members.

Encrypting a plaintext (or cleartext) message disguises its content, enhancing confidentiality. The result is a ciphertext, which decryption can revert to plaintext. A cipher, an algorithm for encryption or decryption, uses a key and a set of well-defined steps that enable decryption when known.

For instance, a message "THE QUICK BROWN FOX" can be encrypted to "QEB NRFZH YOLTK CLU" using a cipher called "Caesar's cipher" with a left shift of 3 places in the alphabet, where the key is 3 (Graph 2.1).

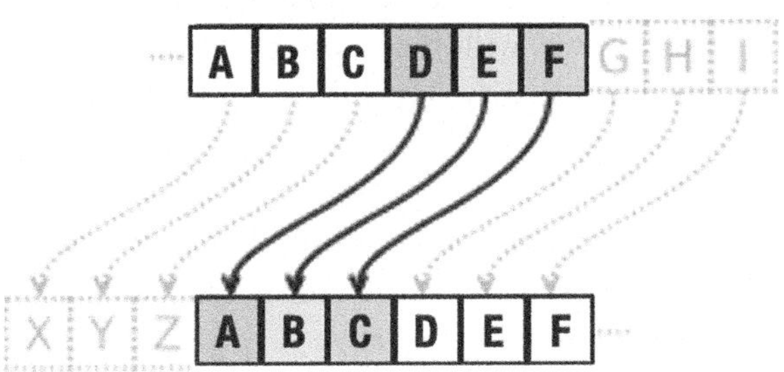

Graph 2.1 Left shift cipher (*Source* Author)

Further elements of cryptography, crucial for digital payment solutions, which we still need to define include:

- **Zero-knowledge proof:** A cryptographic function that permits a prover to demonstrate the truth of a claim to a verifier without divulging any additional information beyond the claim itself and that it is true. For example, one can prove being an adult without revealing identity or birth date.

- **Hash functions:** A cryptographic hash function that returns a fixed-size bit string or hash value for any given data block. Any change to the data will completely alter the hash value. The ideal cryptographic hash function is easy to compute, hiding to recreate the original message, preventing a change to the message without changing the hash, and collision-free, i.e. impossible to find two different messages with the same hash.
- **Symmetric key cryptography:** This encryption system uses a single, shared secret key to encrypt and decrypt a message. The challenge of this concept lies in securely exchanging the secret key between sender and receiver of the message, and then maintaining its secrecy.
- **Asymmetric key cryptography (aka public key cryptography):** Invented by Whitfield Diffie and Martin Hellman to address the key management issue of symmetric key cryptography, this concept uses two separate keys: a public one for encryption and a private one for decryption.

Encryption and **signing** are 2 key functions in asymmetric encryption. They use the public and private keys in different ways. For encryption (to ensure confidentiality), the sender uses the recipient's public key to encrypt the message, ensuring only the intended recipient can decrypt it. In contrast, for signing (to ensure authenticity and integrity), the sender uses his own private key (and the message) to generate a unique digital signature, confirming the message's authenticity and integrity.

In some cryptographic schemes like RSA (Rivest-Shamir-Adleman), the same key pair can be used for both encrypting and signing, while in other schemes this is not the case.

Post-quantum cryptography is a related subject as it will be needed to prevent a serious, negative impact on both encrypting and signing. We will explore that subject separately in an upcoming chapter.

In summary, understanding cryptography is crucial in the digital/crypto money landscape. Grasping these fundamental concepts will enable you to navigate this exciting frontier confidently.

!!! Remember:

Encryption (in asymmetric encryption) uses two different but mathematically related keys, known as the public key and private key as mentioned above. The public key is available to anyone, while the private key is kept secret by the owner.

When someone wants to send an encrypted message to the owner of the public key, they use the recipient's public key to encrypt the message. The message can only be decrypted by the owner of the corresponding private secret key. This ensures that only the intended recipient can read the message.

Signing (in asymmetric encryption) with a public–private key pair, also known as digital signing, is a process of creating a digital signature to ensure the authenticity and integrity of a message or document.

In the signing process, in opposite to what happens for encryption, the sender uses their private secret key to generate a unique digital signature for the message or document, which is then sent along with the original message or document. The recipient can upon receipt use the sender's public key to verify the signature and ensure that the message or document comes from the sender and has not been altered or tampered with during transmission.

In summary:

See Table 2.1.

Table 2.1 Encryption/signature summary

Asymmetric key cryptography	Encrypting	Signing
Target to be protected	Entire digital data	Entire Digital Data or Hash Value of the entire digital data
Public Key used	Encryption	Verification
Private Key used	Decryption	Signing
Objective	Confidentiality	Authenticity & Integrity

Source Author

3

An Introduction to Technology Architectures: Shaping the Future of Payments

Moving on from cryptography to a subject which is touching on the underlying architectures of payment solutions. This is another area where Bitcoin with its blockchain has introduced new possibilities.

Prior to embarking on the exploration of digital payment token solutions, we like to cover first a few basics on technology architectures to facilitate your journey into payment tokens. Here are three different, underlying systems architectures that are important to know.

3.1 Centralized Systems

Centralized systems in IT refer to computing architectures where all processing, data storage, and control functions are managed by a single primary computer or a cluster, usually located within a data center or mainframe. Clients or users access these central computers via a network, leveraging their capability to process data and manage applications.

The advantages of such systems are manifold: streamlined management, simplified backup and recovery procedures, and reduced costs owing to economies of scale. However, centralized systems are not without their limitations. They present a single point of failure, potential performance bottlenecks and may lack flexibility and scalability. Centralized systems, where sensitive data is concentrated, can also be susceptible to security threats or privacy breaches.

In these systems, a central authority exerts full control.

L. V. Schumacher, *Decoding Digital Assets*, https://doi.org/10.1007/978-3-031-54601-3_3

Characteristics of a centralized system:

1. Synchronization with a global clock: In a centralized system, all client nodes synchronize with a global clock, which is maintained by the central node. This ensures that all nodes within the system operate in a coordinated manner.
2. Centralized control: The system is governed by a single central unit that manages and coordinates all other nodes. This central unit serves as the authority for decision-making and resource allocation within the system.
3. Dependence on central node: The failure of the central node can lead to the failure of the entire system. Since the central node serves as the primary point of communication and coordination, its unavailability prevents other nodes from sending or receiving responses or requests effectively.

Example of a centralized system: A Minecraft server.

3.2 Distributed Systems

A distributed system involves multiple interconnected computers or nodes, each having its processing power and storage capacity, working collectively. Examples include most high available websites, distributed databases, and content delivery networks.

These systems function with each node maintaining its independence while collaborating. The governance can be centralized or decentralized.

Characteristics of a distributed system:

1. Resource sharing: A distributed system allows for the sharing of hardware, software, or data across multiple machines or nodes. This enables efficient utilization of resources and promotes collaboration within the system.
2. Simultaneous processing: Multiple machines in a distributed system can process the same function or task simultaneously. This parallel processing capability enhances performance and enables faster execution of tasks.
3. Scalability: Distributed systems are designed to be scalable, meaning they can easily accommodate additional machines or nodes to increase computing and processing capacity. This scalability allows the system to handle growing workloads and adapt to changing demands.
4. Error mitigation: Failures within a distributed system can be better more easily absorbed compared to centralized systems. With multiple nodes

monitoring the system, errors or faults can be identified and isolated, minimizing the impact on the overall system.

5. Transparency: Nodes in a distributed system can access and communicate with other nodes transparently. This transparency ensures that nodes can interact seamlessly, regardless of their physical location or underlying infrastructure.

Example of a distributed system: Google search system.

3.3 Decentralized Systems

Decentralized systems distribute decision-making and control across multiple nodes or entities, eliminating a single, centralized authority. In a decentralized system, any participant can take over any role in the system without any prior authorization. Notably associated with blockchain technology and cryptocurrencies, these systems validate and record transactions across a network rather than relying on a central authority like a bank.

Decentralized systems offer enhanced resilience, security, and fault tolerance by eliminating a single point of failure. Blockchain, and Bitcoin in particular, epitomizes decentralized systems. Here, each network node maintains a complete transaction history, and transactions are validated and approved by consensus rather than a central authority. This design ensures system integrity and security while promoting transparency and accountability.

In decentralized systems, decision-making and control are collaboratively shared, creating a resilient and transparent system.

Characteristics of a decentralized system:

1. Lack of a global clock: In a decentralized system, each node operates independently and has its own clock. There is no centralized global clock that all nodes follow. Each node has its own clock. This allows for greater flexibility and autonomy within the system.
2. Unstoppable computation: In a decentralized system, a single node failure can cause a specific part or subset of the system to fail, but it will not lead to the complete failure of the entire system. This is ensured by the distributed nature of the system, where different nodes can continue to function independently even if some nodes experience failures. For the system to fail, all nodes would have to fail together.

Example of a decentralized system: : Bitcoin, GNU name system, ...

The architecture of a system can have significant impacts on other characteristics of a system, sometimes desired and sometimes not. The consequences of the architecture choice must hence be weighted against other objectives of the system.

Striking a balance between anonymity and decentralization that works for the "owners" of the system is one such example. For instance, Chaum's eCash [132] achieved anonymity via a centralized authority using an interactive blind-signature protocol. Decentralizing such protocols proves difficult. Moreover, opting for decentralization necessitates a mechanism to track transactions and prevent fraud. Public traceability, a crucial feature in Bitcoin, could potentially (respectively did) compromise anonymity.

The critical question, which follows from the above and which will be important to keep in mind as we advance through the chapters, for any CBDC or stablecoin implementation is:

How does centralized, single-entity operation or control (by a bank or central bank for example) of a decentralized system influence the benefits of full distribution or decentralization?

Having covered the key topics of cryptography and information technology in sufficient detail for what is coming, it's now time to transition to the fascinating subjects of PRIVACY and MONEY. We will start with privacy, a foundational value and building block of our society and then we will move on to money.

4

Understanding Privacy

Perhaps surprisingly, one of our first chapters covers privacy. It is a topic of paramount importance in the realm of future monetary forms. This chapter aims to explain the principles of privacy protection as they stand today. It outlines how privacy will profoundly influence the shape and adoption of upcoming monetary systems. It will also make the meaning of the term *privacy* a lot more precise.

Privacy is a term often shrouded in ambiguity with interpretations varying across cultures. It warrants a clear explanation and precise definition. At the end of this chapter, we will all have the same shared understanding of what privacy means.

In any democratic society, privacy plays a vital role because it is directly linked to freedom and democracy. With the onset of digital money and payments, their potential to influence privacy—positively or negatively—becomes significantly potent, contingent on the design of the digital currency system. The past two decades have shown that privacy isn't an inherent feature, and many projects falter in effectively incorporating it. Thus, as we contemplate introducing a new form of currency for all, privacy and its implications demand careful scrutiny and intricate design considerations from the start.

Historically, privacy was chiefly concerned with preventing personal information leaks. Containing key personal data was relatively simple, achieved through rudimentary tools like window curtains or toilet doors. With the spread of information technology and continuous online connectivity, the concept of privacy has expanded significantly to include more complex dimensions.

L. V. Schumacher, *Decoding Digital Assets*, https://doi.org/10.1007/978-3-031-54601-3_4

In the current landscape, privacy extends beyond just preventing information leaks. It empowers individuals with control over their personal data, and the right to demand disclosure, correction, or deletion of their personal information.

The Organization for Economic Cooperation and Development (OECD) Privacy Guidelines [83], established in 1980 and still in effect today, encapsulate the notion of personal information control. These guidelines underpin the privacy protection principles that form the basis for domestic or regional privacy laws in many countries. In 2013, the OECD revised these guidelines to address the challenges brought forth by the expanding internet economy and the increased cross-border flows of personal data.

The OECD privacy guidelines detail several general principles for privacy protection:

1. The Collection Limitation Principle: This limits personal data collection and mandates consent from data subjects.
2. The Purpose Specification Principle: This necessitates specifying the purpose of data collection and usage in advance.
3. The Data Quality Principle: This calls for keeping collected data accurate, complete, and up to date.
4. The Security Safeguards Principle: This stipulates the requirement of protecting personal data with reasonable security measures.
5. The Individual Participation Principle: This grants individuals the right to request data controllers to disclose, correct, or delete personal data.

These guidelines also highlight the principle of **data minimization**, which advocates for collecting and holding only the minimum necessary information for a specific purpose.

Beyond the OECD guidelines, the concept of **privacy by design** has gained traction in privacy protection systems in the European Union (EU) and the United States. This concept underscores proactive measures for privacy protection, embedding privacy protection measures into the architecture of IT systems and business practices, and ensuring visibility, transparency, and user-centricity of privacy protection mechanisms.

Privacy protection is also governed by a variety of rules, including domestic laws, international arrangements, international standards, and self-regulation by industry organizations.

In the EU, the General Data Protection Regulation (GDPR) [84] is legislated in accordance with the OECD guidelines, acknowledging the right to privacy as a fundamental human right.

Similarly, in the United States, the California Consumer Privacy Act (CCPA) [85] has been enacted in California to ensure consumers' right to privacy, with other states following suit.

In summary, privacy protection has evolved from merely preventing information leaks to encompassing individuals' right to control their personal data. The OECD guidelines, privacy by design concepts, and domestic laws in various countries provide a robust framework for privacy protection in the digital age.

Privacy protection is a fundamental ingredient in ensuring a free and democratic future. It's intricately tied to digital money and Central Bank Digital Currencies (CBDCs), which warrants our focus on this crucial subject early on. While we acknowledge that not every country enjoys the same freedoms and democracy, we uphold the belief that all of us strive toward a world that is free and democratic.

One particular challenge we encounter when delving into privacy in the context of CBDC is the myriad of privacy definitions that surface: hard privacy, soft privacy, differential privacy, layered privacy, revocable privacy, realistic privacy, and so forth.

Our approach is to simplify privacy from the onset. There are **only two options when it comes to privacy**:

1. Real privacy (unbreakable and unlinkable anonymity).
2. Trust-based privacy (privacy based on the trust of one or more third parties).

You have "**real privacy**" if your data belongs exclusively to you, and only you can consent to a third party accessing that personal data. Your actions also cannot be linked to each other. One could call this real privacy also hard or trustless privacy.

In contrast, "**trust-based privacy**" forces you to trust a third party to protect your data and not share it with anyone, including themselves. This trusted third party could be your government, your central bank, your bank, or your credit card company. All you can do is trust or hope that these trusted third parties abide by their promises or legal obligations. However, you do not have control over it. This is the current state of privacy for our bank accounts and credit cards. The bank or credit card company holds our personal data but has agreed or is legally obligated not to share it with others.

In this respect, just keep in mind that it took a decade of legal battles before Meta was convicted and fined €1.2 billion [133] in May 2023 for infringing the European GDPR law and abusing the trust of EU users with regard to their privacy.

Confidentiality is an example of trust-based privacy, where a small group of people or companies know the information (e.g. your payment details), but promise not to share it with others (i.e. to keep it for themselves or confidential).

In this book, when we talk about **PRIVACY**, we mean the real privacy of option 1. We will also explore what protection is possible under the trust model of option 2.

When it comes to CBDC systems, the choice between **real privacy** and **trust-based privacy** will be determined at two levels:

1. The government or central bank will decide what kind of privacy they want to allow in the new system. Will it be cryptographically guaranteed, or trust-based?
2. In the absence of mandatory acceptance prescribed by law, the citizens will then decide, by accepting or rejecting the CBDC system, if they agree with the choice presented to them by their government/central bank.

To avoid confusion, we will define additional privacy-related terms that will appear throughout this book. For example, we need to define **anonymity**. We need to articulate what we mean by anonymity, as well as its relationship with similar terms, such as privacy.

Literally, anonymous means "without a name." This implies the absence of any name at all, not just a first or last name.

Consider the Bitcoin system: Neither my first name nor my last name is known in that system, but I am recognized by one or more Bitcoin addresses, which serve as a kind of pseudo-identity. In this book, we will refer to this as **pseudonymity**, as I do have a form of name (albeit unrelated to my real name). Even if I can have multiple pseudonyms, this does not equate to anonymity.

We define anonymity as follows: **Anonymity = Pseudonymity + Unlinkability.** Here, unlinkability implies that the different interactions of the same user with the system should not be linkable to each other.

Consider an example [104] cited by Arvind Narayanan from Princeton University in one of his courses to illustrate the difference:

Reddit, a large social news and discussion platform, allows users to create free accounts, share content, and engage in conversations on various topics under a chosen pseudonym. All their posts are linked to their pseudonym. This is pseudonymous interaction.

On the other hand, 4Chan, an anonymous online community, offers users the ability to make posts with no attribution at all, resulting in fully anonymous interactions.

This brings us to the critical question: Why is pseudonymity insufficient for real privacy?

While pseudonymity may prevent someone from creating a profile of all my interactions on the system and tying it back to my real identity, experience has shown that pseudonymous profiles are quite vulnerable. They may be linked to actual identities at some point. Once this happens, all past, present, and future transactions will be associated with the user's real identity.

For instance, it's often straightforward to link a pseudonymous Bitcoin address with a real-life identity. When dealing with a Bitcoin-related service, such as an online wallet provider, exchange, or merchant, these services usually require your personal information to process transactions. An exchange may request your credit card information for your cryptocurrency purchase, while a merchant will ask for your shipping address.

Even if a direct link doesn't occur, your pseudonymous profile can be deanonymized due to side-channel attacks or indirect leakages of information. This includes metadata like time, location, IP addresses, IMEI numbers, etc., that can be combined to link to the real identity.

For example, an attacker might examine a profile of pseudonymous Bitcoin transactions and correlate the times of day that user is active with other publicly available data. This might reveal a linkage between the pseudonymous Bitcoin profile and a real-world identity.

Transaction graph analysis enriched with other public data has made it possible for companies like Chainalysis, TRM Labs, Elliptic, Elementus, Messari, etc., to easily identify pseudonymous cryptocurrency users. Unmasking pseudonyms is merely a question of effort.

!!!Remember: For a comprehensive understanding of this book and any future work on Central Bank Digital Currencies, it's crucial to remember that when we say privacy, we mean real privacy. It is also important to retain that pseudonymity does not guarantee privacy or anonymity. To achieve those, the stronger property of unlinkability is required.

Anonymity = Pseudonymity + Unlinkability. Anonymity is cryptographically enforced and cannot be broken.

In the end, your personal data either has strong real privacy protections that cannot be unwound (unless with your consent), or you simply trust your government and/or your financial intermediary not to use it or lose it. It's as simple as that. And last but not least:

Privacy that can be removed (without consent) is NO privacy at all!

5

Understanding Money

"Money makes the world go around" This famous line [86] sung by Liza Minelli in the musical Cabaret encapsulates the universal importance of money. But what exactly is money, and where did it originate?

Early human societies relied on commodity money, employing objects with inherent value like shells, beads, or salt for exchange. Coins, stamped with an image or inscription to verify weight and purity, were first minted in the ancient kingdoms of Lydia. They marked a significant evolution in the concept of money. The emergence of paper money was primarily developed in China. It offered a more practical and easily stored form of currency and paper money has persisted to this day.

Economists define money based on three fundamental characteristics [134]. Money should be:

1. **A store of value**: Money can be saved and utilized later, permitting individuals to distribute their purchases over time.
2. **A unit of account**: Money establishes a standard for determining prices.
3. **A medium of exchange**: Money facilitates transactions, enabling the purchase and sale of goods and services.

As societies evolved, so too did the forms of money. It transitioned from commodity money to coins, and then to paper notes. Today, several distinct types of money are in use within our economic landscapes:

L. V. Schumacher, *Decoding Digital Assets*, https://doi.org/10.1007/978-3-031-54601-3_5

1. **Commodity money**: This form of money has intrinsic value, such as gold, silver, oil, or other commodities.
2. **Central bank money** or fiat money: This type of money, unbacked by a commodity, gains its value through government regulation or decree. Modern currencies like the US dollar, euro, or Japanese yen fall under this category.
3. **Digital** or electronic money: This form of money is stored, exchanged, and transacted electronically, with cryptocurrencies, mobile wallets, and bank transfers being common examples.
4. **Representative money**: This is money backed by gold or silver certificates. The gold standard, a system where the value of a currency was pegged to the value of gold, provided a stable basis for international trade until its gradual abandonment during the twentieth century due to economic pressures.
5. **Commercial bank money** or private money: This type of money is created by commercial banks via the process of fractional reserve banking and lending, wherein only a fraction of bank deposits is required to be held in reserve.
6. **Local money**: These are currencies used within specific geographic areas or communities, typically aimed at promoting local economic growth and sustainability.
7. **Alternative money**: These are currencies not issued by a government or central bank and operate independently of traditional banking systems. Bitcoin and other cryptocurrencies are examples of alternative currencies.

Money can also be categorized based on the liability it represents. A liability refers to an obligation that a person or organization owes to another party. For example, commercial bank money is always a liability of a private entity, like a commercial bank, making the exchange of such money inherently challenging due to issues of fungibility and exchangeability of liabilities issued by different banks, as no two banks are equal (Graph 5.1).

These complications—the fact that money from big bank A is not the same as money from small bank B—have been addressed by the concept of the "singleness of money," a cornerstone of the modern monetary system. This concept ensures that the exchange of money isn't affected by varying exchange rates between different types of currencies, whether privately issued (like deposits) or publicly issued (like cash). It is a convertibility promise from private money to public money, that holds the financial system together.

Graph 5.1 Types of liabilities (*Source* Author)

Before the introduction of the "singleness of money" via central banks and central bank-issued settlement assets, **bank note reporters** [135] (see picture below) were periodicals in the mid-nineteenth century used by businesses and individuals to identify counterfeit bank notes and to determine the discount rate for bank notes from distant banks. A dollar from one bank was not necessarily equal to a dollar from another bank. During this free banking era of the United States, before the establishment of the US Federal Reserve Bank, privately issued banknotes were discounted by as much as 20% in distant locations.

THOMPSON'S Bank Note REPORTER.

VERMONT.

Bank note reporter (*Source* Wikipedia)

E-money is another term we encounter in financial discussions. E-money refers to currency that is electronically exchanged and transacted. It includes cryptocurrencies, mobile payment systems, and other electronic payment methods. E-money issuers or e-money institutions (EMIs), which can be banks, financial institutions, or non-bank institutions authorized by relevant financial authorities, issue and manage e-money.

As an e-money institution, the entity is responsible for ensuring that the electronic money issued is backed by funds held in a secure account, complying with applicable laws and regulations. E-money is a liability of the e-money institution. The EMI safeguards customer funds, protects against fraud and misuse, and ensures the smooth operation of electronic payment systems.

Table 5.1 completed in part with data from DCI [136] provides a nice overview on the different types of money, who can access it, and whose liability it is.

Table 5.1 Types of money

	Cash	Central Bank Reserves	Commercial Bank Money	E-money	Cryptocurrency	CBDC
Retail usage	✓	X	✓	✓	✓	✓
Digital & Online transactions	X	✓	✓	✓	✓	✓
Liability of central bank	✓	✓	X	X	X	✓

Source Author

In the next chapter, we will dive deeper into the subject of digital money and payments. We will explore their potential impact on our future and our societies.

6

A Deep Dive into Payments

Venturing into the day-to-day use of money, we arrive at the key subject of payments.

Payments represent the transfer of money, goods, or services from one party, the payer, to another, the payee, often in return for a product, service, or obligation. The mode of payment can vary extensively, ranging from cash, checks, and credit/debit cards to bank transfers, and cryptocurrencies. These transactions are pivotal to financial activities and commerce, as they enable businesses and individuals to exchange value and meet financial commitments.

Payment methods can be broadly categorized into three primary types: retail, wholesale, and cross-border.

Retail payments form the backbone of everyday transactions, such as paying for a meal with a credit card, buying groceries with cash at a supermarket, or using an online payment service provider like PayPal for online shopping at Amazon.com.

Wholesale payments, however, are mostly invisible to the general public. They underpin the financial system's infrastructure, facilitating the transfer and settlement of large-scale funds between large financial institutions.

Cross-border payments, or international payments, involve transactions across different countries, necessitating a synergy among banking systems on either side of the border (and sometimes in-between). These transactions must navigate national boundaries and fluctuating exchange rates.

Cross-border payments bring their own set of challenges and complexities. The creation of the European Union aimed to alleviate these issues by

L. V. Schumacher, *Decoding Digital Assets*, https://doi.org/10.1007/978-3-031-54601-3_6

introducing free movement of money and capital as one of its founding principles. This aspiration led to the development of a common currency, the euro, adopted by currency union of 19 out of the 27 EU member states. This unified approach opened access to a larger market and eliminated currency conversion risks for all parties involved.

However, the euro isn't the only multi-country currency in use today. Three other currency unions exist at the time of writing. The CFA franc, used by a total of 14 countries across two currency unions in West and Central Africa, maintains a fixed exchange rate to the euro. The fourth union, the Eastern Caribbean Currency Union (ECCU), groups eight Caribbean nations that use a shared currency, the Eastern Caribbean dollar, pegged to the US dollar.

Historically, other currency unions have existed, such as the Latin Monetary Union established in 1865 by France, Belgium, Italy, and Switzerland, and the Belgian-Luxembourg Economic Union from 1922, which was ultimately replaced by the introduction of the euro.

While these currency unions often lead to deeper economic and political integration and significantly increase trade, they also come with inherent risks for its participants, as the 2008 financial crisis vividly demonstrated on the back of the Greek population.

In the quest to retain the benefits while avoiding the drawbacks of currency unions, novel concepts have been proposed. These include the "Sur," a joint trading currency suggested by Brazil and Argentina, and a gold-backed currency for international trade proposed by Russia and Iran. Even the idea of a BRICS (Brazil, Russia, India, China, and South Africa) reserve currency has been discussed.

The concept of a cross-border trading currency dates back to the 1944 Bretton Woods conference that set the post-war international monetary order. Economist John Maynard Keynes suggested a global currency, the "Bancor", solely for wholesale trade settlement. The idea was to prevent competitive devaluation and protectionism by having each country balance its trade accounts in bancors instead of relying on their own currencies' exchange rates. This interesting proposal, however, was rejected and the US dollar emerged as the dominant currency for international trade and the global reserve currency.

Cash, the first institutional method of payment and the default physical method for a long time, is still primarily used for retail payments. Its usage, however, is rapidly decreasing, a trend that was already in motion before the COVID-19 pandemic but has since accelerated. Sweden is a prime example of a country moving toward becoming a cashless society.

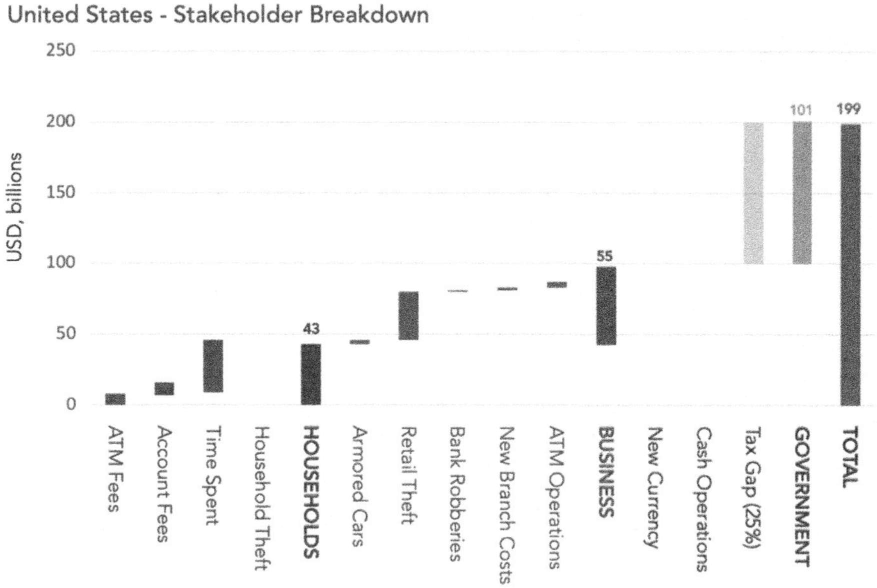

Graph 6.1 Cost of cash in USA (*Source* Adaptation of Institute for Business [93] in the Global Context)

Cash, represented by banknotes and coins, is a bearer instrument belonging to the person who carries it. It facilitates instantaneous transactions without third-party involvement, but it does have downsides: it can be lost, stolen, or destroyed, and it can't be used online. Beyond these practical issues, cash isn't a cost-effective method of payment when considering its total economic impact, from printing and handling to storage and retirement. For example, cash handling costs by major supermarkets are estimated to be at about 1% of cash volume.

A study [93] by the Institute for Business in the Global Context at Tuft's University estimated that the cost of cash in the United States is approximately US$200 billion annually, based on conservative assumptions. This cost is borne unevenly. It is actually highest for poor and unbanked Americans. Businesses lose approximately US$40 billion annually through cash theft, and the government loses an estimated US$100 billion annually in tax revenue from cash transactions (Graph 6.1).

Even though physical currency only made up about 11% of the total value of the money supply of about US$14 trillion in 2018 in the United States, a considerable number of banknotes were in circulation. The majority of the new bills are printed to replace older ones going out of circulation.

Table 6.1 Printing costs of US dollars

Denomination	Printing costs (cents per note)
$1	7.5
$5	12.7
$10	12.4
$20	13.8
$50	13.3
$100	17.0

Source Data by US Federal Reserve Bank

Table 6.2 US dollar notes in circulation

Denomination	Notes in circulation (billion notes)
$1	11.7
$5	2.8
$10	1.9
$20	8.9
$50	1.7
$100	11.5
TOTAL	38.5

Source Data by US Federal Reserve Bank

The tables [95] below based on data by the US Federal Reserve Bank provide details on the printing costs of US dollar notes for each denomination (Table 6.1).

In comparison, a Swiss bank note is significantly more expensive than a US dollar note and costs on average 40 cents [94] a piece.

In 2018, the US Federal Reserve Bank had the following amount of bank notes in circulation [96] (Table 6.2).

Despite these very big numbers of notes in circulation, physical currency made up only about 11% of the total value of the money supply (also called M_2) of about US$14 trillion in 2018 in the United States.

The U.S. Bureau of Engraving and Printing is responsible for printing new dollars. 70% of the newly printed bills replace older notes going out of circulation. The average lifespan [96] of US banknotes is shown in the table below (Table 6.3):

As we have seen before that cash usage is declining, it is digital payments that are increasingly taking the lead. Though digital payments only started gaining traction in the 1990s, they're on a trajectory to make cash entirely obsolete in some countries. Some interesting concepts around digital notes have been created, with bank notes carrying QR codes that allow to upload the value into a digital wallet. This may be in interesting on ramp for digital

Table 6.3 US dollar bank note lifespan

Denomination	Average lifespan (years)
$1	5.8
$5	5.5
$10	4.5
$20	7.9
$50	8.5
$100	15

Source Data by US Federal Reserve Bank

money, if such notes, which become useless after the upload, can be produced in a model that is environmentally friendly and economically viable.

All of this is marking the dawn of a new era in the world of payments, which we will explore in the next chapter.

6.1 Understanding Digital Payments

Digital payments are electronic transactions conducted via digital channels such as computers, mobile devices, or the internet. They replace the exchange of physical currency. These digital systems facilitate the swift, secure, and instant transfer of money for goods and services.

The Electronic Funds Transfer (EFT) was the inaugural digital payment system established in the 1960s and catering mainly to large corporations and financial institutions. The mid-1970s saw credit card companies adopting magnetic strip technology, marking a shift away from paper slips. Subsequently, the rise of the internet and e-commerce in the 1990s brought about innovative digital payment systems like PayPal, enabling easy online transactions and fund transfers.

The early 2000s witnessed the expansion of mobile devices, prompting the advent of mobile payment systems such as Kenya's M-Pesa. Today various digital payment methods exist, including credit and debit cards, mobile payments, bank transfers and cryptocurrencies. All of these have been gaining in market share since the 1990s, thanks to their convenience, speed, and security. The COVID-19 pandemic has further amplified these trends.

However, these digital payment systems are primarily functioning over private digital payment rails. This leads to two significant challenges. These systems can be exclusive, closed-loop systems, and the conversion between different forms of digital money can be complex or even impossible. These private systems were developed to generate profits in a capitalist world, and not as a public service. They also require users to entrust their funds to the operator, which then approves all transactions and may limit fund withdrawals.

These factors have led central banks worldwide to investigate Central Bank Digital Currencies (CBDCs). The goal is to maintain or regain control over the payment infrastructure, especially in countries where cash usage is declining, to preserve sovereignty over their country's financial systems.

When it comes to wholesale payments between banks and central banks, the systems that power those payments include Fedwire, CHIPS, SWIFT, FedNow, ACH, RT1, TARGET2, and TIPS. These systems handle various facets of fund transfers, providing secure, cost-effective platforms for real-time, irrevocable transactions for institutional users.

Turning now from wholesale to retail payments, consumers can choose from various digital and physical payment options. While cash usage has declined over the past two decades, it still maintains a certain market share. Wire transfers, paper checks, prepaid debit cards, credit cards, PayPal, and payment apps all provide alternatives to cash.

Contrary to expectations, digital payments aren't necessarily cheaper than cash. Despite technological advancements and decreasing IT costs, a 2022 report by the BIS revealed that the marginal cost of physical cash payments still remained lower than that of card payments for a €25 transaction. The graph reflects a scenario in which merchants were asked to assess costs for accepting cash, debit card and credit card payments for a €25 transaction over a three- to four-year time horizon. This fact underscores the continued relevance and efficiency of cash transactions alongside their digital counterparts. Nevertheless, we would expect that digital payments will end up being much cheaper than cash in the near future (Graph 6.2).

The whole digital payment world was shaken up in the last decade, starting with the launch of Bitcoin in 2008. This was a new type of money, and it worked in a new way, by eliminating the need for a trusted third party in money transactions. It basically introduced tokenization and with it, a new payment token.

A **payment token** is a digital asset designed to serve as medium of exchange, unit of account, and store of value. It represents a digital surrogate of cash, a payment card, or an account, substituting the physical note, credit card, or account details during transactions. Typically, a payment network or a payment processor generates these tokens, which can then be stored on a digital device or within a digital wallet.

Digital payment tokens are a specific type of digital asset, frequently produced and regulated via blockchain or Distributed Ledger Technology,

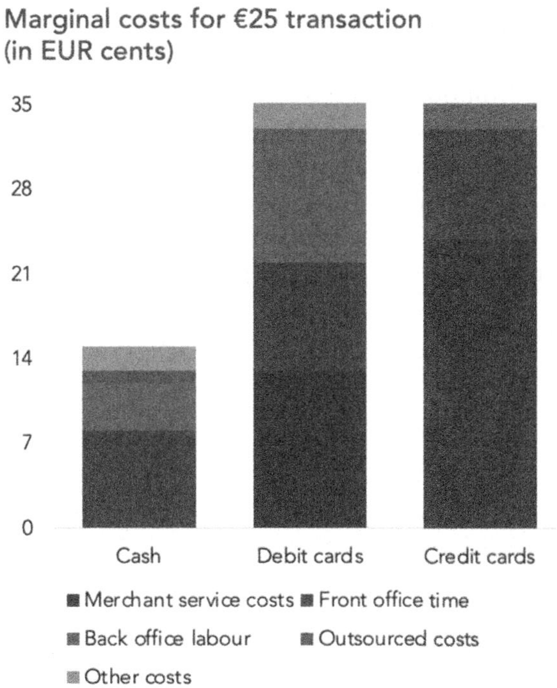

Graph 6.2 Marginal cost per payment (*Source* Adapted with data from BIS)

although not exclusively as demonstrated by digital payment tokens like Chaum's eCash and Taler Systems' GNU Taler. Digital payment tokens can embody various forms of value, including cryptocurrencies such as Bitcoin (BTC), Ethereum (ETH), and Ripple (XRP), as well as stablecoins, which are anchored to a stable asset, often a fiat currency like USD or EUR.

Stored in digital wallets—software applications that empower users to send, receive, and manage their digital assets—digital payment tokens garnered attention due to their potential benefits. These include fostering financial inclusion for the unbanked or underbanked populations, expediting and reducing the cost of cross-border transactions, and facilitating decentralized financial applications (DeFi) that offer innovative financial services and products by disintermediating banks.

It's crucial to mention that many payment tokens, including Bitcoin, were initially designed for use as a medium of exchange. However, at the time of this writing, they are largely perceived as a store of value. This perception may evolve again with the proliferation of Layer 2 payment systems (additional systems that are designed to overcome shortcomings of the base layer by running on top of it) like Lightning as Layer 2 for the base layer Bitcoin, or the GNU Taler depolymerizer. Despite this shift, there remain advantages to categorizing such assets under the broader umbrella of payment tokens.

In the ongoing evolution of crypto-assets, we will concentrate on payment tokens here. They can be categorized into three distinct categories, which we will examine together in the upcoming sections of this book: **cryptocurrencies, stablecoins**, and **Central Bank Digital Currencies**.

But before we get to these payment tokens, we will first discover the institution, that creates our traditional money and ensures it moves around, the central bank.

7

Understanding Central Banks

The foundation of the bustling economic activity we witness is the fiat money issued and backed by central banks. Let's take a deeper look at these institutions.

A **central bank** is a financial institution responsible for managing a country's monetary policy, its currency supply, and its interest rates. Often independent from government influence, central banks carry out their functions effectively without political interference. Well-known examples include the US Federal Reserve, the Bank of Canada, the European Central Bank, the German Bundesbank, the Bank of Japan, the Bank of England, and the People's Bank of China. The World Bank, however, is not a central bank; it's an international financial institution focused on promoting economic development and reducing poverty.

Most countries have a central bank, only some tiny countries and islands don't. Generally, the primary functions of a central bank include:

1. Regulating the country's money supply, defining monetary policies, and setting macroeconomic objectives.
2. Ensuring price stability.
3. Maintaining foreign currency reserves.
4. Supervising the banking system.

Central banks currently issue two forms of money as part of their money supply and monetary policy mandates:

L. V. Schumacher, *Decoding Digital Assets*, https://doi.org/10.1007/978-3-031-54601-3_7

1. **Central bank money** (or central bank reserves): Reserves for select financial market participants, used mainly for interbank transactions and settling large-value transactions between financial institutions.
2. **Physical cash**: Banknotes and coins for the public.

Central bank money, also known as base money or high-powered money, is unique as it is directly issued by a country's central bank and considered the most secure form of money. It is the foundation of the entire money supply of a country. It is different from commercial bank money, which is created through lending and borrowing.

7.1 Generating and Issuing Money

As a country's monetary authority, a central bank regulates the supply of money in the economy. The process of issuing money and accounting for it includes:

1. **Money creation**: Central banks create money through a process known as "open market operations" or "monetary policy operations," typically by buying government securities from banks or other financial institutions. This increases the money supply in circulation.
2. **Reserve requirements**: Central banks set reserve requirements, determining the minimum amount banks must hold in reserve, thereby influencing the amount of money that banks can create through lending.
3. **Accounting for money**: Central banks track the amount of money they have created, recording the corresponding liabilities on their balance sheets. These liabilities represent the money created and held by the public or the banking system.
4. **Monetary policy**: Central banks use tools like interest rates and open market operations to manage money supply, aiming to achieve their monetary policy objectives, such as price stability or economic growth.
5. **Reporting and transparency**: Central banks are often required to report their financial activities and provide regular balance sheet updates to ensure transparency and accountability.

While the process of money issuance can slightly vary based on the central bank and the country's monetary system, the above principles offer a broad overview of how central banks operate.

Central banks also have the power to create money through a process called quantitative easing (QE), which involves purchasing government bonds or other securities, as described above, to stimulate economic growth and stabilize the economy during times of recession or financial crisis. However, QE can lead to inflation if not carefully managed.

As we look toward the future of money, it's crucial to understand how central banks create and distribute physical cash. This process, using the issuance of banknotes as an example, involves:

1. Designing a new banknote series of the currency: Central banks typically work with artists and designers to create designs that feature important cultural and historical figures, symbols, and landmarks.
2. Printing the currency: After finalizing designs, the central bank collaborates with a printing company to produce the currency. The process is intricate, highly secure, and requires specialized equipment.
3. Distributing the currency: Once printed, the currency is stored in the central bank's vaults until needed, then distributed to businesses and individuals through commercial banks and other financial institutions. It is upon distribution that the new currency is recorded in the books of the central bank.

7.2 Legal Mandates of Central Banks

Central banks have a range of legal mandates that vary from country to country, typically including some or all of the following:

1. Conducting monetary policy.
2. Regulating the financial system.
3. Holding foreign exchange reserves.
4. Providing banking services to the government.
5. Supervising payment systems.

These mandates are set out in the central bank's governing legislation or charter and are subject to oversight by government bodies.

Authority to issue a CBDC may or may not be included in a central bank charter. This may be linked to the fact that often the central bank is allowed to issue cash, but not allowed to conduct business that would compete with their banking sector. The graph below shows the results of a survey [4] conducted by the Bank of International Settlements (BIS) on the legal authority of central banks to issue a CBDC (Graph 7.1).

Only about a quarter of the respondents confirmed that their central bank had the authority to issue a CBDC. For those reasons, a legal analysis into the local legislation should always be part of any CBDC project.

The central bank is the ultimate money issuer in a country and is known as the "lender of last resort" as it provides loans to commercial banks or other financial institutions in times of financial crises or emergencies. Central bank money is typically accepted as legal tender for all debts, public and private, and is backed by the full faith and credit of the government.

Legal tender is a form of payment recognized by law as acceptable for the payment of debts and obligations. It refers to any currency or form of money recognized by a government to settle a debt, including banknotes and coins. Legal tender laws vary by country, but in most cases, they stipulate that creditors must accept legal tender currency for the payment of a debt, and debtors have the right to make payment in legal tender. This gives it a unique level of trust and confidence not found in other forms of money.

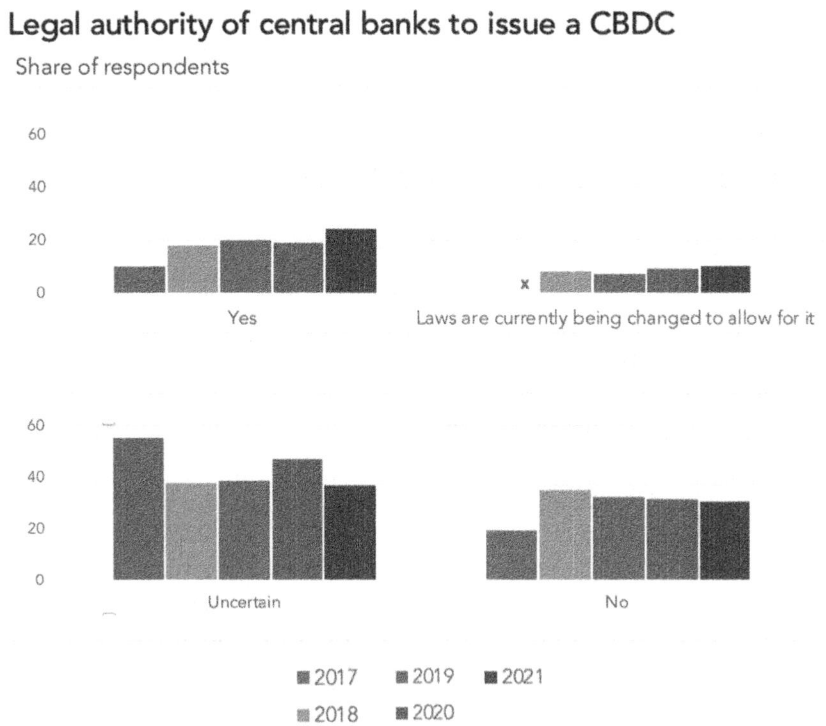

Graph 7.1 Legal authority of central banks to issue CBDC (*Source* Adapted from data by BIS)

The national currency issued by a central bank is typically the legal tender, a form of money that businesses are legally obligated to accept for settling debts and obligations. However, there are exceptions; some countries designate alternative forms of currency, such as foreign currencies, as legal tender under specific circumstances. For example, El Salvador, in September 2021, and the Central African Republic, in April 2022, recognized Bitcoin as legal tender, though the latter rescinded this status in March 2023 through local law N. 22.004.

Even though legal tender must be accepted for debt settlement, it doesn't necessarily mean that all merchants or businesses are obliged to accept it. Interestingly, more vendors today opt not to accept cash, insisting instead on card payments. Legal tender laws differ by country, but commonly, they mandate creditors to accept the country's legal tender for debt payment. Consequently, this imbues legal tender with a unique level of trust and confidence. However, businesses or individuals aren't usually required to accept specific forms of payment, such as credit cards or checks, as these aren't considered legal tender.

7.3 Generating Income

Do central banks generate income? If so, how do they do generate revenues and for whom?

One way to generate revenues for central banks is through emitting cash. Cash isn't just for making payments; it's also how central banks make money. When a person holds physical cash, he/she is giving the central bank an interest-free loan. That is a kind of tax that's directly tied to how much cash the person holds, and it's based on the interest rate. Most people don't realize they're paying such a tax. This central bank revenue is both big and it mostly paid by the poorest people. There is about $8.3 trillion worth of physical money in the world's biggest economies, and assuming an interest rate of 5 percent, it's like a tax of over $400 billion every year on everyone in the world. As mostly poor people hold the majority of cash and use it the most, it is especially tough on them. In addition, when central banks create money, they essentially exchange pieces of paper (currency) for goods and services, and the difference between the cost of producing that currency and the value it represents (face value) is a part of the seigniorage income next to the interest shown above.

Hence, central banks have several revenue streams:

1. Seigniorage: This represents the profit made from both the interest income and the income from the face value of the currency for a central bank. The central bank earns the difference between the cost of producing currency (paper money and coins) and its face value. On top, it collects interest on the emitted currency. Central banks create money by printing or minting currency which generates income for them, and this profit margin is set to increase with the advent of Central Bank Digital Currencies (CBDCs).
2. Interest on reserves: Central banks hold vast reserves, usually as government securities or commercial bank deposits. These reserves accrue interest, providing income for the central bank's operations.
3. Foreign exchange operations: Central banks engage in foreign exchange transactions, like buying and selling foreign currencies. Profits or losses from these transactions depend on market conditions.
4. Open market operations: Central banks influence interest rates and money supply by buying and selling government securities and company shares in the open market. Purchasing at a lower price and selling them at a higher price yields a profit.
5. Fees and commissions: Central banks may levy fees for various services, such as processing payments or managing foreign reserves.

Central banks are typically self-funded, prioritizing price stability and economic growth over profit maximization. Any profits are usually returned to their respective governments.

7.4 Some Economic and Monetary Terms

To navigate discussions around central banks, money, and monetary policy, it's essential to understand a few key terms, like M_0, M_1, and M_2, which denote different measurements of a country's money supply.

M_0 or base money is the most restrictive measure including only physical currency in circulation and reserves held by commercial banks at the central bank.

M_1 is broader, encompassing all components of M_0 plus checking account deposits held by individuals and businesses at commercial banks.

M_2 is the broadest measure, adding savings accounts, money market accounts, and other time deposits to M_1.

Moving onto central banks' future strategies, we find that over half of the approximately 200 central banks worldwide have initiated projects to explore, test, and pilot a new form of central bank money, known as Central Bank

Digital Currencies (CBDCs) next to coins, banknotes, and reserves. These initiatives are poised to reshape our financial future and that of coming generations. To capture the spirit of this transformation, Morten Bech, Head of the BIS Innovation Hub in Switzerland, seemingly took inspiration from former US President Donald Trump's MAGA (Make America Great Again) slogan and coined the formula:

$$CBDC = MM_0GA$$

implying that the introduction of CBDCs is all about revitalizing today's M_0 (cash and central bank reserves) or making M_0 great again.

8

Exploring the Nature of Assets

In this chapter and the next, we will explore what assets are and what kind of assets we find back in the crypto-world. It is important to get a good grasp on what assets are and how these different assets relate to each other from the physical world to the crypto-world. Assets can exist in both, sometimes one is the master and the other its representation.

In the realm of finance and business, the term 'assets' carries significant weight. The more assets you have, the better off you are in general. The International Financial Reporting Standard (IFRS) provides a comprehensive definition of an asset as:

> An **asset** is a resource controlled by the enterprise as a result of past events and from which future economic benefits are expected to flow to the enterprise.

In layman's terms, an asset is anything of value or a resource of value that a company or an individual owns or controls with the expectation that it will provide a future benefit. Assets are crucial components of any business or personal financial health and are often used to fund operations, pay debts, or carry out investments.

Assets are typically categorized based on their ease of conversion into cash. From this perspective, they are either classified as current assets or fixed (non-current) assets.

Current assets, as the name suggests, are assets that can be easily and quickly converted into cash or cash equivalents. They are the lifeblood of a company's operations, providing the necessary liquidity for daily activities. They are often also called liquid assets. Examples of current assets include:

L. V. Schumacher, *Decoding Digital Assets*, https://doi.org/10.1007/978-3-031-54601-3_8

- Cash: This is the most liquid asset and can be used directly to pay for goods, services, or obligations.
- Cash equivalents: These are short-term investments that can be quickly converted into cash, such as treasury bills or money market funds.
- Short-term deposits: These are funds deposited in a financial institution for a specified short period, often earning interest.
- Accounts receivables: These are amounts owed to a company by its customers for goods or services delivered but not yet paid for.
- Inventory: This consists of goods available for sale or raw materials used to produce goods.
- Marketable securities: These are investments like stocks, bonds, or other securities that can be easily sold.

On the other hand, **fixed assets**, also known as non-current assets or long-term assets, are assets that cannot be easily and readily converted into cash. They are typically intended for long-term use and are crucial for a company's long-term sustainability and growth. Fixed assets are illiquid assets. Examples of fixed assets include:

- Land: This is a piece of property owned by a company, often used for operations, or held as an investment.
- Building: These are structures like offices, factories, or warehouses owned by a company and used for business activities.
- Equipment: These are tangible assets like machinery, computers, or vehicles used in the production of goods or delivery of services.
- Patents: These are exclusive rights granted to an inventor or their assignee for a fixed period, providing them the sole right to make, use, or sell an invention.
- Trademarks: These are recognizable signs, logos, or expressions representing a company or product, providing legal protection against their unauthorized use.

Understanding the nature and types of assets is fundamental to grasping the financial health of a business or an individual's economic standing. They form an integral part of the balance sheet and are essential in assessing the value and potential of an enterprise.

The following graph 8 tries to capture assets across the different spheres to provide you with a good overview to start with.

An asset is fungible, if each instance of that asset has the exact same characteristics and is exchangeable. A $5 bill is fungible, with exactly the same

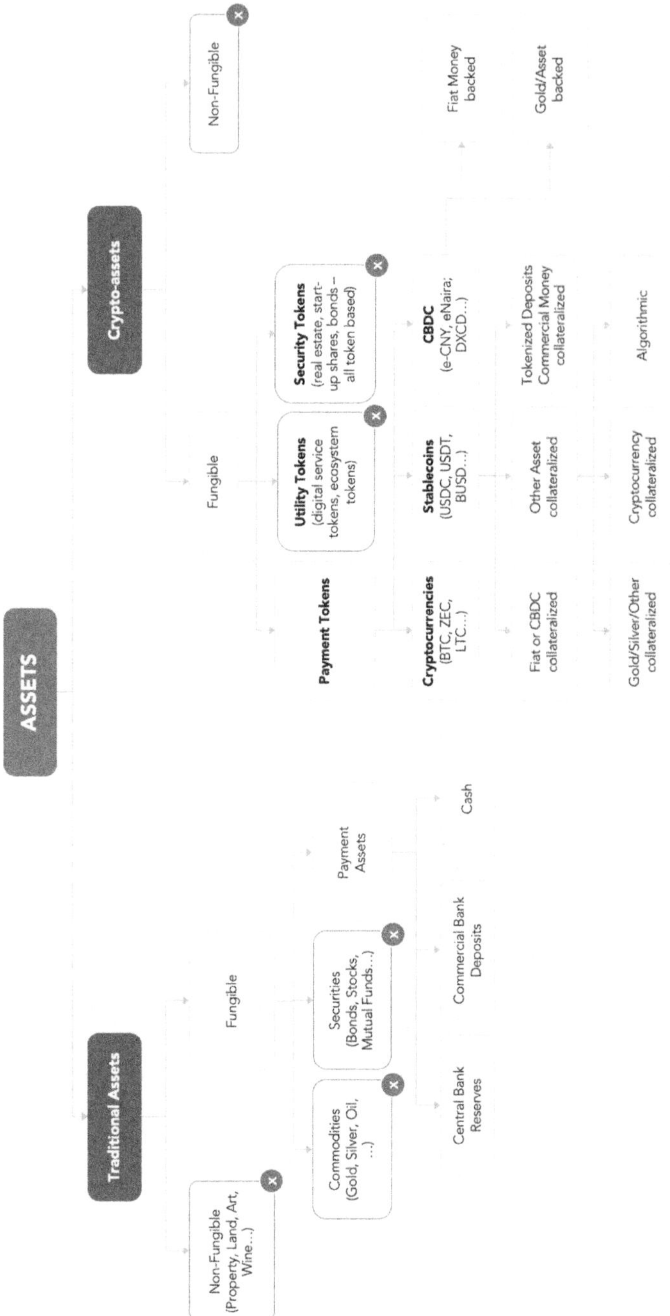

Graph 8.1 Overview of assets (*Source* Adapted from Book of Crypto [1])

characteristics as any other \$5 bill, and it is exchangeable 1:1. An individual will not see ANY difference in using one \$5 bill versus another. An asset is non-fungible if the above is not the case (Graph 8.1).

9

A Primer on Crypto-Assets and the Unavoidable Blockchain

In this chapter we will focus on the subset of crypto-assets. There are 4 types of crypto-assets (all of them represented by digital tokens) and three of them were not designed to contribute to payments and are marked with ⊗ below. We will hence not cover them in detail in this book. If those are of interest, we encourage you to study them in much more detail as there is plenty of literature on the subject (Graph 9.1).

We acknowledge the rising prominence of Non-Fungible Tokens (NFTs), Utility Tokens, and Security Tokens, but our analysis will be concentrated on exploring payment tokens, specifically cryptocurrencies, stablecoins, and Central Bank Digital Currencies (CBDCs). Before delving into these particular tokens, a fundamental understanding of blockchain technology, also known under the larger term 'distributed ledger technology (DLT)', is essential.

Distributed Ledger Technology (DLT) is the overarching term for decentralized databases managed by multiple participants. While all blockchains are DLTs, not all DLTs are blockchains. For now, we will use the two terms interchangeably.

The advent of Bitcoin, triggered by the publication of the Bitcoin white paper [82] in 2008 by the Satoshi Nakamoto, has ushered in an era of crypto-assets, which are all fundamentally rooted in blockchain technology. It's here where our exploration begins.

The essence of a blockchain is its ability to store data from numerous transactions within one distinct block, arranging these blocks sequentially to form a chain. As this chain lengthens, each newly added block is connected to its

L. V. Schumacher, *Decoding Digital Assets*, https://doi.org/10.1007/978-3-031-54601-3_9

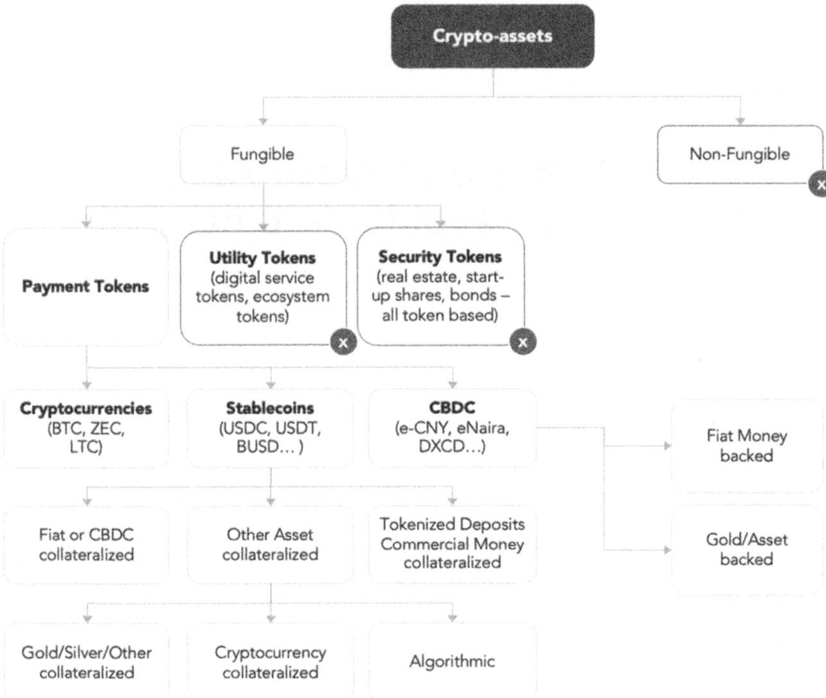

Graph 9.1 Overview of crypto-assets (*Source* Adapted from Book of Crypto [1])

predecessor (parent) block through a unique cryptographic function, generating a reference named a hash. This hash serves a dual purpose: it references the parent block and functions as a unique identifier for the current block. In the Bitcoin blockchain, for example, a hash is a 64-character hexadecimal string that distinctly represents a specific block and all the blocks preceding it. A sample hash for illustrative purposes could look like this:

b6c8dd1b2f6c74e58d7d5961d9a139e34c05b3a8e10b

This hashing process allows for each new block to be validated, verifying its parent block along with every previous block in the chain. Consequently, the growing blockchain fortifies its security, making it exceedingly challenging to manipulate (Graph 9.2).

Altering the data within a single block would necessitate recalculation of the hash of every subsequent block, an incredibly intensive process that renders tampering with the blockchain practically impossible.

Blockchains also have consensus algorithms that are supposed to eliminate the need for a trusted third party. These consensus algorithms run on each

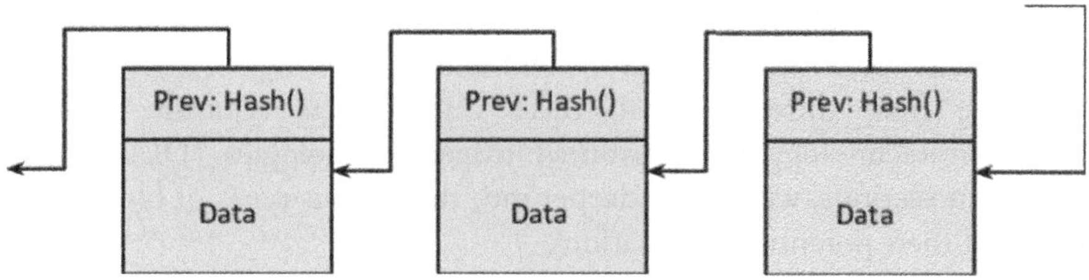

Graph 9.2 Chain of blocks—concept (*Source* Author)

node of the decentralized network and have the role to find agreement on the transactions to be executed. We will explore DLTs and blockchains in further detail in Chapter 14.

Now that we have a basic understanding of blockchain technology, let's briefly review the three types of crypto-assets that we will not investigate further in this volume: Utility Tokens, Security Tokens, and Non-Fungible Tokens.

Utility Tokens are a special breed of crypto tokens, designed to offer access to a specific product or service within a blockchain ecosystem. These tokens are typically issued by companies or organizations to fund the development and upkeep of their blockchain-based offerings. Unlike other tokens, such as Security Tokens, Utility Tokens do not represent ownership in an asset, but grant access to specific functions or features within a blockchain ecosystem. For example, holding a utility token, may give you access to a service offered by the blockchain ecosystem as with Filecoin.

Filecoin is a decentralized storage system. The Filecoin token allows users to buy and sell unused storage on the network. So, if someone wants to store their files on the Filecoin network, they'd use Filecoin tokens to pay for this storage. Conversely, if someone provides storage to the network, they earn Filecoin tokens.

Security Tokens, on the other hand, represent ownership in an asset like a company's stock, real estate, or commodities. These tokens are designed to comply with securities laws and regulations, offering investors legal protections akin to those provided by traditional securities. Their value is tied to the asset they represent, and they are usually issued through an initial coin offering (ICO) or a security token offering (STO).

Lastly, Non-Fungible Tokens (NFTs) are unique digital assets on a blockchain, representing unique items like digital art, collectibles, or virtual real estate. Traditional cryptocurrencies are fungible and interchangeable, but each NFT is distinct and cannot be replicated or divided. NFTs have made waves in various industries like art, gaming, sports, and music, creating fresh opportunities for creators, collectors, and fans.

Despite their differences, all these crypto-assets typically build on blockchain technology or distributed ledger technologies (DLT). In the subsequent sections, we'll delve deeper into the various types of blockchains/ DLTs and their potential implications.

9.1 Exploring the Distinction: Public Blockchains Versus Private Blockchains

A public blockchain, also referred to as a permissionless Distributed Ledger Technology (DLT), operates as a decentralized system open to all. There's no need for approval or authorization from any governing authority. This type of open network allows anyone interested to participate, contribute, and access the information recorded therein.

The framework of a permissionless DLT is designed to record transactions and data on a distributed ledger. This decentralized database is mirrored across all nodes in the network (meaning that all nodes store the full data set). The assurance of security is guaranteed through cryptographic algorithms and consensus mechanisms, such as the most prominent proof of work or proof of stake consensus algorithms. These ensure that transactions are valid and that the ledger remains unaltered and invulnerable to tampering.

The open-door policy of a permissionless DLT is one of its main attractions. It allows anyone to participate in the network without requiring validation or authorization from a central authority. This is particularly beneficial for applications that require resistance to censorship, privacy, and transparency, such as cryptocurrencies or decentralized applications (dApps).

An unusual case is the public-permissioned DLT as defined by Ruiz [129]: "A **public-permissioned** blockchain network is a new type of network filling the gap between the public-permissionless networks (like Bitcoin or Ethereum) and the private consortium networks.... A public-permissioned blockchain network **combines the permissioning from private consortiums with a decentralized governance model**, trying to achieve the best properties of both models."

While today not many central banks seem open for public blockchains and decentralized governance models, it is not impossible that the future may bring a change in thinking on this front, as most of the benefits of blockchains lie in their decentralization and elimination of the trusted third party.

Further, the open nature of a permissionless DLT isn't without challenges. Some of these include scalability, energy consumption, and security concerns. As the network grows with an influx of participants, the computational power required to maintain the ledger increases. This leads to higher energy consumption and potentially slower transaction times. Moreover, the open access exposes the network further to potential attacks from malicious actors who might exploit system vulnerabilities.

On the other side of the coin are private blockchains, also known as permissioned Distributed Ledger Technology. These are decentralized systems where network access and functionalities are limited to a select group of participants, who have been granted permission by a central authority. Essentially, this is a members-only network where participants must be authorized to join, contribute to the system, and access the recorded information.

So it is fair to say that the private blockchains forgo some of the key innovations of the permissionless blockchain, which are access to all and no need for a trusted third party.

In a permissioned DLT, just as in its permissionless counterpart, transactions and data are logged on a distributed ledger. This decentralized database is replicated across all network nodes. Cryptographic algorithms and consensus mechanisms are employed to secure the ledger. They ensure the validity of transactions and the immutability of the ledger. The Table 9.1 summarizes who has read access, write access on the different DLT types as well as who can commit. Committing means to record, validate, and permanently store a piece of information (usually in the form of a transaction or data) onto the DLT.

A significant benefit of a permissioned DLT is its bolstered security and privacy. Due to the restricted network access, control over participant admission is easier, and it's simpler to deter malicious actors from exploiting system vulnerabilities. Moreover, permissioned DLTs can offer additional privacy features, such as encrypted data storage and confidential transactions.

Nevertheless, the exclusive nature of a permissioned DLT can also restrict its potential applications. By losing some of the benefits associated with full decentralization, permissioned DLTs are less suitable for applications that require absolute resistance to censorship or complete decentralization, like cryptocurrencies.

Table 9.1 User access by DLT-type

			Read	Write	Commit	Example
DLT types	Open	Public permissionless	Open to anyone	Anyone	Anyone	Bitcoin, Ethereum
		Public permissioned	Open to anyone	Authorized participants	All or subset of authorized participants	Alastria LaCChain EBSI
	Closed	Consortium (private permissioned)	Restricted to a set of authorized participants	Authorized participants	All or subset of authorized participants	Partior
		Enterprise (private permissioned)	Fully private or restricted to a set of authorized participants	Network operator only	Network operator only	JPM coin

Source Adapted from the Book of Crypto [1]

9.2 Application in Industries

The banking and finance industry has shown significant interest in blockchain technology, specifically in the implementation of permissioned and private blockchains managed by themselves or by consortia, as show in the previous graph.

According to the Graph 9.3, the adoption of blockchain and DLT technology is most prevalent in the banking and finance sector, with the government and insurance industries following behind.

Financial institutions often test out blockchain technology within a closed, secure, and regulated setting, where participants can be properly managed and authenticated.

Notable consortia, offering permissioned DLT technology with distinct specifications and functionalities for entreprises, include the Ethereum Enterprise Alliance, Hyperledger (managed by the Linux Foundation), Corda (managed by R3), and Quorum (managed by Consensys).

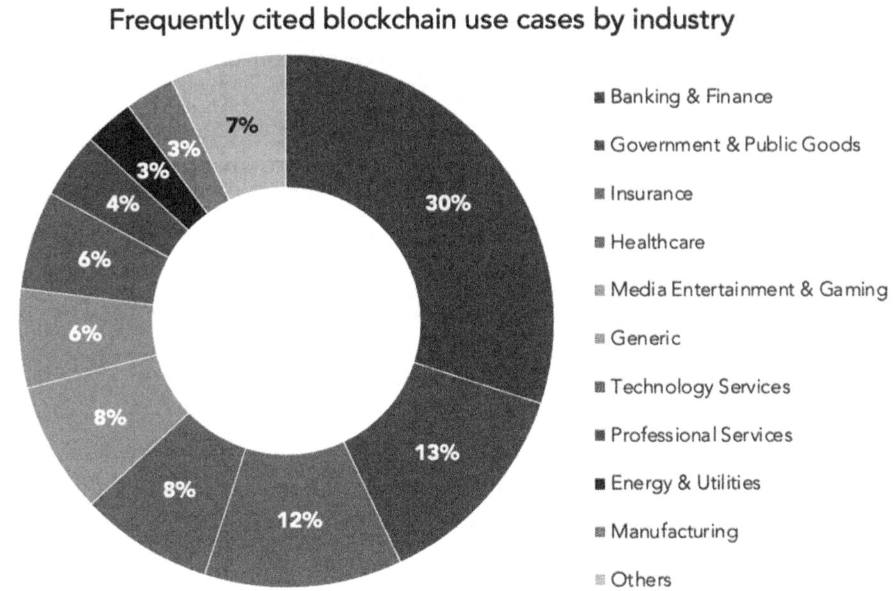

Graph 9.3 Frequently cited blockchain use cases (*Source* Book of Crypto [1])

Not all DLTs and blockchains operate the same, as we will see in the coming chapters. We will illustrate this based on Ethereum and Bitcoin.

9.3 Account-Based Blockchains

An account-based blockchain delineates a unique type of blockchain architecture, expertly designed to manage and keep track of digital asset ownership and transfers via user accounts. In this account-based configuration, each user or account is allocated a unique address on the blockchain. This address serves as a digital vault, used to store and manage their digital assets, such as cryptocurrencies or tokens.

Ethereum (ETH), a prominent cryptocurrency operating on the Ethereum network, exemplifies an account-based blockchain. ETH can be safely stored in digital wallets, which are software applications that empower users to send, receive, and manage their ETH holdings. The interplay between ETH and digital wallets unfolds as follows:

1. The genesis of a wallet: To leverage a digital wallet for ETH management, users must initially establish a wallet. These wallets, accessible online or as downloadable software, usually necessitate the setup of a password or

mnemonic phrase for enhanced security. The wallet serves as a secure store for the private key—a vital secret code necessary for debiting or crediting the account balance recorded on the blockchain.

2. The receipt of ETH: Upon successful creation of a wallet, users can receive ETH by disseminating their address to other participants. An Ethereum address, such as 0xb794f5ea0ba39494ce839613fffba74279579268, functions as a public key within the Ethereum network. When another user dispatches ETH to this address, the transaction is inscribed on the Ethereum blockchain, and the ETH is accordingly credited to the recipient's wallet.
3. The dispatch of ETH: In order to send ETH from a wallet, users need to input the recipient's address into the wallet, specify the desired amount of ETH to be sent, and confirm the transaction. This process involves the user's secret private key, stored securely within the wallet, signing the transaction and broadcasting it to the Ethereum network for processing.

Numerous blockchain networks employ an account-based model, including but not limited to:

1. Ethereum: Ethereum, a widely recognized blockchain network, employs an account-based model. It sustains a database of accounts and their balances. Transactions within this network adjust the balances of both the sender's and the receiver's accounts.
2. Binance Smart Chain: Binance Smart Chain is another blockchain network utilizing the Ethereum Virtual Machine (EVM) and an account-based model.
3. EOS: The EOS blockchain network also adopts an account-based model. Like Ethereum, it maintains a database of accounts and balances, and transactions modify the balances of the sender's and receiver's accounts.
4. Cardano: Cardano, another member of the blockchain network family, uses an account-based model. It maintains a database of accounts and balances but employs a UTXO-like model for its accounting.

Next we will delve into the alternate model of blockchain, which is not account-based but rather built on the UTXO (Unspent Transaction Output) model, akin to Bitcoin.

9.4 UTXO-Based Blockchains

A UTXO (Unspent Transaction Output)-based blockchain is distinguished by its transaction-centric model that meticulously tracks the inputs and outputs of each transaction (TX). Every UTXO signifies the output of a preceding transaction and can be utilized as input for a future transaction. Typically, a UTXO is fully expended into one or multiple new UTXOs. The cryptocurrency Bitcoin functions with UTXOs.

Each Unspent Transaction Output (UTXO) in Bitcoin is associated with a distinct address, such as:

3FZbgi29cpjq2GjdwV8eyHuJJnkLtktZc5

In the Bitcoin network, transactions are a composition of inputs and outputs. When a user dispatches Bitcoin to another user, the transaction inputs comprise UTXOs belonging to the sender, while the outputs manifest as new UTXOs that belong to the recipient. Sometimes, a new UTXO represents change returning to the sender.

For instance, a UTXO of 3 Bitcoin (BTC) under my ownership can be disbursed as a 1 BTC payment to a merchant, creating a new UTXO, and a return of 2 BTC to myself, forming another new UTXO. The original UTXO is entirely spent, giving birth to two fresh UTXOs—one containing 1BTC for the merchant, and the other holding 2BTC in change for me.

Each UTXO is linked with a specific Bitcoin address, a unique identifier employed to receive and send Bitcoin. Although the usage of new addresses is generally recommended, certain scenarios are not conducive to this practice. For instance, addresses for merchant payments or donations displayed on websites often remain static. When a transaction spends a UTXO, the full value of the UTXO is transferred to a new address (or addresses), materializing as new UTXOs. These new UTXOs will have their own unique addresses.

This may appear as a complex user experience, with numerous intricate UTXOs of varying amounts and addresses comprising the total amount of UTXOs owned by the user. While Bitcoin's UTXO model delivers a high level of security and enables efficient transaction processing, managing individual UTXOs can make the user experience less intuitive than that of an account-based blockchain like Ethereum.

However, digital wallets significantly enhance the user experience with UTXOs by offering services like:

1. Wallet balance aggregation: Many Bitcoin wallets enable users to view their total wallet balance instead of individual UTXOs. The wallet automatically aggregates the value of multiple UTXOs to display a single balance, simplifying understanding of Bitcoin holdings.
2. Transaction batching: Some Bitcoin services batch multiple transactions together, consolidating several UTXOs into a single transaction. This reduces transaction fees and simplifies Bitcoin sending.
3. Change address management: When a Bitcoin transaction spends a UTXO, the remaining value is typically sent to a new address as "change." Some wallets automatically manage change addresses to prevent confusion and potential loss of funds.
4. UTXO selection algorithms: Bitcoin wallets can employ algorithms to automatically select the most suitable UTXOs for a given transaction. Some wallets may prioritize spending smaller UTXOs to reduce the total number of UTXOs in a wallet and make it more manageable.

The UTXO model started the blockchain movement with Bitcoin and forms a fundamental design element of many other cryptocurrencies. Several other blockchain networks utilize the UTXO model, including Litecoin, Bitcoin Cash, and Dash.

It's important to note that both account-based and UTXO-based models have their strengths and weaknesses. Different blockchain networks select the model that aligns most closely with their objectives and use cases.

Going forward, we won't differentiate further between these two types of blockchains as for the topics covered in this book, we will consider them basically equivalent. We will simply refer to blockchains as the overarching term. It's crucial to remember that both types of blockchains can only have positive balances, be that in the account or in the UTXO.

10

Unveiling the World of Cryptocurrencies

Cryptocurrencies, as a subset of crypto-assets, are a key element of our explorations in this book. While there is ongoing debate as to whether cryptocurrencies can be classified as actual currencies, they represent a groundbreaking form of digital tokens with distinct characteristics.

Cryptocurrencies share some similarities with traditional currencies, but their unique attributes and limited acceptance as a widely recognized means of payment currently hinder their classification as conventional currencies.

These digital or virtual tokens employ cryptographic techniques to secure transactions and govern the creation of new units. Most cryptocurrencies operate in a decentralized manner, free from the control of central banks or governments. Instead, they rely on blockchain technology—a distributed ledger that records all transactions and is maintained by a network of decentralized computers globally.

The foremost cryptocurrency, Bitcoin, emerged in 2008 under the pseudonym Satoshi Nakamoto, whose true identity remains unknown. Since then, thousands of other cryptocurrencies have entered the scene, each with its own distinct features and intended purposes. Prominent examples include Ethereum, Zcash, and Litecoin.

Bitcoin, as the pioneer of cryptocurrencies, aimed to establish a peer-to-peer payment system and eliminate the need for a trusted intermediary in the issuance and transaction of digital assets. Achieving this objective involved a multitude of individual and decentralized nodes voluntarily joining an open network and utilizing specific consensus algorithms (such as Proof of Work or Proof of Stake) to determine the validity of transactions. These decentralized

L. V. Schumacher, *Decoding Digital Assets*, https://doi.org/10.1007/978-3-031-54601-3_10

consensus mechanisms safeguard the network against censorship and render the role of a trusted intermediary redundant.

It's important to note that the level of decentralization can vary depending on the underlying technology design of each cryptocurrency.

Cryptocurrencies can be bought and sold on specialized cryptocurrency exchanges. These exchanges are the on-ramp, facilitating their uptake and subsequent use for purchasing goods and services from merchants who accept them as a form of payment. Additionally, they can be held as investment assets, with their value subject to market fluctuations.

While cryptocurrencies offer novel perspectives on money and payment systems, they also introduce new risks. Volatility, security concerns, and regulatory uncertainty are among the challenges that arise in this rapidly evolving landscape.

In the subsequent chapters, we will delve deeper into the intricacies of cryptocurrencies. We will explore their underlying technologies, use cases, and the potential impact they may have on the future of finance and beyond. By gaining a comprehensive understanding of cryptocurrencies, readers will be equipped to navigate this transformative digital landscape with confidence.

10.1 Decentralized Cryptocurrencies

Decentralization lies at the core of the original Bitcoin idea and the first cryptocurrency. A decentralized cryptocurrency exhibits the following key attributes:

1. Absence of a central authority: Unlike traditional currencies, decentralized cryptocurrencies operate without the oversight or control of a central authority, such as a government or central bank. This absence of a central authority ensures that decision-making power is distributed across the network, preventing any single entity from exerting undue influence.
2. Peer-to-peer system: Cryptocurrencies facilitate direct transactions between participants without the need for intermediaries. Through a peer-to-peer network, users can interact and engage in transactions directly with one another, fostering a trustless environment where reliance on third parties is eliminated.
3. Distributed network: The transactional records of decentralized cryptocurrencies are stored on a distributed ledger, commonly known as a blockchain. This ledger is replicated across numerous computers, or nodes, within the network. By distributing the ledger across multiple nodes,

decentralization is achieved, ensuring transparency and immutability of the recorded transactions.

4. Open access: Decentralized cryptocurrencies offer open access to anyone who wishes to participate in the network. This inclusivity enables individuals to mine, create addresses, or engage in transactions freely, without requiring permission or authorization. This openness is a fundamental principle of decentralization, promoting the democratization of financial systems.

Bitcoin stands as a prime example of a decentralized cryptocurrency, with the regulations governing its network being transparent and accessible to all. However, while the majority of cryptocurrencies, including Bitcoin and Ethereum, are designed with decentralization in mind, there is a risk that they may experience varying degrees of centralization at certain points.

A notable instance was the concentration of Bitcoin mining, in China, where a significant portion (65%) of the network's mining activities took place in 2021. Bitcoin mining is the process that puts new bitcoins into circulation and verifies, then adds transactions to the blockchain. In other words, the mining process creates new bitcoins and validates transactions between users. This happens by solving complex computational problems. This concentration raised concerns about the potential formation of mining pools (bringing together many miners) that could amass enough computing power to collude and execute a 51% attack.

A 51% attack can occur when a single miner or a group of miners gain control over more than 50% of the total computing (or mining) power of a blockchain network. With this majority control, the attacker can manipulate the network's normal operation, potentially compromising its consensus rules and undermining the integrity of the blockchain.

While decentralization is a core principle of cryptocurrencies, it is crucial to monitor and address any factors that could lead to increased centralization. Safeguarding the decentralized nature of cryptocurrencies helps preserve their core values of transparency, trust, and censorship resistance.

In the subsequent sections, we will explore various aspects of cryptocurrencies, including their underlying technologies, consensus mechanisms, and the role they play in reshaping financial systems and empowering individuals worldwide.

10.2 Centralized Cryptocurrencies

While decentralization is a defining characteristic of cryptocurrencies, certain cryptocurrencies deviate from this principle and are considered centralized. These centralized cryptocurrencies lack the core attributes of decentralization, including the absence of a central authority, a peer-to-peer network, a distributed system, and open access for all participants.

Let's explore some examples of centralized cryptocurrencies and their implications.

1. Stablecoins and Central Bank Digital Currencies (CBDCs): Stablecoins, such as Tether (USDT) or USD Coin (USDC), are intentionally centralized cryptocurrencies designed to maintain a stable value by pegging their price to a specific asset, typically a fiat currency like the US dollar. These stablecoins are often issued and controlled by centralized entities, with reserves held to back the value of the tokens. Similarly, CBDCs, which are digital representations of a country's fiat currency issued by a central bank, operate within a centralized framework under the control of the respective central bank. Although CBDCs may leverage Distributed Ledger Technology (DLT), their centralized nature contradicts the underlying principle of decentralization.
2. Blockchain networks with limited decentralization: Some blockchain networks, such as EOS and NEO, exhibit a degree of centralization due to their consensus mechanisms and network governance structures. These networks may rely on a smaller number of nodes or entities that have significant control over the decision-making process, leading to reduced decentralization compared to other cryptocurrencies. While these networks may offer certain benefits, such as faster transaction processing, the level of decentralization is compromised.
3. Token control and concentration: Decentralization can also be undermined when a single entity or group holds a majority of the tokens within a cryptocurrency ecosystem. Ripple (XRP) serves as an example, where the majority of XRP tokens were initially held by the issuing company. This concentration of tokens diminishes the overall decentralization of the cryptocurrency, as control remains centralized within the hands of a few entities. Similar to centralized cryptocurrencies like CBDCs, the control exerted by the issuer or central party contradicts the ethos of decentralization.

The introduction of centralized cryptocurrencies raises questions regarding the benefits and trade-offs associated with limited decentralization. While centralized models may offer certain advantages in terms of scalability and transaction speed, they come at the expense of trust and reliance on central authorities. Additionally, the use of DLT in a single-owner model, as observed in certain centralized cryptocurrencies, may undermine the very principles of resilience and elimination of trusted third parties that blockchains were initially designed to address.

It is important to critically evaluate the implications and potential risks associated with centralized cryptocurrencies. This is particularly important in relation to the objectives of transparency, trustlessness, and censorship resistance that underpin decentralized systems. As the cryptocurrency landscape continues to evolve, striking a balance between centralized and decentralized models remains a subject of ongoing discussion and exploration.

11

Exploring Stablecoins: Ensuring Stability in a Volatile Crypto Market

Stablecoins are the second type of payment token we explore in this book. Stablecoins are a type of digital asset or cryptocurrency, designed to maintain a stable value relative to a traditional currency, a commodity, or another asset. Unlike traditional cryptocurrencies such as Bitcoin, which can be highly volatile and experience significant price fluctuations, stablecoins aim to provide a more stable and predictable store of value.

We have identified ***3 kinds of stablecoins*** that we will look into deeper:

a. Tokens backed 100% by central bank reserves
b. Tokens backed by other financial or physical assets
c. Tokenized deposits

Stablecoins can be issued both by banks and non-banks. The successful stablecoins to date have all been issued by non-banks as illustrated by Graph 11.1. The issuers are usually much less regulated than banks, while regulators are working hard to catch up, like with the MICA regulation in the European Union. Tokenized deposits on the other hand build on the existing bank accounts and are hence a product of regulated banks.

11.1 Tokens Backed by Central Bank Reserves

Tokens backed 100% by central bank reserves, known as "**Synthetic Central Bank Digital Currency**" (sCBDC), are actually stablecoins with a twist. Unlike true CBDCs, synthetic CBDCs are backed by reserves held by private

L. V. Schumacher, *Decoding Digital Assets*, https://doi.org/10.1007/978-3-031-54601-3_11

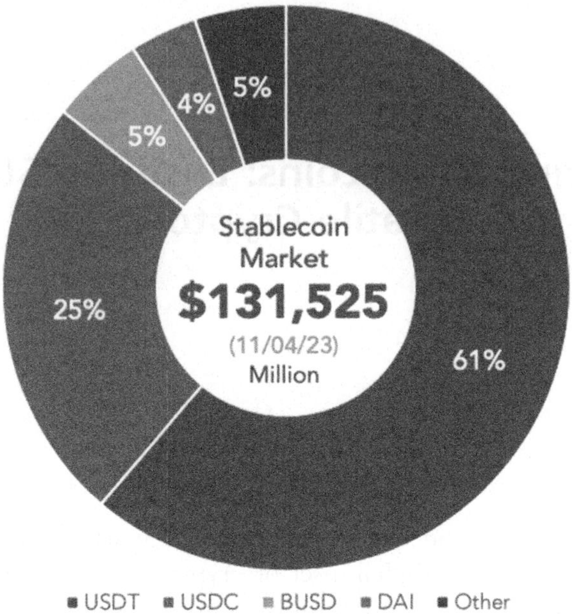

Graph 11.1 Market size by stablecoin, April 2023 (*Source* Market data by DefiLama)

financial institutions at the central bank in a bankruptcy-proof manner. This means that the stablecoin is a claim on the money potentially held in a bankruptcy-proof trust, fully backed by central bank reserves. Access to central bank reserves is essential for the issuing financial institution to create a synthetic CBDC. Examples of synthetic CBDCs include the stablecoin offered by Six Digital Exchange (SDX), which is backed by reserves from the Swiss National Bank.

11.2 Tokens Backed by Other Assets

On the other hand, there are non-central bank reserve backed stablecoins that utilize different mechanisms to maintain price stability.

One type is the "**fiat-collateralized**" stablecoin, which is backed by a fiat currency, such as the US dollar or the Euro, held in a bank account or at another financial institution.

Another type is the "**other-asset-collateralized**" stablecoin, which may be backed by commodities like gold or silver, or by bonds.

Additionally, there are "**crypto-collateralized**" stablecoins, backed by other cryptocurrencies, where the issuer holds a reserve of cryptocurrencies exceeding the value of the stablecoins in circulation to ensure stability.

Lastly, "**algorithmic**" stablecoins, or uncollateralized stablecoins, aim to maintain a stable value through algorithms and smart contracts. They operate using mechanisms such as the rebase model, which adjusts the stablecoin's supply based on its market price, and the coupon model, which incentivizes stablecoin owners to adjust their holdings.

According to data from DefiLama in April 2023, fiat-collateralized stablecoins held the largest market share at 95% (USDT issued by Tether, USDC by Circle, BUSD by Binance and DAI issued by MakerDAO), followed by crypto-collateralized stablecoins and algorithmic stablecoins at 5%. Stablecoins have gained popularity due to their potential to provide stability in transactions and commerce on blockchain networks. They can also serve as a store of value similar to traditional fiat currencies. Some stablecoins have been specifically developed for decentralized finance (DeFi) applications, where they offer liquidity, collateral, and other financial services on blockchain networks.

While stablecoins aim for stability, they are not without risks. The collapse of the algorithmic stablecoin TerraLuna serves as an example of the potential pitfalls. Additionally, recent events such as the drop in Circle's USDC stablecoin value due to the closure of Silicon Valley Bank highlight the inherent risks involved.

Stablecoins, including e-money tokens like USDC, may have higher quality and security than normal bank deposits based on the liquidity coverage ratio (LCR) [98]. The LCR measures a bank's ability to fund cash outflows for 30 days, and stablecoins like USDC have demonstrated higher LCRs compared to systemically relevant banks. However, stablecoins backed by collateral held in banks can still be affected by bank runs, as seen in the Circle case with SVB.

Not every stablecoin can keep up with Circle's LCR, as shown by the numbers of Tether, the issuer of USDT. Tether's audit report [137] published in May 2023 and certified by audit firm BDO, showed about $50 billion in US government bonds, $1.5 billion in Bitcoin and $1.3 billion in precious metals. Considering Bitcoin and precious metals as a stable backing asset, is at least an interesting strategy when stability toward a US$ is the goal. The holders of USDT carry the risk of loss of a downward move in Bitcoin or precious metals, but will not participate in potential gains due to an upward move in the price of Bitcoin and precious metals. The eventual profits from these positions may just go directly to Tether.

As stablecoins gain more market share, the demand and competition for high-quality liquid assets (HQLAs), such as the large share held by central banks today, will intensify. The market for HQLAs and related pricing could experience significant changes as stablecoins continue to grow in popularity and look more and more for HQLAs to constitute their backing assets.

11.3 Tokenized Deposits: Transforming Traditional Banking Deposits into Digital Assets

In this chapter, we delve into the concept of **tokenized deposits**. The concept introduces the conversion of traditional bank deposits or savings accounts into digital tokens. This also means that tokenized deposit projects are usually launched by commercial banks and fall under the existing banking regulation. This is probably one of the main differentiators to stablecoins, that are generally projects of non-banks and hence unregulated or less regulated.

As bank deposits (or commercial bank money) constitute the largest category of money in use, this innovative idea could have a broad impact on our financial system. For instance, the commercial money, underlying potential tokenized deposits, constitutes 75% of all money in the EU and 97% in the UK. In the US, the majority of money exists as bank deposits, with just 11% in cash and 16% in reserve accounts at the Fed. The impact of tokenized deposits on economies could be three times larger than the relevant amounts for Central Bank Digital Currencies (CBDCs).

We commence by exploring the two models proposed by the BIS for private tokenized money [138], examining their mechanics and implications.

The first model, known as the **digital bearer instrument** model, resembles existing asset-backed stablecoins. It operates on the transferability of private money tokens, representing claims on the issuer. While this model offers flexibility, it introduces challenges such as deviations from par value and potential credit risks. In this case, we need to discuss the importance of maintaining singleness of money, as introduced in Chapter 5, and the risks associated with KYC compliance.

The second model, referred to as the **non-bearer instrument** model or "**tokenized deposits**", involves the transfer of liabilities through the existing two-tier monetary system (bank-central bank). This model ensures settlement on the central bank's balance sheet and eliminates doubts about the exchange value. Singleness is preserved through the use of central bank money, with regulatory standards and access to the lender of last resort promoting competition and financial inclusion.

Although these BIS models are still in development, private projects in the tokenized deposit space are actively exploring these concepts. We will review the current landscape and the potential impact of these initiatives.

Furthermore, we address the need for Central Bank Digital Currencies (CBDCs) to fully realize the benefits of the non-bearer instrument model. While CBDCs are yet to be implemented, their crucial role in ensuring singleness of money and facilitating settlement in these models is highlighted.

Tokenized deposits have the potential to revolutionize traditional banking by simplifying payment processes. They enhance security, and offer new opportunities for individuals and businesses. Here are challenges and opportunities associated with this emerging financial innovation.

Tokenized deposits offer investors the possibility to convert traditional bank deposits or savings accounts into digital assets represented by tokens. These transferable tokens, issued and traded on blockchain-based platforms by licensed financial intermediaries, provide investors with greater flexibility (like available 24/7/365) and access to a wider range of financial services (like instant settlement). While tokenized deposits have a minimal impact on banks' balance sheets, they have the potential to reshape the banking sector by introducing innovative solutions.

A deposit token represents a claim against the issuing institution and serves as the economic equivalent of existing deposits. These tokens facilitate payment transactions, trade settlement between digital assets, and act as a store of value and means of exchange on Distributed Ledger Technologies (DLTs) and other platforms.

While tokenized deposits operate in a new technical format, they are subject to existing regulations and supervision applicable to commercial banks. These regulations include minimum capital and liquidity requirements. They impose technology risk management and ensure the prudential and operational integrity of deposit-taking and other banking activities. However, it is crucial to understand the regulatory framework governing tokenized deposits in each jurisdiction, as they may carry risks such as volatility and the lack of regulatory oversight. Investors should be aware that tokenized deposits may not be covered by deposit insurance programs, necessitating careful consideration and due diligence.

As said, tokenized deposits hold significant potential, as they represent a substantial portion of the money supply in our economies. Furthermore, tokenized deposits can support credit creation through fractional reserve banking, contributing to economic growth.

Tokenized deposits even offer benefits beyond credit creation. They address liquidity management challenges and enhance cross-border interbank payments by providing greater accessibility, transparency, and security. The tokenized deposits also allow streamlining transactions and automating complex payment operations. By utilizing Distributed Ledger Technology (DLT), commercial bank money payments can leverage smart contracts, achieve instant and atomic transaction settlement, and enhance transparency of transaction statuses.

Hence tokenized deposits have the potential to revolutionize traditional banking by offering greater flexibility, accessibility, and efficiency. Embracing DLT and smart contracts enables the transformation of payment systems, liquidity management, and cross-border transactions. This again leads to a more seamless and secure financial ecosystem.

Tokenized deposits offer a range of benefits, including continuous trading, reduced transaction costs, and increased transparency. These digital assets can provide investors with ownership of a portion of the underlying deposit and are held directly or by custodians, such as banks or financial institutions. Investors receive regular interest payments based on the interest earned on the deposit. The tokens themselves can be traded around the clock on the platforms, enhancing liquidity and flexibility.

Tokenized deposits function through various characteristics that determine their nature and transferability. We pass here on the digital bearer instrument without DLT and differentiate 2 main characteristics and 3 designs on how tokenized deposits can be implemented on a DLT.

In the first case, the deposit token is the digital twin or copy of the deposit account, and the amount owned is determined by the balance in the deposit account. This is called non-native deposit accounts.

Non-native deposit accounts involve claims on deposit accounts recorded on the DLT, with on-chain activity serving as an indicator of off-chain transfers. Non-native deposit tokens represent transferable tokens issued as claims against the issuing institution, where the value transfer occurs off-chain and is triggered by on-chain token transfers.

The second case introduces native deposit accounts. These have value transferred when funds move on the DLT, with the master record residing on-chain (i.e. on the DLT). Native deposit tokens have the token itself representing the deposit, with the master record on-chain and the token holder as the owner. This means that the value on the DLT is not a digital copy of your asset, but it is what you own.

Financial institutions have the flexibility to adopt different DLT designs for introducing DLT-based deposits. These designs can be categorized into three broad types according to an Oliver Wyman/JP Morgan publication [60]:

1. Single bank blockchain/DLT:
   This approach involves a single financial institution utilizing its own private blockchain for tokenized deposits. The institution operates and maintains the blockchain. It provides a closed ecosystem for deposit token transactions.
2. Shared blockchain/DLT:
   In a shared blockchain model, multiple financial institutions collaborate to establish a common blockchain infrastructure for tokenized deposits. This allows for interoperability and streamlined processes among participating institutions. It also adds efficiency and accessibility.
3. Universal blockchain/DLT:
   A universal blockchain approach extends beyond the financial sector, involving various stakeholders, including financial institutions, regulatory bodies, and other relevant parties. This broader adoption aims to create a standardized and inclusive ecosystem for tokenized deposits, promoting transparency and market integrity (Table 11.1).

As DLT technology continues to evolve, the adoption of tokenized deposits in various DLT designs presents new opportunities for investors and

Table 11.1 DLT Types in deposit tokens

	Single Bank DLT	Shared DLT	Universal DLT
Key features	Intrabank value transfers	Interbank settlement and clearing of value	Networks connected to open DLTs, creating global connectivity for clearing and settlement
Users	Single Bank clients only	Commercial banks and corporate enterprises, allowed by the consortium running the shared DLT	Any entity allowed within the defined restrictions of the token issuer on the universal DLT
Illustrative use cases	JPM Coin	Partior consortium USDF consortium	MAS/JPM SGD deposit token SBA Token

Source Author's adaptation from [60]

financial institutions alike, fostering a more seamless and digitized banking experience.

One critical aspect that remains unresolved in the realm of tokenized deposits is the singleness of money, or how banks will ensure fungibility between different banking-backed tokens. The goal of many of these projects is to enable multi-bank-enabled tokenized deposits, but achieving seamless fungibility poses a significant challenge. The liability of a token lies with the issuing bank, and the risk profiles of different banks may impact the fungibility and pricing of their tokens.

The settlement process becomes more complex in the deposit business of commercial banks, as deposits are liabilities of specific banks. When sending funds from one bank to another, a settlement mechanism is necessary. Payments between banks are typically settled using central bank money, either through netting during a settlement cycle or instantly through systems like RTGS (Real-Time Gross Settlement).

However, if there is no central bank money available for deposit token settlement, the singleness question arises: Will tokens from different banks retain the same value, or will the financial troubles of one bank affect the value of its token compared to others?

For instance, in March 2023, would investors have preferred a token from JPMorgan (JPM) over a token from Silicon Valley Bank (SVB)? I think the answer is clear, everyone would have preferred the JPM token.

Unanswered questions also remain regarding the treatment of tokens on the receiving bank's balance sheet and the implications for clients. If a client of Bank B receives a token from Bank A, will they automatically become a client of Bank A as Bank A is the issuer of the token? Addressing these questions comprehensively is crucial before tokenized deposits can fully realize their potential.

Resolving the challenges related to fungibility, settlement mechanisms, and client implications will pave the way for wider adoption of tokenized deposits, providing investors with increased accessibility, efficiency, and transparency in the digital asset landscape.

One proposed solution to ensure fungibility is outlined in the work on the Giralgeldtoken (deposit token) by Deutsche Kreditwirtschaft (DK), which introduces three governance mechanisms [139]:

a. 100% backing of the token with central bank money
b. A multi-bank consortium launching the token and backing it with combined centrally held assets from all participating banks
c. Utilizing settlement assets such as CBDC

Another potential solution is offered by Fnality and similar platforms, which enable tokenization of central bank money and provide the necessary settlement assets. While Fnality's focus may not be specifically on tokenized deposits, their approach allows for the issuance of synthetic wholesale CBDC, integrating it into their platform to facilitate the settlement of tokenized deposits.

Several successful proof of concept (PoC) projects and initiatives have emerged, showcasing the potential of tokenized deposits and their integration with blockchain technology. Basically all of them focus on financial intermediaries and businesses, not on the retail consumer. The developments aim to enhance efficiency, improve traditional banking services, and facilitate secure transactions in the digital asset landscape. Let's explore some notable projects:

1. IberPay's Digital Euro PoC: IberPay [91], a Spanish payment provider, conducted a PoC using a hybrid model that combines token-based bearer Central Bank Digital Currency (CBDC) and account-based digital currency. The PoC utilized Iberpay's Red-i interbank blockchain network, which operates on Hyperledger Besu.
2. The Regulated Liability Network (RLN): Created by Citibank and SWIFT, RLN (140) emphasizes the importance of a settlement asset for tokenized deposits. The platform aims to enable transactions between banks by settling liabilities using Central Bank Digital Currency (CBDC). While RLN plans to settle in gross using a wholesale CBDC, such assets are not currently available.
3. USDF Consortium: Comprising 11 regional US banks, the consortium focuses on developing a digital dollar through blockchain technology. They utilize a private permissioned version of the Provenance blockchain to create a "tokenized deposit" representing existing bank deposits. USDF aims to enhance traditional banking services and expand access to secure and affordable financial solutions.
4. Digital Interbank Network by Tassat: Tassat introduced the Digital Interbank Network, enabling real-time 24/7 settlement of payments among U.S. banks using tokenized bank money as digital dollars. This blockchain-based payments network focuses on B2B use cases and operates within the existing regulatory framework of the U.S. banking system.
5. Partior Consortium: JP Morgan, DBS, and Standard Chartered Bank formed the Partior consortium, aiming to tokenize central bank money

on a shared permissioned Distributed Ledger Technology (DLT) platform. Their focus is on creating a settlement asset for the Real-Time Gross Settlement (RTGS) system.

6. Fnality: Supported by leading financial institutions, Fnality aims to improve liquidity management by creating a payment solution using blockchain and Distributed Ledger Technology (DLT). While not focusing specifically on tokenized deposits, Fnality provides a tokenization of central bank money, offering a reliable source of value similar to fiat currency.
7. Onyx by JPMorgan [60]: Onyx operates a digital assets platform based on a permissioned version of the Ethereum blockchain. They facilitate the issuance and trading of tokens, including JPM coin, which represents ownership of assets on JPM blockchain accounts. Onyx also explores deposit tokens, representing existing bank deposits recorded on a blockchain while maintaining regulatory safeguards.
8. GNU Taler Tokens backed by a German commercial bank: This project falls under the BIS model 1 of the digital bearer instrument, where the token is much more cash-like, generated from bank deposits. The tokens are backed by the balance sheet of the bank, or in the best case by a bank-owned bankruptcy remote reserve at the central bank (making it a synthetic CBDC). It allows for programmable money issuance, but the proposed system in Germany is not based on a DLT.
9. Project Guardian [141] by the Monetary Authority of Singapore (MAS): Led by DBS Bank, JP Morgan, and Marketnode, Project Guardian explores decentralized finance (DeFi) applications in wholesale funding markets. The project aims to enable secured borrowing and lending through smart contracts on a <u>public</u> blockchain-based network, utilizing tokenized bonds and deposits.
10. Swiss Banking Association (SBA): SBA [142] proposes a deposit token, a form of programmable money issued by Swiss banks. These tokens are digital representations of funds held in segregated deposit accounts and are backed by real assets. The SBA envisions their use for peer-to-peer transactions, merchant payments, and integration into existing payment systems. In contrast to the JPM coin, SBA sees a joint token through a special-purpose vehicle on a <u>public</u> blockchain as the way to go. Payment services would run over a Layer 2 solution. Open issues remain with regard to legal and regulatory requirements and the classification of a deposit token in Switzerland, as well as confidentiality and privacy questions.

11. Deutsche Kreditwirtschaft (DK): DK [139] is exploring the issuance of tokenized deposits directly on customer blockchains. In collaboration with DZ Bank, Commerzbank, Helaba, and Unicredit, they are conducting a proof of concept for deposit tokens. The project utilizes a commercial bank money token (CBMT) model, leveraging third-party DLT networks. This project is mostly focused on addressing industry needs, which involve extensive process automation through the usage of DLT, smart contracts and microtransactions. The proposed CBMT should be complementary to a retail CBDC and an answer to the competition from stablecoins. The DK paper is technology agnostic and high level, but introduces some novel ideas like:

    - being available directly on Industry DLTs (CBMT is multi-DLT capable)
    - being agnostic of wallet owners and payment processors
    - clearing & settlement mechanisms between banks are fully transparent (CBMT is a multi-issuer concept).

    Tokenized commercial bank money could significantly optimize Distributed Ledger Technology (DLT)-based business-to-business (B2B) use cases by increasing efficiency, security, and transparency:

    - Delivery-versus-Payment (DvP): In supply chain finance, trade finance, and securities settlement, DvP is a key business process. It ensures that delivery of goods is made only when the payment is received.
    - Pay-per-use cases: With pay-per-use models, customers pay only for what they use.
    - Smart contract-initiated payments: Smart contracts are essentially programmable contracts that can be set to automatically execute when certain conditions are met.
    - Continuous payment streams: Tokenized commercial bank money could allow for real-time, continuous payment streams, an innovation that could radically change how workers are paid or how subscriptions are billed.

These innovative projects aim to address various aspects of tokenized deposits, including fungibility, settlement mechanisms, interoperability with traditional banking infrastructure, and regulatory compliance.

It is interesting to observe that nearly all projects were initially based on permissioned blockchains, but more recently models have started popping up that propose the usage of the main public blockchains, and even digital bearer instruments.

While many challenges remain, these initiatives demonstrate the ongoing development and exploration of tokenized deposits to unlock their full potential in modern financial ecosystems.

11.3.1 Enhancing Cross-Border Payments with Tokenized Deposits and Unified Ledgers

Efficiency and transparency in payments vary across different contexts. While solutions like SEPA and SEPA Instant have made European payments efficient, cross-border transactions face greater complexity, for example in a transaction from Jamaica to Uzbekistan, where the correspondent banking system needs to play a vital role. Multiple hops, multiple regulators, and disparate systems among banks, correspondent banks, and central banks introduce sequential steps, potential issues, and a lack of transparency.

To address these challenges, the concept of a public–private unified ledger as a settlement system has been proposed. Agustín Carstens, General Manager of the BIS, highlighted the potential of Central Bank Digital Currencies (CBDCs) and asset tokenization in a keynote speech [114] at the Monetary Authority of Singapore. He emphasized the need for a **unified ledger** with a common programming environment, combining the strengths of the central bank and private sector. This partnership would provide a technologically superior representation of money, enabling automated transactions, interoperability, and cost-effective products that foster financial inclusion.

The unified ledger would preserve the existing roles of the central bank and private sector, with the former issuing central bank money and ensuring payment finality through settlement on its balance sheet. The latter would engage in consumer-facing activities. By bringing together CBDCs and tokenized deposits on a unified ledger, greater efficiency and innovation could be achieved. This approach does not necessitate decentralized or permissionless platforms, but rather a collaboration that maintains trust and enables technological advancements by restricting access.

Many projects in this domain plan to leverage smart contracts for account management, utilizing blockchains as the account system. The tokens representing liabilities of respective banks can be implemented on their individual blockchains, connected via a meta blockchain, or issued on a shared common blockchain. However, the issue of fungibility between tokens from different banks remains unresolved. Mr. Carstens and others have proposed solutions to address this challenge, recognizing the need for innovative approaches to unlock the full potential of tokenized deposits.

In conclusion, the utilization of tokenized deposits in banks offers numerous benefits such as enhanced accessibility, transparency, and security.

As such, a global enterprise using the JPM Coin, can move money between countries instantly and 24/7/365. The success is shown by the fact that in October 2023, JP Morgan told Bloomberg that JPM Coin has reached a volume of US$1 billion daily.

A five-party transaction will benefit from the atomicity offered by such solutions, meaning that either all five transactions will be executed together or none will, providing a lot of security and transparency, where today it often happens that not all five parts of a deal get executed at the same time (all or none) and the transaction ends up in limbo for a while.

However, the establishment of solutions that ensure fungibility between tokens issued by different banks is crucial. As efforts continue in designing, developing, testing, and adopting such solutions, the transformative potential of tokenized deposits in revolutionizing cross-border payments can be fully realized.

Part II

Decoding Central Bank Digital Currencies

12

Central Bank Digital Currencies (CBDCs): Exploring Characteristics, Risks and Benefits

In addition to stablecoins, **Central Bank Digital Currencies (CBDCs)** have gained significant attention as a promising form of payment token. Governments worldwide are actively exploring the issuance of their own digital currencies, pegged to the local fiat currency. This chapter, and those that follow, will delve into CBDCs, exploring their unique characteristics, risks, and benefits.

CBDC, short for Central Bank Digital Currency, represents the third type of payment token discussed in this book. It is a digital form of currency issued and backed by a central bank, designed to function as legal tender. Conceptually, CBDCs can be seen as digital counterparts to physical banknotes and coins, or as digitized versions of the reserves held by financial institutions at the central bank. As a result, CBDCs represent a new form of central bank money, supported by the stability of central bank reserves and possessing the necessary trust characteristics to coexist alongside existing forms of currency.

CBDCs should not be confused with decentralized cryptocurrencies like Bitcoin or Ethereum, as they operate on distinct principles. Unlike cryptocurrencies, CBDCs are centralized, issued by central banks, and backed by the government's creditworthiness. This backing ensures the reliability and stability of CBDCs as a digital currency, setting them apart from cryptocurrencies that lack government or central authority support. It's important to note that the money held in bank accounts or used with credit cards is commercial bank money, which carries higher risk as it is only backed by the respective bank or credit card provider, not the central bank.

L. V. Schumacher, *Decoding Digital Assets*, https://doi.org/10.1007/978-3-031-54601-3_12

The introduction of CBDCs raises various challenges and risks that need to be addressed. The potential centralization resulting from CBDC implementation has drawn attention, as it could further concentrate power in the financial system. Additionally, the design of CBDCs that store transaction data in a centralized ledger or repository may present unprecedented security risks and privacy concerns. Cybercriminals could target such centralized databases, and the mass surveillance possibilities offered by CBDCs may infringe upon individual freedoms.

Mitigating the risks associated with CBDCs requires careful consideration and trade-offs. Technological tools exist to address these concerns, but they may come with their own drawbacks. Therefore, it is crucial to define the essential features and benefits a CBDC must deliver before proceeding with an implementation.

CBDCs have emerged as a promising form of digital currency, offering reliability and stability backed by central bank reserves and government creditworthiness. Their implementation may present challenges and risks like privacy, programmability, and offline usage. Addressing these concerns through thoughtful design and technological measures is essential. By carefully navigating the complexities, CBDCs done right have the potential to revolutionize our financial landscape while safeguarding privacy, maintaining individual freedoms, and fostering financial inclusion.

12.1 Types of CBDC

The money flower conceived by the BIS provides a great overview of the different forms of money available and a good introduction into the CBDC topic.

The money flower graph shows cash as a non-digital token/value-based item. This means that physical money, like paper bills and coins, represents a certain value. Here's why this is important:

Physical representation: Cash is something you can touch and hold. It's a physical object (a token) that represents an amount of value. A $10 bill, for example, is a token that represents $10 worth of value.

Trust and acceptance: When you use cash, the person you're giving it to doesn't need to check your bank account to see if you have the money. The cash itself is the value. This is different from using a check or a credit card, where the value is not in the physical object itself but in the promise that the bank will pay that amount.

Immediate transaction: With cash, the transaction is immediate. When you hand over the money, the other person gets it right then and there. There's no delay like there might be with other forms of payment that need banks to process them.
No need for personal information: Using cash doesn't require personal information or a digital record. This is like when you use game tokens; the token is all that matters, not who is holding it.

Cash being "token-based" means that it is a physical representation of value, like tokens in a game (like the fake paper money in a Monopoly game), and it allows for immediate, direct transactions without the need for personal information or further processing. Similar characteristics can be applied to the other tokens shown in the graph, with the only difference that some of these are digital files versus physical paper notes or metal coins.

"Widely accessible" means that this category is available to many parties, like the citizens of a country for example.

There are two main types of CBDCs being explored and launched across the world at the time of this writing. The Graph 12.1 captures them in 3 highlighted areas:

> ***Retail CBDCs*** for citizens are shown as *"CB accounts (general purpose)"* and *"CB digital tokens (general purpose),"* and ***wholesale CBDCs*** for banks are shown as *"CB digital tokens (wholesale only)."*

12.1.1 Wholesale CBDCs

Wholesale Central Bank Digital Currencies (abbreviated wCBDCs) refer to a type of CBDC that is accessible only to financial institutions that hold reserve accounts with a central bank. These institutions usually include commercial banks, investment funds, and other authorized financial entities.

The purpose of a wCBDC is primarily to enhance the efficiency and security of transactions between these financial institutions that already have established accounts with the central bank. This can involve activities such as interbank payments and securities settlement.

Wholesale CBDCs are only available to a select group of participants, unlike retail CBDCs, which are designed for use by the general public (i.e. the people).

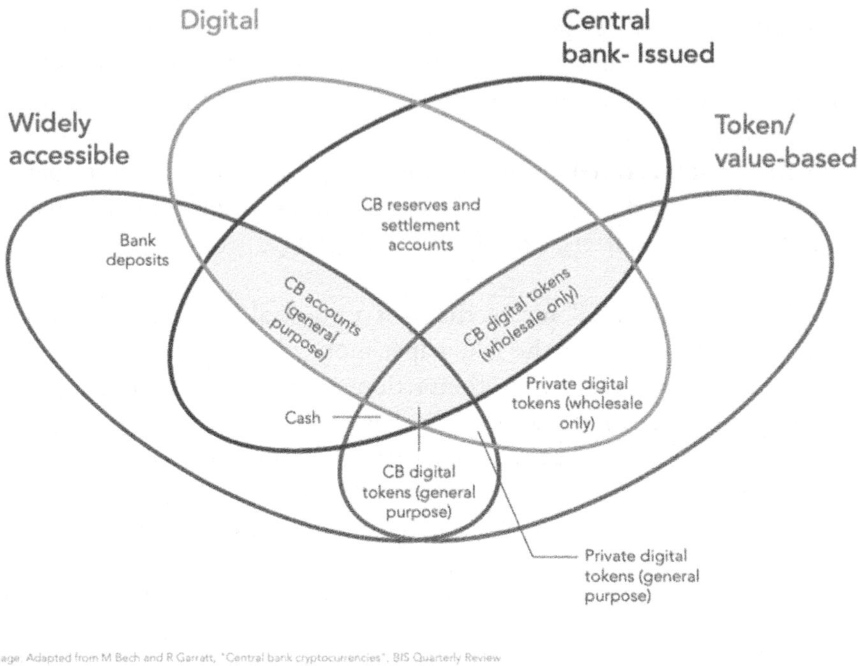

Graph 12.1 Money flower (*Source* BIS Quarterly Review)

12.1.2 Retail CBDCs

Retail CBDCs (abbreviated rCBDC) are designed for use by everyone and are intended to be a digital equivalent of physical currency.

According to the image of the money flower above conceived by the BIS, retail CBDCs can be created as **central bank accounts** (CB accounts (general purpose)) or as **central bank digital tokens** (CB digital tokens (general purpose)).

We do believe that this representation is one level of simplification too much. In order to eliminate confusion down the road, when it comes to characteristics and possible technical realizations, we find it necessary to split the ***CB digital token (general purpose)*** category conceived by the BIS in their money flower graph into two categories: one for designs with actual digital tokens (without blockchains), like the eCash or GNU Taker token, and another one for designs with blockchains and digital signing keys, similar to cryptocurrencies, like Bitcoin.

Both categories have the commonality that a digital file (the actual token or a secret signing key) exclusively gives access to the money, but the rest of the solutions (and their characteristics) are significantly different and that makes it necessary to separate the two from each other.

That provides us with 3 categories of retail CBDCs:

a. **Token-based CBDCs**:
   These are digital tokens that are held by the user as cash-like bearer instruments representing central bank money, and which can be used for peer-to-peer transactions. Token-based money is the actual "***digital cash,***" of which an early version was already conceived in 1990s by Prof. David Chaum with eCash. These tokens only exist in your digital wallet, in the same way the physical banknote only exists in your purse, and there are no corresponding account or ledger entries.
b. **Account-based CBDCs**:
   These are digital representations of the local fiat currency held in an account with the central bank. They are similar to traditional bank accounts, where the balance is calculated as the sum of the ins and outs, but instead of being held with commercial banks, they are held with the central bank. Identification is necessary to access these accounts.
c. **DLT-based CBDCs**:
   Such CBDCs are based on an entry in a digital decentralized ledger or blockchain representing central bank money, which can only be accessed with a digital secret signing key. This secret digital key, which exclusively provides access to the funds represented in the ledger entry corresponding to the digital key, is held by the user in their digital wallet, like a physical key being kept in the pocket of the owner to unlock his safety deposit box. These retail CBDCs are based on a design similar to cryptocurrencies with blockchains, like Bitcoin.

Retail CBDCs will have to compete with existing private payment solutions, including the newer Instant Payment Systems (often also called Fast Payment Systems (FPS) or Real Time Payment (RTP) systems), as they have been deployed in more and more countries. IPS systems are types of financial technology that allow for the immediate transfer of funds between accounts, typically across different banks or financial institutions. They work 24/7 and accelerate the clearance and settlement process between banks and bank accounts. IPS systems are designed to process payments in real time, making the funds available to the recipient almost instantly instead of the usual 2–3 days delay. Retail CBDCs must match the speed of these Instant Payment Systems and their usability to be able to impose themselves as a viable alternative.

It should be understood though that both token-based (digital cash) and DLT-based CBDCs may work without needing clearing and settlement, going from wallet to wallet without involving a bank or a bank account. In the end, this depends on the effective design of the solution.

It is important to acknowledge that Instant Payment Solutions have already been successfully implemented in several jurisdictions, such as Brazil, China, India, Switzerland, and others. Retail CBDC solutions must assess themselves against these established solutions in terms of usability and adoption, as they compete in the same space. This competition is for example a driving force behind the stringent requirements set by the Chinese central bank for their CBDC solution, which will be explored later in this book (Graph 12.2).

When executed effectively, both CBDCs and Instant Payment Systems share several qualities. They provide a huge improvement in usability and enable various providers to introduce new services through multiple interfaces. These arrangements have the potential to benefit users by reducing costs, ensuring universal access, and promoting financial inclusion as future chapters will illustrate.

Furthermore, central banks, as issuers of CBDCs and often also as supervisors of Instant Payment Solutions, potentially play a significant role. They can impose guidance toward establishing enhanced privacy with CBDCs and ensuring responsible usage of payment data.

A central focus will also be on aptly designing the requirements of digital identity in these systems. Current Instant Payment System (IPS) platforms are

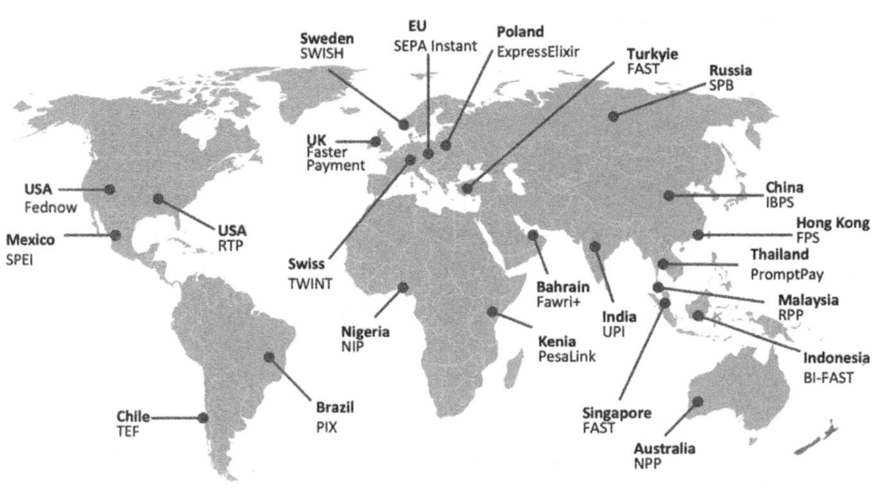

Graph 12.2 Implementations of IPS (*Source* Author)

typically account-based and accessed via identification of the user. They tend to make all transaction data available to their providers. In contrast, central banks have the option with retail CBDCs to adopt a more cash-like (token-based) approach, without the need to link it to identities for secure operation. By creating an open system that prioritizes user privacy and data control, which can be leveraged to dismantle data silos and weaken the market dominance of incumbent private companies (like Visa, Mastercard, PayPal,...) that have exclusive control over user data, a different future payment space can be imagined.

While CBDCs and Instant Payment Systems share numerous common attributes, a significant key distinction, which is not necessarily recognized by the general public at the time of this writing yet, lies in how CBDCs directly extend the unique features of digital central bank money to the general public. In a CBDC system, making a payment only requires transferring a direct claim on the central bank from one user to another, eliminating the need for an intermediary. Transactions are settled directly and in real time on the central bank's balance sheet using central bank money. On the other hand, Instant Payment Solutions enable retail payees to receive immediate access to final funds, but the underlying wholesale settlement between payment service providers may experience delays.

A comparison of cash, the 3 types of retail CBDCs, and Instant Payment Systems in the Table 12.1 adapted from work [202] by the BIS illustrates key similarities and differences that are relevant here.

When it comes to defining the consumer needs in a retail CBDC and its impact on design choices, the BIS has published a first version of the following pyramid [78], originally introduced by Auer & Boehme, to assist in establishing how a CBDC could be defined. The pyramid below has been adapted for a better fit (Graph 12.3).

A CBDC must fulfill consumer needs at least at the same level, and ideally better than existing payment tools, if it expects to be adopted widely. The development of Central Bank Digital Currency specifications should therefore result from considering the consumer needs and those of other stakeholders like banks and merchants. Mapping their requirements should direct the designers toward the necessary-related design choices.

The left of the CBDC pyramid outlines consumer needs and associated features that would make a retail CBDC useful, including cash-like peer-to-peer usability, convenient real-time payments, payments security, privacy, wide accessibility, and ease of use in cross-border payments.

The right side of the pyramid lays out the associated options in design choices.

Table 12.1 Comparison of Cash, CBDC and IPS characteristics

	Cash	Token-based retail CBDC	DLT-based retail CBDC	Account-based retail CBDC	Retail IPS
Safety as a settlement asset	Direct central bank liability	Direct central bank liability	Direct central bank liability	Direct central bank liability	Liability of commercial banks and (in some cases) non-bank PSPs with collateralization and deposit insurance, and potentially non-bank PSPs without deposit insurance
Finality of the retail payment	Immediate upon receipt (but requires physical proximity)	Immediate upon receipt	Immediate upon receipt	Immediate upon confirmation by PSP	Immediate upon confirmation by PSP
Finality of the underlying wholesale payment	No wholesale settlement required	No wholesale settlement required	No wholesale settlement required	No deferred settlement required	Some use deferred clearing/ settlement for interbank exposures; others use RTGS
Costs for users and merchants	Relatively low	Extremely low	Design choice, but must be competitive with cash and other digital payments	Design choice, but must be competitive with cash and other digital payments	Generally low (typically cross-subsidized with other services), can be regulated

	Cash	Token-based retail CBDC	DLT-based retail CBDC	Account-based retail CBDC	Retail IPS
Identification required for access?	None, except for high-value payments in many jurisdictions	None	None	Yes	Yes
Anonymity and confidentiality for users	High; Two-sided anonymity	HighOne-sided or two-sided anonymity	Design choice, mostly medium by being pseudonymous	No anonymity; but trust-based confidentiality protected by system design, bank secrecy and data protection laws	No anonymity; but confidentiality protected by system design, bank secrecy and data protection laws
Offline payments	Yes	Design choice	Design choice	No, unless combined with token-based offline system	No
New digital functions	No	Use in e-commerce, instant, available 24/7, further new functions, including programmable money & payments, and ability to make micro-payments	Use in e-commerce, instant, available 24/7, further new functions, including programmable money & payments	Use in e-commerce, instant, available 24/7, further new functions, including programmable payments	Use in e-commerce, instant, available 24/7, further new functions, including programmable payments

(continued)

Table 12.1 (continued)

	Cash	Token-based retail CBDC	DLT-based retail CBDC	Account-based retail CBDC	Retail IPS
Cross-border use	Yes, with physical transport (subject to limit/regulation)	May be more convenient and cheaper to operate than cash. Subject to design could provide convenient and cheaper access	May be more convenient and cheaper to operate than cash. Subject to design could provide convenient and cheaper access	May be more convenient and cheaper to operate than cash. Subject to design could provide convenient and cheaper access	May interlink with other IPS abroad but requires inter-IPS settlement arrangements

PSP = Payment Service Provider, RTGS = Real Time Gross Settlement system by the central bank

Source Author's adaptation of BIS table from CBDCs—an opportunity for the monetary system

Graph 12.3 CBDC Pyramid (*Source* Adaptation from BIS' CBDC pyramid)

The primary consumer need for a CBDC is that it embodies a cash-like claim on the central bank, ideally transferable in peer-to-peer settings and easily shifting electronic money holdings into cash if requested. And second, it must be fast, resilient, and available.

These two needs—cash-like safety and convenience of use—lead to the foundational design consideration for a retail CBDC, which is the choice of the operational architecture. This includes balancing the consumer's demand for a cash-like claim on the central bank with the convenience that intermediaries provide to the payment system. The consensus across countries as of the writing of this book is that a CBDC should always be a claim on the central bank and that CBDCs should be deployed in a two-tier model, where financial intermediaries and banks take care of KYC, AML, and CFT compliance (in tier one) and the central bank tales care of the rest (in tier two).

The consumer's need for payment safety requires that a CBDC be secure not only from intermediaries' insolvency or technical glitches but also from outages at the central bank. The choice is whether to base this infrastructure on a conventional centrally controlled database or on Distributed Ledger Technology (DLT).

Two additional consumer needs are easy universal access and privacy by default. There is often a perceived trade-off between privacy and ease of access on the one hand, and ease of law enforcement on the other. The associated design choice in the third layer of the pyramid is whether access to the

CBDC is tied to an identity system or through cryptographic schemes, that introduce bearer instruments and do not require identification. The trade-off between privacy and ease of access can be eliminated with the right technology choices and the trade-off between privacy and ease of law enforcement can be minimized as well.

The final consumer need to consider (on the top left of the pyramid) is that CBDCs should enable cross-border payments. This feature could be offered at the wholesale level through technical connections built on current systems or at the retail level, for example by allowing consumers to hold foreign digital currencies directly.

Before ending this chapter, we want to come back to the formula of Morten Bech, where CBDC is making M_0 money great again (CBDC = MM_0GA) and apply what we have seen by expanding his initial formula a little further. As no single central bank has claimed so far that it wants to replace cash, we do want to keep physical cash as the ideal fallback in payments, but augment it with a digital cash complement to cover areas in which cash cannot be used today.

This seems to be the most obvious approach to CBDC success for many countries: Cash will be made great again by combining physical cash (bank notes and coins) with a retail CBDC (rCBDC) for online/digital use, and the already digital central bank reserves may be replaced completely over time with an overall more efficient wholesale CBDC (wCBDC), which takes us to the following refinement of the M_0 of the future:

$$\begin{aligned} \text{CBDC} &= \text{MM}_0\text{GA} \\ \text{M}_0^{\text{Today}} &= \text{Cash} + \text{central bank reserves} \\ \mathbf{M_0^{Future}} &= \mathbf{Cash + rCBDC + wCBDC} \end{aligned}$$

12.2 History and Catalysts for Central Bank Digital Currencies (CBDCs)

The concept of Central Bank Digital Currencies (CBDCs) emerged in the wake of Bitcoin's launch, which sparked discussions among central banks worldwide. This chapter explores the historical context and key factors that have prompted the recent surge in CBDC projects globally.

1. **Technological advancements:** Advancements in blockchain, distributed ledger, and other technologies have paved the way for the creation of secure, efficient, and tamper-proof digital currencies without the need for a trusted third party. While the idea of digital cash was introduced in 1983 by David Chaum, it lacked the necessary computing infrastructure and widespread smartphone adoption for success. Today, central banks are exploring the potential of CBDCs to modernize their payment systems using these technological advancements.
2. **Growth of digital payments:** Digital payments have witnessed significant growth worldwide, accelerated further by the COVID-19 pandemic. Recognizing this shift, many central banks are exploring CBDCs to adapt to the evolving payment landscape and to offer their citizens a more secure and efficient payment system.
3. **Sovereignty of payment solutions and monetary policy:** Central banks are concerned about the risks associated with the decline of cash usage and the entry of Big Tech companies into the payment sector. Sweden's cashless society and the threat of Big Tech, exemplified by Facebook's Libra, have raised a lot of concerns. Issuing CBDCs will allow central banks to maintain control over the financial system, the critical payments infrastructure, and mitigate the risks associated with decentralized cryptocurrencies.
4. **Rise of cryptocurrencies:** The rise of cryptocurrencies, such as Bitcoin, has gained significant attention and operates outside the control of central banks. This has heightened concerns among central banks regarding the potential risks associated with decentralized digital currencies. By introducing their own digital currencies, central banks aim to regain control over the financial system and address the risks posed by cryptocurrencies.
5. **Geopolitical competition:** The emergence of digital currencies has opened up possibilities for an alternative global financial system not reliant on the US dollar. Several countries, particularly China and Russia, view CBDCs as an opportunity to challenge the dominance of the US dollar and establish their currencies as global standards. Geopolitical events, such as the Ukraine conflict and sanctions on Russia, have further fueled the de-dollarization movement. However, given the dollar's current dominance, sustained and widespread changes over a long time will be required before any significant shift occurs.

Table 12.2 illustrates the growth in efforts and activities started by central banks on the CBDC subject, both retail and wholesale.

Table 12.2 Central Bank involvement in CBDCs

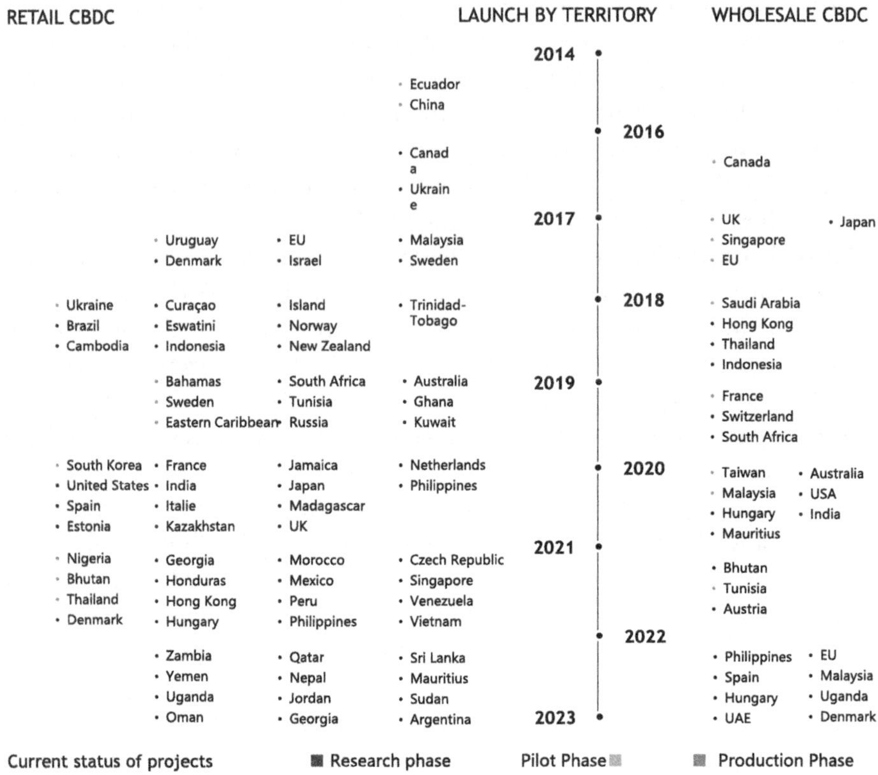

Source Author based on data by CBDCtracker.org

The Graph 12.4, based on data from the Bank of International Settlement's 2022 survey on CBDCs and Digital Tokens [201], gives further insight into the evolution, the focus and type of work undertaken in a CBDC space bustling with activity.

The Rise and Fall of Facebook's Libra and the Impact on CBDC Development

Facebook's announcement of its Libra cryptocurrency in 2019 sent shockwaves through the financial world, sparking discussions on stablecoins and Central Bank Digital Currencies (CBDCs).

While the ultimate vision of Libra was to provide universal access to financial services, one of its more practical and immediate objectives was to address the challenges associated with cross-border payments. The white paper [167] stated:

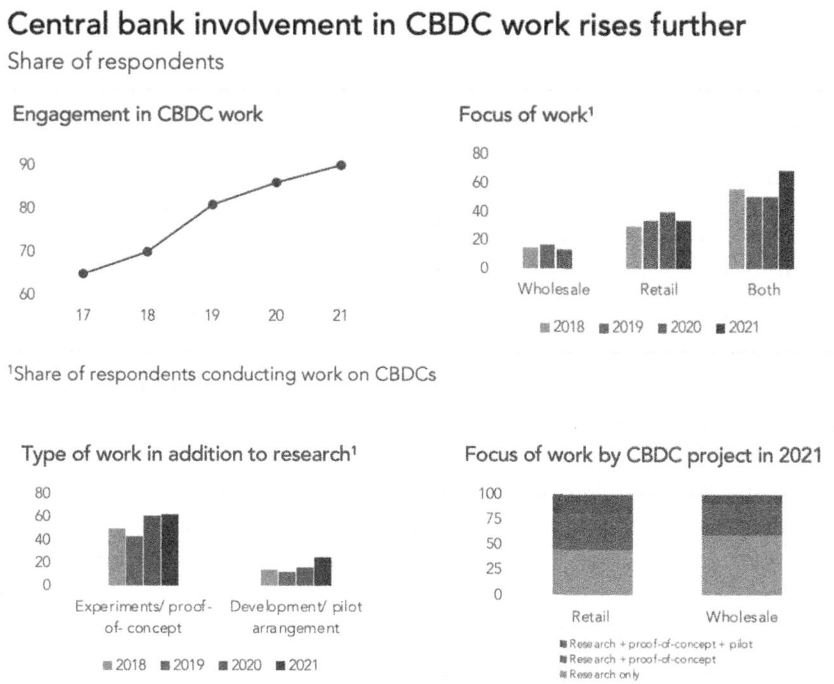

Graph 12.4 CBDC activities (*Source* Data from BIS "2021 central bank survey on CBDCs and digital tokens")

> Moving money around globally, and in a compliant way, should be as easy and cost-effective as — and even safer and more secure than — sending a message or sharing a photo, no matter where you are, what you do, or how much you earn. [12]

With over 2.5 billion users on platforms including Facebook, Instagram, and WhatsApp, Facebook's Libra project held the potential to rapidly introduce and popularize a new global currency. However, a myriad of challenges ultimately led to the downfall of the project. This section dissects the triggers behind the rise and fall of Libra, along with its impact on CBDC development.

1. **Libra's grand vision**: Libra aspired to establish a universally accessible financial infrastructure and digital currency, specifically targeting cross-border payments. It aimed to produce a low-volatility cryptocurrency and transform digital-first applications. Libra had assembled many blue-chip names as founding member, like Mastercard, Visa, PayPal, Stripe, eBay, Uber, Spotify, Vodafone, ... Nevertheless, its potential influence on

existing financial controls and the possible consolidation of power within the Libra Association raised alarm bells.

2. **Ethical and social implications**: The Libra project faced criticism over several ethical and societal matters. These ranged from financial inclusion, privacy, security, and regulatory complexities to monopoly concerns and the ethical motivations behind Facebook's participation. Critics pointed out potential exclusions, data privacy threats, security risks, regulatory hurdles, market monopolization, and the potential profit-driven motives.
3. **Regulatory obstacles**: Libra faced substantial regulatory backlash due to worries about a private corporation administering a global digital currency. Governments and regulatory bodies raised concerns about potential money laundering, terrorist financing, and other unlawful activities. Past missteps by Facebook in managing user data and its involvement in significant scandals further amplified regulatory scrutiny.
4. **Departure of key partners**: As regulatory pressure mounted, key partners such as Mastercard, Visa, eBay, and PayPal pulled out from the Libra project. The withdrawal of these influential players undermined Libra's credibility and significantly lessened its likelihood of success.
5. **Strategic shift**: Faced with mounting challenges, Facebook altered its strategy in April 2020, focusing now on creating multiple stablecoins backed by individual national currencies. Coupled with the rebranding of Libra as "Diem," this shift marked a retreat from the original vision of a singular global currency. The strategic realignment was perceived as a setback, casting doubts about the project's feasibility.
6. **Escalating competition**: The announcement of Libra spurred other tech companies and financial institutions to delve into their own digital currency initiatives, thereby threatening Libra's potential market dominance.

The combination of regulatory resistance, lack of trust, partner withdrawals, change in strategy, and competition ultimately led to the demise of the Libra project. In January 2022, the Diem Association (formerly the Libra Association) began winding down its operations. It sold its assets to California-based company Silvergate Capital for an estimated $200 million.

The rise and fall of Facebook's Libra project significantly influenced the progression of CBDCs. While the initial announcement of Libra spurred a rush toward digital currency exploration, its failure underscored the critical challenges and worries to be addressed. However, the repercussions on central banks were notable as it pushed them to massively expedite their exploration and development of CBDCs.

12.3 Benefits of CBDCs

In this chapter, we explore the numerous benefits that can potentially be derived from Central Bank Digital Currencies (CBDCs). The ten key benefits include:

1. **Financial stability:** CBDCs can mitigate the risk of payment system failures and bank runs by providing an alternative and additional means of payment and store of value. This enhances the stability of the financial system and improves the effectiveness of monetary policy.

SVB—A Bank Run to Remember

One notable incident highlighting the issue of bank runs is the case of Silicon Valley Bank (SBV), which experienced a bank run on March 10, 2023, which led to its closure. At that time, only 10% of the deposits held by SBV were covered by deposit insurance. Without the intervention of the US government, there was a possibility that up to 90% of these deposits could be lost.

During this period, there was some discussion about the concept of providing a 100% guarantee on commercial bank deposits. However, this idea was swiftly dismissed by Janet Yellen, the United States Secretary of the Treasury. Implementing such a guarantee would have had far-reaching and possibly unforeseen consequences throughout the economy. Eventually, a guarantee was nevertheless extended temporarily via the FDIC to prevent further bank runs.

In the context of CBDCs, it is crucial to recognize that if these deposits at SBV had been in the form of CBDCs, the bank run could have been averted, because CBDCs issued by the Federal Reserve Bank of the United States would always be guaranteed deposits at 100%, eliminating the risk associated with bank runs.

2. **Monetary policy implementation:** CBDCs offer central banks more direct control over the money supply and interest rates, enabling more effective implementation of monetary policy. They can be used for targeted distribution of stimulus payments and the implementation of negative interest rates, enhancing the flexibility of monetary policy tools.
3. **Financial inclusion:** CBDCs have the potential to improve financial inclusion by providing access to financial services for the unbanked

and underbanked populations. CBDCs can be accessed through smartphones, even without a traditional bank account, promoting broader financial participation.

4. **Improved domestic payment efficiency:** CBDCs make payments faster, cheaper, and more convenient. They allow direct peer-to-peer transactions without the need for intermediaries, reducing friction and costs in the payment process. The efficiency gains from CBDCs can lead to the disintermediation of certain participants in the current payment landscape.
5. **Cross-border payments efficiency:** CBDC adoption can especially enhance cross-border payments, which are highly complex today. CBDCs can enable interoperability between different payment systems and currencies. They can eliminate the need for intermediaries, reducing settlement times and costs for cross-border transactions.
6. **Payment safety:** CBDCs can offer enhanced security compared to cash or traditional digital payments. Advanced cryptographic techniques can ensure the integrity of transactions, protecting against manipulation and counterfeiting.
7. **Improvements in privacy protections over existing digital payment solutions:** CBDCs can provide stronger privacy protections, offering individuals greater control over their financial data and transactions. Privacy-enhancing features aligned with GDPR requirements can be incorporated, providing individuals with increased confidentiality.
8. **Sovereignty or alternatives to private payment solutions:** CBDCs give central banks greater control over the monetary system and critical payments infrastructure, reducing dependence on private and/or foreign payment providers. They offer countries a way to compete with privately issued digital currencies while maintaining control over the digital monetary system.
9. **Preventing black markets and tax evasion:** CBDCs can be designed to prevent black market activities and tax evasion, promoting a more socially fair economic environment. However, initial adoption in less developed countries that operate mostly black markets without taxation may face challenges due to the short-term tax collection objectives conflicting with existing black markets and the users benefitting of them.
10. **Combatting money laundering:** CBDCs can incorporate features that make it difficult for criminals to exploit them for illicit activities such as money laundering or terrorist financing. This strengthens the integrity of the financial system and reduces the risk of financial instability.

While CBDCs offer a range of benefits, it is essential to acknowledge the potential risks and challenges associated with their implementation. We will discuss these in the next chapters. The Graph 12.5 illustrates how central banks worldwide perceive the benefits of a **retail Central Bank Digital Currency** (rCBDC) for both advanced economies and emerging/developing economies and the evolution between 2018 and 2021.

The Graph 12.6 shows how central banks around the world rate the benefits of a **wholesale Central Bank Currency** (wCBDC) for advanced economies (AE) and emerging markets and developing economies (EMDE) and the evolution between 2018 and 2021.

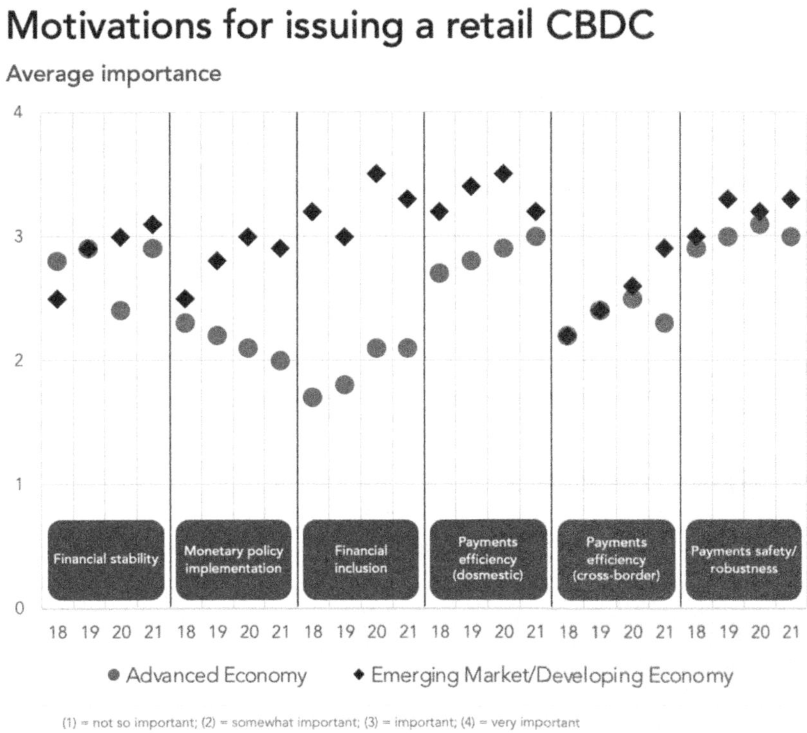

Graph 12.5 Motivations for issuing a retail CBDC—evolution over the years 2018–2021 (*Source* Data from 2021 BIS central bank survey on CBDCs and digital tokens)

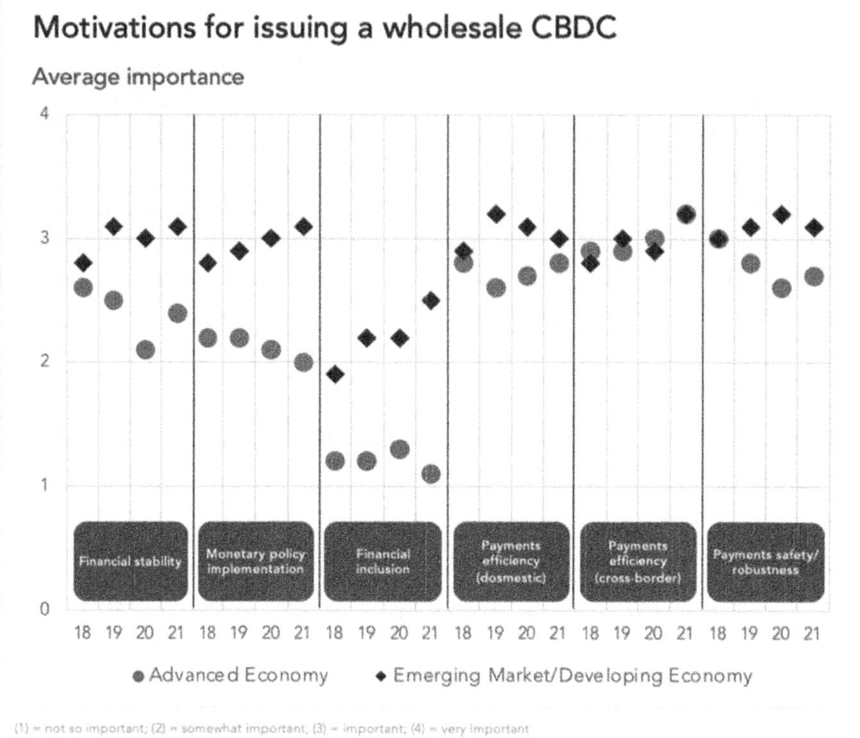

Graph 12.6 Motivations for issuing a wholesale CBDC—evolution over the years 2018–2021 (*Source* Data 2021 BIS central bank survey on CBDCs & digital tokens)

12.4 Risks of CBDCs

In this chapter, we examine the risks associated with the introduction of Central Bank Digital Currencies. Policymakers and researchers are closely monitoring these risks as CBDCs continue to evolve. The 6 key risks we identified are as follows:

1. **Weakening of financial stability**: The introduction of CBDCs may raise concerns about financial stability. If individuals shift their savings from commercial banks (where the savings face a higher risk given that a commercial bank is more likely to default than a central bank as illustrated by the SVB shutdown) to CBDCs (where the savings face no risk as liability of the central bank), it could increase the risk of bank runs during financial crises. This in turn could potentially destabilize the overall financial system. The mobility of the money into a much safer asset would be

significantly enhanced by a CBDC. The recent example of the bank run on Silicon Valley Bank highlights the potential acceleration of such runs if CBDCs were available. Even a decrease in bank deposits could impact overall lending and adversely affecting the economy.
2. **Disintermediation**: This shift in deposits could weaken the funding capabilities of banks, impacting their ability to provide loans and impacting their business. The impact will depend on the design of the CBDC. A CBDC designed like bank accounts and offering similar characteristics could easily be primarily used as store of value and facilitate such disintermediation. A CBDC designed like cash and offering similar characteristics would be less likely to be used as store of value but rather as means of payment, because the risk of carrying $100,000 with you in your physical wallet is higher than what most people would be comfortable with. A successful CBDC could also cause a disruption of existing payment solutions, especially if it is consumer friendly, fast, and free. The adaption of the CBDC as payment solution will to the largest extent consist of a churn of customer of existing payment solution providers (PSPs). These PSPs will see their revenues and profits threatened.
3. **Cybersecurity**: The increased digitization and potential use of Distributed Ledger Technology in CBDC systems introduce new cybersecurity risks. The larger attack surface of distributed ledger systems may make CBDCs more vulnerable to hacking, cyberattacks, and security breaches. Given the potential as a valuable target with unlimited potential as a money printing press, CBDCs must have robust security measures to counter sophisticated hackers, including state actors and criminal organizations.

The Snowden Revelations

The Snowden revelations, which exposed extensive government surveillance programs, had a lasting impact on discussions surrounding privacy and civil liberties. The published documents unveiled the scope and reach of intelligence agencies' surveillance activities, both domestically and internationally. The publicized documents highlighted controversial programs such as the collection of phone records, internet communication interception, and cyber espionage targeting foreign companies, governments, and politicians.

These revelations sparked a global debate on the balance between national security and individual privacy. Critics argued that the surveillance programs infringed upon citizens' rights and violated constitutional protections. Meanwhile, proponents emphasized the importance of these programs for safeguarding national security and claimed that strict oversight ensured targeted surveillance.

The New York Times disclosed based on the Snowden papers that the NSA spends more than $250 million a year on its Sigint Enabling Project, which "*actively engages the U.S. and foreign IT industries to covertly influence and/or overtly leverage their commercial products' designs" to make them "exploitable."*

In addition, a 2014 Washington Post article titled "NSA seeks to build quantum computer that could crack most types of encryption" stated that NSA had a budget of $80 million per year for a research program called "*Penetrating hard targets,*" including research aimed at building a "*cryptologically useful quantum computer.*"

Moreover, the Snowden papers strained international relations, as many countries expressed outrage at discovering that they had been subjects of US surveillance. This breach of trust prompted discussions on sovereignty and cooperation among nations.

Edward Snowden, in a 2019 podcast interview with CoinDesk, shared his concerns about the potential risks associated with Central Bank Digital Currencies. He highlighted the possibility of governments leveraging CBDCs to increase surveillance and control over financial transactions. While acknowledging potential benefits like lower transaction costs and enhanced financial inclusion, Snowden recommended individuals prioritize decentralized and privacy-focused digital currencies, such as Bitcoin, to protect their financial privacy. Referring to the toxicity of metadata, Edward Snowden also famously said at IETF 93 conference in 2019 that:

> *(...) we need to get away from true-name payments on the Internet. The credit card payment system is one of the worst things that happened for the user, in terms of being able to divorce their access from their identity.*

The revelations brought forth by Edward Snowden underscore the need for careful consideration of privacy and personal freedoms when designing and implementing CBDCs. It is essential to address these risks and ensure that robust privacy protections are incorporated into CBDC frameworks to safeguard individuals' rights in the digital age.

4. **Privacy and surveillance**: CBDCs raise concerns about privacy and surveillance. The accumulation of vast amounts of transaction data by a deployed CBDC system could provide governments with unprecedented access to individuals' financial information. Without appropriate privacy

safeguards, this level of monitoring could infringe on personal freedoms and civil liberties. CBDCs can be designed with privacy protections, or they can be designed to allow for extensive monitoring of transactions. The privacy aspects of CBDCs must be carefully considered during the design phase, as retrofitting privacy features later on will not work.

5. **Monetary policy**: The adoption of CBDCs may have implications for monetary policy. The widespread use of CBDCs could alter the transmission mechanism of monetary policy, as it could fundamentally change how monetary policy is conducted and transmitted to the economy (no longer via the intermediary of banks). While it could offer central banks more direct and potentially powerful tools, it also introduces new complexities and uncertainties, particularly in how consumers and businesses would react to these new forms of monetary interaction. Balancing these factors to effectively control inflation and stabilize the economy could be more challenging in a CBDC-dominated financial system.
6. **Operational risks**: The implementation of CBDCs is a complex and time-consuming process, carrying operational risks. Integrating new technologies and systems, conducting extensive testing, and coordinating multiple stakeholders may result in operational challenges and potential disruptions to the financial system.
7. **Lack of adoption**: The success of a retail CBDC depends on adoption. In a digital payment landscape with existing high-quality solutions, a new CBDC must offer additional benefits to convince consumers and merchants to switch from incumbent options. Privacy, zero fees, and instant transactions are potential differentiators over exiting payment solutions. The legal tender status of a CBDC also influences adoption, as granting it similar legal tender status to cash, or even a cash+ like legal tender with mandatory CBDC acceptance on any point of sale system can enhance acceptance.

These risks can of course be mitigated. A cash-like CBDC will encourage a similar usage as cash, with limited amounts for daily use being carried around by individuals for use as means of payment. An account-like CBDC could for example be restricted with holding limits and disincentives above certain thresholds to prevent its use as store of value.

While valid concerns exist regarding privacy and financial freedom with CBDCs, each implementation requires thorough analysis. CBDCs can be designed to protect anonymity, similar to physical cash, or to become tools for mass surveillance. The design choices will ultimately determine the outcome. Data minimization, the fact to NOT collect and to NOT store unnecessary personal data in the commercial bank or central bank systems, is a key principle in addressing surveillance and data leakage risks. If there is one conclusion that all citizens and designers should draw with regard to the risks involved in a CBDC, then it is the following:

If something is technically feasible, it will sooner or later be exploited (with or without legal authorization) via leaks, hacks or government agencies.

The CBDC designs and the planned features will be derived from the policies and targets that are defined in the charters of the central banks. Adaptations of central bank missions to include "*absolute control over the rules and regulations of the use*" of money via the issuance of a CBDC, as envisioned in a speech by Agustín Carstens of the Bank for International Settlements [169] are dangerous, if the central bank can choose to void privacy assurances.

In order to design a secure system, central banks need to adopt a different approach and view themselves as potentially malicious actors when developing a CBDC. Only this perspective will prevent the creation of designs that would entrust the central bank with information and decisions that they should not be, or do not need to be, entrusted with.

The ECB report [170] "*Central Bank Digital Currency: functional scope, pricing and controls*" from December 2021 proposes that the ECB «*may also prefer (...) the ability to control the privacy of payments data,*" which is a fundamental misinterpretation of the concept of privacy as we have seen in Chapter 4. Citizens will only have privacy with a CBDC if they themselves have control over their payment data. Therefore, a central bank claiming "*the ability to control the privacy*" is an oxymoron, because once control is given to anyone else, privacy is lost. Privacy that can be removed (without consent) is NO privacy at all!

These risks emphasize the importance of a well-designed and carefully implemented CBDC framework that addresses potential negative consequences and mitigates risks.

12.5 Fear, Uncertainty and Doubt

While CBDCs have gained attention in the financial world, they have also generated controversy and given rise to fear, uncertainty, and doubt (FUD). This has led to the emergence of certain conspiracy theories surrounding

CBDCs. It is crucial to explore these concerns and understand the factors that have contributed to their formation.

The picture below may illustrate the feeling of many citizens, with an initial positive reaction followed by worries and second thoughts... (Graph 12.7).

One of the primary accusations against CBDCs is the fear of governments gaining complete control over individuals' financial transactions. Skeptics argue that CBDCs could be used as a tool for extensive monitoring and surveillance, potentially infringing on people's privacy.

Another concern revolves around the potential restriction of money and payments through CBDCs, leading to a future where people's ability to buy and sell is tightly controlled, raising dystopian scenarios.

Additionally, there are fears that CBDCs may be part of a larger agenda to eliminate physical cash altogether. This apprehension stems from concerns

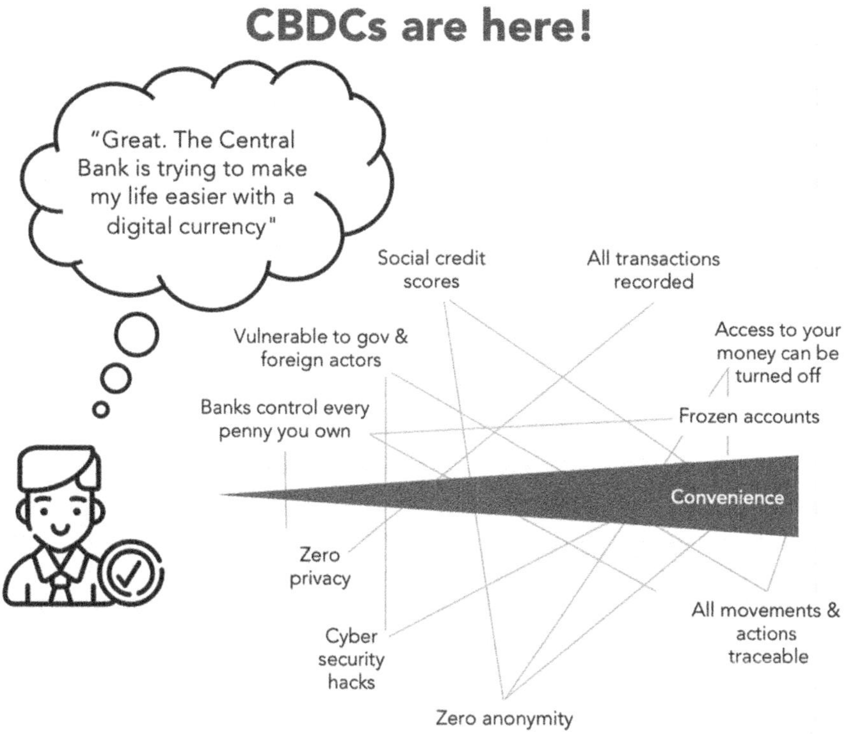

Graph 12.7 CBDCs are here and impact many areas (The lines indicate topics influencing each other) (*Source* Author)

about the loss of financial freedom and increased reliance on the banking system.

Furthermore, some individuals argue that CBDCs could be a stepping-stone toward the establishment of a global currency, ultimately replacing national currencies. This notion implies a more centralized financial system and heightened control over the global economy.

While these concerns and theories paint a worrisome future, it is essential to understand the origins and factors that have fueled these ideas.

By delving deeper into the underlying elements that have contributed to these apprehensions, we can gain a better understanding of the sentiment surrounding CBDCs and engage in informed discussions about their potential implications.

12.5.1 Concerns About Controlling and Restricting Money and Payments

The Snowden revelations shed light on the extensive surveillance capabilities of governments, exemplified by programs such as Section 215 of the US Patriot Act and the Investigatory Powers Act (IPA) in the UK. These revelations serve as a reminder that personal and transaction data collected through CBDCs could be exploited by governmental organizations for security or political purposes.

One concern surrounding CBDCs is the potential for central banks to introduce negative interest rates as a means of encouraging spending, while this is not possible with cash. However, this strategy could lead to a surge in consumption and inflation, negatively impacting the economy. Furthermore, technical challenges may arise, such as the need to impose limits on individual CBDC holdings, which could restrict the number and amounts of payments as knowledge of recipients' CBDC holdings and past transactions would be required to complete payments.

The ability to cut off individuals and organizations from their money presents an effective tool for suppressing the free expression of dissenting opinions, posing a threat to democracy. A few examples are cited here by the critics to highlight the use of similar methods in the past.

WikiLeaks:

In December 2010, WikiLeaks was cut off by Visa and Mastercard in a serious tightening of the financial vice around WikiLeaks, since it released the first portion of a quarter million diplomatic cables a week earlier. PayPal followed suit and blocked payments to the site, and the Swiss

PostFinance closed the accounts of WikiLeaks founder Julian Assange. Cutting off funding to WikiLeaks was an attempt to silence it and prevent it from publishing further embarrassing material to, in this case, the US government.

Canadian truckers' protest:

In February 2022 in Canada, truckers protested with significant support against a tightening of COVID-19 restrictions in several cities, affecting public life. The government then proceeded to cut truckers and donors off from their bank accounts.

The Canadian Emergencies Act of February 2022

The Emergencies Act of February 2022 passed in reaction to these protests gave the Canadian executive the authority to freeze bank accounts without judicial oversight. Shortly after, Canadian Minister of Justice David Lametti used this power to issue warnings on TV, stating that individuals making substantial financial contributions to a political cause he opposes could face extrajudicial asset freezes. Finance Minister Chrystia Freeland followed up in a press conference later in February stating that financial institutions have frozen the accounts of protestors in Ottawa, including people making donations to the truckers. Isabelle Jacques, assistant deputy finance minister, testified at the Commons as follows:

> Conservative MP Philip Lawrence: "*If someone gave $20 to the Freedom Convoy through a crowdsourcing platform, they could have their bank account frozen?*"
> Deputy Minister Isabelle Jacques: "*If that person gave the money after February 15, it is possible. I think that would be in rare circumstances.*"
> MP Lawrence: "*But not impossible?*"
> Deputy Minister Jacques "*It is possible*"

On February 20, 2022, Canadian MP Marc Strahl posted on his Twitter account:

> Briane is a single mom from Chilliwack working a minimum wage job. She gave $50 to the convoy when it was 100% legal. She hasn't participated in any other way. Her bank account has now been frozen. This is who Justin Trudeau is actually targeting with his Emergencies Act orders.

The prospect of such actions taking place in Canada (which we would likely all consider as a highly democratic country) raises concerns about the potential consequences being enabled in less stable democracies, if a CBDC that relies on account-based transactions without privacy protections replaces cash. If these things can happen in Canada, what does that mean for less democratic or dictatorial places?

Financial World Leaders Reinforcing the Concerns

Mr. Agustín Carstens, head of the Bank for International Settlements (BIS), shared his views over adaptations of central bank missions to include "*absolute control over the rules and regulations of the use*" of money via the issuance of a CBDC on October 19, 2020, in his speech on "*Cross-Border Payment – A vision for the future.*"

Mr. Carstens stated that with the CBDC design proposed, the central bank would have the ability to know all details about every payment. Below is the exact statement Mr. Carstens made on stage that day:

> In our analysis on CBDC, in particular to the general use, we tend to establish the equivalence with cash, and there is a huge difference there. For example, in cash, we do not know for example who is using a 100 dollar bill today, who is using a 1000 peso bill today. A key difference with the CBDC is that central banks will have absolute control on the rules and regulations that will determine the use of that expression of central bank liability, and also we will have the technology to enforce that. Those 2 issues are extremely important and that makes a huge difference with respect to what cash is.

Consequently, the central banks would be able to strictly enforce their rules and regulations, which implies they could arbitrarily block payments by private citizens. The repressive potential of a government or central bank with such a capability is so large that it should be firmly rejected from the start.

State Legislation Reinforcing the Concerns in the United States:

On March 20, 2023, Florida Governor Ron DeSantis, presumed 2024 US presidential candidate, issued a law banning both foreign and domestic CBDCs in the US State of Florida, vowing to protect Florida citizens from the Big Brother mass surveillance proposed by Washington, DC. Other states like Indiana have taken similar measures since.

You will find further details on this and similar stories in the upcoming chapter on the digital dollar.

As a result, the key question arises whether central banks should limit the issuance of CBDCs within the confines of their current charters rather than altering their regulatory frameworks. Presently, the US Federal Reserve and Sweden face restrictions in their mandates on maintaining digital account balances for individuals, which is a prudent measure since linking payments to identity (needed to authenticate central bank accounts) is very detrimental to privacy.

While this prohibition prevents the Federal Reserve from creating an account-based retail CBDC, it does not preclude the issuance of a token-based CBDC that respects cash-like privacy. This distinction is critical because the technologies underlying token-based privacy-focused CBDCs do not inherently enable or support asset freezes like those enabled by the Canadian Emergencies Act.

These considerations highlight the importance of carefully designing CBDCs to mitigate risks and protect individual privacy and financial freedoms.

12.5.2 Concerns About Eliminating Physical Currency

The potential elimination of physical currency would have significant implications for the concerns raised above, as there would no longer be a fallback bearer instrument like cash and all assets could be centrally controlled within an IT system. In our increasingly digital world, cash usage is declining, as alternative payment methods offer more convenient user experiences.

Currently, the announced CBDC projects, based on the information shared in their official reports and speeches, state that central banks intend CBDCs to be a complement to cash rather than a replacement. Critics point out that it is crucial to closely monitor this subject as the messaging may reflect what is deemed acceptable in society at a given moment, rather than revealing the ultimate goals of the proponents behind the measure.

Therefore, it is essential for citizens to stay informed about CBDC developments and express what CBDC design they would accept. A privacy-preserving CBDC must incorporate real privacy protections from the outset, with safeguards that cannot be removed. However, critics note that this does not imply that cash usage will remain unrestricted. Many jurisdictions have already introduced growing restrictions on cash usage, even before CBDCs became a prominent topic. Examples include Germany, where citizens must prove the origin of funds for purchases exceeding €10,000 in cash, France, where cash payments are limited to €1000, and Greece, where the limit has been set at an even lower €500 for cash payments. These developments, combined with the retirement of large-denomination banknotes in many countries and the refusal of an increasing number of stores to accept them, may suggest a trend toward the eventual elimination of cash, despite politicians professing otherwise.

Christine Lagarde, head of the ECB, reinforced these beliefs by saying the following on the restrictions of cash usage in an interview with Tucker Carlson on Fox News:

> Now we have in Europe this threshold: Above one thousand Euro, you cannot pay cash. If you do, you are on the gray market. So, you take your risk, you get caught, you get fined or you go to jail.

In the context of CBDCs, the absence of cash presents a very distinct proposition compared to a CBDC that coexists with cash. Real privacy protections within a CBDC become a lot more critical and take on a new level of importance if cash is no longer an option for financial transactions.

12.5.3 Concerns About Introducing a Global Currency

While the concept of establishing a global currency similar to the euro may have some theoretical appeal, the likelihood of countries such as the United States, Russia, and China agreeing on a common global currency is virtually nonexistent. Currently, the United States benefits greatly from the US dollar's status as the dominant global currency, used extensively in international trade, including for oil purchases (commonly referred to as the "petrodollar").

The polarization resulting from the Ukraine conflict has only intensified efforts by Russia and China to distance themselves from reliance on the US dollar, as the American government has utilized the dollar as a tool and seized all Russian assets denominated in dollars. This approach has raised concerns among many countries, potentially leading to a weakening of the dollar's long-term role as a global currency. A report by Eurizon SLJ Capital in April 2023 [115] noted that the US dollar's share in global reserves declined at a rate ten times faster last year than in the previous two decades. While the US dollar still comprises an impressive 58% of total global reserves, this figure has declined from 73% in 2001.

The euro, despite its numerous benefits, has demonstrated the creation of significant central powers that have not always acted in the best interest of its member states' citizens. This was evident during the 2008 financial crisis when the European Commission, European Central Bank (ECB), and International Monetary Fund (IMF), collectively known as "the Troika," imposed stringent austerity measures, structural reforms, and privatization of government assets on Greece and its citizens in order to provide a €110 billion bailout loan and prevent sovereign default.

These examples highlight the challenges and complexities associated with introducing a global currency. The divergent interests, geopolitical dynamics, and historical experiences of major powers make it highly unlikely that they would reach a consensus on a unified global currency.

In conclusion: The concerns surrounding CBDCs are not totally without merit, and it is important to acknowledge the potential trade-offs involved. While Central Bank Digital Currencies hold promise in terms of efficiency and security, they also raise valid concerns about privacy, freedom, and financial stability. The global financial crisis serves as a reminder that pursuing financial stability should not come at the expense of individual liberties and rights.

The design and implementation of CBDCs require careful consideration of the benefits and risks involved in such a project. It is crucial to approach the development of a secure CBDC system with the conservative assumption that all parties, including designers, operators, and even the central bank, could potentially act maliciously.

This book aims to provide a comprehensive understanding of the opportunities and risks associated with CBDCs. It also aims to offer guidance to practitioners in designing and implementing successful CBDC projects.

Furthermore, this book seeks to empower interested citizens by providing them with a thorough understanding of the impact CBDCs can have on their future. By being informed and vigilant, individuals can actively participate in discussions surrounding CBDCs, ensure that their interests are heard and their rights are protected.

12.6 Surveys on CBDCs

12.6.1 ECB 2021 Survey: Privacy Comes Out on Top

On October 12, 2020, the European Central Bank (ECB) launched a "Public consultation on a digital euro [13]" which ran until January 12, 2021.

The consultation included 18 questions aimed at collecting the views of both citizens and professionals. The first part was aimed mainly at citizens in their role as users, while the second targeted primarily financial, payment, and technology professionals with specific knowledge of the economics, regulation, and technology of (retail) payments. However, respondents were invited to provide feedback on the full set of questions.

The Graph 12.8 sets out the results of the more than 8000 responses submitted by participants in the public consultation.

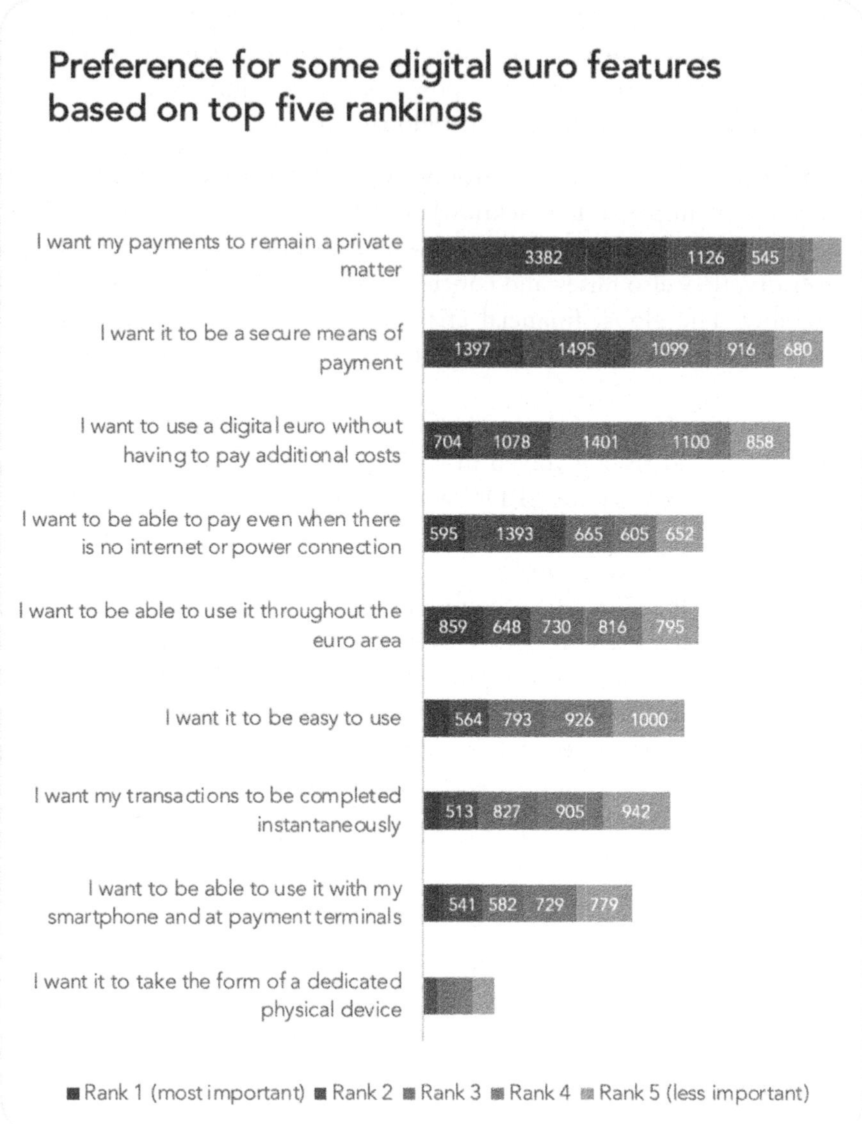

Graph 12.8 Survey: ECB - Public consultation on a digital euro (*Source* Data from ECB: Eurosystem report on the public consultation on a digital euro, April 2021)

The results in summary show the following priorities in the EU for a digital euro:

#1 Privacy	43%
#2 Security	18%
#3 Use throughout EU	11%
#4 No costs	9%

12.6.2 Bundesbank 2021 Survey: Free and Private Transactions Desired

In another survey [14] on the digital euro conducted by the Bundesbank (German central bank), the most important items for Germans with regard to the digital euro are that its **usage is free of cost (#1)**, that **payment data remains private (#2)**, and that it is in line with GDPR, so that **data protection is assured (#3)**. Interesting fact in Germany coming to light in this survey is that a chipcard was preferred to a smartphone by the participants of this survey (Graph 12.9).

12.6.3 Austrian OENB 2022 Survey on the Digital Euro: Safety is #1

The Austrian National Bank (OENB) conducted this survey [67] with 2006 Austrian residents aged 16 and above. They were selected at random from a database of phone numbers in this country of 9 million residents.

The OENB observed that two-thirds of the survey respondents were not familiar with the concept of a digital euro. When asked about their level of interest, 54% showed some degree of interest. Younger respondents tended to anticipate more personal benefits from the launch of a digital euro. However, respondents wanted cash to continue playing a significant role in the future.

CBDC design decisions regarding security and privacy are considered among the most critical for a broad acceptance of CBDC among consumers. **Payment security was ranked #1**, with **transaction data privacy ranked #2.**

The survey results confirmed that the satisfaction level with existing payment options was very high across different types of transactions. Austrian respondents generally preferred identified accounts over anonymous digital equivalents of bearer instruments. Other survey data showed that offline functionality was considered important, and the ability to transfer digital euros directly between individuals was perceived as less significant compared to offline functionality (Graph 12.10).

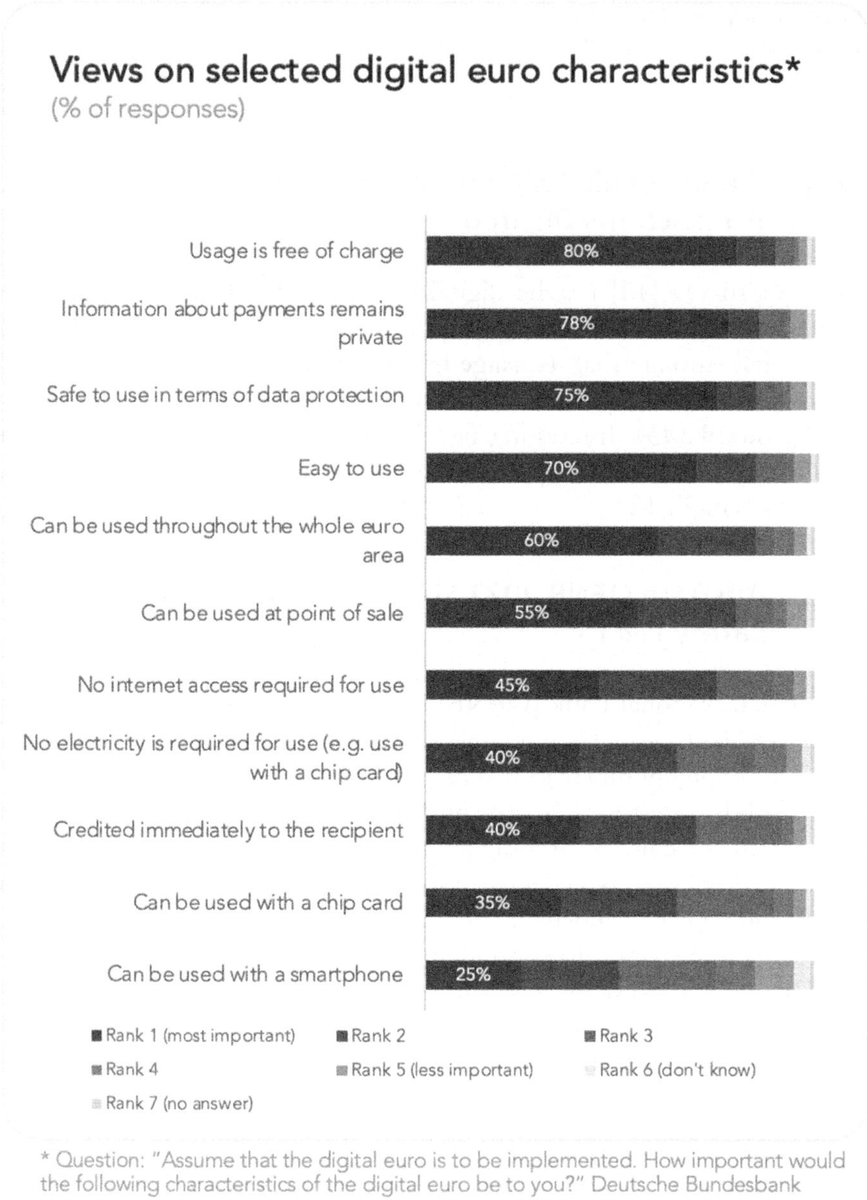

Graph 12.9 Survey: Bundesbank 2021 survey (*Source* Data from Deutsche Bundesbank, Monthly Report: What do households in Germany think about the digital euro? October 2021)

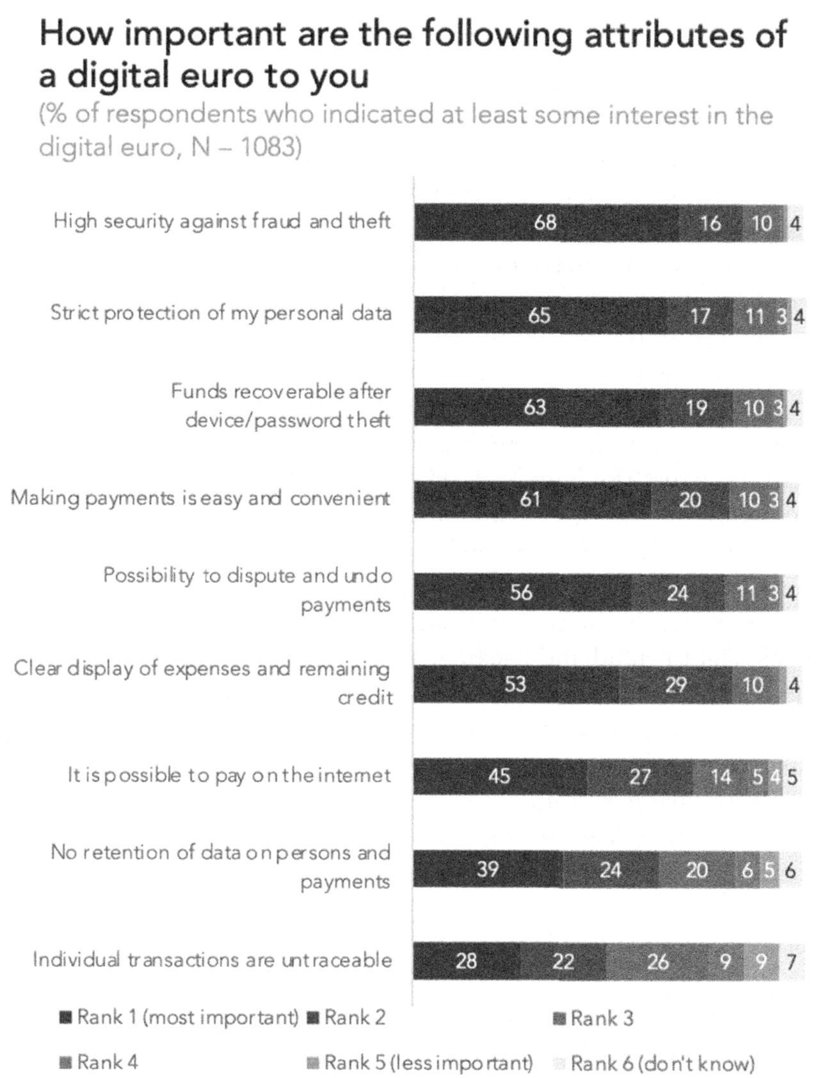

Graph 12.10 Survey: Austrian National Bank (*Source* Data from OENB survey [67])

12.6.4 Kantar Public (ECB) 2022 Survey on New Digital Payment Methods

In March 2022, Kantar Public conducted a comprehensive survey [42] on behalf of the European Central Bank (ECB) that examined new digital payment methods. This was the second such survey carried out and it targeted various demographics across all 19 countries within the eurozone. The respondents included 2160 members of the general public, 142 tech-savvy individuals, 138 merchants and retailers, and 89 people with limited access to banking or the internet. This varied cohort was analyzed to reflect the diverse perspectives within the euro area.

The survey results weren't derived from representative surveys but were based on the evaluation of different focus groups. The results unveiled a preference for universally accepted payment methods for both physical and online stores across the euro area. The participants emphasized the importance of convenience, speed, and user-friendliness in payment solutions. They expressed a desire for comprehensive, one-stop payment solutions that seamlessly integrate all existing payment options.

Safety and security were significant concerns, with participants seeking protection against fraud and hacking, as well as reliable payment authentication methods. Biometric payment verification methods, such as iris scanning technology, received widespread support, and participants desired flexible and customizable privacy settings.

While participants had little knowledge of the digital euro, they generally agreed that banks and/or central banks would be the safest and most reliable providers. They also expressed the opinion that the digital euro should not threaten cash.

The survey uncovered **key insights**:

- Citizens want universally accepted payment methods in online and physical stores across Europe (#1).
- Users prefer instant and contactless person-to-person payments (#2).
- High safety and security standards seen as fundamental for digital payment methods (#3).

On privacy, this survey asked more refined and pointed questions along 3 different privacy scenarios. In the study, potential CBDC users were given three options for financial privacy: high, medium, and low. Each option involved trade-offs between usability and transaction tracking.

The *high privacy option* offered minimal transaction recording, but online shopping/e-commerce was not allowed, and a spending cap of €150 was imposed.

The *medium privacy option* had no spending cap, and transactions could be conducted online or in shops. Non-detailed transaction data would be stored by the bank and only shared with the government as legally required.

The *low privacy option* was similar to the medium one, but the bank would store detailed transaction data, which the user could access, but the bank could use all this data for marketing and advertising purposes as well.

Among these three options, the medium privacy option was the most favored, suggesting that privacy was less of a concern for these participants than for those in the 2021 ECB survey. However, somewhat paradoxically, respondents also indicated a desire for adjustable privacy levels to suit different payment situations.

To gain a more profound understanding of these findings, let us delve into the methodology of the survey. We all are aware that the questions asked can significantly shape the results. A detailed examination of the privacy options presented in the survey reveals some potential biases that may have influenced the participants' preferences.

For instance, the high privacy option was so restricted that it was practically impossible to use it for regular activities like grocery runs, buying clothes, or online shopping. It was also inexplicably excluded from online usage, a characteristic that would likely deter any user. Similarly, the low privacy option allowed banks to use personal data for marketing and advertising, a practice akin to Facebook's business model that many would understandably object to.

This leaves the medium privacy option as the least objectionable by default, despite its inherent contradictions. For example, while it claimed that banks would store personal data and monitor transactions only to be accessed when required by law, it also stated that the bank would not collect or store detailed information about purchases. Such a discrepancy raises questions about the practicality and feasibility of this option.

The survey could also have yielded different results if participants were informed that they could secure real privacy for all their transactions instantly with a single click, something that is technically possible today. It's unlikely that anyone would refuse such an offer, if it was effortless and automatic.

The report also stated: "*Many participants among the general public and the tech-savvy reported not thinking about privacy when making payments: there is a general assumption that much of their purchasing is tracked. Many, particularly the tech-savvy, felt it impossible to have a private digital transaction.*" This assertion underscores a worrying trend where consumers willingly surrender their privacy due to the false belief that maintaining privacy is too arduous or even impossible.

This belief is likely rooted in the long-standing narrative, promoted by IT professionals, that security and privacy necessitate complex and hard-to-do processes. However, the reality is that today's technology allows for secure, private transactions with a single click, while complying with anti-money laundering and combating the financing of terrorism (AML/CFT) regulations.

There is a pressing need to dispel these misconceptions and inform citizens (and maybe even designers of CBDC systems) about the potential of current technology in maintaining privacy and security without adding complexity to their lives. This is especially crucial to prevent them from accepting unnecessary compromises on privacy and security that could negatively impact their futures.

12.6.5 Kantar Public (ECB) 2023 Survey on Digital Wallet Features

In 2023, Kantar Public conducted a survey [171] commissioned by the European Central Bank (ECB) to evaluate the perceptions of citizens regarding digital wallet features. This research spanned from December 2022 to January 2023 and targeted diverse demographic groups.

Across the entire euro area, participants valued functionalities such as **instant peer-to-peer (P2P) payments with no transfer fees (#1)** and **budget management capabilities (#2)** the most. They were also drawn to features not commonly available at the time, like **offline payments (#3)** and **QR code payments (#4)**. Other well-received features included conditional payments, the option of standalone and integrated applications, and merchant dashboard and payout management (which we will see in detail later). Transaction history with limited data, however, was rated lowest by participants.

Within the framework of the study, all digital wallet functionality was linked to a user's bank account. Users authenticated transactions via facial recognition, with each instant P2P payment requiring an additional facial recognition step.

The term "budget management" referred to the ability to pre-fund the digital wallet, much like loading cash into a physical wallet, or to directly connect it to a bank account for automatic deductions during payments. It also allowed users to maintain a specified balance in the wallet.

For offline use, users first needed to preload the wallet, mirroring the way cash is used. QR codes were introduced for in-store or P2P payments: the user would scan the QR code and confirm the payment to the merchant or peer using facial recognition.

Conditional payments referred to pay-on-delivery or pay-per-use options, such as paying for fuel at a gas station only after filling up or paying at a rental car station only after returning the vehicle.

The digital wallet was presented to users either as a standalone app or as an integrated feature in their bank's e-banking app. Regardless of the format, it was tied to their bank account for instantaneous identification.

The dashboard and payout management feature catered specifically to merchants. They could either have immediate credit after each transaction or retain the existing banking practice of waiting for two business days. Furthermore, a merchant could aggregate all digital wallets and receive a lump sum payout. A third option allowed the combining of digital euros with credit card receipts for a transaction plus two days payout. This feature raised questions about why anyone would allow their bank to hold onto their money for an extra two days without any benefit.

The option for a transaction history with limited data would exclude payee information from the history and statements, an option that could be toggled on or off in the wallet. While it seemed to have limited applications, such as hiding transactions from a partner, it did not prevent the bank from having full access to all transaction data.

Merchants indicated their willingness to sign up for the digital euro based on factors such as customer demand, ease of use coupled with security and speed, initial investment requirements, fees, and the level of technological skills needed.

This second Kantar Public survey for the ECB offers intriguing insights, but it also remains in line with the first in its representation of user solutions, seemingly based on an account-based Central Bank Digital Currency (CBDC), and its questionable privacy options. It is somewhat reassuring to note that EU citizens showed minimal interest in the feature of hiding information from family members or significant others.

12.6.6 CATO Institute—US Survey on the Digital Dollar

Based on the most recent United States poll results [172] on rCBDCs conducted by the CATO Institute in April 2023, the attributes Americans prioritize the most for a rCBDC, if implemented, are

#1 avoiding additional costs	**33%**
#2 ensuring privacy	**32%**
#3 higher security than existing methods	**25%**
#4 ease of use	**24%**

Americans would support CBDCs, especially if they reduced money laundering and fraud or if the government could ensure welfare payments were spent on their intended purpose.

Interestingly, the poll also found that 34% of Americans are against the Federal Reserve offering a Central Bank Digital Currency (CBDC). In contrast, only 16% support it. Most Americans, 49%, have not formed an opinion on the digital dollar. This is probably because only 28% of Americans know about CBDCs. A large majority with 72% are not yet familiar with the concept of a digital dollar.

Further, the Cato Institute's 2023 CBDC National Survey [188] conducted in May 2023, a month later than the above study, revealed that a mere 16% of Americans support the introduction of a CBDC. Despite frequently using digital dollars through credit and debit cards, Americans are wary of CBDCs. Unlike digital dollars issued by private banks such as Bank of America or Chase, a CBDC would be the liability of the US Federal Reserve Bank, creating a direct connection between citizens and the government's central bank. The survey indicated that 34% of Americans oppose the idea of the US Federal Reserve introducing a CBDC, while 16% support it. However, a significant 49% remained undecided, likely because only 28% were familiar with CBDCs.

There is also a shared concern across party lines; both Democrats (71%) and Republicans (82%) would resist a CBDC allowing government control over expenditures. Furthermore, a significant majority from both parties would reject a CBDC if the government could monitor their purchases. On the brighter side, Americans were optimistic about a CBDC's potential to enable instant transactions, improve financial inclusion, and support the Federal Reserve during economic downturns. Still, about 25–33% remained neutral.

Both political parties chiefly worried about the government utilizing a CBDC to oversee personal expenses. Alarmingly, 76% of Americans prioritized the potential risks over the potential benefits of CBDCs. Most Americans emphasized privacy (32%) and cost-effectiveness (33%) for a potential CBDC. Subsequent priorities included secure digital transactions (25%) and user-friendliness (24%). A striking 78% of Americans expressed their unlikelihood to use a CBDC, viewing government supervision of their spending as the leading risk.

12.6.7 Further Research and Surveys

In 2021, Gjefle and his associates conducted a study [41] focused primarily on the United States. This research involved in-depth interviews and wider surveys involving over 1400 participants aged 16 years and older. The investigation sought to understand individuals' experiences with existing U.S. payment systems and their attitudes toward privacy.

Simultaneously, a worldwide study [43] was undertaken by the Official Monetary and Financial Institutions Forum (OMFIF) in 2020, encompassing the United States. This comprehensive study garnered responses from over 13,000 participants, aged 16 to 75, across 12 countries. The survey was designed to gauge consumer confidence in digital currency issuers and attitudes toward possible attributes of digital currencies.

Should a CBDC for retail payments be introduced in the United States? Consumers indicated in these surveys three fundamental requirements for such an introduction: dependability, convenience, and security. An in-depth analysis of the surveys revealed more about these desired characteristics:

Dependability: Gjefle's survey found that most consumers prefer a CBDC system that is reliable, consistent, and trustworthy. This implies an operational CBDC platform that ensures 24/7 accessibility and continuity of service. Consumers are strongly disliking situations where the CBDC payment platform is down at a time of need.

Additionally, potential U.S. CBDC users underscored the significance of transaction certainty with an assurance of execution. "Uncertainty" was highlighted as the most persistent pain point for Americans when it came to making payments. Consumers wished for comprehensive visibility into their transactions, including details of the transferred amount, transfer destination, applicable fees, and the timeline (immediate or within a predetermined period). They also demanded explicit information on the amount debited from their account (face value and fees) and the amount credited to the recipient's account (face value minus fees). It can be inferred that consumers favor seeing the transaction's face value and the charges separately and in advance, a marked departure from the current practice where fees are deducted from the total transferred amount, often resulting in a different final amount.

Convenience: U.S. consumers desired a CBDC system that is user-friendly and uncomplicated. The notion is that a CBDC payment app should not mandate having a bank account, a credit history, or an exhaustive identification process. Furthermore, they wanted the CBDC terms and conditions to be simple, straightforward, and consistent.

Survey respondents also emphasized the need for efficient transaction execution, expecting CBDC transactions to be completed within 10 seconds or less. Encouragingly, they were open to transitioning from current payment methods to CBDCs, provided the transactions were free or with minimal charges. This sentiment was particularly pronounced among financially underserved respondents and cash users.

Potential CBDC users also highlighted the need for high-quality customer service, especially in resolving transaction disputes. They expressed the expectation that customer support should include the option of speaking to a human representative.

According to the OMFIF 2020 survey, U.S. consumers hoped for a CBDC that emulates cash in its usability. They desired a free-to-use, widely accepted CBDC that settles transactions quickly, facilitates P2P payments, provides a measure of anonymity, and can be used offline. Additionally, they would like the CBDC to expedite the conversion process between cash and digital currency.

Security emerged as a priority among respondents, with most consumers advocating for a CBDC system that prioritizes it. They wanted their money to be secure, their personal data to be safeguarded, and their transactions to have a degree of privacy.

The Gjefle survey revealed that most U.S. respondents favored a CBDC system that would protect their personal data from hackers and unauthorized usage. This often translated to the preference of holding a CBDC account with a bank. While security was identified as the paramount feature for a digital currency, potential U.S. CBDC users appeared less apprehensive about transaction privacy. They prioritized as follows: security (#1), ease of use (#2), privacy (#3), and cost (#4).

A further study [205] by Prodan, Dabija, and Marincean published in July 2023 analyzed consumer sentiment toward digital currency using Twitter data over 24 months, starting in January 2021. The analysis categorized tweets tagged with "CBDC" as positive (27%), negative (7.8%), or neutral (65.3%). Commonly used words included CBDC, central bank, digital, crypto, and

Bitcoin. The research indicated again that people are to a large extent neutral or ignorant on the subject and that Twitter is an effective tool for central banks to understand public attitudes toward CBDCs and it can aid in shaping policies and communication strategies. The study emphasized the need for transparency and accountability in CBDC development to ensure its wider acceptance and foster an inclusive financial system. The study concluded that while CBDCs offer potential benefits like increased financial inclusion and security, they also present privacy and stability concerns.

In Conclusion

All these surveys confirm that a major part of the citizens are still largely ignorant on the CBDC subject. Efforts to change that and to allow citizens to weigh in with more qualified opinions would be welcome, before citizens are faced with a CBDC solution that they may reject.

These diverse surveys collectively and clearly identify 4 key aspects that citizens prioritize across various geographies:

- **Security**
- **Privacy**
- **Ease of Use**
- **Free (no cost) Usage.**

12.7 Key Features of CBDCs

We will now expand on the features that we have encountered in the previous chapters, in the surveys and that are important in the context of CBDCs. Some of them will be reviewed in significant detail because their understanding is critical as a basis for any design decision. Of course, all these features are also similarly important and applicable in the case of stablecoins and tokenized deposits.

12.7.1 Security Considerations

The foremost consideration in CBDC solutions is security. With CBDC systems potentially becoming prime targets for hackers of all sorts—from state-sponsored actors, criminal organizations, to individual hackers—the stakes are high. Who would not like to have an unlimited money printing press in his basement or his backpocket?

A coordinated cyberattack on large-scale payment infrastructures such as Fedwire could trigger significant worldwide financial disruption. This could result in severe liquidity shortfalls, commercial bank defaults, and system-wide shutdowns, which would severely affect daily transactions and financial stability on a vast scale.

To ward off cyberattacks and mitigate the effects of successful breaches, central banks like the U.S. Federal Reserve Bank have enforced various countermeasures. These include regular contingency testing for high-volume and high-value Fedwire participants, redundancy provisions such as backup data centers and out-of-region personnel, and transaction value limits.

Additional risks to wholesale payments infrastructure involve attacks on the SWIFT messaging system. The hacking of the Bangladesh central bank serves as a potent example of the vulnerabilities in the SWIFT ecosystem and the potential scale of damages when central banks come under attack.

In a significant cyberattack in 2016 [68], hackers exploited weaknesses in the central bank of Bangladesh's network security. However, due to a fortuitous coincidence, most transactions were blocked or reversed and only US$81 million were lost.

The Bank of Bangladesh Hack

The central bank of Bangladesh experienced a significant cyberattack [68] in 2016. The attackers were able to exploit vulnerabilities in the bank's network security and infiltrate the system, then modifying SWIFT (Society for Worldwide Interbank Financial Telecommunication) messages to transfer funds to various bank accounts in the Philippines. The hackers behind the cyberattack on the central bank of Bangladesh in 2016 attempted to steal a total of $951 million from the bank's account at the US Federal Reserve Bank of New York. However, most of these transactions were blocked or reversed, because by the pure luck the name of one of the target banks included the word "Jupiter," which was also the name of a Greek ship on a sanctions list. The sanctions filter flagged the message for further scrutiny. By then, the New York branch of the U.S. central bank had already approved five of the payments for a total of US$101 million. US$20 million were reversed and the attackers were only able to successfully steal $81 million.

From 2015 to 2018, at least ten successful attacks revealed a slew of vulnerabilities in the SWIFT operations in banks [63]. As a response, SWIFT introduced the Customer Security Program (CSP) featuring three primary elements:

1. Securing the local environment.
2. Preventing and detecting fraud in commercial relationships.
3. Consistently sharing information and preparing to counter future cyber threats.

The **SWIFT CSP** introduced the SWIFT Customer Security Controls Framework (CSCF) [116] with about 30 specific controls, some advisory and some mandatory. It had the goal of adopting stronger security standards and improving response times to address potential threats. Despite these measures, reports suggest that the number of incidents has steadily increased since SWIFT's regulations were put in place: more than 60% of banks surveyed said that SWIFT cybercrime has been on the rise, and only 40% of banks were "very confident" that they've detected all fraud attempts that have been aimed at them. This isn't to suggest that the regulations are counterproductive—only that hackers are relentless, and they'll make it their mission to find new ways of stealing credentials and impersonating trusted users and businesses.

The reality is that the measures, which have been annually tightened, are far from sufficient. Despite initially issuing strong guidance to banks and threats of obligatory compliance subject to audits and public shaming, SWIFT hasn't followed through on this threat.

A case in point is "CSP Control 2.4 - Back Office Data Flow Security," which states the following about its control objective and control context in the SWIFT documentation:

> ***Objective***: "*Ensure the confidentiality, integrity and mutual authenticity of data flows between local or remote SWIFT infrastructure components and the back office first hops they connect to.*"
> ***Context***: "*Protection of data flows/connections between the back office first hops, at application level, as seen from the SWIFT secure zone, and the SWIFT infrastructure safeguards against man-in-the-middle, unintended disclosure, modification, and data access while in transit.*"

This control has been advisory (i.e. non-mandatory) with the following note "*SWIFT expects this control to become mandatory in a future version of this document and ...*" since 2017 and its implementation would have eliminated the attack vector used in Bangladesh through end-to-end encryption of all SWIFT messages within a bank. However, six years on, this crucial control still remains advisory.

Banks have possibly resisted these cumbersome efforts imposed by the SWIFT CSP, and SWIFT has seemingly acquiesced, despite the availability of the needed technologies to close these critical vulnerabilities. It is also clear from vendor interactions to place such products, that banks tend to dismiss compliance recommendations that are merely advisory until they become obligatory.

Given the elevated risks involved, prioritizing security is of paramount importance for CBDCs. The initiation of any security efforts should be grounded in a comprehensive threat model.

12.7.1.1 Introducing a Threat Model for Risk Mitigation

A **threat model** is a structured illustration of all the relevant information impacting the security of an application, essentially providing a security-centric view of the application and its surroundings. It's a necessary first step, instrumental in identifying, understanding, and communicating threats and their mitigation strategies within the context of safeguarding CBDC systems and assets. It always needs to cover what the capabilities of adversaries are and what they are trying to achieve in order to prepare for the potential attacks.

The following steps might be involved in constructing a CBDC threat model:

1. Determine the resources or assets that require protection, such as sensitive data, intellectual property, physical infrastructure, or personnel.
2. Identify possible threats to these assets, including malicious actors, natural disasters, technological failures…
3. Evaluate the probability and potential impact of each threat. For instance, a cyberattack might pose a high likelihood and a high impact on sensitive data, while a natural disaster may have a low likelihood but a high impact on physical infrastructure.
4. Rank the threats based on their probability and potential impact. This ranking assists in deciding which threats should be addressed immediately and how resources should be distributed.
5. Formulate a strategy to counteract the identified threats. This strategy could encompass implementing security measures such as access controls, digital signatures, encryption, business continuity plans, disaster recovery plans, or other measures to minimize the risk of an attack or incident.

A representative threat model for a digital cash system could potentially look like this:

1. **Assets**: The assets requiring protection include the digital currency, along with other sensitive information such as secret signing or encryption keys, user identities, transaction histories, and wallet details.
2. **Threats**: Potential threats to the digital cash system might include:
   - Malware and hacking attacks: Hackers could attempt to gain access to user wallets and back-end systems, intercept transactions, or steal sensitive information.
   - Insider threats: An insider with access to the system could misuse their privileges to steal secret keys and digital currency or commit fraud.
   - Physical theft or loss: If the digital currency is stored on a device such as a phone, laptop, USB stick, or portable hard disk, it could be stolen or lost.
   - Distributed denial-of-service (DDoS) attacks: Attackers could attempt to overload the system with traffic, causing it to crash or become unavailable.
   - Blockchain-based attacks: Attackers could attempt to manipulate the blockchain ledger (like a 51% attack) to commit fraud or steal digital currency.
3. **Likelihood and impact**: Each of these threats carries varying probabilities and potential impacts on the digital cash system. For instance, while a distributed denial of service (DDoS) attack might have a high likelihood and a moderate impact, a successful malware attack could cause significant damage but is less likely.
4. **Prioritization**: Threats can be ranked based on their assessed likelihood and impact. For instance, addressing the threat of malware and hacking attacks might top the list, followed by internal threats and physical theft or loss.
5. **Mitigation plan**: A range of security measures might be implemented to counter these threats, including:
   - Privacy by design and data minimization to reduce the stored data that could be stolen or compromised.
   - Strong user authentication and access controls to prevent unauthorized access in case of account-based system.
   - Encryption and secure storage of digital currency and user data.
   - Regular security audits and vulnerability assessments to identify and address weaknesses in the system.
   - Multi-factor authentication for administrators and master-users to prevent insider threats.
   - Air gapped and secured cold storage of master keys in secured locations.

- Backup and recovery plans in case of physical loss or theft of devices.
- DDoS protection and other measures to ensure system availability.
- Robust blockchain consensus mechanisms to prevent tampering and fraudulent activity.

12.7.1.2 Introducing the CIA Triad

Any such strategy must encapsulate the "**CIA triad**" we introduced in Chapter 2. CIA stands for Confidentiality, Integrity, and Availability. The CIA triad is a prevalent model for the construction of secure systems. This is how it applies to CBDCs.

Confidentiality: Confidentiality involves ensuring that sensitive personal and non-personal data is accessible only to participants within the ecosystem who require this information.

In this context, considerations should also incorporate an approach to enhance encryption technologies toward perfect forward secrecy (PFS), which defends the encryption against "Store now, decrypt later" strategies employed by harmful actors (anticipating future quantum computing advancements to enable decryption, for instance). Data minimization is advised for such a system, as this design can considerably limit the exposure of confidential data. After all, data that hasn't been collected cannot be compromised. The preservation of data confidentiality protects against:

- Data loss from the CBDC system.
- Decreased user trust in the CBDC system due to data leaks.

Integrity: The principle of integrity pertains to the protection of user funds, sensitive data, and the supporting systems from unauthorized modification, misuse, or destruction. The integrity of user data remains intact only if the data is authentic, precise, and dependable. Upholding the integrity of data and systems is key in averting situations like:

- Manipulation of data within the CBDC system.
- Monetary losses.
- Diminished user confidence in the CBDC system if funds are not readily accessible.

Availability: Ensuring continuous accessibility of both the core CBDC system and its wider ecosystem is pivotal for resilience. Any new CBDC system should operate continuously, 24 × 7 × 365, with an availability of at least 99.95%, and as close to 100% as achievable.

Maintaining data and system availability is instrumental in safeguarding against the following issues:

- Users' inability to access their funds and data.
- Decline in usage due to frequent outages.

Additional factors of importance for a CBDC system, which extend beyond the scope of the CIA triad, are necessary to be deployed to ensure security.

12.7.1.3 Conducting Cryptography, Security and Code Reviews

The processes of cryptographic evaluation, security inspection, and code assessment, which will be explained below, are essential for any CBDC system to confirm, to the maximum extent possible, the system's security, dependability, and absence of vulnerabilities susceptible to malicious attacks. While these reviews can't guarantee absolute security, they are considered best practice for integrating security into a system.

Given their ability to "print" limitless amounts of money, CBDC systems will be targeted by a wide variety of adversaries. Therefore, comprehensive reviews conducted by highly skilled resources are crucial to bolster security and reduce risks. In these systems, cryptography is a critical component and cryptographic primitives serve as the fundamental components of modern cryptography, providing the necessary tools for secure communication and payments in the face of potential adversaries. A full chapter will be dedicated to cryptographic primitives later in the book.

Cryptographic reviews analyze the cryptographic primitives used and their application. We will discover later in this book why cryptographic primitives play a crucial role in the definition of money tokens.

Security reviews involve scrutinizing the architecture and design of the CBDC system to spot potential security weak points, vulnerabilities, and threats. Such reviews can help identify possible attack vectors and suggest countermeasures to alleviate those risks.

In contrast, code reviews focus on examining the actual code running the CBDC system. Often, it is the flawed implementation of cryptographic principles in the written code that paves the way for vulnerabilities.

Code assessments aim to identify bugs, mistakes, and vulnerabilities in the code, which could be potentially exploited by attackers. Furthermore, they ensure that the code adheres to established coding standards and best practices. Open-source code will assist massively by additionally allowing larger groups of specialists and researchers to scrutinize it, leading to better security.

These evaluations are key elements in the development and implementation of a CBDC system and should be carried out on a regular basis.

12.7.1.4 Addressing Quantum Computing

Cryptocurrencies, stablecoins, and CBDCs rely on the quality of the cryptography that they have been designed and implemented with. The cryptographic primitives used are to a very large extent based on asymmetric key cryptography, as we have already seen in part 1 of the book.

The security of cryptographic algorithms (for signatures, encryption, zero-knowledge proofs…) usually relies upon strong assumptions, which are statements that particular mathematical problems are extremely expensive to solve.

The most common strong assumptions in cryptography include the factorization problem and the computation of discrete logarithms. For both of these problems, quantum algorithms have been developed that would allow these problems to be solved efficiently on a quantum computer. Quantum computers use quantum bits or qbits, which can perform multiple calculations simultaneously, making them much more powerful than classical computers.

As a result, cryptographic algorithms that rely on these assumptions (i.e. asymmetric key cryptography algorithms) would become insecure as soon as a sufficiently powerful quantum computer is built.

Post-quantum cryptography is the study of cryptographic algorithms that do not rely on strong assumptions that could be broken by a quantum algorithm. This is the subject that we care for in the design of digital currencies.

In contrast, **quantum cryptography** is the development of cryptographic algorithms that only run on quantum computers.

In the context of cryptocurrencies, the most widely used signature/encryption algorithm is the elliptic curve digital signature algorithm (ECDSA), which relies on the discrete logarithm problem. ECDSA is currently considered secure because it relies on the difficulty of solving the discrete logarithm problem that classical computers cannot solve efficiently.

Another very common method used to secure our digital data relies on an algorithm, called RSA crypto algorithm, because it was developed by three MIT researchers Ron Rivest, Adi Shamir, and Leonard Adleman. The RSA algorithm can be used for encryption and signing, and is vulnerable to being cracked by a quantum computer. The RSA crypto algorithm relies on the factorization problem, i.e. the immense difficulty of factoring the product of two large prime numbers.

However, quantum computers will solve these problems—the factorization and the discrete logarithm problem—efficiently, making these cryptographic methods vulnerable to attacks.

As such, Shor's algorithm [173] could solve the RSA-based factorization problem, but today's "toy" quantum computers are not reliable enough to run this quantum algorithm. A million qbits would be necessary to run Shor's algorithm, but the most powerful quantum computer barely manages 500 qbits at the time of this writing. One to two decades could be necessary for quantum computers to reach that level.

If CBDCs are not quantum-proof or at least quantum-ready (upgradeable to quantum-proof), then they could at some point in the future—call it Q-Day—be subject to theft or manipulation by quantum computers, which again could undermine the trust and stability of the entire financial system. Hence, it is crucial that CBDCs incorporate quantum-resistant signature/encryption algorithms that are designed to withstand attacks from quantum computers.

CBDCs should be quantum-proof or quantum-ready to protect against potential future security threats posed by quantum computers. As quantum computing technology advances, it is important that central banks remain on the outlook and take proactive steps before Q-Day to ensure the security and resilience of their CBDC system.

The emergence of quantum computing only has a very limited impact on historic, classically signed (not post-quantum) data as typically the digital signatures would have been already validated in the past, when the transaction went through, prior to the emergence of the quantum computer.

Naturally transactions authorized by classical digital signatures after the emergence of quantum computing would be insecure. This creates problems for systems where the ownership of funds is tied to the ability to sign with a long-term private key (as in Bitcoin).

In contrast, systems that rely on classical encryption to keep transaction data private may find that with the emergence of quantum computing the historically confidential data suddenly becomes irrevocably public. Just remember the known "store now, decrypt later" schemes of the National

Security Agency (NSA) to collect and store as much encrypted data as possible and to decrypt it at a later time when technology has sufficiently advanced for it to break the encryption.

Thus, systems should be developed that today use post-quantum encryption, while it is probably sufficient to merely be ready to transition to post-quantum signature algorithms should quantum computing become a reality on Q-Day.

Reasons for not **immediately** deploying systems that are fully post-quantum secure include:

- Computational costs.
- Maturity of post-quantum solutions.
- Availability of post-quantum solutions.

For post-quantum encryption, there currently exist very few choices. Post-quantum signatures exist but tend to be significantly more expensive and post-quantum zero-knowledge proofs for certain claims may not even be known.

Symmetric key cryptography, including symmetric encryption, and hash functions seem so far largely unaffected by the threat of quantum computing. Symmetric key cryptography is for example affected by Grover's algorithm [174], which provides a quadratic speedup compared to the often exponential speed-ups of other quantum algorithms. It can hence be mitigated by simply doubling symmetric key lengths for an adequate protection against quantum attacks. This is easily done, for example by moving from crypto algorithm AES128 to crypto algorithm AES256 by simply doubling the key length from 128 to 256 bits, and has no real downsides in a productive application.

Certain features like privacy and offline usage can have an additional impact on the security of CBDC systems. We will review these consequences in further detail in coming chapters.

!!! Remember: Quantum computers will massively impact asymmetric key cryptography. Post-quantum encryption should be deployed immediately, and post-quantum signatures are needed on Q-Day.

Highest levels of security are not easy nor cheap to implement and to keep up, but there are limitless amounts of money at risk in central banks.

Hence, the most conservative assumptions should be taken with respect to security of central bank systems and therefore, the design of any CBDC system should assume that **ALL parties**, including the system's designers, implementers, and main operators, could be malicious.

12.7.2 Privacy & Confidentiality Considerations

Privacy is a paramount consideration, which is why we began the book with an introductory discussion on the topic in Chapter 4.

Now, we will dive deeper into the subject of privacy, specifically in relation to Central Bank Digital Currencies. Privacy, as an attribute of a CBDC, can unfortunately be defined and interpreted in multiple shades of gray. Essentially, privacy is a multifaceted and often misrepresented or misunderstood feature of a CBDC. The specifics matter immensely, and designers and citizens must be vigilant in understanding the nuances of privacy as communicated in the context of CBDCs.

Privacy is so critical that it may well be the determining factor for the success of any CBDC initiative, depending on the degree of privacy it provides. As we have seen in the surveys and as we will also later see from the US example, early indications suggest that the level of privacy associated with the use of CBDCs will play a decisive role in their acceptance and usage. Even projects in less developed regions may falter due to inadequate adoption stemming from their privacy features or the lack thereof.

Confidentiality, a component of privacy, implies that transactions should be invisible to unauthorized parties (e.g. other banks, payment service providers, telcos…). Confidentiality is generally ensured through the encryption of data in transit over untrusted networks and through encryption of data at rest. Who is in possession of the decryption key is another key variable.

While confidentiality is concerned with shielding data from unauthorized individuals, privacy pertains to the protection of user information, including payment transaction details, even from involved entities such as banks, central banks, and payment processors. Although closely related, these two notions of privacy and confidentiality are distinct. Deciding on an appropriate level of privacy is a technical and political decision with implications for the CBDC system's architecture, design, and adoption.

The incorporation of privacy protections into a Central Bank Digital Currency (CBDC) design is crucial for two main reasons.

Firstly, it is inherently valuable to protect the privacy of end-users. CBDCs are expected to amass enormous volumes of financial data, and some central banks have pledged not to use CBDCs as tools for mass surveillance.

Secondly, a system with strong privacy protections is intrinsically more secure. Without hard privacy measures in place, a system, that collects massive amounts of sensitive user data and experiences a breach, can lead to the exposure of all that data to the attacker and other unauthorized parties, infringing on confidentiality. In contrast, a design that protects privacy, implements stringent data minimization, and/or hides sensitive user data, even from trusted system insiders, can lessen the effects of a breach or insider attack on security and confidentiality as banks or central banks cannot lose data they don't have. This aligns with the recommendation from the previous chapter on security to design any CBDC system as if all participants, including the system's designers, implementers, and main operators, could be malicious.

As evidenced by the European Central Bank survey in 2021 about the most crucial digital euro attributes and confirmed by the American Cato survey in 2023, privacy protections are of utmost importance. Privacy emerged as the top priority in the EU with 43%, surpassing all other features, including security and usability and as #2 in the US with 32%.

It's worth repeating here that it's currently technically feasible to have one-click payments with absolute (unlinkable, cryptographically guaranteed) real privacy for the spender while still meeting anti-money laundering (AML), know your customer (KYC), and counter terrorist financing (CFT) requirements. Blind signatures are one of the possibilities to make that happen.

There are ongoing discussions and pilot programs examining such technological solutions that can safeguard privacy in CBDC payments while complying with AML and KYC requirements. Therefore, there are no technical barriers for citizens to accept less privacy when spending money than they currently have with cash, while at the same time, tax evasion and black markets could be eliminated with the same CBDC. This might seem too good to be true, but it is indeed possible.

However, some countries have announced in their outlines that their CBDC will offer the same level of privacy as current digital payment solutions, effectively replicating the lack of privacy protections from bank accounts, credit cards, and other payment services. This is quite disappointing for informed observers and often misleading for uninformed citizens, as there is zero privacy in current payment solutions.

Similarly misleading are statements that promise total privacy from a central bank, when all personal data is initially collected by commercial banks before a limited subset is then transferred to the central bank. Can one's privacy be genuinely protected in such a scenario? Privacy must be maintained across the entire CBDC ecosystem before privacy can be genuinely claimed.

Even the Chinese CBDC, also known as the digital yuan or e-CNY, has incorporated varying levels of privacy in its pilot program, with tiered levels for balance, transfer, and activity limits. The digital yuan provides five levels of privacy, two of which do not require the disclosure of a user's identity, but only a phone number or email address. Even though this is "only" pseudonym-based privacy (phone number or email address) and can always be traced back to a specific user with enough effort, the privacy offered exceeds that available in leading commercial solutions or credit card schemes.

Initiating a dialogue around privacy must begin with the fundamental question:

From Whom Are We Seeking Privacy?

The response can vary widely depending on the central bank's perspective:

- All third parties.
- Only the transaction counterpart.
- The commercial bank.
- The payment service provider.
- The central bank.
- Government entities and their agencies (like tax authorities, law enforcement, secret services, intelligence agencies, etc.).
- Any combination of the above.

Modern technology can securely implement privacy for any of these scenarios today. However, the technical solutions needed will considerably differ in their design, based on the answer to the pivotal question of whom the users want privacy from (respectively what the central bank wants to offer).

Achieving real privacy, as outlined in Chapter 4, necessitates making deliberate architectural decisions at every stage of a system's design. It is crucial to embed privacy by design and by default from the beginning, as retrofitting a system to ensure data protection and privacy can be a daunting—if not impossible—task later. As such, the design of Bitcoin makes it impossible to implement full anonymity as it is built upon the transparency of transactions.

Real/hard privacy can only be achieved through mathematical or cryptographic means and can never be undone.

Some commonly discussed software-based privacy strategies include secure internet communication protocols, transport encryption (TLS), symmetric and asymmetric encryption, public key infrastructures (PKI), ring signatures, blind signatures, zero-knowledge proofs (ZKP) such as the zero-knowledge succinct non-interactive argument of knowledge (ZK-SNARK) or the zero-knowledge scalable transparent argument of knowledge (ZK-STARK), homomorphic encryption, as well as secure computation and secret sharing methodologies.

Some publications [162] have argued that a CBDC system that offers real privacy would suffer from excessive technical or cryptographic overhead, because encrypted records tend to require more space and computing power. They claimed that "*anonymization on the network layer that all hard-privacy proposals assume adds latency and other inefficiencies because of repeated encryption, decryption, and re-encryption*" and should therefore be sidelined as viable solutions.

We want to rectify that assumption. CBDC solutions, that offer real/hard privacy, without having to rely on encryption and the described disqualifying overhead and latency, exist already today. Solutions with real/hard privacy, like GNU Taler or its predecessor eCash, operate largely without encryption, but rather rely on signatures, blind signatures, and data minimization. These solutions are extremely efficient and can simply rely on the same checks at the on-ramps that apply to cash today. The described solutions offer one-sided spender anonymity and are not anonymizing the receiver. Hence, they make black markets, illegal activities, and tax evasion transparent without sacrificing the spender anonymity (privacy).

It should also be clear that any payment solution that communicates over a network must encrypt its traffic and mitigate man-in-the-middle attacks as a best practice. With Google Chrome no longer supporting (unencrypted) HTTP internet connections [119] and Search, Gmail and Google Drive automatically enforcing a secure connection, applying anything less than secure HTTPS to protect network traffic in a payment solution (independent of its stance on privacy) would be irresponsible even if it may add a tiny bit of latency.

Homomorphic Encryption

Homomorphic encryption is a big deal in cases where private information is collected and stored. Homomorphic encryption is a cryptographic method that enables data to be encrypted so it can be computed by a third party without the necessity for decryption. This ensures that the data remains encrypted throughout the entire computational process, upholding its confidentiality. If a system is holding a significant amount of private data that requires both protection and utilization, homomorphic encryption can contribute to significant privacy enhancements.

Homomorphic encryption can be classified into partially homomorphic encryption (PHE) and fully homomorphic encryption (FHE). PHE permits only a limited number of mathematical operations to be conducted on the encrypted data, like addition or multiplication. Conversely, FHE enables any calculations to be conducted on the encrypted data, rendering it more potent but also computationally demanding.

Homomorphic encryption has a wide range of applications, especially in secure cloud computing, where it allows data to be stored and processed in the cloud while staying encrypted, thereby safeguarding the privacy and security of the data. It also finds utility in other sectors, like secure data outsourcing, privacy-preserving machine learning, and secure multi-party computation (MPC). Nonetheless, due to the computational burden associated with performing computations on encrypted data, homomorphic encryption remains an active research field, with ongoing endeavors to boost its efficiency and practicality for diverse use cases. They may end up playing a role in future CBDC solutions.

This chapter will shine further light on the different flavors of privacy in the hope that, by the time you finish reading, you will know your way around the critical privacy topic and why we believe it is critically important for CBDCs.

12.7.2.1 Privacy Versus Anonymity

Privacy and anonymity, while closely linked, possess distinct definitions. Privacy is the right of individuals to regulate access to their personal information and be safe from unreasonable intrusions into their personal lives. Anonymity, conversely, is the capacity of individuals to remain unidentified or unknown.

Though privacy and anonymity can coincide in certain circumstances, they aren't interchangeable. Anonymity could be considered a tactic or a means to ensure privacy, but it isn't the sole path to achieving privacy. For instance, an individual can maintain privacy in their personal data, such as financial or medical records, without being necessarily anonymous.

Anonymity gains significance in scenarios where individuals aim to safeguard their identity or evade discrimination or retaliation. This is particularly crucial for whistleblowers, political dissidents, or marginalized group members who may confront persecution or violence if their identities are revealed. In the context of payment transactions, anonymity implies that transactions cannot be traced or linked to any individual. Cash is anonymous. This unlinkability is a fundamental characteristic of anonymity. If someone assures anonymity, it comes with mathematical guarantees that the information isn't available and can't be retrieved.

Privacy, on the other hand, holds importance in all daily life aspects, including personal relationships, financial transactions, and interactions with businesses and government entities. As previously discussed, many countries recognize the right to privacy as a fundamental human right, and it's protected by laws and regulations (like the EU GDPR and the OECD) that govern personal information's collection, usage, and sharing. Minimizing personal data exposure starts with concealing information in a separate or secure location, or under pseudonyms (a fictitious name or number) where the information can later be revealed or linked, and it concludes with anonymous information that can't be retrieved.

So, while privacy and anonymity are related concepts, they possess different definitions and applications. Both are crucial for protecting individual rights and fostering a free and open society. Regarding a retail CBDC, real/authentic privacy for citizens will only be attained through a certain degree of anonymity.

We could anticipate that in the EU, similar concepts that led the European Court of Justice (ECJ) to prohibit excessive data collection and data retention by the governments in the past will be applied to CBDCs. The ECJ has ruled that data shouldn't be collected and stored indefinitely just because law enforcement might want to utilize it in the future. Therefore, in 2014, the ECJ invalidated the EU Data Retention Directive. In 2016, the ECJ stated that national laws mandating telecommunications companies to retain data for law enforcement purposes must meet strict requirements, including being necessary and proportionate. In 2020, the ECJ ruled that the Privacy Shield agreement with the United States didn't provide adequate protections for EU citizens' data considering US surveillance laws and practices. The predecessor of Privacy Shield, called Safe Harbor agreement, was already struck down before it and it is likely that any successor will be struck down as well until the US changes its surveillance laws.

While the ECJ's decisions have been a positive driver for privacy at the rule-setting level, the experiences with GDPR and cookie banners [176] in the EU should serve as an important reminder that, even when legislation prescribes the right thing, companies and governments often collect what they want or deploy cookies as they wish, despite the rules in an environment that, except for a few isolated instances, lacks proper enforcement. Entrusting them with more valuable information (i.e. payment data) and expecting them to behave differently when more value is at stake is undoubtedly a very optimistic viewpoint.

This reinforces the point made before that privacy is either mathematically guaranteed or based on trust (and the observance of the law is as well a trust-based matter as the above cookie example illustrates).

12.7.2.2 Risks Associated with Privacy in Payments

Privacy and anonymity in payments hold both advantages and potential pitfalls. They can offer increased freedom and safety for individuals, but if misused, they can also present obstacles for law enforcement, financial entities, and social justice. Here are some key concerns connected to privacy and anonymity in payments:

- **Money laundering**: Privacy and anonymity in payments can inadvertently aid money laundering, which involves making illegally gained proceeds appear legal. Without adequate regulations and monitoring, tracing suspicious transactions and pinpointing the origins of unlawful funds can pose a challenge for law enforcement agencies.
- **Terrorist financing**: Privacy and anonymity in payments could facilitate the financing of terrorist activities, which involves financially supporting terrorist groups. Such groups might employ anonymous payment methods to transfer funds internationally, thus evading law enforcement detection.
- **Tax evasion**: Privacy and anonymity in payments can be manipulated to avoid taxes by hiding income and assets from tax authorities. This could lead to government revenue loss and destabilize the equitable nature of the tax system.
- **Fraud and scams**: Privacy and anonymity in payments can be manipulated by fraudsters and scammers to deceive and steal money from unsuspecting individuals. Anonymous payment methods enable these offenders to maintain anonymity and evade capture.

From these points, it is evident that privacy and anonymity in payments not only offer advantages for individuals but can also create challenges for law enforcement and financial institutions. Striking a balance between the need for privacy and security and the necessity for transparency and regulation is vital in preserving the integrity of the financial system and promoting a fair and just society. However, this does not imply that privacy must be sacrificed for compliance or security. All these aspects can coexist harmoniously for the advancement of a free, fair, and democratic society.

12.7.2.3 Balancing Privacy and Security: An Examination of Different Privacy Mechanisms

As previously discussed, there are numerous nuances when considering privacy in the context of Central Bank Digital Currencies (CBDCs), as outlined in the CBDC publication. Chapter 4 established that real privacy can only be achieved with a degree of anonymity. Without this, citizens are left to trust third parties to respect their privacy, leaving it entirely in the hands of these entities. We have also seen that the decision is not privacy versus security, but that privacy enhances the security of a CBDC system.

Remembering this, we now explore strategies to achieve varying levels of privacy:

1. **Dual-sided anonymity (real privacy)**: This involves complete anonymity of both sender and receiver, including content. Although this provides ultimate privacy in all directions, it also means that none of the previously mentioned risks (money laundering, terrorist financing, tax evasion, and fraud) can be mitigated effectively.
2. **Single-sided anonymity (real privacy)**: Here, either the receiver or sender is anonymous to third parties. A partially transparent model might help mitigate risks, depending on which party retains anonymity. For example, if recipients remain anonymous, risks associated with receiving funds (like money laundering or terrorist financing) cannot be mitigated. Conversely, if the spender remains anonymous, a comprehensive income transparency could potentially reduce all four risks listed above in Sect. 12.7.2.3.
3. **Pseudonymity (trust)**: This strategy allows individuals to use pseudonyms instead of their real identity when transacting. While pseudonymity offers some protection, it's crucial to understand that it's not synonymous with anonymity. Pseudonyms are ultimately linked to an individual's activities and can, with sufficient effort, be traced back to their real identity.
4. **Data segregation/data splits (trust)**: This involves dividing data sets into subsets for different purposes, potentially allowing entities (like a central bank) to claim privacy. However, in the complete CBDC ecosystem, this approach offers zero privacy, as all the data is accessible to some actors, which in turn renders the central bank claim worthless.

To ensure real privacy, it's crucial to define in detail what should be kept private and from whom. Without a clear understanding and privacy integrated by design, the resulting "privacy" could be full of surprises, similar to the holes in Swiss cheese.

Opposite to popular belief, privacy-preserving designs also significantly enhance the security of a CBDC system. They protect the system against breaches and protect the central bank's independence from pressure to release data. The incorporation of data minimization principles prevents the collection of personal, detailed transaction data, ensuring it never becomes available to unauthorized parties. What is not collected, cannot be lost or stolen.

However, a CBDC system with perfect dual-sided anonymity (like Zash or Monero) would be disastrous, as it would only serve criminals and harm societal fairness. Thus, a well-balanced CBDC ecosystem should offer real/hard privacy from all stakeholders without impeding necessary compliance measures. Technically feasible solutions exist that blend real/hard privacy and KYC/AML compliance while offering efficiency and protection.

!!! Remember: (a) When you talk about privacy with regard to a CBDC, you must look at the total ecosystem and validate that there is real/hard privacy from all stakeholders. Otherwise, there is no privacy, and only a system based on the trust of certain third parties.

(b) Solutions that combine both real/hard privacy and KYC/AML compliance are technically possible and in some designs even more efficient than systems without privacy, especially in combination with data minimization. This can be realized very efficiently, without creating a disabling overhead due to the use of cryptography.

(c) A bank or central bank cannot be pressured, by political or other powers, to hand over information that it does not have. Real privacy can therefore significantly enhance the independence of a central bank and shield it from undue pressures.

12.7.3 Deciding on Consensus Mechanisms: Centralized Versus Decentralized Governance

The choice of a consensus mechanism, an essential protocol to validate transactions and maintain consistency, is driven by the need for secure and efficient operation in a digital currency system. This selection process isn't always straightforward as it is contingent upon the governance model being used, i.e. whether it is centralized or decentralized.

One could start with a system design that includes a single validator, whose role is to confirm the authenticity of the payment token or the legitimacy of the transaction. This model is typically seen in systems that use a centralized database. While this method is efficient due to the absence of the need for agreement among multiple validators, it lacks the redundancy of decentralized DLT that ensures continued operation in the face of unexpected issues. If the validator goes offline or functions improperly, it could compromise the system's integrity and availability.

Alternatively, consensus mechanisms can incorporate multiple validators, numbering in the hundreds or even thousands. This approach is characteristic of public cryptocurrencies like Bitcoin or Ethereum. While this design does provide robustness and can ensure system integrity in the event of individual node failures, it tends to be less efficient due to the inherent limitations imposed by network bandwidth and latency.

Thus, the choice of consensus mechanism is critical and requires careful deliberation. It must balance efficiency, security, and robustness, and it must align with the broader governance model of the system.

In the realm of central banking, it is obvious that the overall governance is rather centralized, and very few central banks have indicated appetite to change that, even though DLT systems are under discussion.

!!! **Remember:** The governance model is a significant factor in determining the consensus mechanism. It is, therefore, crucial to consider the governance model first when deciding on how to validate tokens or transactions.

12.7.4 The Imperative of Optimal Settlement Times

Settlement time, commonly referred to as transaction time or latency, is an critical feature of Central Bank Digital Currencies. It is directly tied to the efficiency of the consensus mechanism used. Ideally, instantaneous settlement is sought after, making it a crucial aspect of CBDC designs for several reasons:

1. **Efficiency:** Instantaneous settlement substantially curtails transaction times and costs compared to traditional payment systems, which might take days to settle transactions like wire transfers. With real-time transaction processing, payments become faster and more streamlined, enhancing the overall user experience.
2. **Security:** Instant settlement amplifies the security of transactions by curtailing the window for potential fraudulent or malicious activities. However, this expedited process mandates robust security protocols and systems capable of efficiently tracking instant payments for fraud, anti-money laundering (AML), countering financing of terrorism (CFT), and sanction checks. Neglecting this may paradoxically render the system more vulnerable.
3. **User adoption:** Prompt settlement can augment the adoption and utilization of CBDCs. Consumers are likely to be more receptive toward a digital currency that guarantees speed, security, and convenience. For instance, in

scenarios such as in-store payments or public transport, swift transaction confirmations are crucial to avoid queues and congestion.
4. **Economic advantages:** Instant settlement can confer economic benefits by enhancing financial inclusion, reducing payment costs, and stimulating innovation in the payments industry.

The emergence of Instant Payment Systems (IPS) underscores the necessity for CBDCs to offer rapid settlements to compete effectively. Any lag in settlement time could significantly impair user acceptance when compared to commercial IPS systems like PIX in Brazil, TWINT in Switzerland, Swish in Sweden, etc.

Instant settlement also requires that all security processes inside banks and central banks are locked down and under control. Instant settlement would have led to a loss of about US$1 billion in the Bangladesh hack seen earlier.

Furthermore, it's essential to consider user experience factors. For account-based CBDCs, compliance requirements, such as two-factor authentication prevalent in the EU, may decelerate the transaction process, increasing the steps needed to complete it. Conversely, token-based CBDCs, which require no account authentication or registration, can offer a simple one-click transaction experience. Here, the system only needs to validate the token used for payment, a process which is remarkably swift and straightforward.

However, it's essential to differentiate the requirements for retail CBDCs (rCBDCs) and wholesale CBDCs (wCBDCs). For rCBDCs, instantaneous settlement is practically a stringent requirement to compete with private Instant Payment Solutions. In contrast, for wCBDCs, while instant settlement might be less critical, the capability for prompt settlements at specific times/dates may be pivotal.

Instant or near-instant settlement times are critical for the mass adoption of retail CBDCs, especially in regions where Instant Payment Solutions are already pervasive. As such, all retail projects should aim for transaction confirmations in less than a second.

!!! **Remember:** Prompt settlement at a moment of choice (including now) will be a key feature for any CBDC solution. It is critical that internal processes are secure enough to handle immediate wire transfers, something that would have cost the central bank of Bangladesh US$900 million more, if they had had instant transfer capabilities at the moment of the hack.

12.7.5 Dynamic System Performance and Scalability

System performance and scalability are crucial attributes for CBDCs, intrinsically tied to the speed of consensus achievement and transaction times. A scalable CBDC system can easily adapt its performance based on demand, ensuring seamless transaction processing even during peak periods.

Performance requirements for a CBDC system are contingent upon specific use cases, the adoption rate projected by each central bank, and the total number of participants (both humans and machines) within the system. Therefore, the emphasis should be on designing CBDC systems robust enough to handle peak load times, rather than merely focusing on average transactions volumes.

Performance is typically quantified in terms of transactions per second (TPS). High TPS is integral for CBDCs to:

1. **Satisfy demand:** Given the potential for wide-ranging adoption of CBDCs as a popular payment method, they must be capable of processing a substantial volume of transactions.
2. **Ensure resilience:** A scalable CBDC system is less susceptible to performance degradation during periods of high demand or stress, thus rendering it resilient to potential shocks or disruptions.

To put things in perspective, Bitcoin handles merely 7 TPS, while VISA manages around 1700 TPS on average, peaking at 24,000 TPS. The Chinese CBDC system, the e-CNY, has been designed with an ambitious target of 300,000 TPS.

The scalability of the performance and the ability to enhance it substantially over time becomes critical when considering emerging trends like machine-to-machine payments and microtransactions. These advancements will dramatically increase the number of transactions a CBDC must process. Therefore, a radically different magnitude of transactions per second must be contemplated to future-proof the system. As it's currently impossible to predict when and where such transaction growth will stabilize, opting for models that scale linearly with hardware deployments is a prudent approach.

Transaction speed or settlement time (the duration it takes for a transaction to be completed) is another vital aspect of performance. To ensure a seamless user experience, transaction times under one second for each payment seem a mandatory target that must be maintained as well for very high TPS numbers.

Efficiency is an increasingly pertinent factor, given the unsustainable energy consumption associated with blockchains like Bitcoin and Ethereum

1.0. Especially for use cases involving machine-to-machine interactions, microtransactions, and the Internet of Things (IoT), high throughput and low transaction costs are indispensable.

While scalability will be a significant concern for retail CBDCs (rCBDCs), transaction volume should not pose a problem for wholesale CBDCs (wCBDCs), regardless of the chosen technology type.

!!! **Remember:** Exceptional scalability is vital for CBDCs to fulfill their potential as a secure, efficient, universally accessible, and user-friendly payment method, capable of meeting future demands of the Internet of Things and machine-to-machine transactions.

12.7.6 The Importance of Sovereignty, Freedom and Trust

Sovereignty is a key criterion for any CBDC and in the context of CBDCs involves multiple dimensions, including monetary policy sovereignty, data sovereignty, and technological sovereignty:

1. **Monetary policy sovereignty:** The introduction of CBDCs allows a country's central bank to maintain direct control over its monetary policy. It permits them to directly manage the money supply and apply policy changes in response to economic conditions. This would not be the case with decentralized digital currencies like Bitcoin or with privately issued stablecoins.
2. **Data sovereignty:** CBDCs would ensure that transaction data remains under the jurisdiction of the issuing country, protected by its laws and regulations. This is particularly important given the sensitive nature of financial data and the need to ensure privacy, security, and compliance with regulations such as AML/CFT.
3. **Technological sovereignty:** With a CBDC, the technological infrastructure (both hardware and especially software) supporting the currency is under the control of the central bank or its appointed entities, rather than a foreign and/or private entity. This mitigates the risks of reliance on external systems and ensures that the technology can be developed and maintained without restrictions in line with the nation's interests and needs.

When it comes to technological sovereignty, proprietary software has been described by Richard Stallmann, the inventor of the free/libre software concept, as applying digital shackles to its users. Since this (proprietary) software is entirely controlled by its vendor, it inherently threatens the autonomy and sovereignty of individual users, especially when utilized for critical infrastructure like a CBDC.

Microsoft attempted to overcome this distrust by introducing the "shared-source" concept. This model grants selective access to the source code to establish trust. However, as Huawei discovered, even the open-source nature and the availability of the source code to Google's Android operating system were insufficient when the US government revoked their license as part of a sanctions package.

Open-source software, unlike shared-source software, allows unrestricted distribution and modification. Open source does not restrict any party from selling or giving away the software and allows its users to freely create modifications and derived works.

Where the open-source initiative emphasizes these freedoms as an effective software development methodology that also improves security via transparency, the earlier ***Free Software*** movement stresses that these should be fundamental rights for informational self-determination and sovereignty for all software users. As software licenses typically do not include a rationale but merely determine the rights and obligations for the users of the software, licenses that grant the user the right to run, read, modify, and redistribute are summarily referred to as free/libre open-source software (FLOSS) licenses.

Open-source developers, having selected open-source as a business model, often have no problem also selling proprietary extensions (like a pro version with added features) to create a revenue stream. In contrast, Free Software developers view digital shackles as an injustice and in violation of human rights and would thus refuse to compromise on their values for the sake of profits.

Naturally software under a FLOSS license does not really care about the intentions of its developers and is inherently both free/libre and open-source software.

Oddly enough, free/libre software advocates have no problem with the free software not being gratis, meaning the user having to purchase the software to be granted all of the rights of the free software license. In contrast, the sentiment in the open-source community tends to be that open-source software should also be gratis.

Although open-source software and free/libre open-source software (FLOSS) are often used interchangeably, you now realize that they have subtle differences, which have now hopefully become clear.

Key benefits of open-source or FLOSS software in public projects include:

1. **Transparency & security**:
   Open-source/FLOSS software ensures transparency and security since the source code is publicly available and can be scrutinized by anyone. This doesn't guarantee absolute security but is currently the most effective way to prove software trustworthiness, provided that qualified reviewers are examining the publicly available source code. It is in full compliance with Kerckhoff's principle [177], which is a principle in cryptography that states that a cryptographic system should be secure even if everything about the system, except for its keys, is public knowledge.
2. **Collaboration**:
   Open-source/FLOSS software promotes collaboration, leading to faster development and superior quality software. A community of developers often provides support, resources, and documentation, ensuring the software's software remains up to date and secure long term.
3. **Cost-effectiveness**:
   Open-source/FLOSS software is generally more affordable than proprietary counterparts, primarily due to the absence of licensing fees and vendor lock-ins, reducing long-term costs.
4. **Flexibility**:
   Open-source/FLOSS software offers higher adaptability as anyone can modify it to meet specific needs, ensuring that the software aligns with the public project requirements.

Understanding software licensing differences is crucial for decision-makers in a CBDC project. The appropriate open-source/FLOSS license can prevent dependence on software vendors managing critical infrastructure and can provide substantial freedom.

Open-source/FLOSS software has been gradually becoming mainstream, despite resistance from commercial software lobbies. Red Hat Software, with its Red Hat Linux products, exemplifies a commercially successful open-source project.

Licenses within open-source software are categorized into permissive and non-permissive (copyleft) licenses. While permissive licenses allow unrestricted modifications and redistributions, copyleft licenses enforce more restrictions. The choice between these two licenses depends on the software project's objectives and the involved developers and users' preferences.

Some of the widely used licenses in open-source/free software include the strong copyleft GNU General Public License (GPL), the weak copyleft Mozilla Public License (MPL) and Lesser GNU General Public License (LGPL) and the permissive Apache License, MIT License, and BSD License. Each of these has its distinctive features and level of restrictions or permissions, that we invite you to explore in further detail.

While free/libre and open-source products often prioritize adaptability and flexibility, other factors like security and system resilience are also critical when evaluating components for a CBDC.

Many jurisdictions are encouraging the use of open-source software in publicly funded projects, such as the European Commission's open-source strategy "Think Open" published in June 2022. Several central banks, like Brazil's Central Bank and the Bank of France, are experimenting with open-source software in their CBDC development. The US Federal Reserve has also released its CBDC-related Project Hamilton developments as open-source code under a MIT license for everyone to try and build upon.

The question of trust is crucial when it comes to adopting a Central Bank Digital Currency solution. For people to accept and embrace a CBDC in their daily lives, they need to have trust in its reliability and benefits. There are two options to consider in this regard.

The first option involves a black-box solution where users can only rely on the information shared by their central bank. They have no means to validate the quality of the solution or understand its inner workings. They are unable to monitor modifications. In this scenario, trust is solely based on the assurances provided by the central bank. Users have no access to the code or the ability to scrutinize its functionality.

The second option is an open-source solution where the code is available for all to examine. Qualified reviewers can analyze the code and identify any potential shortcomings or vulnerabilities. Users can make informed decisions about their trust in the system based on these fact-based reviews. All modifications are visible and the code readable. Transparency is key in building trust in this case.

However, the matter of trust goes beyond the initial launch of a black-box CBDC solution. Concerns arise about the possibility of future changes to the system without public knowledge or consent. For instance, a new government or central bank executive team could alter the fundamental characteristics of an initially great system, including introducing mass surveillance, without informing the public. In a black-box CBDC, there are no checks and balances in place to prevent such changes whatsoever.

To mitigate these risks and ensure trust in the system, the solution must be open-source. All updates and changes must be published as open-source before being implemented. Additionally, the complete tool chains used to create the updates must also be public. This allows citizens to verify that the binaries used in the updates correspond to the published source code. By providing this level of transparency, it becomes possible for anyone qualified to ensure that the deployed CBDC systems adhere to the source code and to their intended purpose—and nothing else.

This discussion resonates with cases like the Apple-FBI dispute and accusations against companies like Huawei (by the Americans) and Apple (by the Chinese) regarding potential backdoors for data access on their phones. It highlights the importance of open-source code and complete transparency. This is mandatory to guarantee the trustworthiness and the integrity of CBDC systems.

Open-source or FLOSS code bases for CBDCs can also enhance security testing, especially when combined with long-term bug bounty programs. However, open-source CBDC code bases also require proper funding, attention, and staffing for effective long-term maintenance. For long-term critical infrastructures like CBDCs, avoiding expensive vendor lock-ins by choosing a FLOSS license must be an essential consideration.

!!! **Remember:** CBDC solutions with FLOSS licenses are available and can prevent a critical infrastructure/CBDC project from becoming dependent on a private, commercial enterprise. In our capitalist model, this can entail a hefty price to be paid continuously. In addition, FLOSS solutions contribute massively to having a system that people can trust, without relying on simple, unverifiable promises.

12.7.7 The Power of Extensibility

To guarantee the ability of a CBDC system to foster innovation and cater to future payment needs, it's essential to factor extensibility into its design. During the planning stage, several key elements should be contemplated to enhance the system's potential for future development and evolution. These include:

a. **Open architecture**:
   The CBDC architecture should be structured to allow effortless addition, updating, or substitution of modules. This feature ensures

the system's ongoing adaptability and flexibility, vital for its long-term usability and relevance.

b. **Composability**:

Extensibility in a CBDC system can be further fortified through a composable architectural design approach. This method focuses on creating defined building blocks, akin to Lego bricks, that can be assembled to achieve the required CBDC system functionality. This strategy enables a departure from restrictive, inflexible monolithic structures, offering a dynamic and adaptable system layout.

c. **Open protocol**:

Though not as expansive as free/libre and open-source software, an open protocol for a CBDC denotes that the technical specifications and regulations guiding the issuance, distribution, and usage of the CBDC are publicly available. This information can be accessed and utilized by all interested parties, including developers, businesses, and individual users.

Well-known examples of open protocols include HTTP (Hypertext Transfer Protocol), SMTP (Simple Mail Transfer Protocol), and TCP/IP (Transmission Control Protocol/Internet Protocol). These are crucial for powering the World Wide Web and email systems and connecting devices to the internet.

In the context of a CBDC, an open protocol aims to boost interoperability and user-friendliness by facilitating interaction between various systems and applications and the CBDC network. It can establish a fair competitive landscape for developers and service providers while enabling smooth integration of CBDCs with current payment systems.

An open protocol for a CBDC can also enhance transparency and accountability by providing a clear view into the technical aspects of the CBDC system. This visibility is essential for ensuring the CBDC network's security and integrity and for fostering trust and confidence among users and stakeholders. For instance, an open protocol can allow developers to build new wallets for a CBDC system, provided these third-party wallets are compatible with the open protocol.

By adopting an open protocol for a CBDC, the benefits of the CBDC can be widely distributed and accessible, fostering innovation and competition in the development of CBDC-related products and services.

!!! Remember: The more streamlined the process for central banks and financial intermediaries to add functionality to the CBDC system, the higher the likelihood of its success. An extensible CBDC system fosters innovation and adaptability, catering to evolving financial landscapes and future payment needs.

12.7.8 Bridging Systems Through Interoperability

Today, systems don't exist in isolation; rather, they are intricately connected. Interoperability, hence, is a crucial attribute that makes a Central Bank Digital Currency system swift and user-friendly, and paves the path for widespread acceptance and success.

When planning a CBDC, several layers of interoperability should be considered to ensure seamless interaction between different systems. These include:

1. **Interoperability with central bank RTGS systems**: The CBDC should smoothly integrate with the real-time gross settlement (RTGS) systems of the central bank, enabling instantaneous fund transfers.
2. **Interoperability with commercial bank back-office systems**: The CBDC should work in conjunction with the internal processes and systems of commercial banks, streamlining transactions and record-keeping. Here, standards like EBICS, SEPA, etc., come into play.
3. **Interoperability with private payment rails**: The CBDC should cohere with existing private payment infrastructures, thereby providing users with diverse transaction options.
4. **Interoperability with e-commerce sites/solutions**: The CBDC needs to integrate seamlessly with various e-commerce platforms, facilitating online transactions and broadening its usability.
5. **Interoperability with other financial actors**: Entities such as exchanges, clearinghouses, and financial service providers should be able to interact with the CBDC without friction, fostering an inclusive financial ecosystem.
6. **Interoperability between different CBDC systems**: For instance, the digital dollar should interact with the digital euro smoothly. This cross-platform or cross-border functionality will facilitate international trade and finance.
7. **And more**: The CBDC should be designed with the foresight to integrate with other emerging technologies and systems.

Many of these layers of interoperability will utilize APIs that adopt the ISO 20022 standard for messages exchanged between systems. This international standard provides a universal method for high-quality financial messaging, promoting reliable communication and data exchange.

!!! **Remember**: A well-designed, interoperable CBDC can contribute substantially to a resilient and dynamic financial landscape. Not only will it streamline and secure transactions, but it will also foster innovation and inclusivity in the global financial market.

12.7.9 Exploring Programmability of Money and Payments

Programmability is a controversial and widely discussed aspect of Central Bank Digital Currencies, attracting significant attention for its potential transformative impact on financial transactions.

It's crucial to dissect the concept of programmability into two interconnected yet distinct components:

1. **Programmability of payments.**
2. **Programmability of money.**

The "**programmability of payments**" pertains to automating and customizing payment transactions via software code. This can manifest in the form of recurring payments, conditional payments, and smart contracts, enabling intricate transactions to occur automatically without intermediaries. The functionality of programmable payments is largely recognized and integrated within our current banking and credit card systems, and its incorporation into a CBDC system is generally accepted.

On the contrary, "**programmability of money**" is about customizing and modifying the properties and behaviors of money itself through software code. This could entail programmable inflation rates, automatic interest payments, and dynamic supply adjustments, thereby enabling the monetary system to adapt to specific economic and financial conditions. Furthermore, it could mean setting parameters on money usage, such as its expiration, limitation to specific categories like food or clothing, safe usage constraints for minors, or geographic / temporal restrictions.

For example, the US COVID-19 relief could have been distributed electronically within 48–72 hours and programmability features of CBDC could have ensured that these relief funds had to be spent in specific industry sectors within 120 days to kick-start the economy. Compare this to the efficiency of mailing checks (after an unnecessary discussion if Donald Trump would sign these relief checks himself) and then hoping for the recipients not to deposit, but to spend the money upon receipt.

The notion of programmable money has ignited numerous debates and a divergence of perspectives across jurisdictions. The European Central Bank (ECB), for instance, rules out the idea of "programmable money," asserting that a CBDC with restrictions cannot be termed "money." Instead, such a financial instrument would originate from a source other than the ECB and would be termed a "voucher." Hence, the digital euro will not incorporate programmable money.

Conversely, the Monetary Authority of Singapore (MAS) perceives programmable money as a potent innovation, encouraging its use by financial intermediaries on top of a CBDC. The United Kingdom aligns with this view for its digital pound; however, the Bank of England (BoE) will not implement central bank-initiated programmable features. Rather, it intends to equip the private sector with the requisite infrastructure to introduce programmability features atop the foundational services offered by the BoE.

Although both programmable payments and programmable money involve enhancing the functionality and flexibility of digital currencies through software code, they vary in their scope and focus. Programmability of payments concentrates on automating and streamlining payment transactions, whereas programmability of money targets creating a more adaptable and responsive monetary system.

!!! **Remember:** Programmable payments are nothing new; they have long been a part of our financial system. In contrast, programmable money is a radical innovation brimming with potential benefits. However, it might clash with a central bank's traditional definition of "money" and hence might not be pursued. It is advised to design the system in a manner that enables other participants, like the treasury, the ministry of finance or financial intermediaries, to introduce programmable money, perhaps under a different nomenclature such as "vouchers".

12.7.10 Exploring Fungibility: The Interchangeability of Money

Fungibility is a fundamental property of currency that ensures its units can be freely exchanged with one another. It signifies that each unit of a fungible currency holds identical value and identical characteristics, allowing for seamless interchangeability. For instance, a $20 bill can be used to purchase a product or service just as effectively as any other $20 bill. The value and features of each $20 bill are indistinguishable, enabling them to be exchanged without any distinction.

In the realm of digital assets, a fungible token refers to a type of crypto-asset token that shares the exact characteristics of other tokens within the same asset class. This means that every token holds an equal value and exhibits the same properties as any other token within that crypto-asset category. Examples of fungible tokens include widely recognized currencies such as euros or dollars, as well as shares of a company's common stock, where each unit is entirely interchangeable with any other unit of the same asset.

However, in certain blockchain systems, achieving complete fungibility is not always guaranteed. This is because many tokens retain a traceable history of ownership and transactions, which may impact their perceived value. For instance, a Bitcoin that has been involved in illegal activities like drug trade or extortion might be considered less valuable to a user compared to a "clean" or "virgin" Bitcoin. This issue does not arise with traditional fiat currencies as they do not carry any transactional history.

This distinction is exemplified by institutional investors seeking to acquire newly minted Bitcoins directly from miners or Over-The-Counter (OTC) trading desks [143]. These "virgin" coins are often deemed more valuable than regular coins and can command a premium of 10–20%. Despite the additional costs, financial institutions and conventional investors are inclined to prefer these pristine coins. Consequently, there is a growing demand for newly mined Bitcoins among institutional investors, contributing to the lack of complete fungibility within the cryptocurrency space.

It is essential to recognize that the fungibility of CBDC tokens may be challenged if they carry their entire transaction history. This consideration becomes pivotal in designing a CBDC system that aims to preserve fungibility while addressing the transparency and traceability requirements of a digital currency ecosystem.

!!! **Remember**: Fungibility is possibly challenged if the CBDC tokens carry ownership or transaction history, and this may represent a data privacy issue.

12.7.11 Ensuring Resilience: The Backbone of CBDC Systems

Resilience plays a pivotal role in the design and operation of a robust CBDC system, aiming to prevent disruptions and uphold the availability and integrity of critical data. The pursuit of resilience aligns with the broader objective of maintaining financial stability.

To achieve resilience, a CBDC system must demonstrate the ability to withstand faults or failures across its various components. These faults can stem from infrastructure issues, software-level malfunctions, or protocol-level inconsistencies. They may arise unintentionally, due to random infrastructure failures, or deliberately, caused by misbehaving nodes.

Open-source or FLOSS code bases for CBDCs can also contribute to improving resilience as they are open to reviews from a much larger group of experts, which can even be encouraged with long-term bug bounty programs, and that can lead to improvements in security and resilience.

The measurement of resilience can be assessed through the following factors:

- **Uptime targets:** Establishing defined objectives for the system's operational availability.
- **High fault tolerance levels:** Designing the system to tolerate a wide range of faults without significant disruption.
- **Redundancy (on multiple levels):** Implementing redundant components and backup systems to ensure continuous operations.
- **Fast service recovery:** Enabling swift recovery from disruptive events to minimize downtime.
- **Fast automated data backups and recovery:** Implementing mechanisms to efficiently backup and restore critical data.
- **System modularity:** Embracing modularity to facilitate quick fault fixing and seamless system updates.

The topic of resilience also raises questions about the role of Distributed Ledger Technologies in CBDC systems. DLTs were originally designed to provide a decentralized framework that eliminates the need for a trusted third party, ensuring censorship resistance through decentralized consensus mechanisms and independent nodes in an open network.

However, in the case of CBDCs, where the central bank maintains 100% control over the system, it becomes important to evaluate whether the benefits of DLT, derived from its original design with a fully permissionless and decentralized setup, still hold true. Centralized control introduces a single point of failure, as all nodes are operated by the central bank, eliminating protection against supply chain attacks for example, as all nodes receive software updates from one centralized source.

Further research is needed to determine whether a centrally controlled, permissioned DLT of large scale can attain the same or higher availability compared to industry-proven high-performance database systems that operate at 99.99% availability or higher.

It is essential to consider that designing the CBDC for integration into existing payment channels may not enhance overall resilience. Alternatively, deploying the CBDC on a separate payment rail infrastructure can significantly improve the resilience of payment systems in general.

It is crucial to emphasize that resilience is of paramount importance. While conventional systems have a strong track record, occasional outages can occur, even for renowned platforms like the amazon.com website or payments networks like SWIFT. The performance and resilience of a centrally operated DLT system should be examined to determine if it can surpass the capabilities of conventional systems.

!!! Remember: Resilience is crucial. Conventional systems have a good track record, but they can also go down—this happens to the amazon.com website and also to payments networks once in a blue moon. It remains to be seen if a centrally (-bank) run DLT will fare better than these conventional systems.

12.7.12 Embracing Efficiency: Green Solutions for CBDC Infrastructures

Efficiency stands as a crucial consideration in the development of any CBDC infrastructure. Projects have a focus on minimizing energy consumption and reducing environmental impacts. Solutions that consume excessive amounts of energy for consensus building, such as Bitcoin's energy-intensive proof-of-work algorithms, are not ideal for responsible CBDC projects.

The pursuit of efficiency encompasses several key aspects that contribute to a greener and more sustainable CBDC infrastructure:

1. **Consensus mechanisms:** Selecting energy-efficient consensus mechanisms plays a vital role in minimizing the environmental footprint of a CBDC. Alternative consensus algorithms, such as proof of stake (POS) or practical Byzantine fault tolerance (PBFT), offer more energy-efficient alternatives to the resource-intensive proof-of-work (POW) mechanism.
2. **Power consumption optimization:** Implementing strategies to optimize power consumption within the CBDC infrastructure can lead to significant energy savings. This includes the use of energy-efficient hardware components, data center design optimizations, and algorithmic enhancements to reduce computational requirements.

3. **Sustainable infrastructure:** Building a sustainable infrastructure for CBDC operations involves utilizing renewable energy sources and implementing energy management systems. The adoption of green energy, such as solar or wind power, reduces reliance on fossil fuels and contributes to a more sustainable energy ecosystem.
4. **Transaction efficiency:** Optimizing the efficiency of transactions within the CBDC system helps minimize energy consumption. This can be achieved through an efficient design, batch processing, compressing transaction data, or utilizing off-chain (Layer 2) scaling solutions to reduce the computational load on the network.
5. **Lifecycle assessment:** Conducting a comprehensive lifecycle assessment of the CBDC infrastructure provides insights into its environmental impact at each stage, from design and development to deployment and decommissioning. Identifying areas for improvement and implementing sustainable practices throughout the infrastructure's lifecycle is crucial for long-term environmental sustainability.

Efficiency in CBDC infrastructure not only minimizes the ecological footprint but also presents an opportunity to lead by example in the global push for sustainable finance and responsible technology development. By embracing greener solutions, CBDCs can align with broader environmental goals while promoting financial innovation and inclusion.

!!! **Remember**: Prioritizing efficiency and sustainability in CBDC infrastructure contributes to a greener future and reinforces the responsible implementation of digital currencies.

13

CBDC Examples

Nearly 130 countries, representing over 95% of global GDP, are exploring a CBDC as of October 2023 according to the CBDC Tracker website (Graph 13.1).

Two countries in the Caribbean have fully launched a digital currency, and 12 countries have conducted pilots, including Nigeria and China. China's pilot reaches 260 million people at the time of writing, is set to expand to most of the country later in 2023. The Bahamas were the first mover with its Sand Dollar, and Jamaica is the latest country to launch its CBDC, with the JAM-DEX. Nigeria and the Eastern Caribbean are closely behind in going live with a CBDC in "production."

The latest BIS central bank survey [183] published in July 2023 questioned 86 central banks, covering 86% of the world's population and 92% of global economic output. The efforts of these central banks toward CBDC have seen considerable advancement over the past year. Over half of the banks surveyed were engaged in tangible experiments or involved in the development of a pilot CBDC program. The survey also predicted the "live" circulation of 15 retail and 9 wholesale CBDCs by 2028.

We will take a look at the launched CBDCs, the advanced pilots, and some of the interesting projects that have been conducted so far, in the upcoming pages.

L. V. Schumacher, *Decoding Digital Assets*, https://doi.org/10.1007/978-3-031-54601-3_13

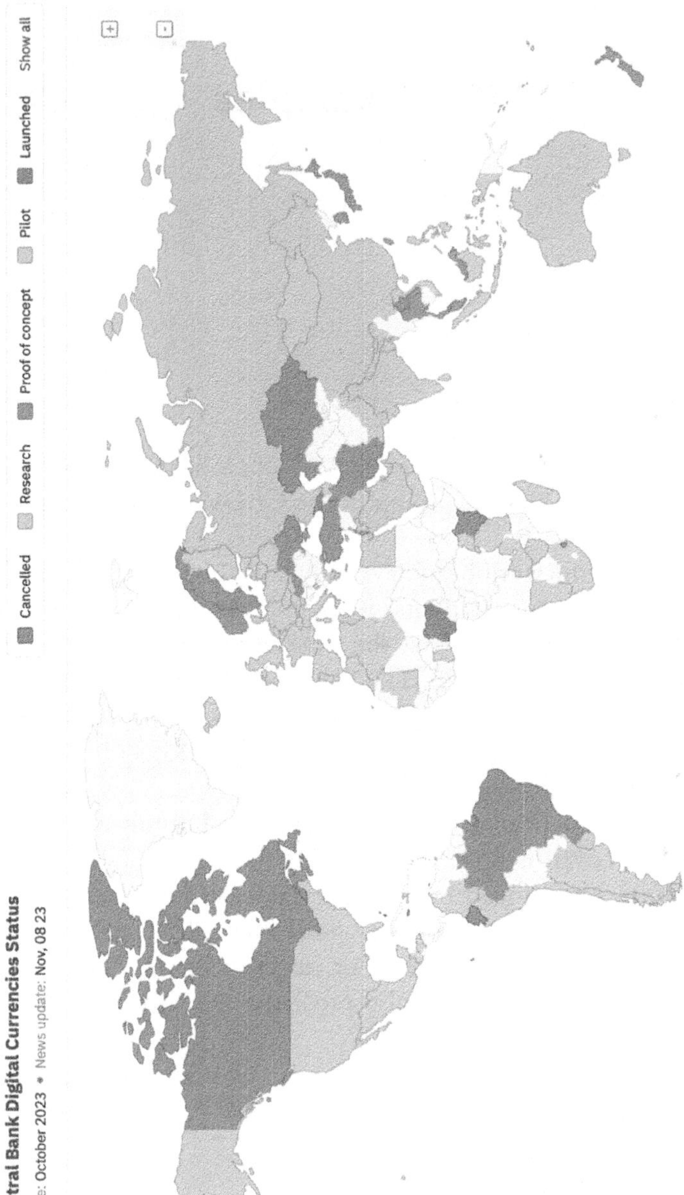

Graph 13.1 Overview of CBDC projects (*Source* https://cbdctracker.org [6])

13.1 Live Examples

13.1.1 The Bahamas: Pioneering the SandDollar CBDC

The archipelagic state of The Bahamas with over 3,000 islands, cays, and islets in the Atlantic Ocean has emerged as a trailblazer in the realm of Central Bank Digital Currency. With a population of approximately 400,000 in 2022, the nation boasts impressive internet access and smartphone penetration rates of 87% and 98%, respectively.

$$1 \text{ Bahamian dollar}(B\$) = 1 \text{ US\$}.$$

In a groundbreaking move on October 20, 2020, The Bahamas launched the world's first state-backed digital currency known as the "SandDollar." This digital version of the Bahamian dollar (B$) is issued by the Central Bank of the Bahamas (CBOB) through authorized financial institutions (AFIs), mirroring the issuance of physical cash.

The CBOB partnered with NZIA Limited as its technology partner for the implementation of the DLT-based SandDollar CBDC.

The SandDollar initiative was driven by multiple goals, including enhancing financial inclusion for communities residing in remote islands and strengthening the resilience of the payments system during natural disasters and pandemics. Additionally, the CBDC aimed to alleviate the high costs associated with cash payments by government agencies to individuals without bank accounts. To this end, plans were put in place to integrate government agencies into the SandDollar network, facilitating digital government payments and reducing related expenses.

The Central Bank of the Bahamas outlined the following goals for its CBDC project:

1. Enhance payment system efficiency through secure transactions and faster settlement speeds.
2. Improve financial inclusion, cost-effectiveness, and accessibility to financial services across the country.
3. Ensure equitable access to payment systems for individuals of all ages, immigration status, and residency.
4. Bolster the nation's defenses against money laundering, counterfeiting, and other illicit activities.

The CBOB has multiple responsibilities in the CBDC scheme, including issuing currency, overseeing holdings, and supporting a centralized Know

Your Customer (KYC)/Identity system. While the CBOB does not offer customer service or endorse digital wallets directly, it manages the record of all digital currency holdings for individuals.

The CBOB also developed an in-house KYC solution for SandDollar wallets, which all institutions can use at no extra cost.

How does the SandDollar work?

Residents that want to participate in the SandDollar can do so either via their smartphone (iOS and Android) or by using a physical payment card to access a digital wallet. SandDollar-integrated wallets have multi-factor authentication features, and all mobile devices must support a passcode or biometric sign-in to access the app and complete transactions. The SandDollar cannot be used outside the country or for foreign exchange operations on its own, reducing its susceptibility for illicit international flows.

The KYC status of a user determines what their wallet allows. The first level of Individual Wallet requires only an email address or phone number and is restricted to a B$500 balance and B$1500 in monthly transactions. The second level of Individual Wallet requires a government photo ID and allows holding balances up to B$5000 and doing monthly transactions up to B$10,000. The third level of wallet is a merchant wallet and requires businesses to provide their license and tax filing, with a holding limit of B$8000 to B$1,000,000 and unlimited transactions. Any excess wallet balances are deposited in users' bank accounts at financial institutions through a dynamic link.

Although the SandDollar had yet to gain widespread adoption, the CBOB acknowledged the risks it posed to financial intermediation, integrity, and cybersecurity. The CBOB has attempted to gain further adoption by ensuring the SandDollar's offline usability, so that citizens could transact even when there is no electricity or cell phone network. Offline functionality was considered critical, but the authorities encountered unanticipated difficulties in achieving it. During the pilot projects, the solution of local "offline" networks built on introducing local redundancies to the main telecommunication system did not achieve the policy goal. The solution's telecommunication masts were vulnerable to the same weather conditions as the main telecommunication system, and the local networks' geographic reach was limited, making payments between islands challenging.

As of January 2022, the CBDC's circulation represented less than 0.1% of the physical currency in circulation. Recognizing the need to increase awareness and usage, a nine-month marketing strategy was launched in Q2 2022, aiming to achieve specific targets related to active wallets, active merchant wallets, and market awareness (Table 13.1).

Table 13.1 SandDollar status and target 2022

	Q1—End of March 2022 (actual)	Q4—End of Dec 2022 (target)
Active wallets	12k	20k
Active merchant wallets	>100	450
Market Awareness	78%	90%

Source Data from CBOB presentation at CBDC conference

To promote higher adoption of SandDollars, various measures were implemented, including cash giveaways for early adopters, merchant discount fees, sponsorship at festivals and events, intensive outreach to Family Islands, a SandDollar-branded mobile unit, and the establishment of the SandDollar Academy. This comprehensive marketing plan, with a budget exceeding B$1 million, aimed to drive increased engagement and usage of the CBDC.

Significant developments were made to the SandDollar system in the first half of 2022, with a focus on commercial bank re-engagement. These developments included Bank Account Integration (ACH), offline capabilities, eKYC, and self-onboarding. Integration of the ACH was completed in 2022, enabling top-up transfers from deposit accounts to native SandDollar wallets through online banking platforms of commercial banks.

By the beginning of the first quarter in 2023, peer-to-peer (P2P) transactions using SandDollar more than doubled compared to the same period in 2022, while peer-to-business (P2B) transactions increased by over three times, with an average transaction amount of B$68.

As of April 2023, there were over 100,000 mobile phone-based wallet accounts in The Bahamas, while approximately 455 out of 1500 businesses with access to merchant services through licensed payment providers were accepting SandDollars. This means that only 1/3 of the deployed merchant wallets were in use in April 2023. The amount of SandDollars in circulation was less than 0.2% of all Bahamian dollars (Table 13.2).

Table 13.2 SandDollars in circulation

Bahamian SandDollar Statistics—March 2023	
SandDollars in circulation	**$1,024,816**
Number of approved digital wallet providers	**9**
Active digital wallet providers	**7**
Number of consumer wallets	**101,636**
Number of merchant wallets	**1512**
Number of active SandDollar merchants	**455**

Source Data from CBOB presentation at CBDC conference

To ensure sustained adoption, the CBOB initiated the recruitment of SandDollar Ambassadors across various regions in The Bahamas, who will play a vital role in promoting the CBDC within their communities. These ambassadors will receive training to offer support to wallet users and merchants, becoming advocates for SandDollar adoption throughout 2023 and 2024.

In an effort to incentivize adoption, the CBOB announced a targeted give-away of B$1 million in SandDollars to early adopters during 2023 and 2024, further encouraging the use of the CBDC.

Through its innovative SandDollar initiative, The Bahamas has positioned itself as a global pioneer in the field of CBDCs, driving financial inclusion, resilience, and efficiency within its payment system, while continuously addressing the challenges, and the opportunities presented by this groundbreaking digital currency.

13.1.2 Jamaica: Advancing the JAM-DEX CBDC

Jamaica, a Caribbean Island nation with a population of 2.8 million, has embraced the potential of Central Bank Digital Currency with its JAM-DEX initiative. With a median age of 30 and an 88% literacy rate, Jamaica has shown a growing digital presence, including a 68.2% internet access rate and 104% mobile phone connections in 2021. Furthermore, 50.6% of the population actively uses social media, predominantly through their mobile phones.

$$\text{JMD\$100} = \text{US\$0.65}.$$

In March 2021, the Bank of Jamaica (BOJA) began testing a prototype CBDC in collaboration with Ireland-based technology vendor eCurrency Mint Inc. within the BOJA's Fintech Regulatory Sandbox. This was followed by an eight-month pilot program from May to December 2021, during which several successful activities were conducted.

The pilot program included the minting of J$230 million (US$1.5 m) worth of digital currency, which was issued to deposit-taking institutions and authorized payment service providers. The Bank of Jamaica also distributed CBDC to wallet providers, including the issuance of J$1 million to its Banking Department and J$5 million to the National Commercial Bank (NCB), marking the first issuance of CBDC to a deposit-taking institution.

The pilot phase involved the onboarding of 57 customers, including small merchants and consumers, through the National Commercial Bank during an NCB-sponsored event called "Market on the Lawn" held in December 2021. Transactions such as person-to-person transfers, remittance transfers, and payments for goods and services by small vendors were successfully completed. Notably, the CBDC's use cases encompassed government salary payments, toll fees, and various retail transactions.

Building upon the success of the pilot program, the Bank of Jamaica expressed its intention to roll out the CBDC, named JAM-DEX (Jamaica Digital Exchange), nationwide in 2022. Amendments to the Bank of Jamaica Act were passed into law in June 2022, designating the CBDC as legal tender at a rate of J$1 to 1 unit of CBDC. The JAM-DEX CBDC focuses on domestic use, excluding cross-border transactions, and does not bear interest.

The key objectives of JAM-DEX were:

1. Facilitating Jamaica's digital transformation by providing quick, safe, and reliable digital retail payments with no transaction fees.
2. Ensuring financial inclusion by granting all citizens access to financial services and products.
3. Enhancing efficiency for banks by reducing costs associated with cash handling and distribution.
4. Streamlining the currency management process for the Bank of Jamaica.
5. Offering a socially optimal mix of retail payment instruments.
6. Promoting greater interoperability between existing electronic retail payment systems.

The JAM-DEX CBDC system operates on a centralized payment system with traditional technology (no DLT), seamlessly integrating with the Bank of Jamaica's Real-Time Gross Settlement System (RTGS). Encryption techniques, digital signatures, and multi-factor authentication mechanisms are supposed to safeguard personal identity and user privacy. JAM-DEX is expected to save the country about seven million US dollar per year, which are currently spent on replacing, storing, and handling cash. However, financial institutions and relevant authorities can track payments under the local Proceeds of Crime Act (POCA) to combat money laundering and the financing of terrorism, meaning that there is no real privacy in the CBDC ecosystem.

The national roll-out of JAM-DEX commenced in 2022 and involved the continued onboarding of customers by the National Commercial Bank, the addition of two more wallet providers, expanding outreach efforts to raise public awareness, and the integration of the government's Social/Welfare Ministry to disburse benefits through JAM-DEX.

As of February 18, 2023, JAM-DEX had successfully onboarded 190,000 customers, including individuals, small merchants, and micro-merchants. The total transaction activity for 2022 reached J$357 million (US$2.3 m).

In 2023/2024, Jamaica plans to implement two additional programs to incentivize the use of JAM-DEX. The Small/Micro Merchant Incentive Program offers J$25,000 of JAM-DEX to the first 10,000 onboarded merchants, while the Wallet-holder Individual Loyalty Program grants consumers 2% cashback on total JAM-DEX purchases, up to a maximum spend of J$5000.

JAM-DEX represents Jamaica's commitment to harnessing the potential of CBDCs for digital transformation, financial inclusion, and more efficient payment systems, further driving Jamaica's progress into the digital era.

13.2 Advanced Pilots

13.2.1 Eastern Caribbean Currency Union: Exploring the DCash CBDC

The Eastern Caribbean Currency Union (ECCU) is operating in the Organization of Eastern Caribbean States (OECS) made up by Antigua and Barbuda, Commonwealth of Dominica, Grenada, Montserrat, Saint Kitts and Nevis, Saint Lucia, Saint Vincent, and the Grenadines. The ECCU introduced its Central Bank Digital Currency, known as DCash (or DXCD) in 2021. The ECCU has a population of 615,724 inhabitants and aims to achieve financial inclusion, economic growth, and competitiveness through its CBDC pilot. Cash and paper checks account for 80% of all transactions in the ECCU.

$$1 \text{ EC\$} = 0.37\text{US\$}.$$

DCash was initiated by BITT, a private software company, and incorporated into the Eastern Caribbean Central Bank's (ECCB) transformation agenda. The pilot program launched in March 2021 with participation of three-quarters of the local financial institutions. It focused on utilizing smart devices for financial transactions between consumers and merchants, as well as people-to-people (P2P) transactions.

Despite the potential benefits of DCash, such as reducing payment costs and decreasing reliance on paper cash and cheques, adoption has been slow and uneven across countries within the ECCU. To gain more experience and feedback, the pilot program is set to continue until June 2023, after which the ECCB will make a decision regarding the issuance of DCash. At the time of this writing, no information was available with regard to the official launch decision yet.

DCash has unique design features. It is utilizing private blockchain technology provided by BITT Inc. and is storing system services on Google Cloud, except for the minting system. The underlying blockchain technology in use is based on Hyperledger Fabric, a private permissioned blockchain, where all participants need to be registered for compliance purposes.

The ECCB holds sole authority to issue and redeem the digital currency and maintains control over its supply. The system operates as a "two-tier system," leveraging the strengths of both the private sector and the central bank to ensure trust and compliance with payment system policies. While the ECCB can observe transactions and the outstanding stock of DCash in each digital wallet, detailed information about the identity of participants or transaction purposes remains withheld from the central bank. Financial institutions, however, can access the full information on their own customers, as they are responsible for maintaining their clients' databases. Here again it is important to realize that inside the full CBDC ecosystem, there is no real privacy.

To mitigate financial stability risks, DCash is designed as a small-value retail instrument, unsuitable for foreign exchange transactions. The size of holdings and transaction values per wallet are limited, and digital wallets do not earn interest to prevent competition with financial institutions' savings accounts. In order to further financial inclusion, it is not necessary to have an account at a financial institution to participate in the DCash scheme. Such unbanked people would obtain a wallet through an agent authorized by the ECCB and those wallets would have an initial transaction threshold of EC$1000 (US$370) [128]. For people with a bank account, the threshold would be higher and set at EC$2700 (US$1000).

The DCash system is deliberately kept separate from the ECCB's core payment systems, banks' operating systems, and the Automated Clearing House to mitigate potential risks. However, this requires further testing after the pilot to assess vulnerabilities and risks when connecting DCash with these payment and operating systems.

In a unique incident for a CBDC, DCash experienced a two-month outage in early 2022 due to operational management issues related to digital certificate renewal/rotation. The ECCB guaranteed all balances during the pilot program, and the outage only affected new transactions and user onboarding, leaving the Distributed Ledger Technology (DLT) and existing data/transactions intact. This incident highlighted the importance of enhancing operational resilience, business continuity plans, and incident response strategies. It also emphasized the significance of clearly defining operational, oversight, and risk management responsibilities between the central bank and technology providers/operators, as well as establishing appropriate governance frameworks.

The ECCU's exploration of DCash represents its commitment to innovation in the digital currency space, aiming to overcome challenges and ensure the CBDC's effectiveness and stability in the Eastern Caribbean region.

13.2.2 Nigeria: Challenges and Developments in the eNaira CBDC Project

Nigeria, with a population of 214 million, embarked on the development of its Central Bank Digital Currency (CBDC) called the eNaira in October 2021. Nigeria had about 195 million mobile subscribers, and it has about 104 million active internet users, of which 33% have active social media accounts.

Mobile internet user penetration has grown from 20% in 2018 to 37% in 2022. Although 81% of adults in Nigeria own a mobile phone, Nigeria has a large unbanked adult-rural population. The financial inclusion rate in the country is about 64%. Interestingly, the crypto currency adoption rate in the country was growing fast and recently measured at 24.2%.

$$1 \text{ Naira (N)} = \text{US\$0.22}.$$

The primary objectives of the eNaira project were financial inclusion, empowerment, poverty reduction, improved foreign exchange position, and enhanced monetary and financial stability policies. The CBDC was expected to bring various benefits, including increased availability and usability of central bank money, a resilient payment ecosystem, financial inclusion, cost reduction in cash processing, improved revenue and tax collection, direct welfare disbursements, efficient cross-border transactions, and facilitation of diaspora remittances.

The eNaira use cases were categorized into core use cases, targeted payments, and additional use cases leveraging the CBDC infrastructure.

Core use cases encompassed person-to-person transactions (P2P), person-to-business (P2B) payments, diaspora remittances, and person-to-government (P2G) transactions.

Targeted payments included social benefit transfers, government-to-person and government-to-merchant payments, and cross-border payments and investments.

The CBDC infrastructure should further support various additional use cases such as lending products, asset tokenization, blockchain identity, supply chain verification, educational credentials, and land titles.

Designed to accommodate the needs of over 200 million citizens, the eNaira is the largest active CBDC project in the world, except for the Chinese e-CNY pilot. Despite local banks' efforts to market the eNaira to their customers, adoption has been slow. By mid-2022, top downloads reached a peak of 291,000 per week, and approximately 226,000 transactions had taken place, amounting to 4 billion Naira (around US$8.7 million) in total value. Individual wallet activity stood at 95.4%, while merchant wallet activity was at 46.5%.

The eNaira was implemented, like ECCU's DCash, by the solution provider BITT Inc. on Hyperledger Fabric blockchain technology.

The eNaira aimed to reduce the influence of the informal cash-based economy in Nigeria and expand the country's tax base by pegging it to a one-to-one exchange rate with the Naira. However, challenges and limitations affected its adoption. The limited functionality of the eNaira app, poor user experience, and spending restrictions for new users without a banking verification number (BVN) hindered widespread usage. Additionally, the eNaira's reliance on mobile data access and the absence of cross-border payment functionality limited its relevance to certain user segments.

For mass adoption, more consumers need to download and fund a wallet. The eNaira needs to provide multiple and superior use cases that appeal to customers, merchants, and other participants in the financial system. To address these challenges and enhance control over the underlying technology, the Central Bank of Nigeria (CBN) has been reportedly in talks with blockchain firm R3 (a market competitor of the initial partner BITT Inc.) in the first half of 2023 to develop its own software for the eNaira [144]. This shift toward open-source software could enable the CBN to maintain full control over the CBDC solution. However, these potential new plans remain somewhat unclear and inconsistent with more recent developments. Specific details and the timeline of this potential partnership could not be confirmed in the subsequent months since the article appeared and the partnership of the CBN with BITT seems to be intact.

In parallel, the Central Bank of Nigeria (CBN) has upgraded the eNaira app [185] in July 2023 to enhance its service offerings and improve user experience. It incorporated Near Field Communication (NFC) technology. This advanced feature establishes seamless communication between two devices, such as a mobile phone and a payment terminal, when they are in close proximity.

During an eNaira sensitization workshop, Joseph Angaye, the CBN team leader, highlighted their commitment to maintaining a top-tier payment infrastructure.

Angaye explained the various benefits eNaira offers, emphasizing the importance of staying digitally advanced in a world that is rapidly transitioning into a digital landscape. The eNaira app's versatility allows for programming specific usage parameters, such as restricting spending to a particular location or specific items.

This programmability proves particularly valuable for executing intervention programs effectively. For instance, funds transferred to farmers for acquiring tools or other designated purposes can be securely programmed within the eNaira app. This ensures that the allocated funds cannot be diverted to unrelated expenses (like "marrying more wives and all").

The CBN's upgrade of the eNaira app with NFC technology reflects their commitment to technological advancement and delivering a seamless, secure, and programmable payment solution for users and stakeholders alike.

Nigeria's eNaira project serves as an important case study in the development and implementation of a CBDC. Overcoming the existing challenges and delivering a comprehensive, user-friendly solution will be critical for the eNaira to achieve mass adoption and effectively contribute to the country's economic growth and financial inclusion goals.

13.2.3 China: Advancements and Impact of the e-CNY CBDC

China, with a population of 1.41 billion, has made significant strides in financial inclusion by giving over 80% of the population access to the financial system by 2017. The country also boasts a high penetration rate of smartphones, reaching almost 72% in 2022. In this context, the People's Bank of

China (PBOC) developed the e-CNY (electronic Chinese Yuan) as a digital version of the national currency.

$$100\text{CNY} = \text{US\$}13.9.$$

Source Adapted from Freepik

The e-CNY [2], also known as Digital Currency Electronic Payment (DCEP) or Digital Yuan, serves as legal tender and is intended to enhance payment and settlement transactions in China, improve efficiency, safety, and convenience, and reduce the country's dependence on foreign currencies. The e-CNY does not utilize blockchain or Distributed Ledger Technologies but is designed to be interoperable with existing payment systems, including bank cards and mobile platforms.

The distribution of the e-CNY follows a two-tier system, where the PBOC transfers the digital currency to commercial banks, which then distribute it to consumers. As of this writing, 35 Chinese commercial banks offer access to the e-CNY and facilitate its usage by the public. The e-CNY's pilot program incorporated varying levels of privacy, with different requirements for identity disclosure and transaction limits. It offers five levels of privacy. The first two levels do not necessitate the disclosure of a user's identity, but only require a phone number or email address. With a phone number alone, a user can obtain a wallet that has a balance limit of 10,000 e-CNY (US$1390), transaction limits of 2000 e-CNY per transaction, and a limit of 5000 e-CNY in transactions per day. Upgrading to higher limits and balances requires a personal ID and banking information [80].

Although the e-CNY has been trialed in several cities and gained acceptance among merchants, its adoption has been relatively low. By the end of 2022, the e-CNY accounted for around 0.13% of the total currency in circulation, and over 4.5 million merchants across China had begun accepting the CBDC. Outstanding levels of Digital Currency Electronic Payment stood at 13.61 billion yuan (US$2 billion) at the end of December 2022. The usage of the digital yuan had not yet met the expectations of the Chinese central bank, highlighting the challenges of widespread adoption.

In early 2023, the e-CNY received an upgrade that introduced offline payments and smart contract capabilities. Offline payments allow users to make transactions without internet access by using NFC technology and enabling contactless payments through smartphones. Known as the "Tap to pay" function, it allows users to complete payments even when their phones are turned off or out of power. By leveraging the near-field communication (NFC) smartphone hardware, the app effectively turns the phone into a hard wallet. Users can activate this function on the app and set payment and transaction limits, with options for payment limits up to 500 e-CNY (US$70) and transaction limits for up to 10 payments. The smart contract feature, implemented on the e-commerce app Meituan, enables users to make purchases and participate in prize draws. Furthermore, investors can use the e-CNY to buy securities through a mobile app provided by Soochow Securities, a local brokerage firm.

China's development and relative success with the e-CNY have influenced discussions and actions in other countries. In the United States, some Republican senators have expressed concerns about the potential national and economic risks associated with the e-CNY and have proposed legislation to restrict its use and its presence in the app stores of Google and Apple.

In May 2023, Mr. Mu Changchu, Director General of China's Central Bank Digital Currency Research Institute, confirmed that blockchains were no option for China. One of the key reasons was settlement time. He explained that Chinese were impatient and used to very fast private Instant Payment Solutions of AliPay and WeChat pay. So even a transaction time of one second, considered reasonable elsewhere, would be totally inacceptable to Chinese users. The PBOC is now aiming for settlements in nanoseconds to be competitive with their e-CNY or it risks rejection by the users in China.

At the end of June 2023, transactions conducted using China's digital yuan reached an impressive 1.8 trillion yuan (equivalent to $250 billion), as reported by People's Bank of China (PBOC) Governor Yi Gong [186]. This marked a significant increase compared to the 100 billion yuan recorded in August of the previous year. Despite this notable growth, Yi highlighted that the e-CNY in circulation accounted for only 0.16% of China's M_0 money supply, which represents the physical cash in circulation. This is compared to 0.13% at the end of 2022.

Nevertheless, Yi emphasized that, despite its small balance, the digital yuan's transaction velocity surpassed that of cash, making it a more efficient means of conducting transactions.

In the third quarter of 2023, the first international oil purchase was conducted with e-CNY when PetroChina bought 1 million barrels of crude and completed thereby the first large international trade to be settled in e-CNY. In addition, the e-CNY app was also extended for tourist to allow them to install the app and buy e-CNY using Visa and Mastercard prior to their departure for China.

China's introduction of the e-CNY aims to modernize the payment system, strengthen financial control, and position itself as a global leader in digital currencies. However, the challenges of adoption and the need for continuous improvements and enhancements remain crucial factors in the e-CNY's journey toward broader acceptance and usage.

13.3 Other Key Projects

13.3.1 Sweden's E-Krona

Sweden, with a population of 10.4 million, has a smartphone penetration of 84.37% and internet penetration of 88.3%. Sweden has experienced a significant decrease in cash usage over the years, with card and instant payments gaining popularity. The proportion of cash payments in the retail sector dropped from almost 40% in 2010 to around 15% in 2016. Approximately two-thirds of consumers claim they can manage without cash, and just as many mostly use cards for payments under 100 Swedish Kronor (SEK).

$$100\text{SEK} = \text{US\$}9.5.$$

It is possible that Sweden will soon become a society where cash is no longer widely accepted. These developments in the Swedish payment market are exceptional when compared internationally.

In response, the Riksbank, Sweden's central bank, began exploring the concept of creating a digital version of the Swedish krona, known as the e-krona. The e-krona aims to provide a safe and efficient means of payment for individuals and businesses, acting as a digital complement to physical cash.

13.3.1.1 Report 1: Initial Concept

The initial proposal for the e-krona in 2017 outlined its purpose and design features. It was intended for smaller payments and would be denominated in Swedish kronor. The e-krona could be held by the public, financial institutions, and companies, operating in real time, 24/7. Two feasible models were identified: a register-based (aka account-based) and a value-based (aka token-based) model, both offering unique advantages.

In the case of a register-based e-krona, the balance is stored in a central database, which allows for transactions between e-krona holders to take place independently of banks' payment systems. However, when money is to be deposited or withdrawn from the e-krona system, interaction with the banking system is required. It is possible to trace a register-based e-krona.

On the other hand, a value-based e-krona has many similarities with the current cash system, where the balance is stored on a card or in an app. If the card or smartphone is destroyed or lost, the balance is also lost, much like losing a wallet with cash in it, unless special security settings have been applied. Depending on its design, a value-based e-krona can be either anonymous or traceable.

Report 1 [21] concluded that the e-krona, as a digital currency, could serve as a government-guaranteed payment method without credit risk, providing a modernized alternative to cash. It would complement existing payment forms and enhance competition in the market. Furthermore, the e-krona could be crucial during crisis situations when relying on private actors in the payment space may be challenging. The report also favored a register-based e-krona over a value-based one due to its (perceived) higher development potential.

13.3.1.2 Report 2: Further Analysis

Published in October 2018, the second report [22] emphasized the alignment of the e-krona with the Riksbank's goal of promoting a secure and effective payment system. However, its design may necessitate modifications to the Sverige's Riksbank Act. While a value-based e-krona is believed to be consistent with the Act, an account-based e-krona would require revisions to the legislation to provide the Riksbank with a definite mandate to issue it.

Report 2 recommended the creation of a technical solution for a value-based e-krona and the initiation of a pilot program to explore different concepts. The pilot program focused on developing a prepaid, non-interest-bearing e-krona with traceable transactions (meaning explicitly without privacy for the users).

13.3.1.3 E-Krona Pilot Phase 1

The Riksbank started to collaborate with Accenture in February 2020 to develop the technical solution for the e-krona pilot program, which was based on a token-based system. The e-krona, functioning as digital token, shares similarities with physical banknotes but has unique characteristics. Only the Riksbank can create and issue e-krona tokens, each with a specific value. Tokens are traceable back to the Riksbank as the sole issuer. Accessing and using e-krona requires a digital wallet connected to a mobile app or card. Tokens can only be used once, and each transaction generates a new token for the recipient while consumed tokens are registered. The e-krona network operates on the R3 Corda platform, utilizing the UTXO model, a decentralized and private DLT network. Participants, including banks and payment service providers, run their own nodes in the network, facilitating the issuance, exchange, distribution, and execution of transactions. The network functions independently of existing payment infrastructures and no new money is created. The network is supplied with liquidity through the Riksbank's settlement system RIX. The first phase of the pilot successfully tested simple transactions. During Phase 1 a first performance evaluation was carried out, which tested whether it was possible to carry out, during a period of 10 minutes, on average 100 mixed transactions per second, with 100,000 users. This proved possible, but the transactions were simple, and the test set-up lacked complex chains of transactions with a larger number of tokens.

13.3.1.4 E-Krona Pilot Phase 2

During the second phase [73] of the e-krona pilot, the Riksbank continued its collaboration with Accenture, focusing on several areas.

- Evaluating and improving performance and scalability in the e-krona network
- Integration with internal systems of potential participants
- Developing offline functionality
- Storing keys and tokens in different ways
- Developing support for addressing payments
- Integration with existing point of sale terminals
- Analysis of the e-krona network infrastructure

Performance tests showed that the implemented solution on the R3 Corda platform could handle transactions per second in simple scenarios, aligning with the current peak loads of existing local payment systems like Swish. However, as the complexity and number of tokens increased, performance decreased. Integration of participants, such as Handelsbanken and Tietoevry, demonstrated the feasibility of a parallel network operating alongside established account and payment systems, enabling direct exchanges and transfers between account credits and e-kronor. The pilot explored wallet models and opportunities for offline payments, although full offline functionality posed risks and required secure elements for token protection. An alias service for addressing payments was implemented, and the integration of e-krona as a means of payment in stores on PoS systems was tested. The legal analysis highlighted the need to address financial confidentiality and data protection concerns related to the transaction history carried in the tokens. Further technical solutions and legal considerations were deemed necessary to resolve these issues.

13.3.1.5 E-Krona Pilot Phase 3

The report on the third phase [145] of the e-krona pilot, published on April 4, 2023, examined the potential implementation of digital central bank money if a launch was decided. The Riksbank collaborated with payment service providers to ensure public access to the e-krona. This phase focused on three areas: developing a cooperation model between the Riksbank and market participants for e-krona distribution, fostering innovation in the payment market, and exploring how an e-krona network could facilitate faster and safer transactions across countries and central bank digital currency networks, known as the Icebreaker project, conducted together with Norges Bank, the Bank of Israel, and the Bank for International Settlements (BIS).

Findings emphasized the need for balance between e-krona objectives and market needs. The pilot has also explored the feasibility of conditional payments using the technical platform, which was successfully tested with a hypothetical customer and car dealer. In terms of programmability, the e-krona's potential for conditional payments was of interest, rather than the possibility of conditional (programmable) money. If money is programmed for specific purposes, it loses its fundamental characteristic of being universally applicable for all payments. The Riksbank's aim for the e-krona is not to exert control over or to restrict its uses. Such actions would be contradictory to the basic function of money and could also infringe on personal privacy. Hence in Sweden, programmable money seems to be out.

The pilot demonstrated the platform's potential for enabling more advanced payment services for users. However, it was discovered that implementing conditional payments may result in increased sharing of user data within the e-krona network, highlighting the need for thorough investigations to protect personal privacy.

The third report [107] contained the following conclusions:

- Conditional (programmable) payments are interesting for an e-krona. No conditional (programmable) money is desired. The tested solution enabled conditional payments.
- The increased transparency of DLT and smart contracts does not eliminate the need for traditional regulation and supervision.
- DLT and smart contracts can facilitate the development and dissemination of new payment services.
- DLT and conditional payments may mean greater sharing of information between network participants, highlighting the need for thorough investigations to protect personal privacy.
- Basic e-krona functionality should be separated from more advanced payment services.

Going forward the Riksbank plans to focus the e-krona work going forward less on continued technical testing of the specific pilot solution and more on investigating the design of an e-krona ahead of the decision on possible issuance, alongside monitoring the international development of central bank digital currencies.

13.3.2 United States' Digital Dollar

The United States had a population of 332 million and a GDP of 23.3 trillion USD in 2021. By 2022, the country had 307 million smartphone users and an internet penetration rate of 89.4%. Research from the Federal Reserve Bank of San Francisco indicated that credit cards accounted for 28% of all payments in 2021, the highest percentage since the study began in 2016. This suggests a growing preference for credit cards over cash and other payment methods. Particularly among higher-income households, the credit card usage rate rises to 34% for those earning \$100,000 to \$149,999 and to 44% for those earning over \$150,000.

Payment fees in the US amount to 2.3% of GDP. Additionally, approximately 14.1% of households (around 18.7 million) are considered "underbanked," while 4.5% (approximately 5.9 million) are "unbanked," meaning they lack a checking or savings account at a bank or credit union, according to the 2021 FDIC National Survey of Unbanked and Underbanked Households [81].

During the initial COVID-19 stimulus legislation, a proposal [146] for a Digital Dollar, along with Digital Dollar Wallets was included. These wallets were intended to be accessible by January 1, 2021. The Digital Dollar was defined as a digital ledger entry representing a dollar amount held as a liability by the US Federal Reserve Bank, as well as an electronic unit of value redeemable by qualifying financial institutions. However, this proposal was ultimately removed from the final stimulus bill and not implemented.

Source Shutterstock

A revived initiative for a digital version of the US dollar has since been proposed. An executive order to this effect was passed by President Biden [88]. This new attempt aims at enabling individuals and businesses to use digital wallets for fast and secure payments, and to potentially reduce reliance on physical cash. This should also promote financial inclusion for those without access to traditional banking systems. The project is currently in the early stages, with ongoing research to assess the potential benefits and risks of a digital dollar and determine the most suitable implementation approach.

The digital dollar project has progressed through several key stages, including:

1. Research: Following the initial COVID-19 proposal, various organizations, such as the Digital Dollar Project [147], a partnership between Accenture and the Digital Dollar Foundation, have conducted research to assess the feasibility and potential benefits of a digital dollar. Whitepapers have been published outlining the potential use cases and technical requirements of a digital dollar.

2. Proposals: Multiple legal bills have been introduced in the U.S. Congress, which aim to establish a digital dollar pilot program.
3. Pilot programs: Several pilot programs have been initiated to explore the potential of a digital dollar.

13.3.2.1 Project Hamilton: Interesting Research in the United States

Project Hamilton is a long-term research project conducted jointly by the Boston Federal Reserve Bank and the Massachusetts Institute of Technology's Digital Currency Initiative (MIT DCI). Its primary objective in Phase 1 was to examine the technical viability of a transaction processor for a central bank digital currency. The project challenged traditional categorizations of CBDC models and emphasized the need for alternative arrangements that offer flexibility in distributing data, accessibility, intermediaries, and institutional roles in CBDC design.

The report from Project Hamilton [148] highlighted the following findings in specific areas:'

1. **Performance:** To support retail transactions at a large scale, a CBDC transaction processor should be capable of processing tens of thousands of transactions per second in real time and accommodate potential growth in payment volumes.
2. **Speed:** To leverage the benefits of faster or real-time payments, the project set a target for 99% of transactions to complete within 5 seconds.
3. **Throughput and scalability:** A CBDC system should handle projected transaction volumes from hundreds of millions of users without requiring intermediaries to aggregate transactions. The project aimed for a minimum target of 100,000 transactions per second based on existing cash and card volumes.
4. **Privacy and data minimization:** The design of a payment system must consider choices related to data privacy, access, and retention. The report emphasizes the importance of exploring strong privacy implications in cryptographic designs. Though exploring the implications of cryptographic designs for strong privacy will be a part of the upcoming Project Hamilton Phase 2 research, Phase 1 focused on design options that limit data access and retention in the central transaction processor.

5. **System design:** Two architectures were implemented for efficient, low-latency, and fault-tolerant transaction processing. The atomizer architecture utilized an ordering server to create a linear history of transactions, while the two-phase commit (2PC) architecture executed non-conflicting transactions in parallel without generating a single, ordered history. Evaluation results demonstrated transaction rates of 1.7 million per second in the 2PC architecture and 170,000 per second in the atomizer design.

While the report drew ideas from blockchain technology, it did not endorse the use of Distributed Ledger Technology in CBDC design. Instead, it described it as unnecessary and argued that other models may perform better. However, it also acknowledged that ongoing advancements in blockchain technology could potentially address these concerns in the future.

It is important to note that Project Hamilton's rejection of DLT was made solely within the scope of the first phase of the investigation, which focused on exploring the feasibility and performance of basic transactions. A future phase 2 will study interoperability, smart contracts, programmability, resilience, offline payments, and the balance between privacy and compliance. Given that these are areas where DLT has shown potential, the report's rejection of the technology in the first phase should be considered provisional.

The report acknowledged that a DLT-based CBDC may be necessary for central banks seeking to distribute trust and governance, and that DLT may be preferable for architectures that involve intermediaries running nodes in the system. This intermediary access could provide pathways for interoperability and compliance measures. The study also emphasized the intricate relationship between technical and policy choices.

It is important to note that all the measured values in the project were based on very similar transactions and a linear distribution between servers, which is not a realistic real-life set-up. A private person will have a very different user profile and transaction volume than does a supermarket or Amazon.com. The distribution of transactions over servers was too simple to allow any real conclusions on performance. The problem will be very different in reality, when suddenly (for example) 30% of the users transact with one specific participant (like Amazon.com).

Prior to concluding, we must mention that the digital dollar project is still in its early developmental stages, and it remains uncertain whether a digital version of the U.S. dollar will be created and how it will be implemented. President Joe Biden has nevertheless issued an executive order on the subject in March 2022:

President Joe Biden's Executive Order EO14067

On March 9, 2022, the US President Joe Biden issued executive order EO14067 [88] in reaction to other CBDC projects around the world. EO14067 prescribes the following policy and actions related to a United States Central Bank Digital Currency (sometimes referred to as "*Biden Bucks*"). We quote:

> The policy of my Administration on a United States CBDC is as follows:
>
> (i) Sovereign money is at the core of a well-functioning financial system, macroeconomic stabilization policies, and economic growth. My Administration places the highest urgency on research and development efforts into the potential design and deployment options of a United States CBDC. These efforts should include assessments of possible benefits and risks for consumers, investors, and businesses; financial stability and systemic risk; payment systems; national security; the ability to exercise human rights; financial inclusion and equity; and the actions required to launch a United States CBDC if doing so is deemed to be in the national interest.
>
> (ii) My Administration sees merit in showcasing United States leadership and participation in international fora related to CBDCs and in multi country conversations and pilot projects involving CBDCs. Any future dollar payment system should be designed in a way that is consistent with United States priorities (as outlined in section 4(a)(i) of this order) and democratic values, including privacy protections, and that ensures the global financial system has appropriate transparency, connectivity, and platform and architecture interoperability or transferability, as appropriate.
>
> (iii) A United States CBDC may have the potential to support efficient and low-cost transactions, particularly for cross border funds transfers and payments, and to foster greater access to the financial system, with fewer of the risks posed by private sector-administered digital assets. A United States CBDC that is interoperable with CBDCs issued by other monetary authorities could facilitate faster and lower-cost cross-border payments and potentially boost economic growth, support the continued centrality of the United States within the international financial system, and help to protect the unique role that the dollar plays in global finance...

While the digital dollar is lagging behind CBDC projects in many other countries, opposition to an American CBDC has gained significant traction and visibility. It stands out compared to more advanced nations' CBDC projects.

13.3.2.2 Significant Opposition Forming

This opposition has been observed through initiatives from the current Republican opposition as well as from some Democratic politicians, whereas the democratic Biden administration is supportive of CBDCs. The following examples shed light on the political campaigning surrounding CBDC opposition in the U.S.

The Tom Emmer Bill [34]

On January 12, 2022, Congressman Tom Emmer (Minnesota) introduced a bill prohibiting the Federal Reserve from issuing a central bank digital currency (CBDC) directly to individuals:

> Requiring users to open up an account at the Fed to access a U.S. CBDC would put the Fed on an insidious path akin to China's digital authoritarianism," Emmer stated. "It is important to note that the Fed does not, and should not, have the authority to offer retail bank accounts. Regardless, any CBDC implemented by the Fed must be open, permissionless, and private. This means that any digital dollar must be accessible to all, transact on a blockchain that is transparent to all, and maintain the privacy elements of cash.

Texas Senator Ted Cruz' Legislation [35]

Upon introducing his own legislation to prevent unilateral Fed control of a US digital currency on March 30, 2022, Senator Ted Cruz (Texas) said:

> The federal government has the ability to encourage and nurture innovation in the cryptocurrency space, or to completely devastate it. This bill goes a long way in making sure big government doesn't attempt to centralize and control cryptocurrency so that it can continue to thrive and prosper in the United States. We should be empowering entrepreneurs, enabling innovation, and increasing individual freedom—not stifling it.

Governor of South Dakota Kristi Noem's Veto [36]

During the March 10, 2023, episode of Tucker Carlson's television program on Fox News, South Dakota Governor Kristi Noem issued a cautionary message to her fellow governors. The context of the discussion was a recent legislative measure passed by South Dakota's legislature, which aimed to redefine currency and establish guidelines for a Central Bank Digital Currency, effectively prohibiting other digital currencies from being utilized within the state. Governor Noem vetoed the bill.

Tulsi Gabbard, 2020 US Presidential Candidate and Former US Representative for Hawaii in the US House of Representatives [66]

Tulsi Gabbard made the following statements in April 2023 in an interview with Tucker Carlson, news anchor, on Fox News:

> This is the latest effort by those in power who are intent on undermining and taking away our liberties. The central bank digital currency is about government sanctioned surveillance and control. It is about them being able to keep track of every single thing we purchase, whether it is a stick of gum or automobile or anything in between.
>
> So if they have all this information and data in this system, where does that lead? It gives them the power to decide ok we do not want to allow you to purchase certain things or we may deem it necessary to freeze your overall account (…) Once we give up our economic autonomy, we no longer have freedom. Once we allow somebody else to control our wallet, they then control our freedom.

Ron DeSantis, Governor of Florida and 2024 Presidential Candidate Legislation [37]

The website of Governor Ron DeSantis contained the following statements posted on March 20, 2023:

> The Biden administration's efforts to inject a Centralized Bank Digital Currency is about surveillance and control," said Governor Ron DeSantis standing behind a large 'Big Brother's Digital Dollar' banner. "Today's announcement will protect Florida consumers and businesses from the reckless adoption of a 'centralized digital dollar' which will stifle innovation and promote government-sanctioned surveillance. Florida will not side with economic central planners; we will not adopt policies that threaten personal economic freedom and security.

> A federally controlled Central Bank Digital Currency is the most recent way the Davos elites are attempting to backdoor woke ideology like Environmental, Social, and Governance (ESG) into the United States financial system, threatening individual privacy and economic freedom. Unlike a decentralized digital currency, a CBDC is directly controlled and issued by the government to consumers, giving government bureaucrats the ability to see all consumer activity and the power to cut off access to goods and services for consumers.

In July 2023, Ron DeSantis doubled down in an interview conducted at "The Summit" by Blazemedia [184] and said:

> For those who don't know what CBDC is: What they want to do, and this is tied in with Davos, World Economic Forum, all of these people, they want to get rid of cash, they want no cryptocurrency, and they want this to be the sole form of legal tender. And they have said this publicly at Davos and these other places: It will allow them to – quote - prohibit undesirable purchases, like fuel and ammunition. And so the minute you give them the power to do this, they are going to impose a social credit system on this country. CBDC is a massive threat to American liberty. On January 20, 2025, it goes to the ashheap of history in this country.

Robert F. Kennedy Jr., Member of the Kennedy Family and 2024 U.S. Presidential Candidate [149]

Robert F. Kennedy Jr. has expressed increasing concerns about a central bank digital currency. Kennedy argues that CBDCs lack anonymity and pose a threat to people's privacy and individual freedoms.

Kennedy said in a lengthy tweet:

> While cash transactions are anonymous, a CBDC will allow the government to surveil all our private financial affairs. The central bank will have the power to enforce dollar limits on our transactions restricting where you can send money, where you can spend it, and when money expires,
>
> A CBDC tied to digital ID and social credit score will allow the government to freeze your assets or limit your spending to approved vendors if you fail to comply with arbitrary diktats, i.e. vaccine mandates,

He claims that a CBDC would allow the government to surveil private financial activities, impose restrictions on transactions, freeze assets, and limit spending based on compliance with arbitrary rules like the vaccine mandates. Kennedy draws parallels between the potential banning and seizing of Bitcoin and historical actions taken by the US government with banning gold ownership in the 1930s under the Gold Confiscation Act (Executive Order EO6102) of President Franklin D. Roosevelt.

Indiana Bans Use of a CBDC As Money in the State [193]

After Florida, Indiana Governor Eric Holcomb signed a bill into law that removes central bank digital currency from the definition of money in the state. Introduced by Senator Chris Garten and supported by a bipartisan coalition of 11 cosponsors, Senate Bill 468 amends Indiana's Uniform Commercial Code to explicitly exclude CBDCs from being considered money. This effectively bans the use of CBDCs as a form of currency in Indiana. The law specifies that CBDCs adopted by the United States government, foreign governments, foreign reserves, or foreign-sanctioned central banks are not included in the definition of money.

Tom Emmer's Second Act—Finally on the Right Track

On September 20, 2023, the CBDC Anti-Surveillance State Act [191] H.R. 5403, proposed by Majority Whip Tom Emmer, was approved by the US House Financial Services Committee. This bill aims to prevent the Federal Reserve from directly or indirectly issuing a CBDC to individuals or holding their accounts. The Secretary of the Treasury would also be prohibited from directing the Federal Reserve to release a CBDC without congressional authorization. Notably, Emmer's legislation allows for a privacy-focused digital currency, potentially aligning with Representative Stephen Lynch's ECASH Act [192] H. R. 5410 from September 12, 2023, which promotes a digital dollar mimicking the privacy of physical cash. In a smart move, Emmer does not throw out the CBDC baby with the bath but distinguishes between a CBDC mass surveillance tool and protecting people's privacy in a CBDC. Emmer's bill therefore leaves the door open for a privacy-preserving digital currency: "this Act and the amendments made by this Act shall not apply to any dollar-denominated currency that is open, permissionless, and private, and fully preserves the privacy protections of United States coins and physical currency."

In conclusion: The introduction of a central bank digital currency (CBDC) in the United States has faced significant politicization, despite lagging far behind other countries' efforts. A key criticism is the lack of real privacy measures from the outset, which has fueled accusations of potential mass surveillance. The Snowden revelations have shown people in great detail what US agencies are capable of when it comes to surveillance and data collection.

The US Federal Reserve's failure to guarantee the American citizen real (hard) privacy while maintaining compliance with anti-money laundering (AML) and know-your-customer (KYC) regulations has given rise to skepticism and fear among potential users and offered politician a nice campaigning platform.

These anti-CBDC messages now pose a challenge even for the potential adoption of a well-designed, privacy-preserving CBDC system in the USA. Only Tom Emmer's most recent initiative takes into account the differences one can find in CBDC designs and leaves the door open for a real privacy-preserving digital cash.

Nevertheless, all these critical initiatives raise serious doubts about the feasibility of a US launch in the next 5–10 years. At a minimum, convincing the US citizens to trust any CBDC will be a serious uphill battle from the moment of this writing.

13.3.3 United Kingdom's Digital Pound

The United Kingdom (UK) is an island with 67.7 million inhabitants. In 2022, about 9 out 10 adults owned a smartphone, which could be used for digital payments online and in stores. In 2021, card payments had a 58% market share, of which 32% were contactless. Cash payments had fallen from 55 to 15% in a decade. 95% of the funds held by individuals were private money held as commercial bank deposits and typically spent electronically. Around 1.2 million UK adults did not have a bank account and one-fifth still preferred cash to pay.

$$1 \text{ GBP}(£) = \text{ US\$ } 1.25$$

These patterns raise concerns about decreasing public access to central bank money, potentially leading to a quite fragmented privately owned monetary system and compromising monetary and financial stability. Additionally, dominance of a few firms in the payments sector could arise if they control new money technologies, posing risks to competition and hindering long-term innovation.

In July 2022, Jon Cunliffe, the Deputy Governor of the Bank of England (BoE) further said that any proposed digital pound would likely be managed through some sort of account rather than working like coins or banknotes.

His comments apparently implied that tokens on a blockchain are not the right thing when it comes to a cash alternative or some form of electronic legal tender for the entire population.

In February 2023, the UK published two papers on the Digital Pound [8, 71] "The digital pound: *a new form of money for households and businesses?*" and a technical workpaper, indicating a shift in its stance, after years of questioning the need for a central bank digital currency.

Let us review the content of these reports:

The proposed digital pound, sometimes also called "Britcoin," should coexist with cash, providing a digital equivalent of banknotes and coins, ensuring privacy and data protection, the paper claims. The Bank of England believes a digital pound will be necessary in the future and has initiated this consultation process to seek public input and develop the necessary technical capabilities (Graph 13.2).

The Bank of England's reasons for considering the introduction of a retail Central Bank Digital Currency include acknowledging the changing landscape of money and payments, ensuring continued access to central bank

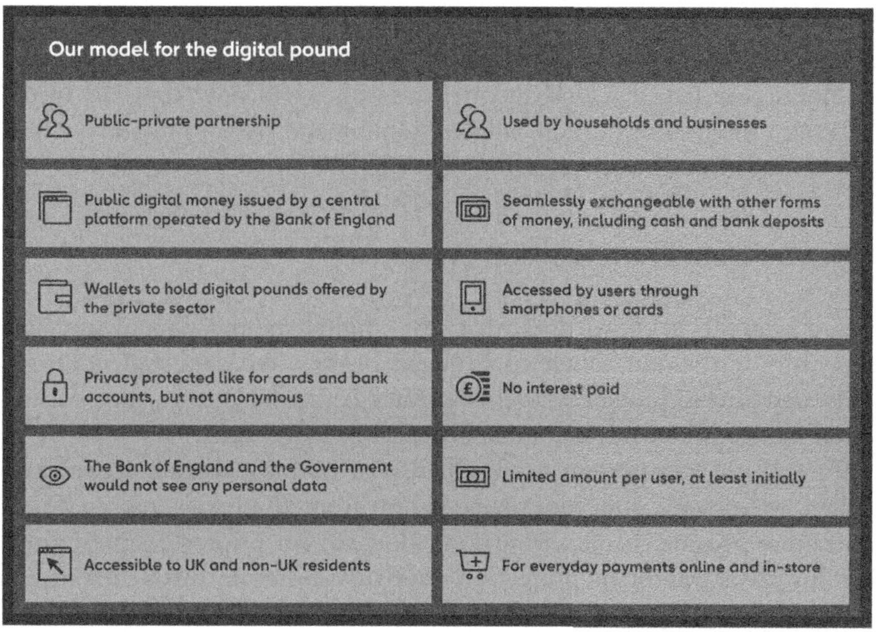

Graph 13.2 Digital pound—BoE model (*Source* [8])[1]

[1] All BoE material shown published under https://www.nationalarchives.gov.uk/doc/open-government-licence/version/3/.

money to maintain confidence and stability in the monetary system, and fostering partnerships with the private sector to drive innovation, provide more choice, and enhance efficiency in domestic payments. As the UK's economy and lifestyles increasingly embrace digital technologies, the BoE sees a CBDC as a means to address these evolving needs and stay aligned with a changing financial landscape.

13.3.3.1 The Platform Model

The model described in the reports is a **two-tier or hybrid CBDC model**, where banks play a role in onboarding, KYC, and AML processes. The Bank of England (BoE) refers to this as a "platform model." If the BoE introduces a digital pound, it will represent a claim on the central bank, similar to physical cash. The BoE will be responsible for providing the digital pound and the central infrastructure, including the "core ledger." Approved non-bank entities or banks in the private sector would have the capability to connect with the central digital pound infrastructure and serve as intermediaries between users and the BoE. These entities can offer digital "pass-through" wallets to end-users, which can be integrated into their existing services. These wallets can ensure user privacy by anonymously recording digital pound holdings on the BoE's core ledger. Consequently, the wallet will only transmit instructions from the user to the core ledger, enabling end-users to interact with the wallets instead of directly engaging with the BoE.

13.3.3.2 Data Protection and Privacy

The document acknowledges that the digital pound would not offer anonymity but would adhere to stringent privacy and data protection standards, and aim to provide a level of privacy comparable to existing forms of digital money, like bank accounts, debit cards, or cheques.

However, it is important to note here that traditional bank accounts and credit cards do not offer any privacy at all from the banks and credit card issuers that provide them, setting a very low bar for privacy despite claiming rigorous privacy and data protection standards earlier in the document.

The Bank of England (BoE) emphasizes the need to combat fraud, money laundering, and terrorism as reasons for not pursuing anonymity, even though there are existing market solutions that can provide single-sided anonymity while fully addressing the mentioned concerns. The proposed digital pound framework suggests that Payment Interface Providers (PIPs) would identify and verify users but would anonymize personal data before sharing it with the BoE. As a result, only the Payment Interface Provider or commercial banks would have full knowledge of users' identities and activities, and the payment system operator, the Bank of England, would not have direct access to personal data.

Instead, the private sector would directly interact with end-users and retain all customer information, similar to the current operations of banks and credit card companies. It is worth noting that banks and credit card companies today have access to all personal and transaction details of their customers, meaning there is zero privacy regarding individuals' personal data.

Under the described model, the Bank of England would only receive anonymized personal data. While this is positive, it does not protect citizens from potential exploitation of personal data by commercial banks or from government surveillance efforts conducted by government agencies like the GCHQ (the UK's NSA equivalent), which can easily collect and consolidate such data from commercial banks for mass surveillance purposes.

The described system offers "privacy" by splitting data into two categories, allowing commercial banks or the Payment Interface Provider to view all transaction details while transferring only limited data to the central bank, justifying that way the claim of "privacy from the central bank".

However, it is crucial to consider privacy from an end-to-end perspective and across the entire CBDC ecosystem to determine if users remain private from all participants and third parties involved. This is certainly not the case for the digital pound.

Privacy that can be undermined by the central bank or government is not real privacy (Graph 13.3). It is no privacy at all.

Therefore, it is important to closely monitor whether the privacy assurances offered are merely strategic marketing to preempt rejection by citizens or if the Bank of England can substantiate them with robust cryptographic measures in a broader context. The current technical document does not provide guarantees regarding overall user privacy; instead, it raises serious concerns, leaving educated readers worried about the potential implications.

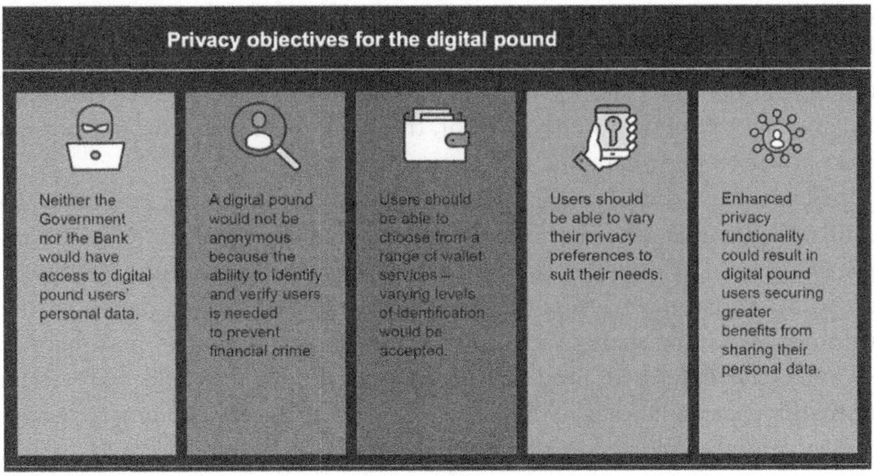

Graph 13.3 Privacy objectives for the digital pound (*Source* BoE [8])

13.3.3.3 User Experience for Households and Businesses

In terms of user experience, the papers outline the following considerations and features:

1. All residents of the UK have the ability to possess and utilize digital pounds.

   Non-residents of the UK, including tourists visiting the country, would also be able to hold and use digital pounds. They can make payments both within and outside the UK, whether with UK or non-UK residents.
2. Digital pound transactions can be conducted through various devices, providing users with flexibility. Payment options include:
   - Smart devices, especially smartphones, but also desktops, laptops, tablets, wearables, and Internet of Things (IoT) devices.
   - Smart cards similar to existing payment cards.
   - E-commerce websites and applications.
   - Point of Sale (PoS) devices commonly found in stores.

   Offline capabilities for the digital pound are being explored, although further investigation is necessary due to the significantly increased risks associated with offline transactions.
3. Initially, the experience of using digital pounds will be designed to resemble existing payment methods. The digital pound system should be compatible with current online and in-store payment technologies, such as card readers.

4. The digital pound will facilitate two key types of payments:
   - Person-to-business (P2B), allowing individuals to make payments to businesses, such as purchasing groceries from a supermarket.
   - Person-to-person (P2P), enabling users to send money to friends or acquaintances.

   The convenience and speed of payment confirmations are essential factors in enhancing the payment experience and will be prioritized.
5. To accommodate a wide range of users and protect financial institutions, there will be limits on the amounts of digital pounds that can be held, typically between £10,000 and £20,000. This threshold allows 75–95% of UK income earners to receive their salaries directly into their digital wallets without exceeding the limit. Additionally, the digital pound will not accrue interest similar to physical cash.
6. Transferring funds between digital pounds and other forms of money should be quick and effortless. Furthermore, the digital pound system should encourage innovation in areas like split payments, batch transactions, and micro-payments (Graph 13.4).

The Bank of England outlined six primary design decisions for the CBDC system:

1. Privacy: The BoE emphasizes the importance of user privacy while balancing the need for intermediaries to access transaction data for their services and regulatory obligations. The BoE correctly states that privacy is fundamental to trust and confidence in the CBDC system. However, the BoE's privacy standards and ambitions are set very low, using bank

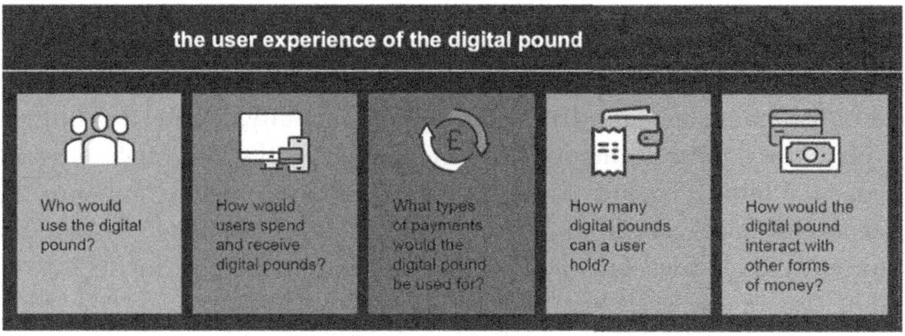

Graph 13.4 User experience of the digital pound (*Source* BoE [8])

accounts and credit/debit cards with zero privacy as the benchmark for the privacy in the digital pound ecosystem.

2. Security: The design of the CBDC system addresses security risks and the potential for cyber threats. While security risks are similar to those of other less attractive payment solutions, additional functionality like offline payments and programmability introduce new risks. The BoE acknowledges these new extra security risks and the need to evaluate and mitigate them early in the design phase to establish a secure and resilient CBDC system.
3. Resilience: The CBDC system must be resilient to disruptions to maintain user confidence, data integrity, and financial stability. The BoE sets initial resilience requirements, including operating 24/7 and exploring the possibility of achieving uptime targets closer to 100%. Current central bank systems like RTGS (Real-Time Gross Settlement) and CHAPS (Clearing House Automated Payment Systems) services have a target uptime of at least 99.95%, which constitutes the minimum expectation for BoE-managed CBDC infrastructure.
4. Performance: The CBDC system should handle a high volume of transactions and ensure fast confirmation and settlement times. The BoE estimates the need for a throughput of approximately 30,000 transactions per second, with confirmation and settlement in under one second, and a future target of 100,000 transactions per second to enable machine-to-machine transactions.
5. Extensibility: The CBDC system should support the introduction of new features without disrupting user services. The BoE suggests options such as open architectures, composability, and free/open-source software to enable intermediaries to implement new functionality.
6. Energy usage: To minimize environmental impact, the CBDC system should be designed to be energy-efficient. The BoE rightfully emphasizes the importance of energy efficiency in its CBDC infrastructure.

Additional points discussed include programmability, where the BoE has no plans to impose limitations on the use of CBDC through programming, and offline payments, which could enhance system resilience, but presents challenges related to double spending and fund validation. The BoE is currently undecided on whether to incorporate offline payments into the CBDC system due to its high-risk profile (Table 13.3).

Regarding the technology, the Bank of England has not made a final decision but has expressed concerns about using permissionless blockchains due to privacy and scalability challenges. They also highlighted potential issues

Table 13.3 Summary of CBDC features and functionality for UK digital pound

Categories	Functionality and features
Payment devices	Smart devices and physical cards Existing online and in-store point-of-sale infrastructure Internet of Things devices Wearables
Wallet management	Opening a wallet Viewing balances
Payments	Peer-to-peer Person-to-business (both in-store and online) Cross-border Offline Scheduled Micropayments Batch payments (like wages)
Interoperability	Moving between CBCD and other forms of money, particularly cash and bank deposits
Economic design	Ability to implement limits policy
Identity, data and privacy	CBCD would not be anonymous No access to users' personal data by the Central Bank Third parties undertake know your customer checks and anti-money laundering (AML) compliance

Source Adapted from **BoE [8]**

with Distributed Ledger Technology, such as transaction processing speed and single points of failure. Based on their current thinking, the BoE may lean toward centrally governed, distributed database technologies as a more efficient and suitable approach.

In terms of timelines, Bank of England deputy governor Jon Cunliffe stated in February 2023 that the chances of a digital pound becoming a reality are better than 50/50. A decision on proceeding to the build phase could be made in 2025/2026 after completion of proofs of concept and architecture and technical designs. It is unlikely that a UK CBDC would become operational before the second half of the decade at the earliest.

In conclusion: The digital pound documents are well done and quite complete. They identify and punt some critical decisions, like offline usage, to the future. But the BoE is exposed to the same risks as the digital dollar was, prior to the "Big Brother's Digital Dollar" attack by Florida Governor Ron DeSantis and others.

Opposition is slowly forming as of this writing, with spray-painted "Stop CBDC" messages across flyovers on the M1 motorway and similar placards opposite the prime minister's office. In addition, a petition has been circulated which collected tens of thousands of signatures across the UK in order to stop CBDCs as a response to the consultation paper above, published by the Bank of England in February 2023. The privacy stance defined in the papers by the BoE is explicitly weak and practically invites a negative popular reaction in the UK, much more than the digital dollar did when it was hit.

13.3.4 European Union's Digital Euro

The European Union (EU) is an economic union of 27 countries with 447 million inhabitants in 2022. Smartphone penetration in the EU was about 77.56%. These smartphones can be used for digital payments online and in stores. Card payments accounted for 49% of total number of non-cash payments in 2022. Cash was used for 59% of point of sale transactions in 2022, down from 72% in 2019. 13 million adult citizens remained unbanked in the EU in 2021, down from close to 31 million in 2017.

$$1 \text{ EUR} (€) = \text{US\$ } 1.08$$

The Eurosystem is the monetary authority of the euro area. At the end of 2022, it consisted of the European Central Bank (ECB) and the national central banks (NCBs) of the 19 European Union (EU) member states that had adopted the euro as their currency. The Eurosystem is responsible for conducting the monetary policy of the euro area, which includes setting interest rates, managing foreign exchange reserves, and promoting the smooth operation of payment systems. This also means that individual countries of the Eurosystem cannot launch a digital euro on their own. The ECB is the central institution of the Eurosystem, and it is responsible for formulating and implementing monetary policy, as well as supervising the banking system in the euro area. The NCBs, which are part of the Eurosystem, implement monetary policy and carry out operations such as the issuance of banknotes and coins.

Source Shutterstock

The European Central Bank (ECB) has been driving the investigation into a digital euro for a while. In October 2020, the ECB published a report called "Report on a digital euro" [150] which outlined the following 14 characteristics for a future digital euro:

13.3.4.1 Core Principles

P1: Convertibility at par: Not a parallel currency to the Euro.
P2: Liability of the Eurosystem: A digital euro is central bank money, and its issuance is controlled by the Eurosystem.
P3: European solution: Widely accessible on equal terms in all euro area countries through supervised service providers
P4: Market neutrality: Not to crowd out private solutions.
P5: Trusted by end-users: Trusted solution from the start and over time.

13.3.4.2 Scenario-Specific Requirements:

R1: Enhanced digital efficiency (if launched to support digitalization): The digital euro should keep pace with state-of-the-art technology at all times in order to best address the needs of the market like usability, convenience, speed, cost efficiency, and programmability. It should be made available through standard interoperable front-end solutions throughout the entire euro area and should be interoperable with private payment solutions.

R2: Cash-like features (if aiming to tackle a decline in the acceptance of cash): To match the key distinctive features of cash, a digital euro aiming to tackle a decline in the acceptance of cash should permit offline payments. Moreover, a digital euro should be easy for vulnerable groups to use, free of charge for basic use by payers and should protect privacy. It should have a strong European branding.

R3: Competitive features (if introduced to limit the uptake of forms of money that are not denominated in euro and/or not appropriately supervised): The digital euro should have features which are at the technological frontier. It should offer the basis for providing functionalities that are at least as attractive as those of the payment solutions available in foreign currencies or through unregulated entities.

R4: Monetary policy option: If considered to be a tool for improving the transmission of monetary policy, the digital euro should be remunerated at interest rate(s) that the central bank can modify over time.

R5: Backup system: If aiming to improve the overall resilience of the payment system, the digital euro should be widely available and transacted via resilient channels that are separate from those of other payment services and can withstand extreme events.

R6: International use (if introduced to increase the international role of the euro): The digital euro should be potentially accessible outside the euro area in a way that is consistent with the objectives of the Eurosystem and convenient to non-euro area residents.

R7a: Cost saving (if launched for cost efficiency): The design of the digital euro should achieve a reduction in the cost of the current payments' ecosystem.

R7b: Environmentally friendly (if launched for environmental reasons): The design of the digital euro should be based on technological solutions that minimize its ecological footprint and improve that of the current payments' ecosystem.

13.3.4.3 General Requirements

R8: Ability to control the amount of digital euro in circulation: The digital euro should be an attractive means of payment but should be designed so as to avoid its use as a form of investment and the associated risk of large shifts from private money (for example bank deposits) to digital euro.

R9: Cooperation with market participants: A project to introduce a digital euro should be carried out in line with best practices in IT project management. The digital euro should then be made available on an equal basis in all euro countries through supervised intermediaries, which could leverage their existing customer-facing services and avoid the costly duplication of processes.

R10: Compliance with the regulatory framework: Although central bank liabilities are not subject to regulation and oversight, in issuing the digital euro the Eurosystem should still aim at complying with regulatory standards, including in the area of payments.

R11: Safety and efficiency in the fulfillment of the Eurosystem's goals: The digital euro should be designed in a safe and efficient way. Its project and operating costs should be estimated and compared with the expected benefits, considering alternative solutions in any future scenario. The provision of non-core services should be left to supervised private entities.

R12: Easy accessibility throughout the euro area. The digital euro should be made available through standardized front-end solutions throughout the entire euro area and should be interoperable with private payment solutions. It should be easily accessible by anyone, including citizens who currently do not participate in the financial system (for example, those who do not have an account at a commercial bank), and should be easy to use. The digital euro would need to coexist with cash.

R13: Conditional use by non-euro area residents: The design of the digital euro should include specific conditions for access and use by non-euro area residents, to ensure that it does not contribute to excessively volatile capital flows or exchange rates. Such conditions could take the form, for instance, of limits or adequate remuneration policies for holdings of digital euro of non-euro area residents.

R14: Cyber resilience: Digital euro services will need to be highly resilient to cyber threats and capable of providing a high level of protection to the financial ecosystem from cyberattacks. In the event of successful attacks, the recovery time should be short, and the integrity of the data protected.

Further reports issued in 2022 and 2023 introduced the following three main reasons for the digital euro project:

(a) Preserving the role of public money as the monetary anchor for the payment system: In a digital era, cash usage is declining, and introducing a digital euro will ensure that central bank-issued electronic payments are accessible to everyone in the Eurozone. This complements cash and maintains central bank money as a stabilizing force in the payments system.

The current hybrid model for payments, which has served society well over a long period of time, involves the central bank providing the monetary base M_0—central bank deposits for banks and cash for the public—while the private sector offers payment solutions based on commercial bank money, such as deposits, to customers. A key aspect of this model is that citizens can convert private money to public money on a one-to-one basis at any time, and they can use public money for payments. This convertibility guarantees trust in both private and public money and protects the currency's function as a unit of account. Public money acts as an anchor that ensures a well-functioning payment system, safeguarding financial stability and trust in the currency.

Making public money available and convenient for purchases throughout the Eurozone enhances the efficiency of the entire payment system. It also reduces the risk of market abuse that can occur when a few private providers dominate the market (Graph 13.5).

(b) Declining use of cash for payments: The widespread adoption of digital payments is challenging the existing hybrid payment model. Cash is being

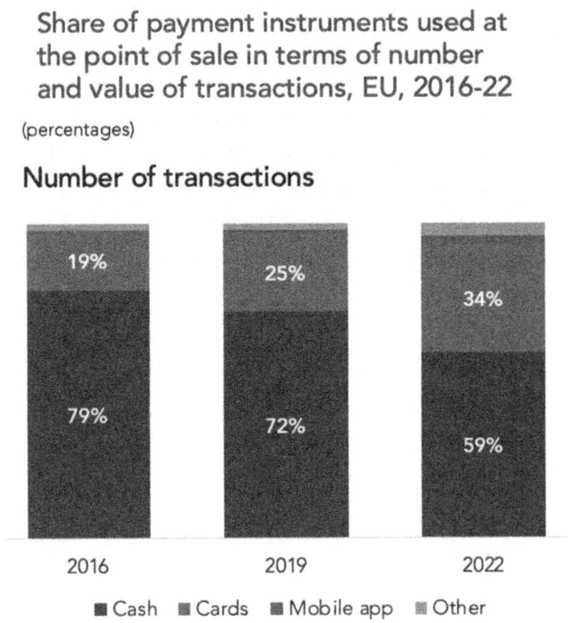

Graph 13.5 Share of payment instruments EU 2016–2022 (*Source* Data provided by ECB)

used less frequently, particularly in e-commerce and contactless transactions. If this trend continues, cash may lose its central role. Maintaining the widespread availability and acceptance of cash protects Europe's strategic autonomy in payments and monetary sovereignty. Cash would still be a fallback solution in the event of geopolitical tensions or if sanctions were imposed against Europe, because most electronic payments solutions are at present run by companies with headquarters outside the European Union, leaving the EU vulnerable. Digital payments are on the rise in the Eurozone and cash usage is on a downward trend as illustrated by the graph above. EU Citizens nevertheless believe it is very important for cash to remain a payment option as illustrated by the graph below (Graph 13.6):

(c) Disruptive digital change: The absence of a public digital money acting as an anchor for digital innovation anchor has led to confusion regarding digital currencies. Crypto-assets are currently inefficient, volatile, and lack convertibility in comparison to central bank money. This exposes the financial system to potential instability. Non-European solutions dominate the EU payments market, and the emergence of CBDCs in major foreign economies undermines the international role of the euro. Introducing a digital euro could enhance the appeal of the currency and promote its global use.

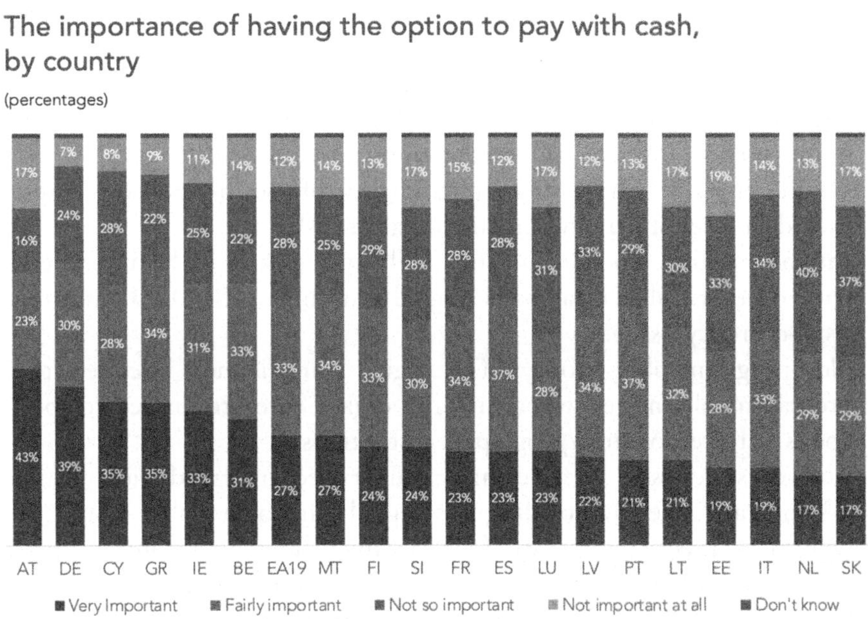

Graph 13.6 Importance of cash option in payments (*Source* Data provided by ECB)

The reports also emphasized key considerations for the digital euro project, including:

- User benefits: A digital euro should provide tangible advantages to users.
- Privacy protection: The highest standards of privacy protection should be upheld, allowing users to choose the amount of information they disclose in compliance with the law.
- Financial inclusion: Widespread distribution of the digital euro should benefit individuals who previously had limited access to financial services, enhancing financial inclusion.
- Safeguards against disruptive behavior: Measures must be in place to prevent excessive use of the digital euro for speculative purposes, which could negatively impact the banking sector and impede efficient lending and financial stability during times of stress.

The publications also highlighted the following features and functionalities of the digital euro project:

1. Privacy protection: The design of the digital euro prioritizes privacy by default, safeguarding personal data and payment information.
2. Limited access to data: The European Central Bank (ECB) will not have access to individuals' holdings, transaction histories, or payment patterns. Intermediaries will have access to data solely for regulatory compliance.
3. Legislative balance: The appropriate balance between privacy and other public policy objectives will be determined by lawmakers.
4. Offline privacy: The offline functionality of the digital euro aims to provide a level of privacy similar to that of cash.
5. Interoperability: The digital euro will be designed to be interoperable with other retail central bank digital currencies (CBDCs), facilitating cross-currency usage.
6. Non-programmable money: The digital euro is not intended to be programmable money, where units of digital euro are limited to specific goods, services, or time/geographic restrictions.
7. Role of supervised intermediaries: Supervised intermediaries will have a significant role in providing the digital euro as a public good. They will act as direct counterparts for individuals, merchants, and businesses, performing all end-user services and driving innovation in payment and financial services within the digital euro ecosystem.

The first point around privacy by default is very encouraging, but the second point already puts the first one into serious doubt. It makes you wonder how many organizations (other than the central bank) will have access to all this data. Privacy by default would mean not collecting most of this information. Offline privacy equal to cash sounds great again, how to realize that in a secure way is the key question, as it is mathematically impossible.

The third Eurosystem report [151] published on April 24, 2023, provided further insights regarding the establishment of a digital euro. Based on this report, the European Commission plans to propose a regulation to establish a digital euro in the second quarter of 2023. The report outlined views on digital euro access, holdings, onboarding, distribution, and services.

As such, the initial release of the digital euro will prioritize euro area residents, merchants, and governments, following standard payment account opening practices. The number of digital euro accounts per individual may be limited to control circulation. Users can access and use the digital euro through existing online banking/payment apps or a dedicated digital euro app. Various payment method, including QR codes, NFC contactless, and aliases/proxies, will be available for different types of payments such as point of sale, person-to-person, and e-commerce transactions.

The core services of the digital euro include account management, payment instrument management, funding/defunding, waterfall/reverse waterfall, transaction initiation, authentication, payment confirmation, refunds, and dispute/exception management. Value-added services can be developed freely by the market participants, but programmable money (i.e. restricted money) is not permitted.

Use cases for the digital euro encompass person-to-person, consumer-to-business, business-initiated, government-related, and machine-initiated payments.

The compensation model includes free basic use for private individuals, economic incentives for acquirers and merchants, comparable incentives for issuers, and the Eurosystem bearing its own costs.

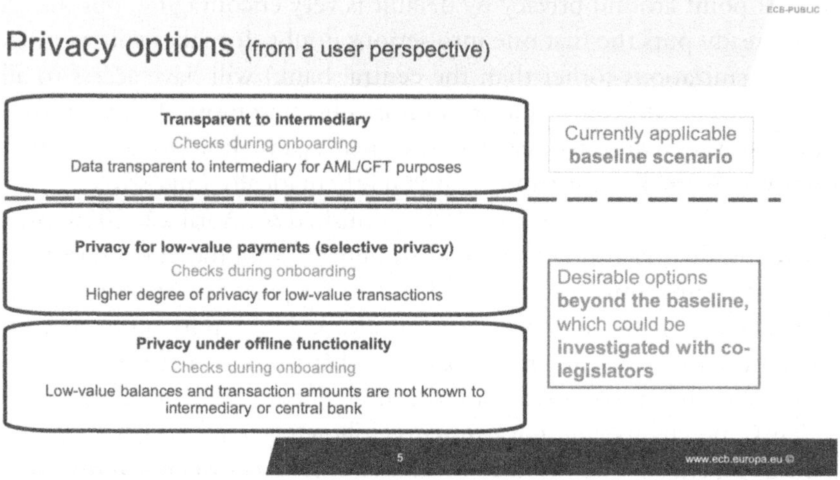

Graph 13.7 Digital euro—privacy options (*Source* Eurogroup Presentation [196]

Regarding privacy, online transactions could offer higher privacy for low-value and low-risk transactions, while offline payments would provide full privacy without transparency to intermediaries or the central bank. Limits will be introduced to prevent excessive use, and a waterfall approach will automatically transfer balances between the digital wallet and the user's bank account when the limits are exceeded (Graph 13.7).

The Eurosystem has the flexibility to use traditional technology, Distributed Ledger Technology, or a combination for settlement activities related to the digital euro. The proposed design will likely result in some type of account-based system, based on the requirements announced.

The presented timeline for the digital euro project included a high-level design in Q3 2023, a decision by the Governing Council in Q4 2023 on a possible realization phase, and a potential issuance of the digital euro by 2027 (Graph 13.8).

The European Central Bank (ECB) released an update with its fourth report [187] in July 2023 on the digital euro project, clarifying that the digital euro will offer essential services without any charges. To ensure widespread adoption and network effects, intermediaries involved in providing services will be duly compensated, similar to existing electronic payment systems. Moreover, legislative safeguards will be implemented to prevent merchants from facing excessive charges by intermediaries. Just as with physical banknotes, the Eurosystem will bear its own costs for the digital euro. The initial roll-out will also only feature peer-to-peer and online transactions. In-store transactions are supposed to follow later.

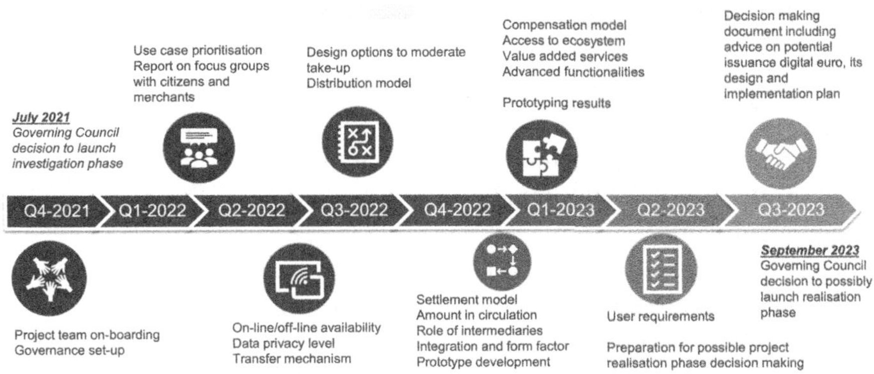

Graph 13.8 Digital euro—timeline (*Source* Eurogroup Presentation [196])

The digital euro will be equipped with both online and offline functionalities, ensuring a seamless user experience from the very beginning. Offline transactions will be secured using "secure hardware" to mitigate the risks of hacking and counterfeiting. Transactions will be settled immediately between devices, and payments received will be transferable to another device without requiring an internet connection. Additionally, the Eurosystem still believes that it prioritizes user privacy, when it will not have access to users' personal details or their payment patterns during transactions but the PSPs will.

On July 18, 2023, the ECB further announced that it would start wholesale digital euro pilots in 2024 and on October 18, 2023, they announced the advancement of the digital euro project into a next phase, now called the preparation phase. This phase is set to commence on November 1, 2023, and is expected to span two years initially. During this period, the focus will be on finalizing the digital euro rulebook, selecting potential providers for the development of a digital euro platform and infrastructure, as well as conducting testing and experimentation. The goal is to create a digital euro that aligns with both the Eurosystem's requirements and user expectations, including considerations like user experience, privacy, financial inclusion, and environmental impact. After this two-year period, the Governing Council will assess the progress and decide whether to proceed to the next stage, potentially leading to the issuance and rollout of a digital euro.

13.3.4.4 In Conclusion

The following are the key reasons for launching a digital euro:

1. Preserving public access to central bank money: The digital euro aims to ensure that central bank money remains widely accessible to users in the digitalized world.
2. Strengthening strategic autonomy: By reducing dependence on non-European payment solutions, the digital euro will enhance the euro area's independence and promote economic efficiency by curbing market abuses.
3. Meeting retail payment needs: The digital euro is designed to cater to the retail payment requirements of the euro area, aiming to make it usable everywhere within the region, similar to euro banknotes.

It looks very likely that the digital euro will adopt an account-based approach. It is important to just distill the published information to the lowest level, and not get distracted with published experiments, like the creation of a settlement prototype called N€XT [127] based on UTXOs without a DLT as part of the digital euro effort.

The discussed limits, the linked bank accounts, the waterfall function when the "wallet or account" is too full or too empty and the planned KYC all point to the need of managing a balance linked to an individual (aka an account) to fulfill the announced targets. The mobile apps for digital euro also appear to become web-apps, indicating that all wallets may be custodial wallets hosted in a cloud within an account-based system. It will be interesting to see the offline plans in detail with regard to privacy and security. Programmable money is explicitly excluded from the digital euro unless added by a payment service provider (PSP) as additional functionality.

Is privacy truly preserved in the full digital euro scheme, or is your private data only protected from the central bank, while all data remains transparent to other players such as commercial banks, financial intermediaries, government agencies, and law enforcement? The design of the digital euro, as described in the reports, has not removed concerns about the possibilities for mass surveillance yet. It nevertheless may deserve a differentiated judgment between the online and the offline solutions that were outlined in their last stocktake published in October 2023. The offline solution may end up closer to a real "digital cash" solution, if it is not rendered useless by low limits or by an imperfect technical implementation.

If further details of the digital euro do not adequately address the privacy concerns raised, it is only a matter of time before similar objections like in the United States arise within the EU. The digital euro's characteristics will deviate significantly from cash and may not align with the spirit of the EU's General Data Protection Regulation (GDPR). Opposition from the political realm and from civil liberties advocates can be expected to challenge such a design before its adoption.

Although the ECB shows a stronger commitment, compared to the US Federal Reserve Bank, toward implementing a central bank digital currency, EU citizens are likely to resist a digital euro that could be misused for mass surveillance, lacks significant advantages over existing payment methods, relies on existing payment service providers with no incentive to compromise their profit margins, fails to address financial inclusion, and is always tied to both a bank account and an ID.

Based on the information available, the digital euro seems to offer more facts to EU citizens to conclude that privacy is insufficient, than the digital dollar did, when it was referred to as "Big Brother's Digital Dollar" by Florida Governor Ron DeSantis as seen in Sect. 13.3.2.

European citizens are encouraged to watch this topic closely and exercise their democratic responsibilities by expressing their opinions and expectations publicly and to their elected representatives before it is too late.

13.4 Summary of Use Cases Presented Across CBDC Projects

After analyzing 25 publications from central banks regarding retail central bank digital currencies (rCBDCs) published before Q1 2023, the following ranked table of **use cases** has been compiled, with the **person-to-person** payment use case being the most frequently mentioned (Table 13.4).

The same 25 publications on retail CBDC resulted in the following ranked table of the highest number of mentions for rCBDC **features** (Table 13.5):

It is intriguing to note that offline usage is mentioned most frequently, despite the associated security risks it presents and which we will visit in detail later on in Sect. 15.4.15. Programmability of money still ranks fourth, even though several central banks, including those of the EU, UK, and Sweden, have stated that restricting the usage of money is not an acceptable feature for their respective central bank currencies.

An analysis of several publications by central banks on the topic of wholesale CBDC revealed the following key mentions that consistently appeared at the top of the list.

Table 13.4 CBDC retail use cases prioritized by number of mentions

	Retail use cases
1	P2P—person to person
2	P2B—person to business (physical store)
3	G2P—government to person
4	P2G—person to government
5	P2B—person to business (e-commerce)
6	B2B—business to business
7	B2P—business to person (salaries, refunds,...)
8	G2B—government to business
9	M2M—machine to machine/M2X—machine to other
10	B2G—business to government

Source Author

Table 13.5 CBDC retail features prioritized by number of mentions

	Retail features
1	Offline usage
2	Programmability of payments
3	Privacy protection
4	Programmability of money

Source Author

Table 13.6 CBDC wholesale use cases

	Wholesale use cases	
1	Minting	Conversion from Central Bank Reserves to wCBDC
2	Issuing	Sending wCBDC to Commercial Banks
3	Burning	Redemption of wCBDC back into Central Bank Reserves
4	Transferring	Sending wCBDC from Bank A to Bank B
5	DvP	Delivery versus Payment transactions
6	PvP	Payment versus Payment transactions

Source Author

Notably, cross-border functionality was consistently highlighted as additional detail in the Delivery versus Payment (DvP) and Payment versus Payment (PvP) use cases, emphasizing the importance of these use cases beyond domestic usage (Table 13.6).

Part III

Designing Retail and Wholesale CBDCs

14

Technology Choices and Design Options

14.1 A Multitude of Design Options

We will explore a multitude of design options for new payments solutions in this chapter. There are many more than the usual options that come to mind. As analyzed by the Atlantic Council in an excellent paper [89], we concur with many of their findings and expand upon them in this chapter:

1. There is a wide range of design options available for CBDCs beyond the typical choices of centralized databases, distributed ledgers, and offline tokens. Numerous combinations are possible, and both ledger and token-based systems can incorporate real privacy protection through cryptographic measures, albeit with some variations in feature coverage.
2. CBDCs can achieve a balance between robust user privacy and regulatory oversight. It is feasible to design systems where users enjoy a reasonable level of real privacy while regulatory authorities can ensure compliance objectives are met.
3. Privacy-preserving currency designs offer security advantages. Deployments of privacy-preserving CBDCs that initially refrain from collecting or subsequently restrict sensitive user data, even from trusted insiders, can significantly reduce the severity of security breaches. What is not collected, cannot be stolen!
4. Adherence to best practices in system design is crucial, including the use of proven consensus protocols and cryptographic primitives. Distributed security protocols, such as those employed in securing distributed ledgers, introduce new challenges and trade-offs. It is essential to utilize well-tested

L. V. Schumacher, *Decoding Digital Assets*, https://doi.org/10.1007/978-3-031-54601-3_14

protocols with provable security guarantees as foundational components in CBDC deployments, while designing the system security to withstand malicious behavior from all involved parties, including the central bank.

14.2 Technical Stack

The technology stack for a Central Bank Digital Currency comprises several layers, each serving a specific purpose (Graph 14.1).

At the lowest level, there are the servers that host the entire CBDC system. These servers can be deployed in secured data centers or in a private cloud infrastructure. In some cases, particularly for smaller countries or less technologically advanced central banks, Infrastructure as a Service (IaaS) may be a viable option. If a Distributed Ledger Technology (DLT) is utilized, this may involve setting up multiple locations to accommodate the different nodes. It is crucial to ensure redundancy and have backup infrastructure in place. As with any critical infrastructure, it is recommended to run these servers within the country's borders to maintain sovereignty, control, and security.

The second layer encompasses the software required to operate the CBDC system. This includes operating systems, such as Linux (open-source),

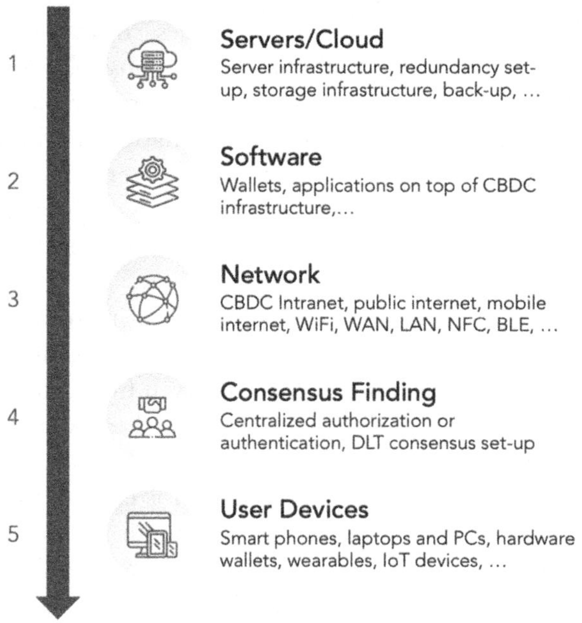

Graph 14.1 CBDC technical stack (*Source* Author)

Microsoft Windows (proprietary), or IBM z/OS (proprietary), then the database or DLT plus the applications necessary on top for tasks like minting, issuing, operating, monitoring, and auditing the CBDC. This layer may combine in-house software developments with commercial software packages. These software components run on the servers or in the cloud infrastructure. Additionally, there will be another set of software deployed at the user and on their devices, such as wallets, to interact with the CBDC system.

The third layer consists of the network infrastructure that connects the various components of the CBDC system. This network can be open (internet) or closed (private network). It must in all cases ensure secure and reliable communication between servers, applications, and end-user devices.

The fourth layer involves the consensus building mechanism, especially if a DLT is employed. Consensus protocols enable agreement on the state of the CBDC ledger across the network of nodes, ensuring the integrity and immutability of transactions.

Lastly, the fifth layer encompasses the end-user devices, such as smartphones, tablets, or computers, through which individuals interact with the CBDC. These devices host the user-facing applications, such as digital wallets, allowing users to manage their CBDC holdings and make transactions.

The choice of technology should be driven by the specific requirements derived from the identified use cases and key features of the CBDC. It is essential to align technology decisions with the functional and operational needs of the CBDC system to ensure its effectiveness and security. It is also important that the critical elements of a payment system, like life cycle management, security, and data protection for example, are evaluated in detail on each level.

14.2.1 Exploring Technology Choices: Databases vs. Distributed Ledger Technologies

In this section, we explore the technology options available for Central Bank Digital Currencies, focusing on the comparison between traditional databases and Distributed Ledger Technologies (DLTs). We emphasize that the selection of technology should be driven by the specific requirements of the CBDC and its use cases, without advocating for one technology over the other.

When evaluating the performance of databases and DLTs, it is essential to take into account the following factors:

1. **Speed:** Databases excel in transaction processing speed, optimized to handle large volumes of transactions quickly and efficiently. In contrast, DLTs prioritize security and immutability, which may lead to slower transaction processing speeds.
2. **Scalability:** Databases demonstrate high scalability, capable of efficiently handling large amounts of data and high transaction volumes. While DLTs can also scale, achieving the same level of scalability may require additional infrastructure and network resources.
3. **Consensus mechanisms:** DLTs employ consensus mechanisms to ensure transaction validity and maintain ledger integrity. These mechanisms, while critical for security, can introduce computational overhead and potentially slow down transaction processing, particularly in systems with numerous participants. It is crucial to rely on well-tested and peer-reviewed consensus protocols to mitigate risks.
4. **Security:** DLTs are renowned for their robust security and immutability, making them ideal for applications requiring trust and transparency. Databases, while secure, may be more susceptible to security breaches and data tampering due to their centralized architecture. However, it's important to note that the security of DLTs depends on the chosen deployment model, as permissioned DLTs may differ significantly in security characteristics from fully decentralized and permissionless setups.
5. **Flexibility:** Databases offer high flexibility, enabling customization to meet specific application requirements. DLTs, while also flexible, may present challenges in customization and may necessitate additional development resources to implement new features and functionalities.

The choice between databases and DLTs for a CBDC hinges on the specific requirements, trade-offs, and priorities of the digital currency project. Databases typically offer superior speed and scalability, while DLTs, in their standard deployment, emphasize security and immutability. We will further explore these topics in subsequent chapters to provide a more comprehensive understanding of both technologies and their applicability to CBDCs.

14.3 Exploring Distributed Ledger Technology for CBDCs

In this section, we take a closer look at the concept of Distributed Ledger Technology (DLT) and its distinction from blockchains. While the terms are often used interchangeably, it is important to understand that DLT is a broader category encompassing various decentralized database systems, while blockchains represent a specific type of DLT. We will explore some notable examples of DLTs, including those that do not utilize a blockchain structure.

Distributed Ledger Technology is the overarching term for decentralized databases managed by multiple participants. It offers a transparent and immutable record of transactions and provides a mechanism for consensus among network participants. It enables trust and removes the need for intermediaries by allowing participants to validate and store data in a synchronized and distributed manner.

While all blockchains are DLTs, not all DLTs are blockchains. Blockchain refers to a specific subcategory of DLT characterized by its chain of blocks, each containing a set of transactions. However, there are numerous DLT networks that utilize alternative structures and consensus mechanisms, offering unique features and benefits.

Here are some of these alternative DLT solutions:

1. Hedera Hashgraph: Hedera Hashgraph is a DLT network that employs a Directed Acyclic Graph (DAG) data structure. It utilizes a consensus algorithm called Hashgraph, designed for enhanced speed and security compared to traditional blockchain consensus mechanisms. This DAG-based approach offers improved performance while maintaining the benefits of decentralization.
2. IOTA: IOTA is another example of a non-blockchain DLT that utilizes a Directed Acyclic Graph (DAG) known as the Tangle. It provides a scalable and feeless platform for the Internet of Things (IoT), enabling secure and efficient machine-to-machine transactions.

Non-blockchain DLTs, such as DAG-based solutions, offer advantages in terms of scalability, transaction speed, and energy efficiency. By utilizing alternative consensus mechanisms and data structures, these DLTs can provide innovative solutions for specific use cases.

While blockchain is a well-known and widely used form of DLT, it is crucial to recognize that other DLT solutions exist. As the development of CBDCs progresses, exploring various DLT options becomes essential to select the technology that best aligns with the requirements and objectives of the digital currency project.

14.3.1 Exploring Blockchains and Consensus Algorithms

In this section, we delve into the world of blockchains and highlight diverse characteristics and features of different blockchain networks. We will showcase a few notable blockchains, such as Solana, Polkadot, Cardano, and Algorand, to illustrate their unique capabilities. Additionally, we will discuss the common features shared by most blockchains and introduce the blockchain trilemma, which presents the challenges in achieving optimal scalability, security, and decentralization.

Several blockchains differ significantly from the main Ethereum (using Proof of Stake) and Bitcoin (using Proof of Work) blockchains, and we are mentioning some of them here to illustrate that point.

1. Solana: Solana is a high-performance blockchain that uses a unique consensus algorithm called Proof of History (PoH), which allows it to handle a higher number of transactions per second than Ethereum or Bitcoin.
2. Polkadot: Polkadot is a sharded blockchain that enables interoperability between different blockchain networks, allowing them to communicate with one another.
3. Cardano: Cardano is a blockchain that uses a Proof of Stake (PoS) consensus algorithm and is designed to be more energy-efficient than Bitcoin.
4. Algorand: Algorand is a blockchain that uses a pure PoS consensus algorithm, which enables it to achieve high transaction speeds and low fees.

In summary: While each blockchain possesses its own unique characteristics, there are several common features shared among most blockchain networks:

1. **Immutability:** Blockchain's cryptographic techniques ensure that once data is added to the ledger, it becomes immutable and tamper-proof.
2. **Decentralization:** Most blockchains operate without a central authority, with participants holding copies of the ledger. The degree of decentralization can vary across different blockchains.
3. **Transparency:** Blockchain enables transparent verification of transactions, allowing users to verify the integrity of the ledger at any time.
4. **Consensus-Driven:** Consensus mechanisms play a vital role in blockchain networks, ensuring agreement among participants before updating and

sharing the ledger. Notable consensus algorithms include Proof of Work (PoW), Proof of Stake (PoS), and Delegated Proof of Stake (DPoS).

14.3.2 The Blockchain Trilemma

The blockchain trilemma highlights the challenge of simultaneously advancing scalability, security, and decentralization in a blockchain network. Achieving substantial progress in two of these areas often necessitates trade-offs in the third.

For example, well-established blockchains like Bitcoin and Ethereum prioritize security and decentralization but may face scalability limitations. Conversely, blockchain systems that prioritize transaction speed and scalability may compromise decentralization.

The blockchain landscape encompasses diverse blockchains with unique features and consensus algorithms. Each blockchain offers distinct advantages and trade-offs in terms of scalability, security, and decentralization. Understanding these differences is crucial in selecting the most suitable blockchain solution for specific use cases. Additionally, addressing the blockchain trilemma remains a key challenge, with ongoing efforts to strike a balance between scalability, security, and decentralization in future blockchain developments.

14.3.2.1 Gaining Performance with Sharding

As we have seen that Bitcoin and Ethereum prioritize security and decentralization, therefore face scalability limitations. Ethereum has taken a first step to improve the situation by moving from Proof of Work (PoW) to Proof of Stake (PoS) consensus algorithms. A next step to increase performance in Ethereum will be the introduction of sharding.

This does not only apply to Ethereum. Making DLTs perform faster is probably the most critical topic that almost all DLTs are working on, trying to figure out how to mitigate the constraints of the Bitcoin Trilemma.

Sharding is a key technique typically used in blockchain-based Distributed Ledger Technologies to improve scalability and performance. Sharding has become prominent as performance enhancing technology, due to the Ethereum 2.0 project, which plans to introduce sharding in the near future. Some other DLTs are already using sharding. Here is a short overview:

1. Ethereum:
   Ethereum is one of the most widely used blockchain-based DLTs, and its developers are currently working on implementing sharding to improve the network's scalability. Sharding is not scheduled to be implemented on Ethereum until H2 2023 as part of "The Surge," phase 2 of the Ethereum 2.0 project.
2. Zilliqa:
   Zilliqa is a blockchain-based DLT that is specifically designed for high-throughput applications, and it uses sharding to achieve its scalability goals.
3. Elrond:
   Elrond is a blockchain-based DLT that also uses sharding to improve its scalability and performance. The network's architecture is designed to allow fast and secure transactions, even as the number of users and transactions on the network grows.
4. Polkadot:
   Polkadot is a multi-chain DLT that uses sharding to enable multiple parallel chains to operate on the same network. This allows for better scalability and interoperability between different blockchain-based systems.
5. Harmony:
   Harmony is a blockchain-based DLT that uses sharding to enable faster transaction processing and better scalability. The network uses a unique sharding approach called "Secure Sharding" that is designed to improve the security and performance of the network.

As the demand for faster and more efficient DLTs continues to grow, it is likely that more DLTs will adopt sharding and other scaling solutions to meet these needs. It is to be expected that further progress will be made on these subjects in the coming years as there is a lot of focus on the topic.

14.3.3 Permissioned/Private Versus Permissionless/Public

The first differentiation that we need to look at in DLTs is the difference between the original permissionless/public blockchain ala Bitcoin, where everyone can participate and the private restricted (i.e. permissioned) version, where only selected participants are allowed and these are cleared by a central authority.

We can differentiate a little bit further and introduce a permissioned model that is a bit more inclusive and particularly interesting when "ownership" of the system is a problematic subject, because it allows for a decentralized governance model. This is the permissioned consortium model.

Hence most DLT or blockchain efforts can be grouped into 3 categories, the first being public blockchains, the second being private blockchains, and finally consortium blockchains.

Table 14.1 provides the details of the 3 categories with regard to what type of network they represent, and how they work.

14.4 Exploring Databases for CBDCs

A database (DB) is a collection of data that is organized and stored in a way that allows for efficient retrieval, management, and manipulation of the data. Databases are used to store and manage data for a wide range of applications, from small personal applications to large-scale enterprise systems.

A database typically consists of one or more tables, which are collections of data organized into rows and columns. Each row in a table represents a record, and each column represents a field or attribute of the record. For example, a database for a customer relationship management (CRM) system might have a table of customers, where each row represents a customer and each column represents an attribute of the customer such as their name, address, and phone number.

Databases are typically managed by a **database management system** (DBMS), which provides tools for creating, querying, updating, and deleting data from the database. Some popular examples of DBMSs include MySQL, Postgres, Oracle, Microsoft SQL Server, and MongoDB.

Databases can be broadly classified into two types: **relational databases** and **non-relational databases**. Relational databases store data in tables that are related to each other through a set of predefined relationships, while non-relational databases store data in a more flexible, unstructured format.

To illustrate the level of performance possible for databases, we quote an Oracle statement [152] from 2018, proudly announcing that their Online Transaction Processing (OLTP) database cranked out 144m SQL transactions/second and 1.2bn SQL statements/second.

There are several ways to achieve **redundancy** in a database, which involves having multiple copies of the data to ensure that it is available even if one copy fails. The specific method used depends on the database system and the requirements of the application. Here are some common ways to achieve redundancy:

Table 14.1 Different types of DLT

	Public DLT	Private DLT	Consortium/Permissioned DLT
Network type	Decentralized	Partially decentralized (least decentralized)	Partially decentralized
Work model	Anyone anywhere in the world can read and write on the network. Data is validated by every participant ("node") in the network, thus making it very secure	Permissions to read and write data onto the Blockchain are controlled by a single "highly trusted" organization—the owner of the blockchain (i.e. a bank or central bank)	Permissions to verify, read and write on the blockchain controlled by a few predetermined nodes. The choice of predetermined nodes can be different for every entity on the blockchain. (i.e. central banks for crossborder payments)
Benefits	Secure as the entire network verifies transactions. Transparent as all transactions are made public with individual pseudonymity. Fully decentralized ownership	Effcient as verification is done by just owner of the blockchain. Private as the owner can control who has access to read or write on the blockchain, Centralized ownership	Efficient as relatively lesser nodes verify transactions. Private as read and write access can be controlled by the predetermined nodes. No consolidation of controlling power. Decentralized ownership between consortium members

	Public DLT	Private DLT	Consortium/Permissioned DLT
Challenges	Inefficient as all nodes need to verify the transaction	Controlling power is consolidated to a single organization. Difficult to align many organizations to use the same blockchain	
Access to DLT	Anyone	Single organization	Multiple selected organizations
Participants	Permissionless & Pseudonymous	Permissioned & based on known identities	Permissioned & based on known identities
Security	Consensus Mechanism Proof-of-Work Proof-of-Stake	Pre-approved participants. Voting-based consensus	Pre-approved participants. Voting-based consensus
Transaction 5peed	Slow	Fastest	Faster
Read from DLT	Open to anyone	Fully private or restricted to a limited set of authorized nodes	Restricted to an authorized set of participants
Write to DLT	Anyone	Owner/Operator only	Authorized participants
Commit to DLT	Anyone	Owner/Operator only	All or subset of authorized participants

Source Adaptation based on JP Morgan/Onyx/Oliver Wyman table

1. **Replication**:
   In database replication, the data is copied from one database to another in real time, usually over a network connection. This ensures that there is always a backup copy of the data in case the primary database fails.
2. **Clustering**:
   In database clustering, multiple servers are used to run the database system, with each server holding a copy of the data. If one server fails, the other servers can take over to ensure continued availability of the data.
3. **Mirroring**:
   In database mirroring, the data is written to two or more disks simultaneously, so that if one disk fails, the other disks can be used to retrieve the data.
4. **Sharding**:
   Sharding is a technique that can also be used for databases. It is used to horizontally partition a database into smaller, more manageable pieces called shards. In sharding, the data in a database is divided across multiple servers or nodes, each of which contains only a subset of the data. This allows for better scalability and performance, as the workload is distributed across multiple machines.

   When a database is sharded, each shard typically contains a specific subset of the data, such as a particular range of values or a specific geographic region. Queries and transactions that only require data from a single shard can be processed quickly, without having to involve the other shards. However, queries that require data from multiple shards may take longer to process, as they require coordination and communication between the different nodes.

   However, sharding can also introduce challenges, such as increased complexity in managing and querying the data, and increased communication overhead between the shards. Properly designing and implementing a sharded database system requires careful consideration of these trade-offs and the specific needs of the application.

Regarding **uptime**, world-class uptime typically refers to having **99.999% availability**, also known as "five nines." This means that a system is available 99.999% of the time, with a maximum downtime of around 5.26 minutes per year. Achieving this level of uptime requires a combination of redundancy, fault-tolerant architecture, and proactive maintenance and monitoring.

As reference, the Bitcoin blockchain has had an availability of 99.986% since its launch on January 3, 2009. SWIFTnet operated by the SWIFT consortium has shown an availability of 99.999% in the past years.

A database system can be a good fit for a Central Bank Digital Currency because it can provide a secure and reliable platform for managing the transactions associated with the currency.

Some of the key features that make a database system well-suited for a CBDC include:

1. **Scalability**:
   A database system can easily scale to accommodate large volumes of transactions and user accounts, which is important for a currency that could potentially be used by millions of people.
2. **Security**:
   Database systems have built-in security features that can help protect against fraud, cyberattacks, and other threats to the integrity of the currency.
3. **Consistency**:
   Database systems ensure that transactions are recorded accurately and consistently, which is important for maintaining the integrity of the currency and preventing errors or discrepancies.
4. **Accessibility**:
   A database system can be accessed from anywhere with an internet connection, which would make it easy for people to use the CBDC from their mobile devices or other devices.
5. **Analytics**:
   Database systems can provide valuable insights into the usage patterns and behavior of CBDC users, which could help central banks better understand how the currency is used or how macro trends are developing and make informed decisions about its design and implementation.

While a standard database system has many benefits for managing a Central Bank Digital Currency, there are some potential drawbacks as well. Here are some reasons why a database system might not be the best choice for a CBDC:

1. **Centralization**:
   A standard database system is centralized, meaning that all transactions and balances are recorded and managed by a single entity (e.g. the central

bank). This could potentially create a single point of failure or be vulnerable to cyberattacks or other forms of manipulation. It may not offer the resilience a DLT can provide.

2. **Security**:
   While database systems have built-in security features, they may not be sufficient to protect against sophisticated cyber threats that could target a CBDC. Additionally, the centralized nature of a database system could make it a more attractive target for hackers or other malicious actors although it may have less attack surface than a decentralized system.
3. **Privacy**:
   A database system may not provide sufficient privacy protections for CBDC users, especially if it is designed to record and track every transaction in detail and in real time. This could be a concern for people who value their financial privacy and do not want their transactions to be monitored or tracked or have it all stolen in a hack.

In summary: A database system has many advantages for managing a CBDC, but it is important to consider the potential drawbacks as well and to weigh these against other potential solutions to ensure that the chosen system fits its requirements and is secure, scalable, and user-friendly. Of course, there are mitigations for all of the listed downsides.

14.5 Hybrids of Distributed Ledger Technology and Centralized Databases

After having reviewed DLTs and databases in detail, it is important to point out that it is also possible to combine DLT technology with database technology in a CBDC system.

Here are some features that a hybrid system could potentially offer:

1. **Decentralization**:
   A hybrid system could combine the benefits of both database and DLT systems, providing the security and scalability of a database while also offering the decentralization and transparency of a DLT. This could help address concerns about a centralized system being vulnerable to cyberattacks or other forms of manipulation.
2. **Speed and scalability**:
   A hybrid system could potentially offer faster transaction processing times and better scalability than a pure DLT system, while still retaining some of the benefits of decentralization, like resilience.

3. **Privacy**:
   A hybrid system could be designed to provide greater privacy protections for CBDC users than a pure DLT system, by limiting the amount of personal information that is recorded on the ledger.
4. **Innovation**:
   A hybrid system could offer greater flexibility and innovation than a pure database system, by allowing for the introduction of new features and functionalities that are not possible with a standard database.

A hybrid system could offer a compelling combination of features that address some of the limitations of pure database or DLT systems, while providing a secure and reliable platform for managing a CBDC. A database component as part of a Layer 2 solution could enable an underlying DLT with new combined functionalities.

Several solution providers already offer such hybrid combinations today, for example GNU Taler can run as a Layer 2 on top of the Bitcoin and Ethereum blockchains for fast, easy, and privacy-preserving day-to-day payments.

14.6 Account-Based Solutions, Token-Based Solutions, DLT-Based Solutions

Another technical aspect that we need to visit is the technical realization of the CBDC as a **token- or value-based** system (like physical cash) versus an **account- or register-based** system (like bank accounts). While these were the only 2 options available twenty years ago and this was an easy distinction to make in the past, the advent of DLT technology has made that differentiation more complex, with the bearer instrument characteristic which we will discover in the respective chapter adding confusion on top.

14.6.1 Token- or Value-Based Solutions

The word ***token*** has become a popular term and is used in many different contexts, which can easily lead to confusion. As we have seen before, even cash is a token. It is therefore very important to consider the context in which the word is used and what the (digital) token effectively delivers.

For example, there is the "identity token":

When a user authenticates through a federated identity system, such as Facebook or Google, they are issued an identity token. This token acts as a digital representation of the user's authentication status, and in some cases, it might also encompass a set of their basic attributes. Often encoded in formats like JSON Web Token (JWT), the token serves a crucial function: whenever the user attempts to access a service or platform within the federated system, they present this token as evidence of their authentication. The receiving service, in turn, can verify the token's authenticity and integrity, typically by matching its signature with the identity provider's (IdP) public key. One of the notable benefits of such a system is Single Sign-On (SSO). Users authenticate just once with the IdP, and then they can seamlessly access multiple services using their issued identity token, greatly simplifying the user experience.

Or a bit closer to payments, there is for example the "session token":

Some smart people got confused in the token discussion by the session token used to secure, for example, an ApplePay transaction (with ApplePay being an account-based system). In many online payment contexts, a session token might be used to represent a transaction or authentication session. This can be a one-time-use token or a temporary token that expires after a short duration. The use of such tokens ensures that even if a malicious actor intercepts a token, its short lifespan or one-time-use nature makes it useless for any other purpose.

Such session tokens are security artifacts needed for secure communication and have nothing in common with the token-based money (like the eCash or the GNU Taler token which are the equivalent of a physical banknote for the holder) that we are talking about in this book.

An additional complication stems from the fact that some blockchain projects describe themselves as "token-based." This stems from them comparing themselves to account-based systems, but they unfortunately forget to include in their comparison the existence of "real" cash-like tokens, as used by eCash and GNU Taler, that existed long before blockchains came along. Therefore, we believe that in the end, we need to differentiate between 3 types of solutions as mentioned earlier. The next paragraphs will further explain why this is the case.

The subject of this book is tokens that represent an asset in a payment transaction. It is important to realize that such tokens have nothing in common, but the name, with the two token examples (session token and identity token) described above.

Token-based or value-based money is a form of currency, where the value is directly tied to the physical asset or commodity that the token represents. These tokens can be physical or digital, and they are used as a means of exchange for goods and services. Examples of token- or value-based money include gold coins, silver coins, and paper currency. Token- or value-based money can also refer to digital assets, where the value is captured in the token that you carry in your digital wallet. Examples of token- or value-based money in the digital realm are the abovementioned 1990's eCash, and its current version the GNU Taler token. These tokens can be used without any need for authentication/identification of the user, just like physical cash for the spender.

14.6.2 Account- or Register-Based Solutions

Account-based or register-based money refers to a type of financial system where the ownership and transfer of money are recorded in a central register or account and accessed through the identification of the owner. In this system, money is not physically transferred between individuals or entities, but rather, it is transferred electronically through accounts, by debiting one and crediting the other.

Examples of account-based or register-based money include bank deposits, electronic fund transfers, and credit card transactions. Most of our current traditional financial systems are account-based. In each of these cases, the transfer of funds is recorded in the account, the ownership of the funds is determined by the account holder's identity and his holdings are determined by the sum of in/out transactions that have been conducted on the account (i.e. by the balance of these transactions). Access to the funds happens via authentication (most often multi-factor authentication).

Account-based money is sometimes considered more secure than token-based bearer instruments because the transfer of funds is carefully tracked and recorded, making it easier to trace and prevent fraud and other criminal activity. However, this type of money can also be vulnerable to cyberattacks and hacking, which compromises the integrity of the electronic account. This means that a hack can wipe out all the money in the account. To protect against these risks, financial institutions often employ sophisticated security measures and protocols to safeguard electronic transactions and account information, and this can make usability worse or even prevent parts of the population (like children or the elderly) from participating.

Any account-based system can easily be used for mass surveillance, as it collects in detail all the in- and out-transactions of each person's account.

It is also important to point out that, as mentioned in Sect. 12.5.1, some central banks (for example, the United States (USA) and Sweden) are legally forbidden from issuing account-based CBDC as that would compete too strongly with the private sector banking system and its account-based system.

14.6.3 DLT-Based Solutions

For a discussion without confusion between the 2 previous categories, it is necessary to introduce a third option, the DLT-based solution. Many publications have assigned the DLT-based solution into the token-based category. This is likely due to an incomplete picture of the available solution and the likely ignorance of real cash-like token-based solutions, like eCash and GNU Taler. The following paragraphs, which compare the three solutions, will provide a clear understanding why such a third category called DLT-based solutions is necessary.

14.6.4 Comparison of Token-, Account- and DLT-Based Solutions

The consequences of one versus the other are major for a CBDC and the features it can offer. Especially big is the potential impact on privacy. Therefore, we will explore these differences in further detail. We hope to bring clarity to the subject and to provide a coherent overview that makes sense going forward.
Here are the 3 types of solutions for retail CBDCs that were outlined:

> **Account-based**: Your money is in an account at the bank, and you can access it with your ID card and the goodwill of the bank.
> **DLT-based**: Your money is in the storage locker at the station (i.e. on the blockchain ledger) and can be accessed by anyone who has the key to the locker (or blockchain ledger). No ID required.
> **Token-based**: Your money is in your wallet, and anyone with access to the wallet can spend it immediately without the need for any other accessory. No ID required. No key required.

Attention: Do not confuse an account- or register-based banking system with an account-based blockchain, like Ethereum, where the control of the financial instrument is in the hands of the bearer of the private signing key. Although Ethereum (ETH) is sometimes called an account-based blockchain in comparison to the UTXO-based Bitcoin, it would not be considered an account-based CBDC system in the case of ETH self-custody.

DLT-based solutions can be represented as a separate category on a spectrum, placed in between account/register-based solutions and token/value-based solutions, as shown in Graph 14.2.

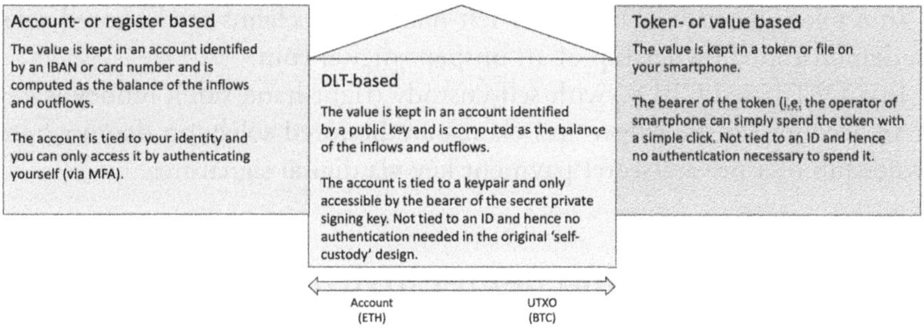

Graph 14.2 3 types of rCBDC (v1) (*Source* Author)

The above distinction into 3 categories of CBDC solution is critically important, and that is why the following chart graphically depicts once more, in a different way, the differences between account-based, token-based, and DLT-based rCBDC systems, as seen above and in previous chapters (Graph 14.3).

In an account-based CBDC (upper left-hand side), ownership is tied to an identity, and transactions are authorized via identification and the necessary collaboration of the bank.

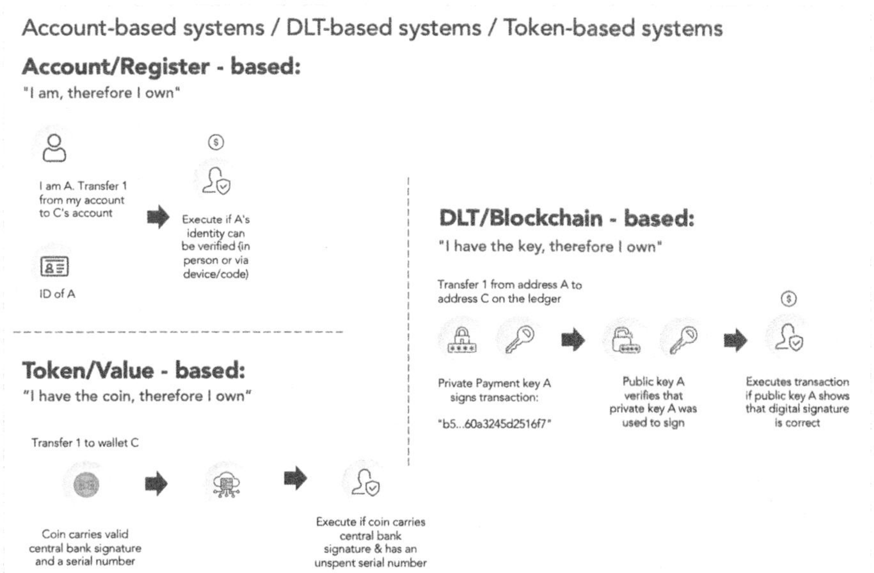

Graph 14.3 3 types of rCBDC (v2) (*Source* Author's adaptation based on a graph by BIS)

In a token-based CBDC (lower left-hand side), claims are honored solely on demonstrated ownership of an unspent digital coin.

In a DLT-based CBDC with self-custody (right-hand side), money is kept in an account on the ledger and claims are honored solely on demonstrated ownership of a private/secret payment key via digital signatures.

14.7 Understanding Bearer Instruments

Money as a bearer instrument refers to a type of financial instrument, where possession of the physical instrument is equivalent to ownership of the money it represents. This means that whoever holds the instrument is considered the owner of the money, regardless of whether they are the legitimate owner or not. Physical cash is the perfect example of a bearer instrument.

Bearer instruments can be easily transferred from one person to another without the need for any formal registration, log-in, identification/authentication or transfer process. All the system needs to do is to check if the bearer instrument (token, coin, bank note…) is valid. In the case of physical cash, people do this in general by the look and feel of the bank note.

In the digital world, this simple check (valid or not) can be very important toward offering an unmatched one-click usability, allowing financial inclusion for young, old, physically or visually impaired, …

Twenty years ago, this was very simple—bearer instruments had to be token/value-based, which, like cash, you carry in your (physical or digital) wallet with you. The only other options available were account-based, like bank accounts, which had to be accessed via personal identification (i.e. authentication of the user).

With the advent of blockchain solutions, this definition has become a little more complicated and the lines between the 2 have been blurred. Let me explain.

The original ideas behind Bitcoin was for money to be kept on the blockchain and that the owner could only move it by signing with a secret private payment key in his possession. The bearer of the (token/value-based) coins/bank notes and the bearer of the secret private payment key are the de facto owners of the cash and the bitcoins.

But that is where the commonality ends and the lines cross.

In keeping it simple, you can also imagine the blockchain like an account system, appropriately called ledger, where the so-called UTXO is identified by a Bitcoin address (for example 3FZbgi29cpjq2GjdwV8eyHuJJnkLtktZc5)

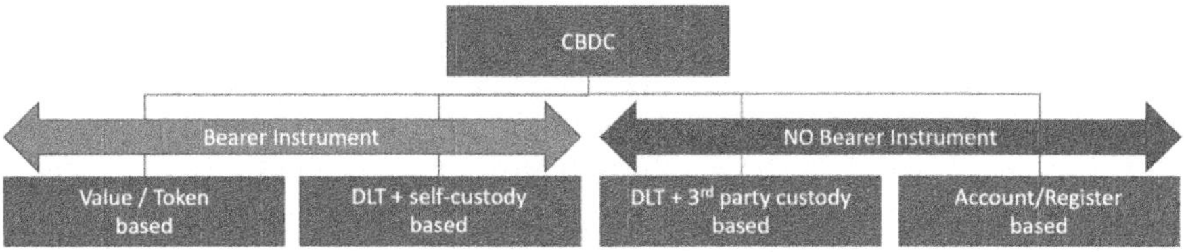

Graph 14.4 Bearer/non-bearer instruments (*Source* Author)

versus an IBAN number (for example CH9300762011623852957 in Switzerland) for traditional bank accounts.

While I need to identify myself to log into my IBAN account, in the case of Bitcoin all I need to make a transaction, is possession of the secret/private payment key. I can keep this key safe myself (self-custody) or I can entrust this key to a professional third party in the hope that they do a better job of safekeeping. In order to rely on such a third party, I will entrust the third party with my secret personal key, and also trust that they will follow my instructions in the future. I will need to identify myself to the third-party custodian in case I want to instruct them to do a transaction on my behalf.

I hope this clarifies the new options that have appeared over time, and how to classify them into bearer/non-bearer instruments (Graph 14.4).

To illustrate this further, let's take the GNU Taler token. It is the proverbial bearer instrument, emerging from the first eCash token 30 years ago. Whoever holds a valid (=unspent) GNU Taler token is the owner of such token, exactly the same as the holder of a US$20 note or a €1 coin is its owner. Whoever holds the token can simply spend it without the need for any additional authentication as it is, like cash, not tied to any identity.

Ethereum (ETH) with self-custody is considered a bearer instrument, as ownership of the token is determined by whoever possesses the private payment key associated with the Ethereum address on the ledger where the token is represented. This means that whoever has access to the secret private payment key and can sign with it, can transfer ETH tokens out of the account to another Ethereum address account without the need for any additional verification or authorization.

But, if Ethereum is used with third-party custody, then we would presume it is no bearer instrument anymore because the ETH owner needs to identify himself to access his account at the custodian, who will then access the secret private payment key held in custody on behalf of the owner to sign and execute the planned transaction. Such a solution should hence be classified as an account-based solution.

Bitcoin (BTC) with self-custody is also considered a bearer instrument. It's a decentralized digital currency that operates on a peer-to-peer network, and ownership is determined by whoever possesses the secret private payment key associated with the Bitcoin address of the UTXO. This means that whoever has access to the private key and can sign with it, can spend the existing UTXO and credit the value to new UTXO addresses without the need for any additional verification or authorization.

Similar to ETH, if BTC is used with third-party custody, then we would again presume it is no longer a bearer instrument because the BTC owner needs to identify himself to access his account at the custodian, who will then access the private key on behalf of the owner to sign and execute the planned transaction. Such a BTC solution should also be classified as an account-based solution.

Now you may ask, what happens if I hand my eCash or GNU Taler tokens over to a custodian? In that case, we have the exact same transaction as we have with physical cash today. You hand your token/cash to a bank and the bank becomes the owner of the GNU Taler token/the physical cash and it creates an entry under your name in a bank account-based system.

It is important to note here that the use of bearer instruments is sometimes considered to make users more vulnerable to theft or loss, since whoever has possession of the instrument has control over it. Therefore, any CBDC based on bearer instruments should store these bearer instruments in a secure wallet and offer the user a secure and privacy-preserving way to backup and restore them. On the other hand, the benefit of a bearer instrument is that it allows to do extremely fast payments, as the system does not need a user to register with anyone, log in, perform a complicated multi-factor authentication (MFA), etc. ID-theft has no consequences for a bearer token, while it allows the hacker to completely empty the bank account, which usually contains more money than the wallet in our back pocket.

14.8 Exploring Design Choices for CBDC Implementations

As we have seen, CBDC designs can take various forms, ranging anywhere from centralized databases to distributed ledgers, and can be further classified as token-based, DLT-based or account-based models. This section explores nine different combinations that can be considered for CBDC implementations and takes into account key factors such as privacy, transparency, and security.

Table 14.2 Design options and their characteristics

	Integrity	Authorization	Privacy	Resilience	Performance
Database with account balances	Relies on central validator	Authentication of user	Toward validators: none. Toward 3rd parties: communication leakage.	Sender needs to be online. Infrastructure needs to be operational. Transaction can be reverted.	Low communication requirements for all parties. High throughput Low latency.
Public DLT/Blockchain with plaintext transactions	Relies on a set of validators collectively	Possession of private payment key	Toward validators: none. Toward third parties: communication leakage.	Sender needs to be online. Infrastructure needs to be operational. Transaction cannot be reverted.	Validators need to run consensus protocol. User may need to download entire ledger. Slow throughput and high latency.
Public DLT/Blockchain with privacy-preserving zero-knowledge transactions	Relies on a set of validators collectively	Possession of private payment key	Toward validators: full. Toward third parties: communication leakage.	Sender needs to be online. Infrastructure needs to be operational. Transaction cannot be reverted.	Validators need to run consensus protocol. User may need to download entire ledger. Slow throughput and high latency
Permissioned DLT with plaintext payment tokens	Relies on a set of validators collectively	Possession of private payment key	Toward validator: none. Toward third parties: communication leakage.	Sender needs to be online. Infrastructure needs to be operational. Transaction can be reverted with 51%	Validators need to run consensus protocol. Low communication cost for users. Moderate throughput and latency.
Permissioned DLT with privacy-preserving payment tokens	Relies on a set of validators collectively	Possession of private payment key	Toward validators: full. Toward third parties: communication leakage.	Sender needs to be online. Infrastructure needs to be operational. Transaction cannot be reverted.	Validators do not need consensus. Users download and upload account commitments. High throughput Low latency.
Exposed payment tokens	Relies on one or more validators	Possession of unspent coin	Toward validators: none. Toward third parties: full.	One party needs to be online. Infrastructure needs to be operational.	Low communication requirements. Validators do not need consensus. Users need to download and upload coins. High throughput. Low latency.
Privacy-preserving payment tokens	Relies on one or more validators	Possession of unspent coin	Toward validators: sender privacy Toward third parties: full.	One party needs to be online for secure transaction. Infrastructure needs to be operational. Transactions cannot be reverted. Change can be given with some solutions	Low communication requirements. Validators do not need consensus. Users need to download and upload coins. High throughput. Low latency.
Secure hardware clients*	Relies on correctness of hardware modules	Possession of hardware module	Toward validators: n/a. Toward third parties: full.	Offline payments are possible. Transactions cannot be reverted.	Only local communication between users. Throughput not an issue. Low latency.
Secure software clients	Relies on correctness of software modules	Possession of software module	Toward validators: n/a. Toward third parties: full.	Offline payments are possible. Transactions cannot be reverted.	Only local communication between users. Throughput not an issue. Low latency.

Source Author's Adaptation
*With offline we mean full offline. / Color codes: Blue, Green = beneficial, Red = constraining

1. **Database with account balances**: This design option resembles traditional banking systems, where a standard database stores plaintext account information for each account holder. An example is the Jamaican CBDC Jam-Dex.

2. **Public DLT/Blockchain with plaintext transactions**: Permissionless Distributed Ledger Technologies (DLTs) like Bitcoin and Ethereum store transaction details in plaintext on the blockchain, offering transparency to all participants. However, user pseudonymity may be easily compromised through analysis tools like Chainalysis et al.
3. **Public DLT/Blockchain with privacy-preserving zero-knowledge transactions**: Permissionless DLTs can also employ zero-knowledge proofs to hide user and transaction information, providing enhanced privacy. However, the two-sided anonymity inherent in these DLTs may pose regulatory challenges as it also protects criminals. Examples include Zcash and Monero.
4. **Permissioned DLT with plaintext payment tokens**: A permissioned DLT, such as the R3 Corda, combines the benefits of identifying users on the DLT while maintaining plaintext transactions. However, this design may not prioritize privacy. An example is the Swedish e-Krona.
5. **Permissioned DLT with privacy-preserving payment tokens**: This design option utilizes a permissioned distributed ledger that employs privacy-preserving tokens to sign balance updates on distributed nodes, offering a reasonable level of privacy for a CBDC implementation. An example is Platypus.
6. **Exposed payment tokens**: In this scenario, a system issues tokens where certain information is exposed to one or more third parties, such as the central bank. An example is eCash 2.0.
7. **Privacy-preserving payment tokens**: This design ensures that no third party has access to information regarding the issued tokens, holders, or spenders, maintaining a high level of privacy while recipients are transparent for compliance reasons and the avoidance of tax evasion, illegal business, and black markets. An example is GNU Taler with its blind signatures.
8. **Secure hardware clients**: CBDC implementations can leverage secure hardware clients, which offer offline transaction capabilities. Privacy can be maintained during offline transactions, although personal data may be collected and uploaded once connectivity is restored. Risks associated with secure hardware will be discussed in a later chapter. An example is Whispercash.
9. **Secure software clients**: Certain proposals suggest deploying CBDC on secure software, although the risks associated with secure software on standard devices should be carefully evaluated. Privacy can be preserved during offline transactions, with the potential for data collection upon reestablishing connectivity. More later. An example is Crunchfish.

In conclusion: Design choices for CBDC implementations encompass a wide range of options. The selection of a particular design should be guided by the specific requirements and objectives of the CBDC project. Each design option presents unique advantages and challenges, requiring careful consideration to strike the right balance between privacy, transparency, and security in a CBDC ecosystem. These 3 key aspects do not constitute a trilemma. More privacy also leads to more security as we have seen, and the needed transparency can be defined for compliant operations without sacrificing the other two (Table 14.2).

14.9 Exploring Digital Wallets for CBDC

Digital wallets play a crucial role in managing digital currencies, including CBDCs. They offer convenience, security, and accessibility for users. This section delves deeper into the different types of digital wallets available, highlighting their characteristics and associated risks. Additionally, the features and considerations of each wallet type are discussed to assist users and designers in making informed choices.

1. **Mobile wallets:** Mobile wallets are installed on smartphones or tablets, allowing users to store digital payment cards, including credit and debit cards, loyalty cards, and cryptocurrencies. They are compatible with iOS and Android ecosystems. Mobile wallets can also facilitate e-commerce payments through QR codes displayed on computers, when supported by websites.
2. **Desktop wallets:** Desktop wallets are software packages installed on personal computers or laptops. They provide secure storage and management of cryptocurrencies. Desktop wallets can be further enhanced for long-term storage by using air-gapped computers, turning them into a type of "hardware wallet." They are compatible with various operating systems like Microsoft Windows, Apple OS/X, and Linux.
3. **Browser wallets:** Browser wallets are a sub-category of desktop wallets, typically in the form of browser plug-ins. They enable secure storage, management, and transfer of digital currencies directly from web browsers. Browser wallets aim to simplify e-commerce transactions. Compatibility extends to operating systems such as Windows, OS/X, and Linux, as well as popular browsers like Google Chrome, Mozilla Firefox, Microsoft Edge, Brave, Opera, and Chromium.

4. **Cloud wallets** (Web-based Wallets or Custodial Wallets): Web-based wallets are accessed through web browsers, with the actual wallet residing in the cloud. They allow users to store and manage cryptocurrencies and are often used for trading or exchanging digital currencies. While convenient, web-based wallets have a worse security track record compared to other wallet types, and are potentially more vulnerable to hacking or phishing attacks.
5. **Hardware wallets:** Hardware wallets are physical devices designed specifically for storing currencies securely. They offer the highest level of security as they are offline and require physical access for transactions. Some hardware wallets incorporate secure hardware components to prevent device replication and counter duplication of funds. However, they can be expensive and susceptible to loss or damage.

With desktop or mobile wallets, users have complete ownership and control over their coins or payment keys through self-custody. This allows users to decide when and where to spend CBDC and grants advanced control features such as setting transaction fees. However, users are responsible for wallet security, maintenance, and safeguarding their computer or smartphone.

In contrast, web wallets or web-based mobile apps shift the responsibility of maintaining wallets and security updates to service providers. While offering convenience, users surrender ownership and control over their coins or payment keys, relying on the provider to ensure their safety. Advanced control features may be limited, and accessing transaction details might require a separate block explorer to monitor transactions and activities. However, users are relieved of security and maintenance tasks and are not required to own and maintain dedicated hardware.

Hot wallets and cold wallets describe the connectivity of digital wallets to the internet.

- **Hot wallets:** Hot wallets, including mobile wallets, web-based wallets, desktop wallets, and browser wallets, are connected to the internet. They offer quick access to funds and facilitate daily use and trading. However, hot wallets are more susceptible to hacking and cyberattacks due to their online connectivity.
- **Cold wallets:** Cold wallets, such as hardware wallets, paper wallets, and offline storage devices, are not connected to the internet. They provide a higher level of security and are ideal for long-term storage. Cold wallets are often used as backups to hot wallets. Although less convenient for daily use, they offer enhanced protection against unauthorized access.

Key mobile wallet features could include the following with prioritization according to the CBDC design:

1. **Secure storage:** Mobile wallets offer secure storage for digital currencies, ensuring the protection of coins, private keys, and sensitive information. Encryption techniques and advanced security measures are employed to safeguard funds.
2. **Multi-currency support:** Mobile wallets can support various digital currencies, allowing users to manage and store different cryptocurrencies within a single app. This feature enables flexibility and convenience for users with diverse digital assets.
3. **QR code payments:** Mobile wallets often incorporate QR code scanning capabilities, enabling users to make contactless payments by scanning QR codes at merchants' point of sale terminals or on e-commerce websites. This feature simplifies the payment process and enhances transaction efficiency.
4. **Peer-to-peer transactions:** Mobile wallets facilitate peer-to-peer transactions, allowing users to send and receive digital currencies directly to and from other wallet users. This feature eliminates the need for intermediaries or traditional banking channels, enabling quick and seamless transactions.
5. **Transaction history:** Mobile wallets provide users with a transaction history log, allowing them to track and review their past transactions. This feature offers transparency and enables users to monitor their spending and account activity.
6. **Security features:** Mobile wallets prioritize security by implementing optional features such as biometric authentication (fingerprint or facial recognition), PIN codes, or password protection. These measures enhance the overall security of the wallet and protect against unauthorized access.
7. **Wallet backup and recovery:** Mobile wallets often provide options for wallet backup and recovery. Users can create a backup of their wallet data, including private keys, in case of device loss, damage, or theft. This feature ensures that funds can be restored in a new device or in case of wallet restoration.
8. **User-friendly interface:** Mobile wallets prioritize user experience by offering intuitive interfaces, easy-to-navigate menus, and clear transaction management. The goal is to make managing digital currencies accessible to users of varying technical expertise.

9. **Push notifications:** Mobile wallets may send push notifications to users, alerting them about important wallet updates, transaction confirmations, or security-related information.
10. **Customization options:** Mobile wallets often offer customization options, allowing users to personalize their wallet interface, set preferences, and adjust settings according to their preferences.

Digital wallets play a vital role in managing CBDCs and other digital currencies. The choice of wallet type depends on individual preferences, security requirements, and usage patterns. It is essential to select reputable wallet providers and practice proper backup and security measures to ensure the safety of funds. Considering factors such as convenience, security, and ownership, users can make informed decisions when choosing the most suitable digital wallet for their CBDC needs.

Interesting questions and realization challenges to ponder with regard to rCBDCs wallets include: Should the number of wallets per person be restricted? If more than 1 wallet per person is allowed, should the wallets synchronize their balances or remain independent?

14.10 Money Custody: Not Your Keys, Not Your Coins?

After the wallets, we will now explore the custody options for our digital money. Starting with what is available for cryptocurrencies, we can then build on that foundation to explore what could be applicable to CBDCs.

There are several custody options available for cryptocurrencies, each with its own benefits and risks. Here are some of the most common custody options:

1. **Self-custody**:
   This involves holding your cryptocurrencies in a personal wallet that you control, such as a hardware wallet, software wallet, or paper wallet. The benefits of self-custody include complete control over your assets, no reliance on third-party custodians, and the ability to hold private keys offline for enhanced security. Self-custody is coined by the famous expression in the crypto-world: "***NOT YOUR KEYS, NOT YOUR COINS!,***" meaning that if you do not have control of your private/secret keys, you do not have control of your crypto-assets. Self-custody is the underlying concept of bearer instruments.

However, self-custody comes with risks such as the possibility of losing access to your wallet or private keys, and the potential lack of insurance coverage in case of theft or loss.

Self-custody is also the method of custody that DeFi and decentralized exchanges were designed for. Decentralized exchanges (DEX) offer alternatives for those looking to avoid centralized intermediaries. These are peer-to-peer platforms that allow users to trade cryptocurrencies without the need for a centralized intermediary. Users typically hold their cryptocurrencies in a personal wallet and connect directly with other traders to buy and sell assets. The other benefits of decentralized exchanges include enhanced security and the ability to trade without revealing personal information. However, decentralized exchanges are still in their early stages of development and can be less user-friendly than centralized exchanges.

2. **Custody with centralized exchanges or the central bank**:
These are online platforms that allow users to buy, sell, and trade cryptocurrencies. When using a centralized exchange, users typically store their cryptocurrencies in a wallet controlled by the exchange. The benefits of centralized exchanges include ease of use, liquidity, and the ability to trade a wide range of cryptocurrencies.

   However, centralized exchanges are also vulnerable to hacks, theft, insider manipulation, and insolvency, which all can result in the loss of user funds. The case of FTX and its fall is a perfect example of the risks that come with a centralized exchange and the related custody. Alameda, a subsidiary of FTX had used $8bn of FTX customer funds, traded with and lost a large part of them. When people wanted to withdraw their cryptocurrency, that money was no longer around for FTX to return to their customers. This finally led to the bankruptcy of FTX. There is no backstop for customers in such a bankruptcy, unlike for bank or brokerage account holders. The customers will have to fight it out with every other creditor of the exchange, because they have no special protections or preferred claims. The accountholders at FTX did not have the same treatment that the accountholders of SVB were able to enjoy, when things went south.

   Some have argued the collapse of the centralized FTX exchange is a triumph for "decentralized finance," or DeFi, which uses computer code to build versions of financial services that don't rely on trust or a central party.

3. **Custodial services (or third-party custody)**:
These are third-party companies that offer custody services for cryptocurrencies. These companies typically store cryptocurrencies in cold storage (offline) wallets for enhanced security. The benefits of custodial services

include professional management, insurance coverage, and enhanced security measures. However, custodial services need to be trusted as they will hold your secret keys. They also come with fees and the risk of insolvency or loss of assets due to hacking or theft.

In summary: Overall, the choice of a custody option will depend on individual preferences and risk tolerances. Self-custody is often preferred by those who prioritize security and control over their assets, while centralized exchanges and custodial services are popular among those who value ease of use and professional management. It should be mentioned here that anything, but self-custody, will have negative impacts on the privacy offered by the solution.

It is important to do thorough research and carefully consider the risks and benefits of each option before making a custody decision.

14.11 Backups: Protecting Your Digital Assets

Backups are of utmost importance in any digital asset system, and regulatory bodies may even require them to be part of any payment solution. While offering backup services may be sufficient, users should always have the option to decide whether they want to utilize these services. Regardless, it is crucial to prioritize backups as a high-quality service, because the security of a user's money or assets are at stake.

Different levels of backup are possible:

a. **Wallet and secret key backup:** For self-custody scenarios, backing up the wallet and secret/private signing keys is paramount. In blockchain-based systems, the loss of the secret payment key could result in the complete loss of the asset, unless a backup exists and can be restored. Disturbingly, it is estimated that billions of dollars' worth of Bitcoin is locked on the blockchain because users have lost their secret keys.
b. **Data backup for hosted solutions:** In the case of third-party custody or centralized exchanges, backups of the data stored on the providers' servers are crucial. Regularly testing the restoration of these backups should be a standard business procedure for regulated providers.

It's important to note that offering privacy-preserving backups for self-custody scenarios is challenging. These services can potentially leak private information, including wallet contents, secret payment keys, or user identities. It is hence important to prioritize privacy-preserving backups, especially in the case a privacy-preserving CBDC, in order not to erase any hard-earned privacy protection implemented with the CBDC system.

Simplistic backup ideas, such as storing the wallet backup in iCloud or Google Cloud, pose severe privacy risks. Cloud services are inherently tied to user accounts, enabling automatic identification. Unless the contents are encrypted prior to upload using keys exclusively held by the user, the data is not secure against unauthorized access either. It is widely known that cloud services like Apple's iCloud may encrypt stored data, but the decryption keys are under Apple's control, accessible to authorities upon request or to anyone deemed appropriate by Apple.

Uploading backup data via encrypted HTTPS and then storing it on an encrypted hard disk may seem secure to inexperienced users, but it adds minimal privacy or protection. Such measures only safeguard against insider threats of someone stealing the hard disk, or from eavesdropping during the upload, which both fall short of comprehensive protection.

To avoid potential leakages, it is highly recommended to adopt a backup service that utilizes secret sharing mechanisms to slice the secret material into chunks. These partial chunks should be augmented with authentication information and encrypted with multiple layers of encryption. This approach can ensure secure retrieval with most privacy preserved, by decrypting the first layer of encryption to access the authentication information, and after successful authentication, allows to retrieve the differently encrypted parts. The different partial secrets can then be decrypted and reassembled on the user's private computer.

None of these options are trivial, as the experience of Ledger, the leading French maker of hardware wallets shows. In June 2023, Ledger announced a new service, Ledger Recover [179], to allow users to store encrypted backups of their seed phrases in shards with 3 custodians, as fallback if they lose their seed phrase. For a restoration, only 2 out of the 3 encrypted shards would be necessary. This service required an initial know-your-customer verification with 2 KYC services retained by Ledger in order to get your private/secret key restored later. This means Ledger is forcing users to attach IDs to crypto wallets—which is highly undesired in a space where hardware wallets used to be viewed as a way to store crypto anonymously.

The Ledger products were especially criticized [178] because the company had previously stated that the seed phrase could never leave the device (which it now easily can with a simple firmware modification) and also for not offering transparency on what they were doing by not offering an open-source solution of their hardware wallets. This is a subject that we will explore further in Sect. 15.4.15 on hardware security.

Open-source solutions, which solve the same problem as Ledger's recover service, but without any need for a KYC provider and usable in an easy privacy-protecting way, exist today. One such example is called GNU Anastasis [180].

All CBDC projects should consider incorporating similar concepts and solutions in their backup designs to prioritize user privacy and data protection. The security and privacy requirements that must be applied to the backup process are of the exact same complexity and importance than those applied to the CBDC solution itself.

By implementing privacy-preserving backup mechanisms, users can mitigate the risks associated with data breaches, unauthorized access, and loss of digital assets.

14.12 Safeguarding Transactions: The Role of Cryptographic Primitives

Cryptographic primitives serve as the fundamental components of modern cryptography, providing the necessary tools for secure communication in the face of potential adversaries. Encryption algorithms, decryption algorithms, digital signatures, message authentication codes, and key agreement protocols are all examples of these essential primitives.

In the context of cryptocurrencies and Central Bank Digital Currencies, cryptographic primitives play a vital role in ensuring the security and privacy of transactions. For instance, in Bitcoin and other cryptocurrencies, these primitives enable users to engage in payments without relying on trusted intermediaries, like banks or governments. Instead, transactions are verified by a decentralized network of nodes, leveraging cryptographic primitives to guarantee their security and immutability.

14.12.1 Illustrating Cryptographic Primitives in Different DLT and Non-DLT Solutions

To illustrate these primitives a little further, let us look at two practical cases.

Bitcoin, as an example, relies on several cryptographic primitives to function effectively. Here are key primitives utilized in Bitcoin for secure operation:

1. **Cryptographic Hash Functions:** Bitcoin utilizes cryptographic hash functions like SHA-256 to generate digital fingerprints of transactions and blocks within the blockchain. These fingerprints are crucial in preserving the integrity and immutability of the blockchain.
2. **Public Key Cryptography:** Public key cryptography, specifically the Elliptic Curve Digital Signature Algorithm (ECDSA), is employed in Bitcoin to create digital signatures that authenticate transactions. Users possess a public key for verification and a private key for signing transactions.
3. **Merkle Trees:** Bitcoin implements Merkle trees to facilitate efficient verification of transaction inclusion in a block. By creating a hierarchical structure of hashes, nodes can verify the authenticity of transactions without the need to download and process the entire blockchain.
4. **Proof of Work:** Bitcoin's consensus algorithm, known as proof of work, relies on cryptographic primitives to require miners to solve complex mathematical problems. By completing this work, miners validate transactions and add them to the blockchain. This process demands significant computational power, making it challenging for malicious actors to manipulate the blockchain.

The second example shows the cryptographic primitives in use in a non-DLT digital payment solution, based on the privacy-preserving token of GNU Taler [153]. The following cryptographic primitives are in use: cryptographic hash functions, blind signatures, Schnorr signatures, Diffie-Hellman key agreement protocol, and cut-and-choose zero-knowledge proofs. These well-established cryptographic primitives contribute critically to the security and privacy of the GNU Taler system.

14.12.2 The Impact of Quantum Computing

The potential impact of quantum computing on cryptography was already addressed in detail in Sect. 12.7.1.4. Quantum computers have the potential to affect factorization and discrete logarithm problems, which are strong assumptions at the foundation of public key cryptography or asymmetric key cryptography.

Encryption and digital signatures, both essential in ensuring the security of transactions, could be compromised by quantum computers, affecting past and future data.

To mitigate this risk, it is crucial to design systems that incorporate well-proven cryptographic primitives and allow for easy substitution with quantum-resistant instantiations when necessary. As we have seen earlier, when it comes to encryption, the ideal moment to start using post-quantum would be now to prevent the "store it now and decrypt it later" threat. When it comes to signing, Q-day would be the latest acceptable moment to have post-quantum solutions implemented.

14.12.3 The Importance of Robust Cryptographic Primitives

Cryptographic primitives or crypto primitives serve as vital safeguards for the security and privacy of digital currencies, including cryptocurrencies and CBDCs. As the use of digital currencies continues to grow, crypto primitives will play an increasingly significant role in ensuring the integrity and trustworthiness of these systems. It is essential to choose cryptographic primitives that have been thoroughly tested and proven to be secure. And that is not an easy thing to do, as will be illustrated shortly.

Over several decades, the U.S. National Institute of Standards and Technology (NIST), responsible for creating cryptographic standards for non-national security U.S. government agencies, had established itself as the primary global authority for cryptographic standards. However, in 2013, Edward Snowden revealed some interesting insights in the papers he published on the work of the NIST and its collaboration with the intelligence community.

The Dual Elliptic Curve Deterministic Random Bit Generator (Dual_EC_DRBG)

The Snowden papers revealed that the National Security Agency (NSA) had compromised the security of a NIST cryptographic standard—the Dual_EC_DRBG—by building in so-called back doors. This allowed for the simple decryption of what was believed to be securely encrypted communications.

This was neither the first nor the last time that the NIST was caught collaborating with the NSA on encryption standards, as the following examples show:

The Data Encryption Standard (DES)

In 1968, the National Bureau of Standards (NBS), later renamed the National Institute of Standards and Technology (NIST), sought help from the NSA in developing a U.S. government encryption standard. An internal NSA history book [195], portions of which were released to the public after journalistic efforts which I recommend everyone with doubts on the subject to read, revealed that the NSA had influenced public standards to ensure they could break them. The intention was to narrow down encryption to a single algorithm, limiting competition and potential threats to NSA.

The NSA collaborated with NBS and IBM's Walter Tuchman on the Data Encryption Standard (DES). While Tuchman was deeply involved in its development, the public story conveyed in the 1970s was different. Tuchman publicly denied NSA involvement, saying the DES algorithm was developed solely by IBM. Similarly, NSA director Bobby Inman in 1979 denied allegations of NSA interference or weakening the DES.

However, the key evidence of NSA's interference was their push for a reduction in key size from 64 to 48 bits. They finally settled on 56 bits in DES, making it more vulnerable. Cryptographers Whit Diffie and Marty Hellman wrote a detailed paper in 1977 on how DES could be broken using a machine costing $20 million with 1970s technology, even before the DES standard was established. They anticipated that technological advances would significantly reduce the cost of breaking the DES encryption. Despite this prediction, the NSA did not acknowledge any security issues and the NIST established the standard and DES remained an official U.S. government standard until 2005.

The Digital Signature Algorithm (DSA)

NIST continued to issue cryptographic standards, including a notable one for a Digital Signature Algorithm (DSA), proposed by the NSA in 1991. This proposed DSA had an apparent flaw: its 512-bit key size. Given the cryptographic system of DSA and mathematical structures known in 1991, this size was insufficient for security. Despite seeming stronger than the 56-bit DES key, DSA's attack algorithms were more complex and hadn't been deeply analyzed, with subsequent advancements further complicating things. DSA also had other, less evident flaws, including potential back doors and pitfalls for those implementing it. Ron Rivest, the R in RSA, commented in 1992 that DSA allowed that "*the poor user is given enough rope with which to hang himself*."

Originally, NIST introduced DSA as its proposal, without mentioning NSA. However, a Freedom of Information Act (FOIA) lawsuit by the Computer Professionals for Social Responsibility (CPSR) disclosed NSA's secret design of the DSA. Due to public criticism, in 1994, NIST permitted larger keys in the DSA standard, but these were still capped at 1024 bits, which was notably less secure than available alternatives like 128 bits for AES. DSA's other flaws remained unaddressed. A specific issue Rivest had pointed out was publicly exploited in 2010 against Sony PlayStation's security system that used ECDSA, a DSA variant. This problem was likely exploited in secret against many more valuable targets.

The latest chapter in the story of the NIST and cryptographic standards involves post-quantum algorithms.

Post-Quantum—KYBER-512

In 2022, NIST announced plans to standardize a particular cryptosystem, called Kyber-512. As justification, NIST issued claims regarding the security level of Kyber-512 [198]. In 2023, NIST issued a draft standard for Kyber-512 in the context of the NIST Post-Quantum Cryptography Standardization Project (NISTPQC). The published level of security was based on high-school level mathematical errors, basically saying $2^{40} + 2^{40} = 2^{80}$. Unfortunately, the right answer should be 2^{41}.

This was such a severe and indefensible miscalculation for a cryptographic standardization agency that Prof. Daniel J. Bernstein, the creator of Post-Quantum Cryptography, was convinced that an authority of this stature would not make such a mistake and therefore requested access to "*the full NISTPQC records*" and "*all records of NIST/NSA meetings mentioning the word 'quantum.'*" In the end, his seventh FOIA-based lawsuit [197] generated the requested access. It turned out, from the analysis of the documents, that the influence of the NSA on the creation of Kyber-512 was much greater than was publicly visible.

15

Architecting a Retail CBDC

Retail Central Bank Digital Currencies (rCBDCs) are intended for broad public use and are digital counterparts of existing coins and banknotes. Building on the foundational knowledge we've amassed about CBDCs thus far, we will now immerse ourselves in the intricacies of the retail CBDC solutions being devised and deliberated globally.

15.1 Objectives of a Retail CBDC

Outlined below are key objectives, previously discussed in depth in Sect. 12.3, which encapsulate the interest behind CBDC projects in general. Each retail CBDC (rCBDC) project selects a subset of these objectives, prioritizing them based on the unique circumstances and needs of their respective country.

1. Ensuring financial stability.
2. Implementing monetary policy.
3. Promoting financial inclusion.
4. Enhancing domestic payment efficiency.
5. Boosting cross-border payments efficiency.
6. Ensuring payment safety.
7. Strengthening privacy protections.
8. Establishing sovereignty or alternatives to private payment solutions.
9. Preventing illicit markets and tax evasion.
10. Combatting money laundering.

L. V. Schumacher, *Decoding Digital Assets*, https://doi.org/10.1007/978-3-031-54601-3_15

The selected objectives for any rCBDC must distinctly highlight the additional tangible benefits it offers over available private payment solutions in the market.

The definition of money given in Chapter 5 listed 3 characteristics: #1 store of value, #2 unit of account, and #3 medium of exchange/means of payment. Any rCBDC is automatically defined as unit of account. A retail CBDC is inherently designed to be an additional means of payment for citizens. That leaves the question about being a store of value. Table 15.1 will provide a comparison between retail CBDC, physical cash, and bank accounts with regard to the store of value feature.

As elaborated in studies, including some discussed in Sect. 12.6, consumers value broad acceptance, user-friendliness, low costs, speed, security, privacy, and consumer protection in payment methods.

Merchants, on the other hand, prioritize affordability, ease of use, and seamless integration with existing systems.

The adoption journey will be particularly challenging in developed markets, urging users to shift from good to great existing private payment solutions to a new rCBDC solution. This will prove extra strenuous or will outright fail, if the new rCBDC solution doesn't clearly demonstrate tangible benefits over existing private retail payment solutions offered by incumbents.

15.2 Operating Model for rCBDC

Pondering over the operating model of a rCBDC solution tailored to individual countries is critical.

One possible approach is for the central bank to shoulder both the implementation and operational costs, mirroring the introduction of a retail CBDC akin to physical cash, where all expenses are borne by the central bank. The central bank can even profit further from the seigniorage of issuing (digital) cash, as explored in Sect. 7.3. This approach is expected to be the prevalent model for CBDC introductions in developed nations.

However, in the less developed world, there are instances where central banks may not be equipped to finance such projects. As a result, they may consider cost-free proofs of concept and pilot programs without public tenders, thereby opening up possibilities for establishing joint ventures with firms capable of supplying and implementing the solution. This scenario could pave the way for providers to negotiate transactional fees for system usage. Yet, it could also imply that the proofs of concept and pilot programs need to be financed by the provider and executed without charge, in order

Table 15.1 Store of value properties

Store of value properties of cash, CBDCs and bank deposits

	Cash	**CBDCs**		**Commercial bank sight deposits** (current accounts)
		Token-based DLT-based	Account-based	
Claim structure	Claim on central bank	Claim on central bank		Claim on a bank
Risks	Loss, theft & fraud	Loss, theft, fraud & cyber risk	Fraud & cyber risk ID theft	Fraud & cyber risk, illiquidity & insolvency
Backstop	Full	Full	Full	Deposit insurance (up to a limit and often with a lag for payout)
Are holdings anonymous?	Yes	At least pseudonymous	No	No
Interest rate remuneration	No	Can be set by central bank[a]		Set by banks, market-based
Interest rate tiering depending on household-specific holdings	No	No	Yes	Set by banks
Caps on holdings per household possible?	No, as holdings are anonymous. However, safety and practical limits lead to de facto limits on holdings	No, as holdings are pseudonymous/anonymous Wire transfers to same wallet can be limited	Yes	Generally no caps or limits (but possible)

[a]Not for offline use tokens

Source Adapted from BIS—Opportunity for the monetary system [1] to qualify for a chance at being the provider of the CBDC's final production solution. Any such model of a public–private partnership should be evaluated in detail in order to clearly assess the winners and losers in such models. Early savings could turn into a high price to pay by the end-users/tax payers in the long term.

In both cases, significant resistance and lobbying from existing payment providers and local banks, who see their profit margins in danger, is to be expected. The operating model needs to be well thought out and in order to drive adoption and success must not be limiting the benefits of customers and merchants to protect the $2 trillion in payment fees currently collected by these financial intermediaries. The risk of these unavoidable pressures affecting the final operating model should not be underestimated.

The ensuing sections (along with the appendix) delineate the primary operational models for rCBDCs that have been proposed and scrutinized by researchers and policymakers. These models exhibit variations in the division of responsibilities between public entities and private actors, particularly in terms of their impact on the onboarding of new users (Know Your Customer or "KYC" process), and their respective roles in managing the execution of payments.

15.3 Use Cases for Retail CBDC

As seen in Sect. 13.4, the following payment flows can be supported by a rCBDC solution. Each rCBDC project will most likely proceed to a prioritization of these use cases prior to embarking on the next step in the project (Table 15.2).

Table 15.2 Use cases for retail CBDC

Available use cases for retail CBDC	
P2P	Support of person to person
P2B—Physical store	Support of person to business—Physical store
P2B—Remote or e-commerce	Support of person to business—e-commerce
P2G	Support of person to government
G2P	Support of government to person
B2B	Business to business
B2P	Business to person
B2G	Business to government
G2B	Government to business
M2X	Machine to (machine/person/business/government)

Source Author

15.3.1 P2P—Person-to-Person Payments

This use case is highly preferred by users when it comes to retail CBDCs and has been incorporated into each of the CBDC projects detailed in Chapter 13 of this book.

Users expect these transactions to be immediate and cost-free, thus aligning with existing Instant Payment Solutions such as UPI, AliPay, WeChat Pay, PIX, TWINT, Zelle, Venmo, and more. Users also anticipate the ability to employ aliases for such payments, like phone numbers, emails, or usernames.

However, it's worth noting that uncontrolled free and instant transactions could potentially expose the system to denial-of-service attacks. Malicious users could flood the system with a large number of such free transactions, thereby potentially causing a system shutdown or financial drain on the operator (unless it's the central bank).

Further intriguing questions that carry significant implications need addressing. Will the feature function if one user is offline, or if both users are offline? How many offline transactions can a single user execute? The responses to these questions are crucial in defining the system's operation and resilience.

15.3.2 P2B—Person-to-Business Payments

This consideration needs to be divided into two categories: (1) physical payments in brick-and-mortar stores and (2) remote payments on e-commerce platforms.

Physical in-store payments necessitate integration with existing point of sale solutions or the introduction of new technologies to facilitate payments in the store. Various means can be utilized to achieve this, ranging from static QR codes (the most cost-effective option) to Android or iOS-based Point of Sale (POS) systems employing dynamic QR codes, NFC, Bluetooth, and more.

This also prompts the question of offline transactions: Do both the consumer and merchant need to be connected to the internet? Is it enough if only one party is online, or can the transaction occur offline altogether?

In the case of remote payments (akin to card-not-present transactions for credit card users), technology that facilitates easy internet use will be necessary. Displaying QR codes on e-commerce sites, generating payment links, and enabling one-click payments are viable options. For individuals possessing both a computer and a CBDC-enabled smartphone, scanning the QR code displayed in the browser on the computer screen with a smartphone is also a feasible solution. However, for those with only a single smartphone engaging in mobile (e-)commerce on their device, QR codes are not a working solution.

15.3.3 P2G—Person-to-Government Payments

These types of transactions could encompass a variety of financial interactions between individuals and governmental entities. These could include paying income taxes, acquiring licenses, settling fines, and more.

Person-to-government payments through digital currency could significantly streamline the process of transacting with government entities, increasing efficiency and reducing bureaucracy. Moreover, this could open the possibility for real-time tax collection.

P2G could lead to improved transparency, faster settlements, and reduced administrative burden for both the government and citizens, while enhancing compliance and effectiveness in the collection of public revenues.

15.3.4 G2P—Government-to-Person Payments

Government-to-person transactions might encompass social security payments, child allowances, COVID-19 aid, refugee allowances, and other forms of direct monetary aid. For privacy-preserving designs and those that allow installation of wallets without identification, it will first necessitate the identification of the individual before any disbursement can occur. However, this may present a highly efficient method of distribution compared to traditional means, such as the slow and problematic delivery of US COVID-19 aid checks through postal mail.

In these scenarios, the effective and value-added application of programmable money could lead to significantly improved outcomes. For instance, the US Treasury could have issued instant US$900 vouchers (also known as programmable money) into digital wallets. By setting a 90-day expiration date and restricting their use to necessary items like food, groceries, utilities… an immediate economic impact during the crisis could have been achieved. Government-to-person payments can also act as a significant driving force for adoption.

15.3.5 B2B—Business-to-Business Payments

These types of transactions represent an essential component of the financial ecosystem, facilitating the exchange of payments for goods and services between companies. B2B payments can involve several scenarios, such as settling invoices for purchased merchandise, paying for services rendered by other businesses, or completing transactions related to supply chain processes.

Incorporating CBDCs into B2B payments could significantly streamline operations, enhance efficiency, and offer real-time transaction processing. This could be especially beneficial for international transactions, which often involve multiple intermediaries and incur high fees and lengthy processing times. The implementation of CBDCs could simplify this process by providing a direct, more cost-effective, and faster method of transaction.

Furthermore, B2B payments using CBDCs can also pave the way for programmable money functionalities. For instance, smart contracts could be utilized to automate payment processes based on predefined conditions, including requests to pay/invoicing and increasing transactional security. This could revolutionize various aspects of business operations such as supply chain management, contractual agreements, and accounts payable and receivable processes.

While the nature of B2B payments may overlap with the domain of wholesale CBDC operations, they still represent a significant facet of the retail CBDC landscape, especially for small to medium-sized businesses. Hence, it is critical to consider their inclusion in the design of a comprehensive rCBDC solution.

15.3.6 B2P—Business-to-Person Payments

B2P transactions encompass a wide range of financial exchanges from businesses to individuals. Such payments could include salary disbursements to employees, refunds to customers for returned goods, cashback rewards, and more.

Incorporating rCBDCs into B2P payments could dramatically streamline these processes and enhance transparency. For instance, with digital salary payments, the need for physical checks or complex banking procedures could be eliminated. Employees would receive their wages instantly, with minimal fees and transaction times.

Similarly, for refunds and returns, businesses could issue instant reimbursements directly to customers' digital wallets, making the returns process more efficient and improving the customer experience. It could also promote trust between businesses and consumers due to the increased transparency and speed of such transactions.

Moreover, programmable money functionalities of CBDCs can further optimize B2P transactions. For instance, automated disbursement of salaries could be set up using smart contracts, reducing administrative efforts and errors.

Another potential benefit of CBDCs in B2P payments relates to financial inclusion. For individuals who are unbanked or underbanked, receiving payments such as salaries or refunds through CBDCs could provide a secure, accessible alternative to traditional banking mechanisms, thus promoting financial inclusivity.

Overall, B2P transactions using CBDCs could offer more efficient, secure, and inclusive payment solutions, transforming the traditional landscape of financial interactions between businesses and individuals.

15.3.7 B2G—Business-to-Government Payments

B2G transactions make up financial exchanges from businesses to governmental entities. These transactions may involve the remittance of income taxes, sales or value-added taxes (VAT), property taxes, social security contributions, payments for licenses or permits, and fines, among others.

rCBDCs could help streamline the process of paying for licenses, permits, or fines. Businesses would be able to directly transfer the necessary funds to the relevant government agencies, reducing transaction times and improving traceability.

The programmability of rCBDCs could also be harnessed to automate B2G transactions. Another key aspect is the potential impact of rCBDCs on VAT or sales tax remittances.

15.3.8 G2B—Government-to-Business Payments

G2B transactions refer to the financial exchanges from governmental entities to businesses. These payments encompass a multitude of scenarios, including procurement invoice settlements, disbursement of grants and subsidies, provision of employee benefits, value-added tax (VAT) refunds, and more.

Integrating CBDCs into G2B payments has the potential to revolutionize these processes, enhancing efficiency, reducing costs, and boosting transparency. In the case of grants and subsidies, rCBDCs can be used to directly deposit funds into businesses' digital wallets. This instant transmission not only speeds up the process but also improves the traceability and accountability of public funds.

Furthermore, the use of rCBDCs in VAT refunds could simplify the usually complex and time-consuming process. Businesses could receive their VAT refunds faster, thereby improving their cash flow management. Moreover, it could potentially streamline tax administration and reduce instances of tax evasion.

The programmability feature of rCBDCs can also be leveraged to automate G2B payments. For example, smart contracts could be implemented to release funds automatically once certain predetermined conditions are met, reducing administrative burdens and ensuring compliance with terms and conditions.

In essence, rCBDCs in G2B transactions can transform the way governments interact financially with businesses.

15.3.9 M2X—Machine to Machine/Person/Business

M2X, or Machine-to-Anything, payments have the potential to revolutionize the way transactions are conducted in our increasingly interconnected world. As our environments become more imbued with technology, it's becoming common for machines, applications, and devices to interact and transact with each other, as well as with people and businesses.

Take, for instance, the prospect of your vehicle autonomously paying for tolls, parking, or electric charging services. rCBDCs could facilitate seamless and instantaneous microtransactions for every kilometer you drive, each minute you park, or per unit of electricity consumed. Similarly, your smartphone could automatically handle payments for content consumption, such as paying for every second of a YouTube video you watch or collecting funds for any bit of personal data you agree to share.

These machine-to-machine scenarios involve microtransactions that, due to their frequency, could quickly scale to a transaction-per-second (TPS) rate that far exceeds any scenario involving only human participants. Consequently, the technological requirements for managing a very high volume of transactions would be significantly elevated.

In the broader context of the Internet of Things (IoT), rCBDCs could enable new ways of value transfer, such as your smart refrigerator directly paying for grocery restocks, or your home automation system settling utility bills.

Importantly, this evolution toward machine-initiated payments requires robust security measures to prevent unauthorized transactions and to ensure privacy and trust in the system. Additionally, regulatory frameworks would need to adapt to this new environment where machines can hold and transact digital money.

In conclusion: We can say that after the prioritization of the use cases for the respective CBDC project, these use cases all need to be documented in client journeys, which in turn will then make clear all the additional processes that need to be fulfilled by external actors and/or systems, and it will allow to define and illustrate the functional requirements or features necessary to realize the planned solution.

15.4 Features of a rCBDC

The successful implementation of the use cases we've discussed for retail CBDCs depends fundamentally on the careful design of their features. In this segment, we delve into the specifics of how these features can be configured to maximize the benefits of rCBDCs, and we weigh the pros and cons of different design decisions.

We return to the 12 key features previously discussed in Sect. 12.7 "Key Features of CBDCs." However, we won't be reiterating the same details as before in this book. Instead, we'll focus on elucidating additional aspects that are unique to retail CBDCs and have an impact on these features.

Following that, we'll introduce and examine 10 more features that are specifically pertinent to the design of a retail CBDC. Each of these elements can contribute to the potential of rCBDCs to transform the financial landscape, providing greater convenience, security, and inclusivity for all users.

This thorough exploration of rCBDC features aims to provide a comprehensive understanding of how they can shape the future of digital currencies and payment systems, and the considerations that must be kept in mind to ensure their successful implementation and adoption.

15.4.1 Security

Retail payment systems can face a number of cybersecurity threats, including credit and debit card fraud which, in 2018, resulted in roughly $25 billion in damages globally. To address these concerns, retail payment risk management strategies often comply with industry standards such as the Payment Card Industry Data Security Standard (PCI-DSS). In order to counteract phishing and user errors, many platforms have implemented safeguards like unique user credentials, multi-factor authentication, fraud detection, micro validation, tokenization, and encryption.

Security requirements for a retail CBDC system will likely be considerably more stringent due to a significantly higher user count, often reaching into the millions. This contrasts sharply with a wholesale CBDC system, where the number of participating financial intermediaries may be as low as 100 and will rarely exceed 5,000. That means it is impossible to lock down a retail system in the same way as it is possible to do for a wholesale system and prevent malicious users from connecting and exploring the system for vulnerabilities.

It's also vital to acknowledge that transitioning solutions from one user model to another isn't always without repercussions. For instance, Bitcoin was designed to securely facilitate peer-to-peer transactions without requiring a trusted third party, achieved through intricate decentralization and consensus mechanisms. However, if we were to adapt the Bitcoin model for a CBDC, it would be misguided to assume that the benefits Bitcoin offered would remain the same in a system operated solely by a single trusted entity—in this case, the central bank. The threat model would undoubtedly change from the Bitcoin scenario to the central bank scenario, and the implications of such a shift warrant meticulous analysis.

Section 15.4.15, which explores the unique challenge of facilitating offline transactions in a rCBDC, will delve further into security-related considerations.

15.4.2 Privacy

Privacy in a retail CBDC context holds a fundamentally different significance compared to a wholesale CBDC (wCBDC), where privacy from other participants may be a primary concern. In a retail environment, the degree of privacy protection within a rCBDC ecosystem can potentially make or break the core principles of a democratic society.

As we've previously discussed in Chapter 4 and Sect. 12.7.2, "privacy" can be realized in various ways, each with differing levels of assurance against data collection, association, linkage, or exploitation. Only systems offering anonymity (either two-sided or one-sided) can ensure real privacy, assuming the cryptographic tools used for anonymization are reliable. All other models inherently rely on trust for privacy.

To lessen the risk of data privacy breaches in the creation of a CBDC, it's essential to embed robust data privacy measures from the onset and throughout all stages, including planning, implementation, and operational phases.

Payments and Digital IDs

On the opposite end of the spectrum of solutions that embed robust data privacy measures, we find solutions that suggest tying digital payments to digital identities. Here any concept of privacy, be that anonymity or pseudonymity, is eliminated for good.

When payment systems require personal information such as name, address, phone number, or identification number, it creates a trail of data that can be used to track individuals' spending habits and financial activities.

This information can be vulnerable to theft or misuse, especially if the payment system is not adequately secured. Moreover, if this information falls into the wrong hands, it can be used for fraudulent activities, identity theft, and other criminal activities.

Furthermore, in some countries, people may not have official identification documents, and thus they may not be able to participate in digital payment systems that require identification. This can create a digital divide and hinder financial inclusion.

Lastly, some people may be uncomfortable with the idea of their financial transactions being monitored or tracked, and they may prefer to keep their financial activities private.

Even today, this information is already collected and traded, unbeknownst to most credit card users, for massive amounts of money, as it was reported in 2018 by Bloomberg [154] that Google and Mastercard had cut a secret deal, allowing Google to track retail sales and link online ads to in-store purchases, in which Mastercard sold its credit card data to Google.

!!! Remember: Tying digital payments to digital identities is the end of real privacy.

The following strategies, comprehensively covered in Sect. 12.7 "Key Features of CBDCs," are methods for achieving privacy in CBDC systems. If you require further clarifications, we recommend revisiting Sect. 12.7:

1. **Guaranteed full dual-sided anonymity:**
   - Anonymity for both sender, receiver, and transaction content.
   - Anonymity for both transaction parties—sender and receiver.
2. **Guaranteed single-sided anonymity:**

- Spender anonymity with receiver transparency.
- Receiver anonymity with spender transparency.

3. **Trust-based pseudonymity:**
   - This involves use of pseudonyms to maintain privacy while keeping track of transactions.
4. **Trust-based data segregation or data splits:**
   - This method involves dividing up data to maintain privacy, with trust in the system operators necessary for this approach to be effective.

As we have seen before, on the one end, two-sided anonymity is not reconcilable with a socially just and law-abiding world, as such a solution would cater perfectly to a world of illegal business, black markets, and tax evasion. Receiver anonymity as well has mostly similar downsides in the big picture.

On the other end, data segregation adds no additional privacy than currently exists in existing payment systems, while offering the central bank a politically correct position of claiming "privacy" without any real effect in the full CBDC ecosystem.

That leaves us with one-sided spender anonymity and pseudonymity as potentially reasonable choices improving the current state of privacy in payments—the first one being **real, hard,** or **absolute**, and the second one **trust-based**.

Anonymity versus Pseudonymity

Let us come back to these two terms, which we already encountered before and some of this may already have been absorbed. We consider these characteristics important and worth spending some more time on.

Anonymity and pseudonymity are both terms used to describe situations in which a person's identity is hidden or obscured, but there are some important differences between them.

Anonymity refers to a situation in which a person's identity is completely hidden or unknown. When someone is anonymous, it is impossible to trace their actions back to them, as their identity is completely hidden. In the case of anonymity, actions by the same actor can also not be linked.

Pseudonymity, on the other hand, refers to a situation in which a person uses a false or fictitious name or identity. This can be achieved by using a nickname, a username, or a pen name. While the person's true identity is not known, their actions may be traced back to their pseudonymous identity. For example, if someone posts a comment on a website using a pseudonym, the website's administrators may be able to track that person's activity on the site, even though they don't know the person's true identity. Pseudonymity guarantees are often and easily broken [175] and that should not be forgotten in this discussion.

There are several important differences between anonymity and pseudonymity. Anonymity provides real privacy and allows people to engage in activities without fear of being identified. Pseudonymity, on the other hand, provides some level of privacy, but may still allow for identification and traceability with a certain amount of effort. Pseudonymity rises and falls with the level of trust in the tools or the responsible third parties, who can ultimately remove the protection when desired.

In conclusion, anonymity and pseudonymity are both ways of hiding or obscuring a person's identity, but they have different levels of privacy and accountability. Anonymity completely and irrevocably hides a person's identity, while pseudonymity allows for some level of protection, but still allows for traceability and identification after the fact.

In order for a retail CBDC solution not to be at risk of being labeled "Big Brother's Digital Currency," [37] the privacy approach should provide for at least one-sided anonymity with cryptographic guarantees, i.e. it must offer unlinkable and time-proof protection of personal and transaction details. Only then a fact-based defense of its CBDC against these attacks by DeSantis & colleagues is possible for a central bank. Otherwise only a **"Trust me…"** strategy remains to convince the citizen end-users to adopt the CBDC.

15.4.3 Consensus Mechanisms

When it comes to retail CBDCs, it's crucial that the consensus mechanism is not just reliable, but also quick and efficient. In such a context, speed is of the essence for ensuring a smooth and satisfactory user experience. This means we can't afford to wait as long as Bitcoin's 10 minutes or even Polkadot's 12 seconds for consensus to be reached.

In retail situations, system designs that rely on a single validator to confirm the validity of the payment token, or the legitimacy of the transaction, tend to have an edge. This is largely due to their speed compared to a consensus-finding mechanism that involves dozens of nodes in a DLT setup.

The time required to reach consensus directly impacts the next item—settlement time or latency. This is a crucial factor to consider, as any significant delay in this regard could hamper the overall functionality and user experience of the rCBDC system. Therefore, adopting an efficient consensus mechanism is vital to ensure the smooth operation of a retail CBDC.

15.4.4 Settlement/Transaction Time

Instant settlement or fast transactions times are a critical feature for rCBDC systems. For general in-store processing, settlement within 1–2 seconds seems sufficient. For paying at the subway turnstile, one to two seconds to conclude a transaction would lead to severe backups, and therefore sub-second settlement times are necessary to be competitive with innovative approaches such as those deployed in the London Tube for example.

Once new business models like pay-per-use and machine-to-machine microtransactions (cent and sub-cent transactions) become mainstream, extremely fast settlement times are critical to accommodate this type of future business transaction. It is mandatory to plan for parallel processing of transactions at high speeds in today's system designs already to prevent a potential overload of the system, when these types of transactions make the volumes soar exponentially.

Remember the statements mentioned earlier by Mr. Mu Changchu, director of the PBOC DCI regarding the target settlement time for Chinese e-CNY transactions being nanoseconds. Compare this with the DLT numbers of 10 minutes for Bitcoin, 6.4 minutes for Ethereum under POS [155], 12 seconds for Polkadot, 4 seconds for Ripple, 1 second for Avalanche, and 0.5 seconds for Solana.

The settlement or transaction time directly influences the next feature, which is the performance and scalability of a rCBDC system.

15.4.5 Performance/Scalability

Performance is an important design element for an rCBDC system. A system that is too slow will not attract users (see previous remarks on China's e-CNY) and the performance of the system must be able to grow without deterioration when the number of users and transactions that come with success grow exponentially. This ability to grow as needed without running into architectural barriers is called scalability.

Performance is often measured in **transactions per second** (TPS).

In the payment systems we find deployed in the world today, we see very wide differences in the peak performances when it comes to these TPS numbers. Here are some current examples:

- In the cryptocurrency space [156], Bitcoin has 7 TPS, Ethereum has 27 TPS, Avalanche claims 4′500, Polygon 7′000 TPS, and Solana 50′000.
- Visa claims it can process 24′000 TPS at its peak and it does on average 1′700 TPS [156].
- MasterCard claims it can do 5′000 TPS [157].
- The Digital Pound design specification is for a minimum of 30′000 TPS, with a possible upper limit of 100′000 TPS [71].
- The People's Bank of China, the Chinese central bank, started with 10′000 and had a design specification for their e-CNY of 300′000 TPS [158].
- AliPay, the Chinese private digital payment solution, at its peak, processes 544′000 TPS and on average 2′025 TPS [46].

Cost per transaction is another critical number that is somewhat related to the TPS performance of a system. To calculate these costs, one should calculate what is necessary in CPU performance, in bandwidth, in legally required storage of the data for 5–10 years and multiply that with the necessary amount of redundancy planned.

The cost per transaction is even more important when it comes to microtransactions. When the user is supposed to make a micropayment of 0.1 cent to a merchant, then this is only economically feasible if the cost of execution such a transaction is several magnitudes lower. Otherwise microtransactions become unviable.

Power consumption, which has become a hot topic due to the great success of Bitcoin and the intensive computational needs of the proof of work consensus mechanism. It was estimated in March 2023 that Bitcoin's total energy consumption could be 103 terawatt hours (TWh) a year, equal to the power consumption of Kazakhstan.

For illustration, 337,421 Visa transactions can be powered by the average energy consumed for a single Bitcoin transaction (501.51 kWh).

15.4.6 Sovereignty

We have covered Sovereignty in detail in Sect. 12.7.6. With open-source/FLOSS software on the retail end, both citizens, merchants, and financial intermediaries can create new feature enhanced wallets and Point of Sale (PoS) systems, without being restricted or shut out from addressing their specific requirements by restrictive software licenses, as long as they adhere to the open protocol of the rCBDC system.

15.4.7 Extensibility

To ensure that a rCBDC system can support innovation and meet future payment needs, it is important to design it with extensibility in mind. Because of the large numbers of participants involved, it is even more important to consider the need for open-source or open-protocol solutions to reduce any long term and expensive dependance on a solution provider and give both citizens, merchants, and financial intermediaries the option to create new feature enhanced wallets and PoS systems as required.

15.4.8 Interoperability

As seen before, it is interoperability which makes a rCBDC system fast, easy to use and hence opens the doors for widespread adoption. The first layer of interoperability lies within the central bank itself.

By taking a look at the ECB's IT system landscape, we can broadly identify three categories of systems where integration is likely:

Core systems:
These include the systems that support the ECB's core functions, such as the Eurosystem's payment and settlement systems (TARGET2 and TARGET2-Securities), the Monetary Policy Data Warehouse, and the European Central Credit Register.
Integration into TARGET2 is highly likely.
Support systems (mostly SAP)
These include the systems that support the ECB's operations and activities, such as the Human Resource Management System, the Financial Accounting System, and the ECB's intranet and communication systems.
Integration into the SAP financial accounting system is highly likely.
Oversight systems:
These include the systems that support the ECB's supervisory activities, such as the Supervisory Data Management System, the Supervisory Information System, and the AnaCredit system.
Integration into the supervisory systems for monitoring is highly likely.

In addition, there is interoperability with systems outside of the central bank, that need to be taken into account when designing a retail CBDC:

- Interoperability with the commercial bank back-end, KYC, and AML systems.

- Interoperability with other payment rails.
- Interoperability with e-commerce sites/solutions.
- Interoperability with other financial actors, like exchanges, etc.

Many of these APIs will adopt the financial services standard of ISO20022 for the messages between systems.

15.4.9 Programmability

The concept of programmability can be split into two key aspects in the context of a rCBDC: "**Programmable Payments**" and "**Programmable Money.**"

Programmable payments are universally recognized as beneficial for a CBDC implementation, given that similar features are already extensively integrated into the existing solutions offered by private entities such as banks, e-money institutions, and payment service providers.

On the other hand, programmable money draws a wider range of views and debates. Although it appears to offer significant potential for governmental uses (for instance, direct distribution of pandemic relief funds in the form of digital currency, which must be spent within a specified period to stimulate the economy or in specific sectors thereof), several central banks express reservations about the potential for money to be restricted in its use (such as limitations to specific product categories or the inclusion of expiry dates).

This issue pertains only to rCBDCs, whereas the feature of programmability is not contested but rather highly sought after in wholesale CBDCs (wCBDCs).

The ultimate manifestation of programmability in rCBDCs will depend on how it is implemented. If a central bank, taking the European Central Bank (ECB) as an example, is wary of and eschews this feature, it might inadvertently close off numerous opportunities for other ministries or financial intermediaries. These entities might gain significant advantage from such functionality, even if the resultant circulating product needs to be termed differently, like "vouchers" for instance.

Before moving on, we need to address a few basic key questions with regard to the mentioned programmability.

How much programming should be allowed? is a key question in this chapter. Different solutions offer different programmability options. Bitcoin is very restricted in its SWIFT programming language, while Ethereum with its Solidity language and smart contract options is very flexible and open in that respect. This programmability criterium must be well defined before any system solution is selected.

Who is allowed to program payments and money? is another key question that needs to be answered? With programming, we understand actually writing software code, like smart contracts. Shall access to programming be completely open as in Ethereum, where every ETH user can program a smart contract by himself? When we consider the innate human skills in writing secure software code, this may not be the wisest approach for an operation at large scale without issues.

Shall only the central bank be able to create programmable features? One option could be for the central bank to approach the subject in such a way that it gives the end-user configuration options in the features programmed by the central bank. This could ensure higher quality while offering options. Allowing banks and financial intermediaries to add programmed features is another idea that has been proposed in the literature. Some central banks are also considering passing this programming opportunity to private providers.

15.4.10 Fungibility

Fungibility in money refers to the property of a currency that allows it to be interchangeable with other units of the same currency as we have seen in 12.7.10. This has of course the largest impact on a rCBDC, as in this case the history of the money can potentially impact its perceived value. Retail CBDC that came from a drug deal or rCBDC that emanated from a government social security payment may be valued very differently.

There is a potential impact on privacy and a lack of data minimization, as the technical realization of a token that carries with it the history of its owners and transactions (where no 2 tokens are 100% fungible) compared to a token that carries absolutely no history.

Carrying transaction history in a token may also create legal and data protection issues for such a rCBDC as documented in the Swedish e-krona project.

15.4.11 Resilience

A rCBDC system should demonstrate exceptional resilience, considering it is expected to operate uninterruptedly 24/7/365. Given that the public's need to make payments doesn't cease outside of regular business hours or on weekends, ensuring seamless operation in the retail sector is particularly crucial.

Therefore, measures to prevent system interruptions and to maintain constant availability and accuracy of the data required for a retail CBDC operation are highly important. SWIFTnet [159] has had a 99.999% availability and (on July 10, 2023) Bitcoin had 99.988% uptime since inception [160].

15.4.12 Efficiency

Any rCBDC infrastructure must be designed with a green mindset and with extremely high energy efficiency goals as any such solution is designed for a high number of transactions and for high speed to make the user experience pleasant.

rCBDC solutions that rely on high energy consumption for reasons like consensus building, with Bitcoin being the worst example due to its energy intensive proof of work algorithm and an energy consumption equal to the country of Kazakhstan, are problematic because the energy consumption will be proportional to the number of transactions and therefore only solutions that are highly energy efficient can be considered for a productive launch and to remain sustainable if success drives the transaction volumes through the roof.

15.4.13 Accessibility

A rCBDC system should be designed to cater to a vast spectrum of users, making it as inclusive as possible. It should be designed not just for those with access to conventional banking services, but especially for those in areas with limited financial services. The system should aim to cover those left out by the current private payment solutions, which are becoming increasingly complex to use (including registration, login, multi-factor authentication, etc.).

We have transitioned from a simple password setup to additional SMS codes, and now, we often need one or more specific provider apps installed on our smartphones plus some body parts. These developments are increasingly complicating the payment process and often lead to the exclusion of certain demographic groups, such as the visually impaired, individuals with motor control issues, the young, and the elderly. They often are incapable to leverage these cutting-edge payment systems. Therefore, any retail CBDC system should prioritize accessibility and inclusivity in its design.

15.4.14 Tax Collection & Income Transparency

The potential of a rCBDC to facilitate tax collection varies depending on its specific design. As discussed under the "Privacy" section, only fully anonymous or one-sided anonymous solutions, where the recipient remains anonymous, prevent tax collection and income transparency. However, these types of solutions tend to attract illicit activities and are likely to be deemed unsuitable for rCBDC implementations by regulatory authorities.

Tax collection and income transparency can be achieved while still preserving spender privacy through cryptographic technologies. This approach offers users a level of real privacy they currently cannot find in private payment solutions, and it is socially responsible to consider a solution that ensures everyone contributes their fair share toward societal betterment, even if this pertains to a sensitive topic such as tax payments. If everyone paid their taxes fairly, our societies would likely be more prosperous and a better place.

It's worth noting that, as confirmed by several case studies, some countries, particularly in the developing world, might prefer not to link the concept of tax collection to the introduction of a CBDC. This is especially true when large segments of their economies operate outside the tax system, and any association of tax collection goals with a rCBDC could compromise its acceptance and adoption.

Successful CBDC and digital payment projects have been launched in countries not wanting to associate their CBDC with future equitable tax collection. However, the solutions chosen did mostly not incorporate robust privacy protections that would render the collection and use of available data for future tax purposes impossible.

15.4.15 Offline Payments

Offline digital payments are a frequently named requirement in the white-papers and proofs of concept documents for rCBDCs. An International Monetary Fund (IMF) paper [65] even goes as far as suggesting that "In many regions, internet-free access may be a make-or-break feature for central bank digital currencies." Central banks perceive offline functionality as a potential approach to accomplish the goals of financial inclusion, resilience, and privacy.

A BIS survey [161] has shown that central banks consider the ability to make offline payments using rCBDCs an important feature, with 49%

considering it to be vital and 49% considering it to be advantageous (Graph 15.1).

The survey also highlighted the expectations of cash resemblance, financial inclusion, and resilience linked to the requirements of an offline rCBDC (Graph 15.2).

On cash resemblance, numerous central banks consider it crucial for rCBDCs and cash to have some comparable user experience and functionalities. Some experts suggest that users should have the ability to make rCBDC payments offline, even if online systems are available, in a similar manner to cash payments. On privacy, offline use has the potential to offer real, hard, cash-like privacy as it is not connected, at a minimum when the transaction takes place offline. The BIS survey reconfirms the importance of privacy offline with 44% of central banks stating that the level of privacy for offline payments should be greater than for online payments. 56% wanted it to be the same, while no central banks wanted it to be lower.

The cash resemblance on privacy can still disappear after the transaction, if the offline device collects all private transaction details and shares them with a central system that reconciles identities, when the device reconnects.

On financial inclusion, offline rCBDC payments should be feasible whenever technically possible. The necessity for offline payments is particularly critical in nations where feature phones are more prevalent than smartphones and in regions where there is no internet connectivity and/or electricity.

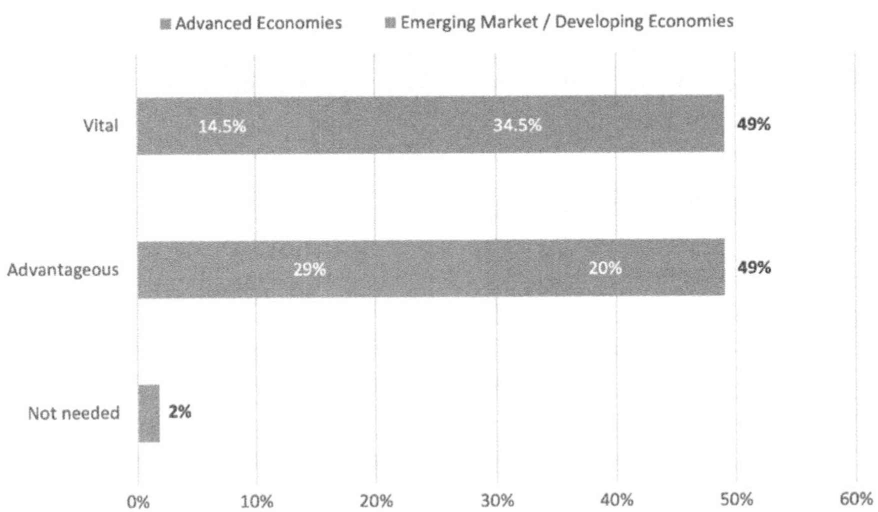

Graph 15.1 Should offline payments with CBDC be possible (*Note* This graph shows both the fraction of total answers and how the answers differ between AEs and EMDEs. *Source* BIS central bank survey on offline payments with CBDC)

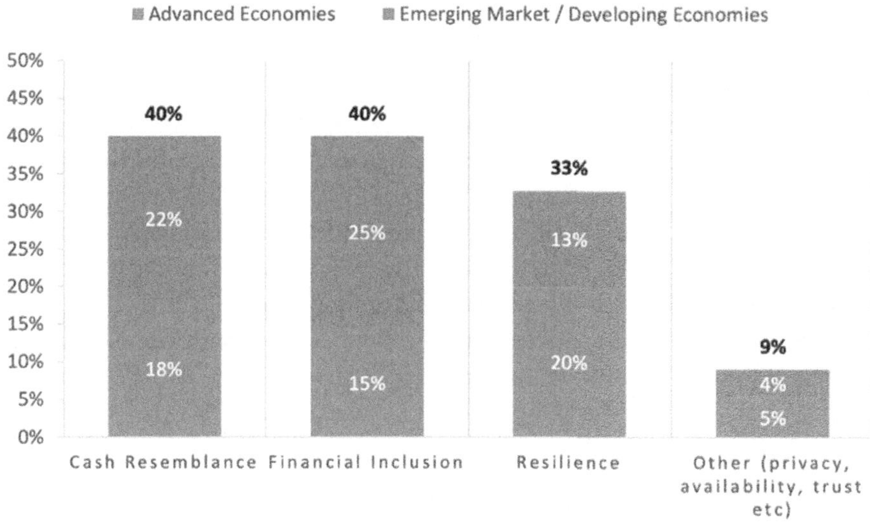

Graph 15.2 What are the main goals for offline CBDC? (*Note* Survey respondents could select more than one option, so the total does not add up to 100%. *Source* BIS central bank survey on offline payments with CBDC)

Offline rCBDC payments should be accessible to unbanked users and for retail payments.

On resilience, it is clear that an offline rCBDC will increase resilience as it adds a new option to make payments to whatever existed before.

Privacy is also an item that can be influenced by offline solutions. The improvement in privacy will depend on the technical realization of the solution as we will soon see in this chapter.

The survey showed that 56% of central banks believed merchants who accepted rCBDCs also needed to accept them in offline mode. Such a stance raises immediately questions about liability. If merchants are forced to accept an inherently insecure method of payment, who will in the end be liable for the damages it will entail?

While it is easy to understand why developing countries, that are missing significant online infrastructure coverage, are looking into this subject, a larger question remains on the need for offline payments in developed countries with great mobile and internet coverage, if the central banks do not plan on eliminating physical cash from our economies.

15.4.15.1 Historic Developments

Offline digital payments go back quite a bit and the first projects started at the same time as the commercial internet. In 1993, the Bank of Finland introduced the Avant stored-value card, which had the capability of offline payments through a specialized card reader device. However, despite its innovative features, the Avant card failed to gain widespread popularity. Similarly, in 1995, National Westminster Bank in the UK piloted a similar stored-value payment system called Mondex, but it did not gain significant traction either. I had the opportunity to use a solution called ChipKnip in the Netherlands in 2004. Mondex was gradually shut down in the early 2000s, Avant was dropped in 2006 and ChipKnip did not survive either.

15.4.15.2 What Represents an Offline Payment?

What offline digital payments actually represent in the different stakeholder's minds is not always simple to extract and the definitions in publications go all over the place. In order to consider the offline solution a benefit in case of catastrophes, it must be considered usable in the absence of power and connectivity. Hurricanes and earthquakes usually do not discriminate between services, and in such cases, it must be assumed that neither internet, telecoms, nor power will be available.

For that reason, we are establishing in Table 15.3 all the options that could fall under the "offline" moniker with regard to rCBDCs. We also have added the power dimension to the list, as connectivity outages and power outages can sometimes go together, especially in the case of natural catastrophes, like hurricanes, earthquakes, and similar events.

For some authors, offline means that one of the 2 participants in a payment transaction (the buyer or the seller) is not connected to the internet. For others, it means that both sides are completely off-grid and not connected to anything. A third definition would find the buyer unconnected, but the merchant connected to server infrastructure via a LAN or WAN.

As described in Table 15.3 for offline payments, both the buyer and seller can be offline, and in other models, only one can be offline, for the transaction to be successful.

With ***offline*** we mean in this book no connectivity at all—not to the internet, not to telecoms network (1G-5G) nor to private local area (LAN)/ wide area (WAN) networks.

With ***no power*** we mean in this book no electrical power, and we exclude all devices that need to be re-charged more often than every three months. We

Table 15.3 Offline scenarios

	Scenario
1	**Customer offline** (no internet, telecom or LAN/WAN connectivity), merchant online
2	**Merchant offline** (no internet, telecom or WAN/LAN connectivity), customer online
3	**Both customer & merchant offline** (no internet, telecom or LAN/WAN connectivity)
4	Electricity out & connectivity out for **customer**
5	Electricity out & connectivity out for **merchant**
6	**Merchant offline** & **Customer no power** - > customer offline (see case 3)
7	**Customer offline** & **Merchant no power** - > Merchant offline (see case 3)
8	Electricity out & connectivity out for **all (customer & merchant)**

Source Author

consider devices that have battery power for longer than 3 months without recharging as a working solution in an offline case (i.e. an RSA token, which has a battery life of 3 years).

We will review the eight different offline options one by one:

Use case 1: Customer offline:
When the customer is offline, a transaction can still take place by routing the consumer communication for the transaction through the merchant's device for validation and settlement. Consumer consent may be a requirement that must be investigated prior to implementation.

!!! **Remember**: Customer offline is technically no issue and solved by routing the transaction through the merchant.

Use case 2: Merchant offline:
When the merchant is offline, a transaction can still take place by routing the merchant communication for the transaction through the consumer's device for validation and settlement.

The merchant can also be offline and display a static QR code, so that the customer can just scan the code and pay like that. This setup has been part of the success of digital payments by AliPay and WeChat Pay in China.

The merchant can also acquire a €10 smartkey that will display the exact same number than the paying device of the customer, to guarantee that a payment was successfully made to him.

With a more advanced smartkey/smartcard, the merchant can even enter the purchase amount and the display of the same code on both devices will guarantee that the right amount was paid by the customer. GNU Taler can offer such functionality for example.

!!! **Remember**: Merchant offline is technically no issue and has multiple solutions. Merchants can even be offline all the time without problems, available solutions are very simple and cheap to deploy.

Use case 3: Merchant and customer offline:
When the merchant and customer are both offline, smartcards will work as offline rCBDC. They can communicate based on the battery power and ensure transfer of funds from one device to the next.

In each of these cases, an additional difficulty can be the absence of electricity. When we say no power, we mean no electricity supply and the smartphone or other battery is drained.

Use case 4: Customer offline and no power:
When customer is offline and without power, regular payment cards with metal contacts are powered up when inserted in merchant device and remain usable.

A second card type is the contactless smart card, in which the card communicates with and is powered by the reader through RF induction technology (at data rates of 106–848 kbit/s). These cards require only proximity to an antenna to communicate. Like smart cards with contacts, contactless cards do not have an internal power source. Instead, they use an inductor to capture some of the incident radio-frequency interrogation signal, rectify it, and use it to power the card's electronics. These cards also remain usable in this scenario.

This NFC functionality can also be implemented on smartphones and work in passive mode, i.e. without power. This feature was introduced by the Chinese e-CNY on Android phones in Q1 2023.

Both regular and contactless cards, as well as smartphones with the right NFC features to interact on empty battery, will function in this use case. You will learn more about NFC in Sect. 15.6.

Use case 5: Merchant offline and no power:
In this case, the merchant can display a static QR code for which no power is needed. Just a paper sticker will do, but is not without risk, as the merchant cannot check his system for a confirmation and needs to rely on the payer's information.

The merchant can remediate that risk and use a battery powered €10 smartkey or smartfob

Smartfobs(*Source* Shutterstock)

with long lasting batteries that will display the exact same number than the device of the customer, to guarantee that a payment was successfully made to him.

With a more advanced smartcard, the merchant can enter the amount and the display of the equal code on both devices will guarantee even that the right amount was paid by the customer.

Both smart key/smart card solutions will work fully offline and as long as the devices have battery.

Use case 6: Merchant offline and customer no power -> customer offline:
A customer with no power will also be without connectivity, as connectivity necessitates power. This is similar to use case 3 with both merchant and customer being offline and without power. Please see use case 3.

Use case 7: Customer offline and Merchant no power -> merchant offline:
A merchant with no power will also be without connectivity, as connectivity necessitates power. Hence this is similar to use case 3 with both merchant and customer being offline and without power. Please see use case 3.

Use case 8: Merchant and customer offline and no power:
In this scenario, only long-lasting battery powered smartcards (or similar) will work as offline rCBDC. They can communicate based on the battery power in the cards and ensure transfer of funds from one device to the next.

In catastrophic situations like the recent earthquakes in Turkey and Syria, cash may still prove to be the go-to solution and the offline rCBDC might at best be a complimentary solution to physical cash. The biggest challenge of offline solutions is that they have not been implemented in large-scale projects yet and hence have not proven their worth and safety.

15.4.15.3 Forms of Offline Payments

As already indicated, in this book **"offline usage in rCBDC"** means all parties, buyer and seller, payer and receiver, are completely without connectivity to either internet, telecoms, or any other network.

Other elements to consider in the discussion around offline payments are the duration of the offline period, the transitivity desired in the system, and the number of payments that can be done.

Transitivity means the ability to immediately re-spend funds that were received offline, without connecting to the outside world. Transitivity implies that each transaction is fully settled in real-time, transferring the funds from sender to recipient, who can re-spend the funds right away.

When it comes to duration, we can differentiate between

1. **Intermittent offline:** rCBDC solutions, that allow users to still transact during shorter intermittent offline periods when there is temporarily no connectivity (internet, telecom, WAN/LAN). Such a system would basically be an extension of an online rCBDC system, and the offline transactions would only settle when connectivity is restored. Until that online settlement is completed, the recipient cannot use the funds he received. This model can also be referred to as **staged offline** [161].
2. **Fully offline:** rCBDC solutions, that allow users to transact during longer offline periods when connectivity is unavailable. This would entail transitive offline transactions, meaning I could pay Paul offline, Paul could then use those funds immediately and pay Mary with them, all without any connectivity over longer periods of time.

   Built-in and hardcoded limits, for example on total amounts transacted, on total number of transactions, or on time elapsed since last connection could limit the functioning of the wallet and force a synchronization with the central CBDC system for risk/security management purposes. This could be called **extended offline**.

In fully offline CBDC solutions, there is no requirement for the payer and payee to connect to a ledger system in order to execute a transaction. Any payment is instantly credited to the payee, enabling them to use it for spending purposes, in a transitive manner, at the conclusion of the transaction. This offline final settlement process allows both parties to remain fully disconnected from the system for an indefinite period of time.

15.4.15.4 Can Offline Payments Be Secure?

The introduction of any form of rCBDC comes with new risks, and one of the more challenging and riskiest features to implement in a retail CBDC is the functionality of two-sided offline payments.

This is due to a theorem in computer science called the **CAP theorem**, which any central bank should be aware of.

The CAP Theorem

In a distributed computer system, it is impossible to simultaneously provide more than two out of the following three guarantees:

- Consistency:
  Every read receives the most recent write or an error.
- Availability:
  Every request receives a response, without guarantee that it contains the most recent version of the information.
- Partition tolerance:
  The system continues to function even when network partitions occur.

The CAP theorem in distributed computing refers to the trade-offs between consistency, availability, and partition tolerance (offline usage) in a distributed system. While it is desirable for a distributed system to achieve all three properties, it is impossible to do so simultaneously. Instead, a distributed system can only provide two of these properties at the same time while compromising on the third. In 2002, the MIT mathematicians Seth Gilbert and Nancy Lynch published the formal proof for this theorem.

In other words, it is not possible for a distributed system to be both consistent and available, if certain parts of it become disconnected.

Consistency requires that all nodes in a distributed system see the same data at the same time, while availability requires that every request made to the system receives a response, without guaranteeing that the response contains the most recent data. Partition tolerance, on the other hand, requires that the system can continue to function even if network failures occur and communication between nodes is lost.

In the context of electronic payment systems and rCBDCs, this means that it is impossible to simultaneously protect against double spending (consistency) while operating offline (partition tolerance). To overcome this technical limitation, some of the existing electronic payment systems rely on intermediaries like credit card networks, which assume financial risk and charge fees to handle potential inconsistencies in the state update process. If the central bank were to operate the system independently, it would need to bear this risk and the related costs itself or declare someone else (the merchant, PSP or customer) liable in its rule book.

Therefore, sufficient mitigations must be found via a defense in-depth strategy to make any exploitation of this proven vulnerability hard and expensive, and to reduce the amount of double spend/fraud that will result from introducing offline payments. It is essential to understand the trade-offs and limitations in designing a robust and efficient rCBDC system that can meet the needs of all stakeholders.

The approach for mitigation in the intermittent offline approach is to just allow the initiation of one payment transaction, which can only be completed when connectivity returns. However, the added value of such a model, compared to an online model with standard industry availability, seems very limited.

Mitigations for fully offline electronic payment systems with its mathematically proven vulnerability can only take two forms:

1. **Surrendering control** over computing resources to prevent double spending, which is typically done through **secure hardware** elements that restrict user access to certain device functions. **Secure software** as well as a combination of **hardware and software** are other less mature solutions that have been proposed as possible options for this remediation too.
2. **Identifying the user retroactively**, after network connectivity is restored. The system then attempts to recover the losses from the party responsible for the double spending.

There are no other options apparent to make offline transactions secure. So let us look at these available options in detail and analyze how reality presents itself compared to these strategies. We will cover in sequential order, secure hardware, secure software, and retroactive action against fraudsters and their challenges in real life.

15.4.15.5 The Track Record of Secure Hardware Elements

Secure hardware elements are one of two ways to mitigate the risks introduced with offline payments. How reliable are they?

There are three main categories of secure hardware: Secure Element (SE), Trusted Platform Module (TPM), and Trusted Execution Environment (TEE).

Secure Element (SE) is commonly used in smartphones and provides a dedicated component for secure execution and storage of cryptographic applications. It can be embedded in a SIM card, phone manufacturer's chip, or a removable microSD card. SE has limitations in terms of application issuance, storage capacity, and processing capabilities, which may hinder large-scale deployment. Usually, secure elements are certified to high levels of security assurance and offer a range of tamper-resistant qualities [161].

Trusted Platform Module (TPM), originally designed for laptops, is a micro-controller with cryptographic capabilities for complex operations. Storage capacity is limited in TPM, allowing only cryptographic operations compared to SE, which can perform any application operation.

Trusted Execution Environment (TEE) is a proposition to overcome SE issues by combining hardware and software parts. It provides a secure storage and processing environment with higher capacities than SE. The hardware part includes a processor that isolates sensitive applications from regular ones, while the software part consists of two separate operating systems (OS): a Rich OS and a Secure OS that are isolated from each other. The Secure OS uses a limited instruction set for security verification and validation. TEE is present on most modern smartphones, with major mobile processor manufacturers like ARM integrating it. However, TEE solutions need to address challenges such as physical attacks, secure boot to prevent rootkit, and secure channels for user interactions with smartphones. TEEs offer generally more functionality, but a lower level of tamper resistance than an SE and are certified to lower levels of security assurance [161].

With regard to these secure hardware elements needed to protect from double spending in offline scenarios, Grothoff and Dold analyzed in their paper *"Why a digital euro should be online first and bearer-based"* [26] the different hardware security platforms that were available in 2016 and vulnerabilities published over the following three years. The results included significant vulnerabilities affecting all major hardware security architectures (Intel, Samsung, ARM, AMD, and SIM cards) within the 3-year span analyzed, throwing not the best light on sustainable hardware security. For more information on these vulnerabilities, please see references [47–58] listed at the back of this book.

Below we provide short descriptions of the more notable hardware vulnerabilities related to secure hardware platforms in the recent past:

1. **Meltdown:**
   These major vulnerabilities affected many modern processors, including those used in secure hardware and secure enclaves. It allowed attackers to access sensitive data stored in the memory of other processes running on the same machine.
2. **Foreshadow:**
   This vulnerability, also known as L1 Terminal Fault (L1TF), affected Intel processors and allowed attackers to read data stored in a secure enclave.
3. **ZombieLoad:**
   This vulnerability affected Intel processors and allowed attackers to leak data stored in the processor's memory, including data from secure enclaves.
4. **Plundervolt:**
   This vulnerability allowed attackers to manipulate the voltage of a processor to inject faults and cause it to execute malicious code, including code running inside a secure enclave.
5. **MDS (Microarchitectural Data Sampling):**
   This vulnerability affected processors and allowed attackers to read sensitive data from other processes running on the same machine, including data from secure enclaves.
6. **Spectre (and its variants):**
   Spectre is another major vulnerability that affected many modern processors, including those used in secure hardware and secure enclaves. Several variants of the original Spectre vulnerability were unearthed since the original discovery, including Spectre v2, SpectreRSB, SpectreSWAP.... All allowed attackers to bypass security measures and gain access to sensitive data stored in secure enclaves.

Many of these vulnerabilities have been mitigated as good as possible through software updates and hardware modifications. It is important to understand that a software update allows to modify the vulnerable device, a hardware modification usually only fixes the problem in the next version of the device (like in smartphones or computers), meaning the affected device is "*unrecoverable*" and remains compromised.

The security validation of hardware devices is usually provided by certifications to increase trust in those devices.

FIPS 140–2 [182] is one such a standard that is quite common. FIPS 140–2, the Federal Information Processing Standard, is recognized as the standard that confirms the efficiency of cryptographic hardware. When a product holds a FIPS 140–2 certification, it is an assurance that the product has undergone rigorous testing and official validation by the United States and Canada. FIPS 140–2 has garnered global acceptance across governmental and non-governmental sectors alike. This widespread adoption attests to its practicality as a security benchmark and its reputation as a viable best practice in the field of cryptography. The four levels of security standard FIPS140-2 for cryptographic modules are defined as follows:

Level 1 necessitates the use of production-grade equipment and algorithms that have been tested externally.
Level 2 introduces additional requirements, such as physical tamper-evidence and role-based authentication. Any software implementations at this level must operate on an Operating System that is approved to Common Criteria at EAL2.
Level 3 imposes further conditions such as physical tamper-resistance, identity-based authentication, and the mandate for a physical or logical separation between the interfaces that allow "critical security parameters" to enter and exit the module. It is also required that private keys can only be transferred in and out in an encrypted form.
Level 4 escalates the physical security requirements even more. It necessitates tamper-active capabilities, which means the device must be capable of erasing its contents if it detects an array of environmental attacks.

CC EAL certification [181] is another such certification. An Evaluation Assurance Level (EAL) is a category ranking assigned to an IT product or system after a Common Criteria security evaluation. The level indicates to what extent the product or system was tested (Table 15.4).

Unfortunately, certifications are not always contributing the level of comfort that they were designed for. More on this topic will follow in the chapter on crypto primitives.

Therefore, it is recommended to be careful with relying too heavily on certifications. The Enron financial statements were also certified regularly….

Table 15.4 CC EAL levels

EAL Level	Description
EAL 1	Functionally tested
EAL 2	Structurally tested
EAL 3	Methodically tested and checked
EAL 4	Methodically designed, tested and reviewed
EAL 5	Semi-formally designed and tested
EAL 6	Semi-formally verified design and tested
EAL 7	Formally verified design and tested

Source Author based on EAL data

Any hardware-security-based approach for offline payments should hence always account in their disaster planning for a vulnerability in the deployed hardware during its life cycle, making an urgent full replacement of all devices necessary.

Let us look at some interesting stories since 2010.

Source Shutterstock

The RSA attack [45] from 2011, which started with a phishing email, is a good example as all RSA hardware tokens, deployed globally by banks and enterprises, had to be replaced. Credit Suisse, as part of the many affected businesses around the globe, did send me a new RSA token for a bank account too.

To further illustrate the gravity of the problem with hardware vulnerabilities, let us look at what Google published as key observation in their report on an attack on ARMs secure hardware *TrustZone* in 2017. ARM TrustZone technology offered a system-wide approach to security with hardware-enforced isolation built into the CPU. It provided that way a starting point for establishing a device root of trust based on Platform Security Architecture (PSA) guidelines:

> *"Unfortunately, the design issue outlined in this blog post is difficult to address, and at times cannot be fixed without introducing additional dedicated hardware or performing operations that risk rendering devices unusable."* [117]

These kinds of catastrophic consequences are not uncommon for the types of vulnerability of interest. They do not happen only once in a decade, as shown by ARM's competition.

In late 2015, Intel unveiled SGX (Software Guard eXtensions), a highly anticipated feature for its × 86 processors. SGX consists of a set of instructions that enable the execution of applications, or specific parts of an application, within a secure container known as an Enclave. Enclaves were intended to offer protection against other applications or privileged system software, including the operating system, hypervisor, or BIOS. This was supposed to bring enhanced security to devices by isolating critical code and data from potential threats or unauthorized access. Even Signal, the secure end-to-end encrypted messenger app, and its related Mobilecoin jumped on the bandwagon and announced that they would build the security of their coins and wallets on SGX.

In 2022, Intel made the decision to remove support for SGX (Software Guard eXtensions) in its 12th Generation Intel Core 11,000 and 12,000 processors. This change is reflected in the datasheets below published for the 11th and 12th generation of Core desktop processors, where SGX was listed as a deprecated technology and no longer available.

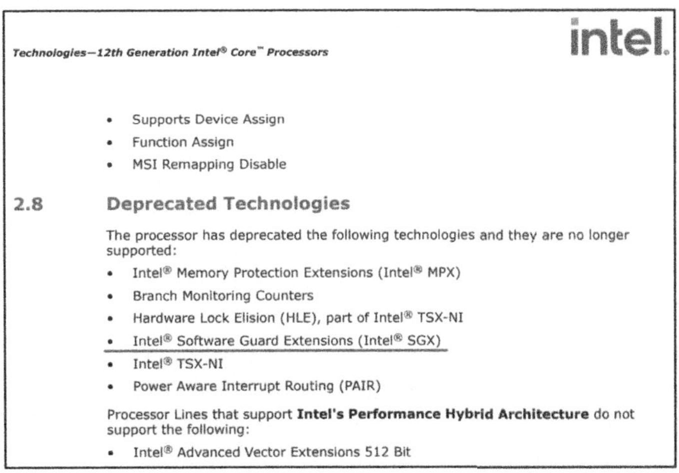

Technologies—12th Generation Intel® Core™ Processors

intel.

- Supports Device Assign
- Function Assign
- MSI Remapping Disable

2.8 Deprecated Technologies

The processor has deprecated the following technologies and they are no longer supported:

- Intel® Memory Protection Extensions (Intel® MPX)
- Branch Monitoring Counters
- Hardware Lock Elision (HLE), part of Intel® TSX-NI
- Intel® Software Guard Extensions (Intel® SGX)
- Intel® TSX-NI
- Power Aware Interrupt Routing (PAIR)

Processor Lines that support **Intel's Performance Hybrid Architecture** do not support the following:

- Intel® Advanced Vector Extensions 512 Bit

Source Intel Presentation

Intel discontinued support for SGX (Software Guard eXtensions) due to successful targeting by security researchers, who uncovered multiple vulnerabilities and attack methods. These discoveries had implications for Intel's brand and positioning as a leader in the security field and potentially raised liability concerns. Some examples of attacks that targeted Intel SGX include:

- Prime + Probe attack discovered in 2017.
- Spectre-like attack disclosed in 2018.
- Enclave attack discovered by researchers in 2019.
- MicroScope replay attack.
- Plundervolt injection attack.
- Load Value Injection (LVI).
- SGAxe attack on the CPU cache resulting in the leak of the enclave's content.

In the end, Intel had more to gain from abandoning SGX as the never-ending vulnerability publications harmed its reputation far worse than abandoning the technology.

For illustration purposes with regard to certification as seen before, the NIST **Certificate #3672 attesting** FIPS 140–2 was issued in 2020 by the NIST computer security resource center [120] (CSRC) for a product based on the Intel SGX technology we just reviewed. The found certificate referring to SGX is still active until June 17, 2025, despite SGX being broken and retired since 2022.

On May 26, 2023, a company of cybersecurity professionals [123] posted a video online, which showed how to hack into the popular Trezor T hardware wallet in their possession. Trezor T was breached by an unpatchable hardware vulnerability in the STM32 chip by STMicroelectronics, that allowed to dump the embedded flash and one-time programmable (OTP) data.

And the discovery of apocalyptic hardware vulnerabilities continues, as the writing on this book progresses. In the initial days of August 2023, a group of researchers made public their identification [189] of a fresh and potent transient execution attack named "Inception." This attack had the capability to divulge privileged secrets and sensitive data through unprivileged processes on all AMD Zen CPUs, including the most recent iterations. Importantly, this data leakage remained achievable even in cases where all previously established mitigations against well-known speculative execution vulnerabilities like Spectre, an important vulnerability which we encountered already earlier, and transient control-flow hijacks, such as Automatic IBRS, have been diligently implemented.

Intel, seemingly not wanting to be left without news coverage next to its competitors, made headlines around the same time. Researchers' findings [190] led to the conclusion that the majority of superscalar Intel CPUs were susceptible to an attack called "Gather Data Sampling," potentially exposing users' data across different security domains. It is important to note that the previously employed defense mechanisms were ineffective. Furthermore, the recent CPUs analyzed not only lacked robust security measures according to the report, but also exhibited more pronounced data leakage compared to older generations. This increased vulnerability made them easier targets for exploitation, as exemplified by instances of leaking secret encryption keys.

!!! Remember: Hardware security has a spotty track record when it comes to staying vulnerability-free over the technology's life span, and the worst aspect of it all is that in many cases, the security issues can simply not be fixed, as shown above in multiple examples. Device replacements are in most cases the only effective remediation. I hope the above listing is sufficiently exhaustive to bring home the potential risks of offline solutions.

15.4.15.6 Secure Software (only) as Solution for Offline Payments?

After reviewing the hardware situation in the previous sections, another approach that is offered in the market today consists of using secure software components.

These environments are supposed to provide virtual secure environments integrated into a digital device, without the need for physical components to be distributed or used. Installations can be done remotely, and updates can also be deployed in contrast to secure hardware, making such software-based solutions certainly more scalable than hardware-based solutions.

However, it's worth noting that software-based offline CBDC systems may be more susceptible to compromise by malware or tampering, as they rely solely on software, and reengineering of software is a lot easier to achieve than the reengineering of hardware.

Software-based trusted environments seem most fitting for trusted applications on smartphones. As we—the human species—have not managed to develop any secure software until this day, not for our smartphones nor for our computers, as is proven by the continuous need of up-to-date anti-virus and advanced threat protection software on all our devices to prevent malicious exploitation, we recommend a lot of caution with secure software solutions for offline payments.

Secure software solutions typically offer lower levels of tamper resistance than Secure Elements or Trusted Execution Environments. One way to secure the software solution further is to integrate it with the secure hardware that is present on the device. Unfortunately, that only lifts the security protection to the level of secure hardware with the described challenges above.

In between the hardware and software, we still find another layer that can cause problems: Firmware. Firmware is a type of software that is embedded into a hardware device, providing low-level control for the device's specific hardware. Firmware can be thought of as the intermediary software that facilitates communication between the hardware and the operating system in a computing device.

AMD fTPM is, like Intel's PTT, a firmware-based trust platform module that is an alternative to the physical TPM 2.0. In April 2023, a new class of attacks against these firmware trusted platform modules (fTPMs) was published in a paper called "faulTPM: Exposing AMD fTPMs' deepest secrets, [99]" in which the researchers show an attack compromising Intel's main competitor AMD's Secure Processor, which constitutes the trusted execution environment (TEE) for AMD's fTPMs.

Intel's competing PTT platform had already a vulnerability in 2018, when Intel performed a security review of its Intel PTT. As a result [122], Intel identified a similar vulnerability in the Intel PTT module that may allow information disclosure of certain Intel PTT data via physical access.

The discoveries of flaws in the secure hardware, software, and firmware just keep coming and that should also be the expectation going forward.

In both secure hardware and secure software, the entire supply chain poses another rather large attack surface and additional risks, as the most efficient attacks are those that happen at the beginning of the development process and that hence affect all devices. Remember the Solarwind supply chain attack of 2020, where criminal hackers deployed malicious code into Solarwind's software, which was then deployed by thousands of enterprises and government agencies worldwide.

Rather than breaking into a single device, compromising the chips, firmware, or software that go into all devices is significantly more efficient as it compromises not only one device but all of them. The unlimited pot of money to be stolen in case of a CBDC will motivate attackers of all kinds to participate in this challenge.

Also keep in mind, when talking about supply chain security, that most hardware chips are produced in East Asia, particularly in Taiwan and China, and that most software is provided by US companies. The issues related to this situation are easily illustrated by the accusations of stealing secrets, endangering national security, and lying to the US government raised [121] by the Americans against the Chinese tech company Huawei. The Americans fear Chinese backdoors in all of these Huawei devices, going as far as to ban them. The Chinese concerns are likely no different with regard to American technology like Apple's.

In summary: After reviewing secure hardware and secure software, which can help us protect fully offline payment operations, it must be understood that any hacker, successfully breaching his single offline CBDC device in the privacy of his basement, might also remove any and all limits that the device was pre-configured with, as well as potentially increase the available funds balance to an amount of his liking. It is therefore important to deploy a defense in-depth strategy to at least mitigate the impact and the speed at which fraud can take place. The central bank's threat model must also include an action item to react to every deployed offline device potentially being hacked and turned into a central bank printing press with unlimited potential.

This raises also the question about the liability of such attacks? Will the central bank absorb the losses itself, push them to users and merchants, or will it turn to the provider of the offline solution to recover the losses?

15.4.15.7 Addressing Fraud Retroactively

Let us now look how implementable the final option to make offline payment safe and usable is. Identifying cheating users retroactively, after network connectivity is restored, the transactions are uploaded, and the verification took place.

This verification process will flag the fraudulent transactions. These can be quickly assigned to the perpetrators in the case of a plain text CBDC system. In privacy-preserving systems with possible conditional deanonymization, the process will be longer with the judicial authorizations necessary prior to the subsequent identification.

If the system allows for fraudulent transactions to take place while the user is offline, the judicial and executive branches of government must be able to receive and handle the complaint volume, pursue the fraudsters, and attempt to recover the losses. This means the necessary hotlines are in place, and the necessary cops are ready and available to chase the fraudsters if the systems are supposed to gain the confidence of the users.

Now imagine offline devices with a transitive payment option (allowing multiple transactions) and unlimited subsequent offline payment transactions. This will blow up the problem complexity to a different level.

For illustration purposes, we will develop the above scenario in context with some developments out of California to provide you with a better basis to extrapolate how this may or may not work out.

In California, the amount of money in play to move a criminal charge from a misdemeanor (lesser criminal act) to a felony (crime of high seriousness) used to be US$450 until 2014. California then voted by referendum on November 4, 2014, on a new law called Proposition 47 [101]. The reasons for this law proposal were overflowing prisons, insufficient number of cops to deal with the 2014 crime volume and too many homeless people. The proposition was considered a good idea, even endorsed by the New York Times and the Los Angeles Times. The proposition passed successfully. By November 2015, California had reduced the state's prison population by 13′000 and was saving the state $150 million per year.

The proposition lifted the misdemeanor level from US$450 to US$950. As a consequence, large retailers in California [101] reported already in 2016, a larger than threefold increase in shoplifting. In addition to shoplifting, Proposition 47 also contributed by 2018 to a jump in car burglaries and other thefts in San Francisco.

Things did not improve since and in April 2023, the high-end grocery chain Whole Foods [102] closed its flagship store in San Francisco over employee safety concerns, and a months later, in May 2023, Nordstrom decided to shut down both of its downtown San Francisco stores. Since 2020, a total of 20 retailers in or near San Francisco's Union Square announced closures. Overall robberies were up 13% for 2023… with law enforcement unable to fight this "petty" crime surge.

So, based on what was just covered, let us try to summarize the potential consequences:

Offline payments and the track record of secure hardware raise the rather likely possibility of a central bank having to replace all the secure hardware elements provided to its citizens in case of a vulnerability. The old hardware may simply have to be thrown out and replaced with a new hardware in a time-sensitive manner. While this may still be financially digestible every 5–10 years in case of a $10 hardware token, it becomes totally inconceivable if personal smartphones or computers are affected by vulnerabilities in their hardware, like Intel, AMD, and ARM in the case of the Meltdown and Spectre vulnerabilities.

Secure software, as a possible alternative to secure hardware, is an even riskier undertaking and in the best case only brings us up to the risk profile of secure hardware described above.

Reducing fraud in a widely used offline rCBDC after the crimes happened, will be an intensive effort and the above illustration from California should at a minimum cause a reflection and not lead to overly optimistic scenarios.

Do we believe that our local law enforcement is equipped to address this unavoidable offline fraud problem that we might be facing? Can law enforcement reasonably identify the bad actors after the facts and then prosecute them in such a way that the victim recovers his/her money quickly?

Who will act in California if the fraud remains under US$950 per occurrence? If the past serves as guide and the individual incidents remain below US$950, it is unlikely much will happen on the prosecution side without the establishment of a significant future police staff increase to handle these cases expeditiously. And if the police and the judicial system cannot enforce lawful usage of an offline CBDC, it might spiral out of control quickly and turn into a large mess.

This brings us to the question of liability: Who is actually liable if a user gets defrauded with an inherently unsecure offline payment solution? Is he/she stuck with the loss personally or should that be a liability of the entity (i.e. the central bank or the provider) that introduced such a device? Should there be insurance for such cases, like with the FDIC? How complex will such constructs become?

Retail CBDC decision-makers must compare the risks and complications of introducing offline tools with just keeping cash for many of the offline scenarios. In countries that are well served with internet and mobile networks, the added value of offline payments should be especially scrutinized with regard to the potential risks and extra costs. Skipping offline functionality in developed economies would also be a further commitment to the future of physical cash and remove the related fears and conspiracy theories (see Sect. 12.5).

The recent large-scale earthquake in Turkey and Syria has shown that in such terrible disasters nothing other than physical cash is likely to remain usable. Even accessibility of cash becomes a challenge. An offline-enabled digital Turkish Lira would not have helped, would it?

Despite significant benefits possible in resilience, financial inclusion and real privacy, the risks of offline functionality must be recognized correctly by central banks because they have been mathematically proven, and mitigations for incidents must be planned and budgeted in the business case of a rCBDC solution.

!!! Remember:

1. If designed properly, offline rCBDC functionality could offer hard cash-like privacy and better resilience. Inclusion of people in unconnected areas can also be improved.

2. As it is mathematically proven that offline transactions cannot be 100% secure, central banks choosing that road should think about defense in depth, a CBDC insurance scheme, and other ways to handle the losses related to some unavoidable fraud.
3. Central banks should assume that, if breaking the restrictive computing element's security properties gives users the ability to access virtually unlimited funds, they will end up breaking it, as hardware (and software) protections tend to fall against well-equipped adversaries with plenty of time and expertise. "Everyone" will be interested in hacking an offline-enabled piece of hardware that is fully accessible in private in order to create his/her own portable "central bank printing facility."
4. A defense in-depth strategy (with hardware security modules, software integrity checks, transaction limits, ...) must be adopted in order to make it as hard as possible for hackers to succeed in exploiting a breach, and to keep the illegal outflows as limited as possible. For example, if a token does not accept more than €500 per transaction or €1000 per day, a "fully hacked" token may still generate unlimited funds but spending them has been constrained to €500 per transaction and throttled in time. This may give law enforcement a higher chance of catching up with the bad guys.

15.4.16 Micropayments

A micropayment refers to a monetary transaction involving minimal sums, even fractions of a penny. This feature can serve as a unique selling proposition (USP) for a retail Central Bank Digital Currency. Historically, the implementation of micropayments posed challenges due to high transaction costs tied to payment processors like credit card companies or PayPal, often charging between 20 and 30 cents per transaction, rendering transactions under $1 prohibitively costly.

Consider the following personal example to illustrate potential micropayment scenarios: In my frequent usage of Twitter, I often encounter interesting articles linked in tweets. However, upon clicking these links, I am often greeted by a paywall, asking for registration or credit card information. In every case, I leave the page. Now, imagine if instead of a paywall, a prompt appears requesting 10 cents to access the article, payable with a single click. This kind of convenience would certainly incentivize me to purchase and read all the articles that initially piqued my interest.

This kind of setup could potentially benefit writers and publishers struggling to maintain revenue streams in the face of dwindling subscriptions and the scraps of income gleaned from advertising giants.

The advent of the internet was meant to facilitate the explosion of micropayment-driven services, but this concept has been overshadowed by advertising-funded services for the past three decades. A well-designed rCBDC could potentially alter this trajectory.

Micropayments open up the possibility for pay-as-you-go models and can easily be integrated into the Internet of Things (IoT) and machine-to-machine transactions.

Machine-to-machine payments refer to automated transactions between machines' digital wallets, eliminating the need for human intervention. For instance, autonomous vehicles, industrial machinery, and other devices could utilize digital currency streaming to automatically handle real-time expenses, such as fuel, maintenance, road tolls, parking fees, and insurance.

!!! **Remember:** Microtransactions can be another USP for retail CBDCs. Until this day, existing payment solutions have not been able to compute small transactions (cents and fractions of a cent) fast and in an economically viable fashion.

Microtransactions will also quickly expand to the Internet of Things and machine-to-machine transactions, which will lead in turn to an explosion in the number of transactions and the need for rCBDC transaction performance numbers of a higher magnitude.

15.4.17 Cross-Border Payments

Cross-border payments are a new opportunity for rCBDCs, and the table below illustrates the frictions that CBDCs should address in the retail space (Graph 15.3).

I just want to take my attendance at the 2023 CBDC conference in Istanbul to illustrate the potential in addressing cross-border payments (also called foreign exchange) with a CBDC. Having landed at IST airport, I first went to a currency exchange vendor to procure some Turkish Lira for my Swiss Francs. The offer provided an exchange at an all-in cost (exchange rate plus fee) around 15%. I considered that a rip-off and decided that I would instead withdraw some money from a local ATM machine. I was quite surprised when the screen presented me with a 9% fee. I also refused that transaction and decided to rely on my credit card only. My Swiss bank,

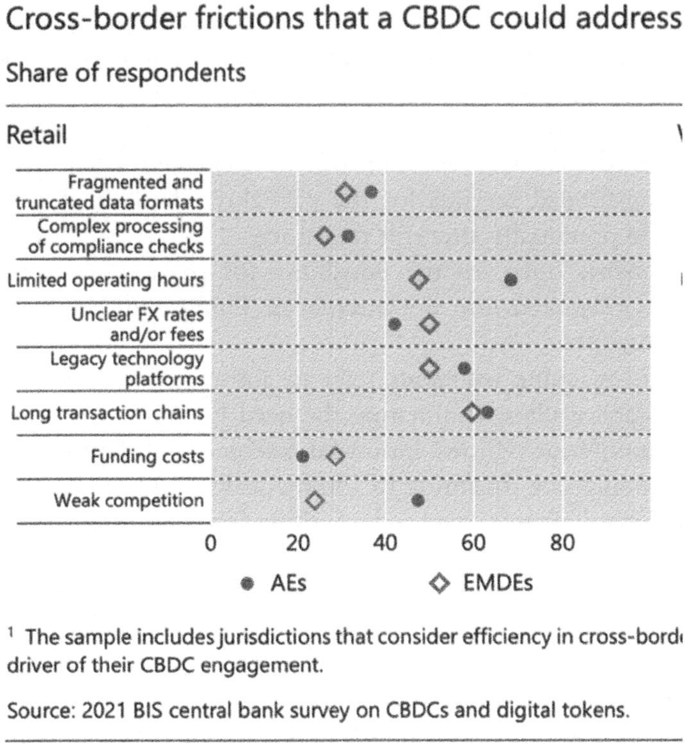

Graph 15.3 Cross-border frictions that rCBDC could address (*Note* The sample includes jurisdictions that consider efficiency in cross-border driver of their CBCD engagement. *Source* 2021 BIS central bank survey on CBDCs and digital tokens)

the credit card issuer, still charged me a fee of 1.75% per transaction and a mediocre exchange rate, while the merchant was hit with his share of fees.

According to a Citibank publication and the McKinsey Global Payments Map [194], consumer foreign exchange provides (mostly banks) a yearly revenue of $75 billion. This represents a massive one-third of all cross-border payment fees, because retail payments deliver much higher margins, despite their small share of only 2% in cross-border payments flows compared to 98% share for business-to-business cross-border payment flows. I hope these figures illustrate the amount of money in play cross-border, and why cross-border functionality is such a hot topic in the future of money technologies we are exploring. Below explains some of the reasons for the high costs.

Cross-border payments, which involve the transfer of money between different countries or regions, are generally expensive and complex due to the following factors:

1. **Weak competition with unclear FX rates and/or fees:**
   When making cross-border payments, currencies often need to be exchanged from one currency to another. Currency exchange rates can fluctuate, and financial institutions may charge fees or apply markups on the exchange rate, resulting in additional costs for the sender and the recipient. Competition on FX offerings is not necessarily available in all geographies and for all users.
2. **Complex processing and regulatory compliance checks:**
   Cross-border payments are subject to various regulations and compliance requirements in different countries. Financial institutions need to ensure that they comply with anti-money laundering (AML) and know-your-customer (KYC) regulations, which may involve additional documentation, verification, and reporting processes. Compliance with these regulations adds complexity and costs to international payments. Cross-border payments need to comply with sanctions and embargo laws imposed by the different countries involved in the transaction. This may involve additional screening and verification processes to ensure that the payment does not violate any sanctions or embargo laws, adding complexity and costs.
3. **Long transaction chains with intermediary banks:**
   Cross-border payments often involve multiple banks as intermediaries (also called correspondent banks—see insert below) in the payment process. Each bank may charge fees for processing the payment, and the payment may pass through several intermediary banks before reaching the recipient, resulting in delays and additional costs.
4. **Payment networks and clearing systems:**
   Cross-border payments may go through different payment networks and clearing systems, each with its own rules, protocols, and fees. This can add complexity to the payment process and result in additional costs.
5. **Time zones and limited operating hours:**
   Cross-border payments may face challenges related to different time zones and working hours in different countries. This can result in delays in processing and settling cross-border payments, adding complexity and costs.
6. **Technology and infrastructure:**
   Cross-border payments require reliable and secure technology and infrastructure to transfer funds across different countries. However, not all countries may have the same level of technological capabilities or infrastructure, and these different legacy technologies can result in delays, errors, and additional costs.

7. **Dispute resolution and customer support:**

   In case of any issues or disputes with cross-border payments, resolving them can be complicated due to different legal systems, languages, and jurisdictions involved. This can result in additional costs for dispute resolution and customer support.

   Resolving problems in cross-border payments can really be highly frustrating even between developed countries, as I have witnessed personally with an intra-Europe wire transfer late last year from Luxembourg to a Switzerland. The money left the account of the Luxembourg company, kept at Luxembourg sender bank BCEE, a day after the instructions were entered into the e-banking system. The money was debited and vanished…. It was then missing in the ether for a while.

   When the Swiss company complained about their unpaid invoice after 45 days the issue surfaced for the first time. It took an unimaginable number of people at the recipient bank UBS not being responsible, or not allowed to talk to me as I wasn't the recipient. My bank did not get any responses either to their inquiries and the recipient (the UBS customer) was told I needed to sort it out on my end. So much for a majorly dysfunctional support organization. 3 weeks of blame shifting, and some investigating finally located the money in a compliance holding account at the recipient bank UBS's subsidiary in Frankfurt, Germany. It was with UBS all along and took another month of calls and emails from both companies and the Luxembourg bank before the funds were released by UBS and the money finally hit the recipient's account at UBS Switzerland. This transaction from Luxembourg to Switzerland took over 3 months to settle and an explanation what happened or an apology for the mess are still missing. It would have been easier and cheaper—considering all the time spend on phone calls and emails—to drive the cash to Switzerland.

The Correspondent Banking System

The Correspondent Banking System is used for processing cross-border payments between different countries or regions. In this system, banks maintain correspondent relationships with each other to facilitate the transfer of funds on behalf of their customers. One bank, known as the correspondent bank, holds accounts on behalf of other banks, known as respondent banks, in different jurisdictions. Respondent banks rely on these correspondent banks to process payments on their behalf (Graph 15.4).

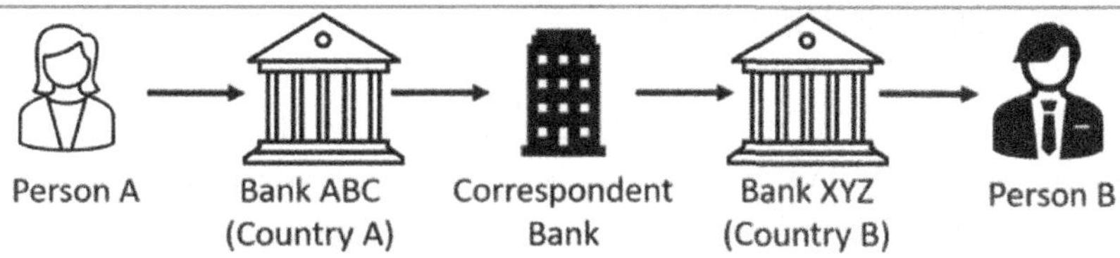

Graph 15.4 Correspondent banking (*Source* Author)

When a corporate or individual initiates a cross-border payment, their bank (the respondent bank) sends the payment instructions to their correspondent bank. The correspondent bank then processes the payment on behalf of the respondent bank, which includes settling the payment through various channels such as SWIFT (Society for Worldwide Interbank Financial Telecommunication) or local clearing systems. The correspondent bank may also provide foreign exchange services if needed, converting the funds into the appropriate currency for the recipient.

However, the correspondent banking system has some challenges. As mentioned earlier, it may involve sequential processing across multiple intermediaries, each with their own operating hours, messaging standards, and pre-funding requirements. This can result in delays, lack of transparency, and trapped balances in nostro/vostro accounts, which are accounts that correspondent banks hold with each other in different currencies. Nostro account means the bank's account with a correspondent bank and vostro the opposite. Moreover, the system may introduce settlement and credit risks, as well as additional transaction costs.

Despite these challenges, correspondent banking remains a key mechanism for facilitating cross-border payments, particularly for large-value transactions, and this offers a huge opportunity for innovation, disintermediation, and automation.

!!! **Remember:** Overall, the combination of many factors like currency exchange, regulatory compliance, intermediary banks, payment networks, time zones, sanctions laws, technology and infrastructure, and dispute resolution challenges can make cross-border payments expensive and complex for businesses and individuals alike. Qualified customer service personnel could a key ingredient to make the process somewhat smoother in case of issues. Cross-border transactions are one of the biggest prizes that can be harvested by a working CBDC solution, but they should not be considered a low hanging fruit.

15.4.18 Transaction Limits

A token- or value-based rCBDC will encourage a similar usage as cash, with limited amounts for daily use being carried around by individuals as means of payment. An account-based rCBDC could, for example, be restricted with holding limits and disincentives above certain thresholds to prevent its use as store of value.

Limits of different kinds have been in discussion in the different rCBDC projects around the world, to address the risks of fraud and money laundering on one side, and of bank disintermediation, where deposits move from the commercial banks to the central bank, on the other side.

Ideas include transaction limits on how much money can be wired into a rCBDC wallet or account, how much money can be held in a rCBDC and how much or how often can be transacted in a day, week, or month. Below are the limits according to the BIS [204] of some CBDC projects that are live in production or close to it (Table 15.5).

15.4.19 Auditability

The CBDC systems should be auditable with automated tools. Such tools for auditability can be developed and deployed with auditors or regulators, or these can be DLT analysis tools if the data is available and readable on chain. It should in any case be easy to conduct these regular or real-time audits to make sure that all the transactions are in order, the issued money corresponds to the reserves and so forth.

15.4.20 Know Your Customer (KYC) & Anti-Money-Laundering (AML)

KYC and AML checks are critical functions for every rCBDC system. The realization of these functionalities can be achieved in 2 different ways.

Should the central bank decide to go with a two-tier or hybrid setup, where the commercial banks will conduct the AML and KYC tasks, then it is necessary for the rCBDC system to integrate into the KYC and AML systems that the bank is already operating for its traditional business. No commercial bank will be interested in operating a second different KYC system for CBDC next to their traditional KYC system. That means the rCBDC system must offer the necessary APIs to make the required system integration simple.

Table 15.5 CBDC account/wallet transaction limit tiers

Jurisdiction	Basic CBDC account			Standard CBDC account		
	ID requirements	Transaction limits	Linked to bank account?	ID requirements	Transaction limits	Linked to bank account?
Bahamas	Phone number verified with one-time password	Wallets can hold up to 500 B$. Aggregate transaction value of 1,500 per month	No	Govt issued ID	Can hold up to 8000 B$. Aggregate transactions of 100,000 annually	No
China	Phone number verified with OTP	Single payment limit 2,000, daily cumulative limit 5,000, balance limit of 10,000 CNY	No	Govt issued ID	Cat 1: no limits with in-person ID verification; Cat 2 / Cat 3: single payment limit 5,000 / 50,000 CNY, daily cumulative limit 10,000 / 100,000 CNY, balance limit 20,000 / 500,000 CNY	Yes, but not for Category 3
Eastern Caribbean	Govt issued ID	1,000 EC$ per month	No	Govt issued ID	2,700 EC$ per month	Yes

Source BIS report FSI4 [204]

If the rCBDC is intent on operating a direct CBDC model without intermediaries, then the rCBDC system can either again integrate into a third-party KYC/AML tool provided by the central bank via procurement, or the rCBDC needs to be expanded with the necessary KYC/AML functionality inside the rCBDC system, which would represent significant additional development efforts on top of the rCBDC functionality.

15.4.21 Rights & Obligations

We have already touched on this subject in the chapter on offline usage, but it needs to be considered for the full scope of the project. It is very important to clearly define the roles and responsibilities of all actors in the CBDC ecosystem before launching it. What will the central bank be responsible for, what will the roles and responsibilities of the banks and/or financial intermediaries be, what will the responsibilities of the merchants be, and finally what responsibilities will remain with the users?

Who will be liable for what if something goes wrong? As we have seen before, who will absorb the loss in the case of a fraudulent offline transaction? The merchant who accepted the higher risk offline payment, or the bank respectively the central bank who own and operate the system and signed off on the implemented (maybe flawed) design?

Is a conceptually equivalent of the U.S. Federal Deposit Insurance Corporation (FDIC) for bank deposits necessary to insure the digital money in the wallets against fraud? Who would fund this new organization? Would it be the customers via the bank profits like in the case of the FDIC? How would it work in each of the design options?

All these questions need to be answered and communicated clearly before a CBDC is even launched.

15.4.22 Kill Switch: Nice to Have?

Last but not least is the requirement for an emergency kill switch, for a red button, that will stop the system, preventing any new transactions and initiate an organized, automated return of rCBDC in circulation in exchange for bank deposits or cash.

Unless this scenario is planned, the features programmed, the business processes designed and crisis management communication and responsibilities defined, any major breach could turn whole countries into utter chaos.

This is not an item to ignore in a rCBDC project where large portions of the population are affected.

15.5 Platform Support/Form Factors

When it comes to introducing a rCBDC, here is a list of form factors that could be considered for such a project launch (Graph 15.5).

The first form factor and the oldest on the list is the feature phone, which does not have internet capabilities. The feature phone solution will have to be an "additional" system next to the DLT or digital token system, because such a device cannot handle the necessary features of a CBDC token or a private signing key. It can only operate via SMS or USSD or by calling certain numbers and placing the payment order in an intermediated centralized or cloud solution.

The Android and iOS smartphones will most likely be the #1 digital payment devices. They will be able to operate via links, QR codes, Bluetooth or NFC with a digital wallet installed. They work great for P2P and P2B in stores. They are not ideal for conducting mobile e-commerce transactions, because they are unable to scan a QR code shown on their own displays. Smartphones are, on the other hand, well suited to scan QR codes that are displayed for e-commerce in a computer's browser.

Wallets in laptops and desktops may be a solution for e-commerce, but browser wallet plug-ins may be a better and more usable solution to

Graph 15.5 Form factors for CBDC (*Source* Author)

conduct e-commerce on your computer or laptop. The plug-ins will need to be compatible with the main browsers in use today, like Chrome, Edge, Safari, Firefox, …. Such a set up will make it unnecessary for consumers to need both a computer and a smartphone in order to conduct e-commerce transactions.

Cloud hosted solutions are another approach to rCBDCs with custodial wallets. This nevertheless comes with a centralization of all keys/assets in a central web-service and necessitates full trust in the operator. This central storage of all keys/assets also makes it the riskiest form factor and an attractive target for attackers.

Smart cards can be used online but are mostly mentioned when offline payments are a subject. We have reviewed them in detail in the secure hardware chapter. The cost of such devices can be significant with a Whispercash smart card costing US$70 [163] for example or a Ledger cold wallet costing around €150 [164].

Wearables like smartwatches are another possible form factor, and the success of the Apple wallet on their smartwatches is a good illustration of the potential of these devices.

Internet of Things (IoT) and embedded devices are the next frontier, introducing instant machine-to-machine payments with microtransactions (down to fractions of a cent) and with pay-as-you-go models. For example, the IOTA DLT focuses on IoT and in the non-DLT space, the GNU Taler solution can serve as example, where a project to port their payment token technology onto embedded devices for IoT was funded by a European government.

15.6 Technologies for Payment Initiation

The technologies that can enable payments for retail activities for citizens are the following:

<u>QR codes</u>

QR stands for quick response. It is a machine-readable code consisting of an array of black and white squares, typically used for storing URLs or other information for reading by a camera on a smartphone or computer. QR codes are probably the technology with highest potential because of the low cost, ease of use, simplicity, and ubiquity.

QR codes can be static or dynamic.

Source Author

NFC

NFC stands for Near Field Communication. NFC functionality is becoming more and more standard on new higher end smartphones. It will probably take a little longer before it will be available on any smartphone device.

NFC is a subset of RFID technology and uses radio waves to communicate data wirelessly. RFID is a technology that uses its radio waves to identify and track objects. It consists of a reader, which sends a signal to a tag or transponder, and the tag responds with information. RFID tags can be passive (no battery) or active (powered by a battery), and they can communicate over a longer range than NFC tags.

NFC, on the other hand, operates on the same frequency (13.56 MHz). However, NFC is designed for communication over very short distances (typically a few centimeters), and it is used primarily for contactless payments, access control, and data transfers between two devices.

Bluetooth/BLE

Bluetooth is available on most smartphones today and can handle a lot of data, but quickly consumes battery life. Bluetooth Low Energy (BLE) is used for applications that do not need to exchange large amounts of data and can run on very little battery power.

Invoice by Payment Link

An invoice payment link is a simple way to request payment from clients paying for goods and services. It is basically a "Pay Now" or "Pay Invoice" button which will be included in an email sent to customers with the invoice due.

RFC 8905 [100] is a standard that defines a "payto" Uniform Resource Identifier (URI) scheme to designate targets for payments. A unified URI scheme for all payment target types allows applications to offer user interactions with URIs that represent payment targets, simplifying the introduction of new payment systems and applications. A simple click on the link will populate the full payment instructions in your e-banking app for example. It is the payment equivalent to the "mailto" URI for emails, where clicking on it opens your email application and puts the recipient in the TO: field.

USSD Codes

USSD stand for Unstructured Supplementary Service Data and USSD codes can be used for payment processing. It involves initiating a transaction by sending a text message to a designated service provider. Upon receiving the text message, the service provider takes the necessary action, such as charging the purchase amount to an online payment system or adding it to the user's phone bill. Once the payment is processed, the merchant releases the goods or services, and the funds are transferred to the company's account. For digital goods, Multimedia Messaging Service (MMS) is commonly used to deliver files along with SMS. If the purchase is for a physical item, the receipt may be sent through SMS or MMS.

15.7 Forms of Retail CBDC

rCBDCs can take different forms and we will attempt to provide a good insight into how these different models may look like, what they are based upon and how we can best assess their advantages and downsides.

Based on a recent study by the IMF, all six current pilots and projects for rCBDCs fall into the "intermediated" category [165]. The CBDC Tracker by the Atlantic Council (2022) further reveals that out of 119 ongoing projects, none are actively pursuing the unilateral model, with 75 still remaining undecided. It is hence likely that any operational CBDC will probably resemble the "intermediated model" the closest.

Below are the models that we see for rCBDC projects and implementations:

15.7.1 Synthetic CBDC Model

The synthetic model, although not a true CBDC, involves the issuance of currency by a private sector entity, such as a stablecoin or an e-money issuer, with the currency being their liability. However, the currency is backed by central bank funds. Central banks handle wholesale payments between e-money issuers and/or other banks (Graph 15.6).

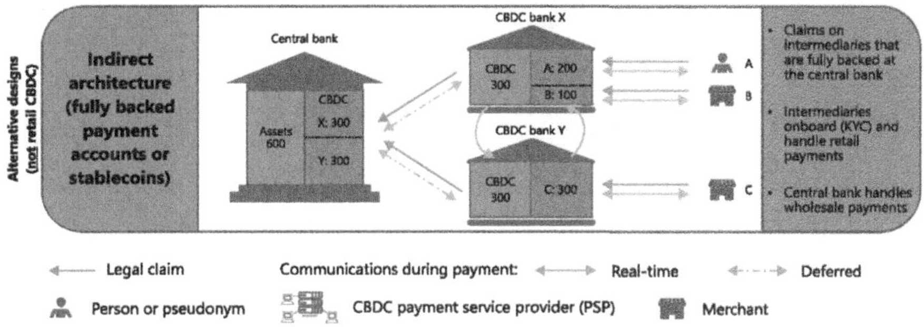

Graph 15.6 Synthetic CBDC model (*Source* BIS)

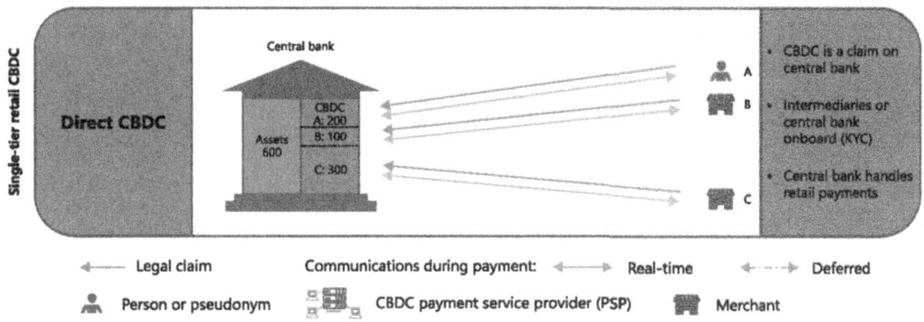

Graph 15.7 Direct CBDC model (*Source* BIS)

15.7.2 Direct CBDC Model

The direct rCBDC model refers to a unilateral approach where the central bank manages all necessary operating functions for currency within its own organization (Onboarding, KYC, AML, …). This involves real-time payment handling and maintaining the necessary records to keep the system running, with the rCBDC being exclusively the central bank's liability (Graph 15.7).

15.7.3 Two-Tier Hybrid CBDC Model #1

The hybrid rCBDC model #1 represents an intermediate solution that enables direct claims on the central bank while real-time payments are processed by intermediaries. Under this framework, the central bank maintains a record of all retail CBDC holdings, which allows for the transfer of holdings from one payment service provider to another in the event of a technical malfunction (Graph 15.8).

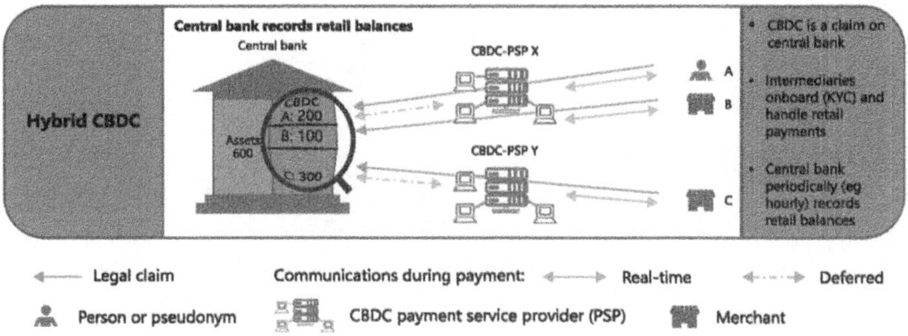

Graph 15.8 Two-tier hybrid CBDC model 1 (*Source* BIS)

15.7.4 Two-Tier hybrid CBDC Model #2

In the second two-tier hybrid model, the currency is issued by and is a liability of the central bank, but the operational roles of onboarding incl. KYC are assigned to intermediaries. Instead of a manual issuance of series of CBDC, here the central bank operates the central system which automatically and on demand issues rCBDC (up to a certain total limit) against incoming funds from the end-user's bank account directly to the end-user's wallet and in real-time updates the ledger of spend tokens by end-users. This model does not change any of the processes for money issuance and supply in place prior to the launch of the rCBDC—they remain exactly as they were before. The rCBDC system will only issue and retire rCBDC automatically on demand (against commercial money, cash, or reserves) in real-time up to an optional limit, that can be set by the central bank. This set up is fully automated and without human interaction, just as the RTGS systems of today (Graph 15.9).

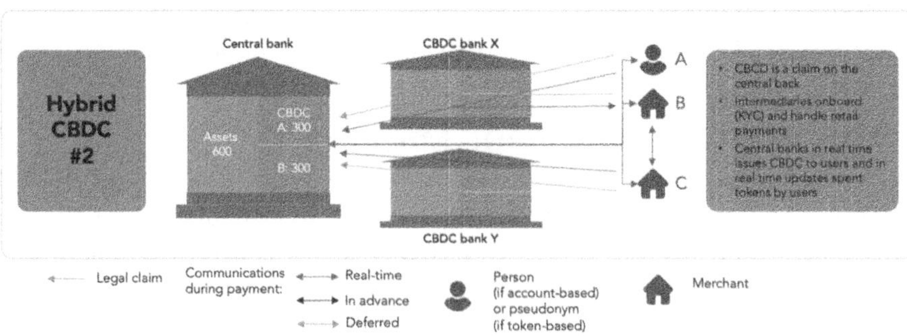

Graph 15.9 Two-tier hybrid CBDC model 2 (*Source* Author)

15.7.5 Two-Tier Hybrid CBDC Model #3

In the third two-tier hybrid model, the currency is issued by and is a liability of the central bank, but some or all operational roles are assigned to intermediaries. The central bank issues rCBDC to banks, who store it to respond to demand, ask for more, or return it. This is a direct digital copy of the physical bank note process. This rather manual process involves the central bank teams specifically defining and issuing series and/or denominations, that are then distributed to banks for further distribution to end-users based on demand. The process of defining and issuing banknotes is not automated and does not take full advantage of today's automation possibilities in the digital world. Here the central bank needs to define new processes for rCBDC issuance and monitor the stocks of unremunerated rCBDC at the participating banks, which need to be kept around the clock (cannot be redeposited overnight) because of the 365/7/24 nature of a rCBDC (Graph 15.10).

15.8 Architectures

According to the BIS central bank survey results of 2021 [4] shown below, most central banks clearly foresee a role for the private sector in their retail CBDC projects.

Nearly 80% also see integration with existing payment systems as part of their project. The survey does not specify if this will exclude a new sovereign independent payment rail for the CBDC next to existing private payment or if it will involve both.

The #1 role for the private sector seen by the central banks is the onboarding of clients with KYC, the central banks certainly not wanting to get involved with the individual users to get them onto the system. This was

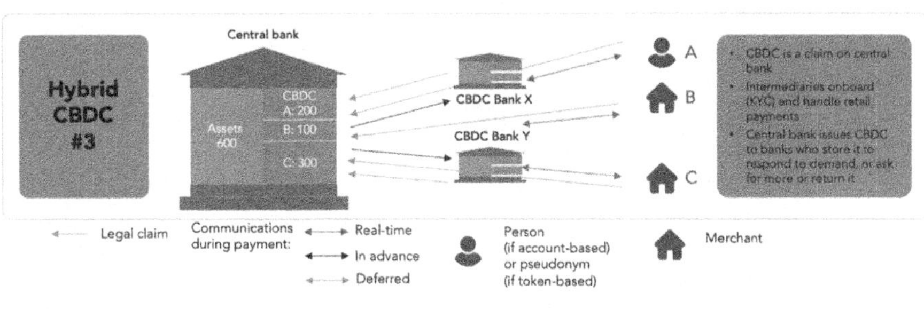

Graph 15.10 Two-tier hybrid CBDC model 3 (*Source* Author)

well illustrated in the survey by the BIS [200] and reflected in the 2 Graphs 15.11 and 15.12.

The next graph based on a BIS original [199] maps out four possible combinations of whether a CBDC infrastructure is distributed or centralized (with a combination of both also possible in a hybrid model) and whether the system is account/register based (accessible via identification/authentication) or token/value based (accessible via possession of a bearer coin or a private payment key). All four combinations are possible for any rCBDC infrastructure (no matter if direct, indirect, or hybrid), but in the different architectures, the central bank and the private sector operate different parts of the respective infrastructure.

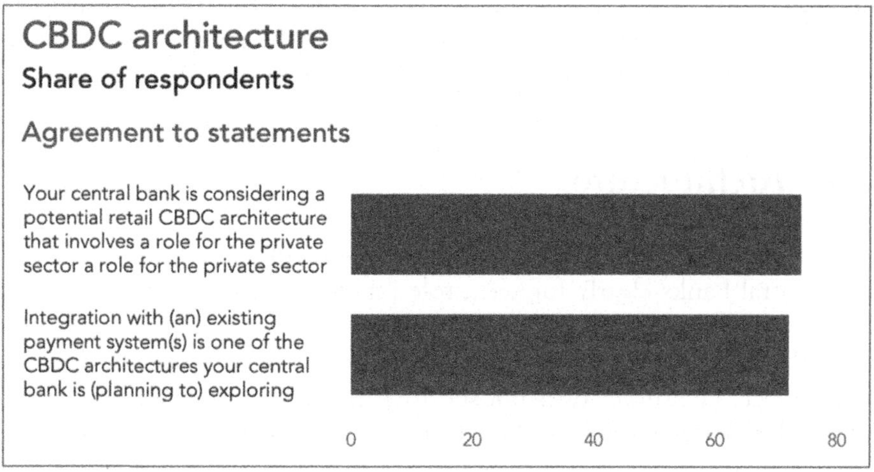

Graph 15.11 CBDC architecture (*Source* Data from BIS [4])

Graph 15.12 Role for the private sector (*Source* Data from BIS [4])

The 4 combinations depicted, numbered by white number in black circles, will be re-used in several of the following graphs. Just remember that anywhere you see these white numbers 1–4 in black circles, across this Sect. 15.8, they refer to Graph 15.13.

We now apply a different view to the 4 combinations and start with the bearer instrument view. As we have seen in previous chapters, with a bearer instrument, possession of the physical instrument is equivalent to ownership of the money it is associated with. Cash is the best example of a bearer instrument, as whoever holds the banknote can spend it.

Category 1 corresponds to traditional bank accounts, accessed through identification.

Category 2 corresponds to pure tokens (no DLT).

Category 3 corresponds to a new category, based on a DLT but accessed via identification (hence similar to accounts where identification is necessary for access).

Category 4 corresponds most to the traditional blockchains, where possession of a private key is necessary and sufficient for access.

In the digital payment space, the GNU Taler token of Category 2 is probably the most proverbial bearer instrument, emerging from the first eCash token 30 years ago. Whoever holds a valid (=unspent) GNU Taler token is the owner of such token and can spend it.

Ethereum (ETH) or Bitcoin (BTC) with self-custody (Category 4) are considered bearer instruments, as ownership of the token is determined by whoever possesses the private payment key.

But, if Ethereum or Bitcoin are used with custodial (third-party) custody, then the owner needs to access his account at the custodian first (hence no

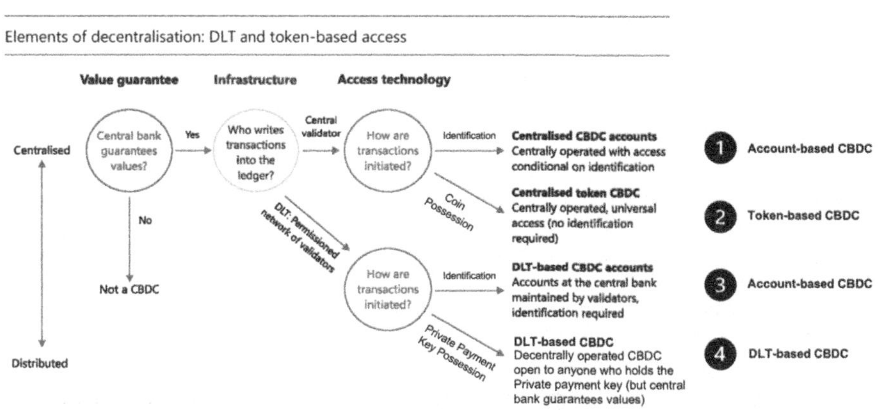

Graph 15.13 Account, DLT or Token-based access (*Source* Author's adaptation of a BIS model [199])

longer a bearer instrument), who will then access the private payment key on his system in the account and then, on behalf of the owner, execute the transaction. For us, these systems qualify as account-based systems. In the graph above, this is a variant of 3, where identification is necessary to access the DLT (here via identification by a custodian, in permissioned DLT-based CBDC with a newly defined authentication process).

Another important difference that we want to make here is the fact that account-based CBDC systems (like banking systems) can carry negative balances, while value-based tokens, like GNU Taler, and DLT-based tokens, like ETH and BTC, can only carry positive values (Graph 15.14).

An additional differentiation can come from the fact that some tokens can be used in disintermediated form (no need for an intermediary), such as cash or a fully offline CBDC token. Others again are intermediated, like GNU Taler, eCash… where a validation takes place prior to the transaction getting executed.

Some of these tokens can be unlinkable (like the GNU Taler, Zcash, Monero, Platypus…) which is a key characteristic for real/hard privacy, while others like BTC, ETH are pseudonymous and hence linkable.

At the bottom of Graph 15.13, you find back the numbers linking the 6 types to the 4 categories established earlier in Graph 15.12.

Table 15.6 attempts to summarize the key benefits and major issues that the different options offer. We have grouped them into 4 CBDC categories from Graph 15.12 based on the previous chapters of this book:

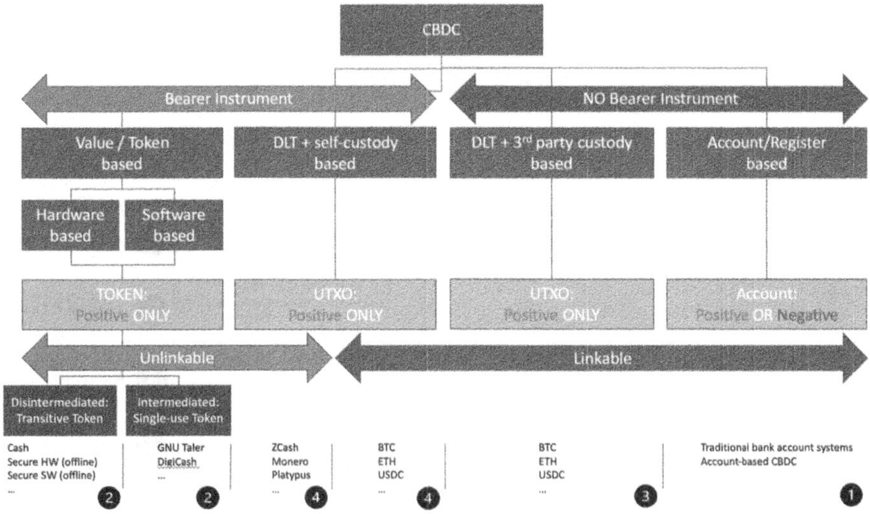

Graph 15.14 Linkable and unlinkable bearer instruments (*Source* Author)

Table 15.6 Comparison of technology options

	(1) Traditional Payment System	(3) (4) Distributed Ledger Technology	(2) Software Bearer Token	(2) Hardware Bearer Token
Key Benefits	Efficiency (domestic) Time to market	• Resilience • Programmability • Cross-border governance	• Privacy • Efficiency • Cost • Micropayments • Scalability • Programmability	• Offline payments • Privacy
Major Issues	Privacy Innovation Financial inclusion Private gardens Centralized No offline	• Efficiency • Privacy • Smart contract complexity • Scalability • No offline	• Untrusted offline mode (secure HW mitigates) • Centralized (DLT option mitigates)	• Security • Upgradability • Cost

Source Author

- Traditional payment system, like those in use today.
- DLT solutions.
- Software bearer tokens, which can exist either online, offline or as a combination of both. They can be realized with a centralized database or with a DLT back-end as options.
- Hardware bearer tokens, which are usually an offline payment solution. They are considered "fully offline" in this table.

15.9 Adoption

Ensuring adoption is critical to success in the case of a rCBDC. A consumer solution that does not gain widespread acceptance is doomed. As some of the early examples of CBDC have shown, adoption is not an easy goal to reach.

A retail CBDC needs to attract both users and merchants in parallel streams. Significant user sign-up without sufficient merchants that accept the rCBDC will lead to failure, as well as too many merchants without the necessary customers to provide a return on the setup investment in the new technology. Merchants will obviously line up with success and customer demand, but no initial success is possible without sufficient merchants and/or government services onboarded on launch day.

Let us explore what a central bank can do to facilitate adoption of its CBDC initiative.

Table 15.7 Staffing of CBDC projects

Central bank & project	Team size
Central Bank of the Bahamas—SandDollar	15
Bank of Canada	50
People's Bank of China—e-CNY	300
Eastern Caribbean Centra Bank—DCash	12
Riksbank—e-krona	20

Source Data from [165]

15.9.1 Train Central Bank Staff

It is important to train the central bank staff in the general subject of CBDCs, so that they understand all the possibilities and risks that a CBDC introduction can bring. This will allow them to make informed decisions on the use cases and features that are desired by the citizens and the central bank. They can pre-select use cases and a feature set that they believe is best suited for the country. In April 2023, the Bank of England started hiring 30 people for the digital pound project [64]. Below is a Table 15.7 with data [165] that shows the teams that were deployed on some other rCBDC projects.

15.9.2 Define a Value Proposition for Users and Merchants

Understanding your local payments market through interaction with merchants and users will provide insight on the challenges faced by all stakeholders in that environment of current digital payments. Based on those findings, validate or revise the pre-selection, determine the targets for the project and the new additional value propositions that the CBDC solution will have for the users and merchants you want to attract. They both need good and tangible reasons to switch away from the existing incumbents and their payment solutions. For example, in developed markets with good existing payment solutions, spender privacy at a higher level could be a differentiator and unique value proposition (USP). For merchants, no or low fees and no compliance challenges like PCI-DSS could be a USP. Merely replicating the features of existing digital payment systems will not attract users, nor will it contribute to further financial inclusion.

It is also very important to analyze and understand how the conceived solution (different designs will have different impacts) will impact and benefit the different segments of society, for example the poor and elderly, those in areas with poor connectivity, and those that wish to stay with physical cash.

These items need to be understood and communicated clearly prior to the launch of a CBDC project, no matter where we are geographically.

15.9.3 Define Operating Model with the Central Bank

The operating model and the costs that will be allocated to the different stakeholders in the CBDC ecosystem are an important aspect, that can make the difference between success and failure. No or low costs for users and merchants seems to be a safe bet here, fund the solution with the savings from less cash expenses and the extra seigniorage that the CBDC will bring in.

Is a synthetic, one-tier or two-tier CBDC operating model desired? The banks and payment service providers must be integrated accordingly in a way that creates value for them as well.

If the introduction of a CBDC is supposed to bring benefits to users and merchants, it will have to come at the expense of the current financial intermediaries. The existing players like Visa, Mastercard, card issuing banks, etc. will likely use all their lobbying power to prevent any loss of business, so be prepared for it. The benefits of a sovereign alternative in payment infrastructure should be worth fighting for.

15.9.4 Define the CBDC Business Processes with the Central Bank

The processes defined in the rCBDC solution must be validated with the central banks and fit into the local environment. For example, does the central bank desire a digital copy of their physical cash creation (series, # of notes per denomination, etc.) and of the distribution processes (distribution of digital cash to banks, and management of available denominations per bank, …)?

Or does the central bank want to maximize the full digitization potential and launch a CBDC that operates automatically and on demand without human intervention, similarly to their RTGS systems, where the only human input may be a limit on the maximum of rCBDC that can be issued? All scenarios, manual or automated, must be designed, approved, and tested in detail by the project team.

15.9.5 Verify the User Features and Benefits with Both Users and Merchants

Test the actual features with the users and the merchants in proofs of concept and pilots. Be careful with the results of other's surveys as the quality of the insights depends too much on the quality of the questions asked as we have seen in Sect. 12.6. Merchants can be helped in driving adoption by making the CBDC a legal tender and possibly even going one step further to a cash$^+$ legal tender and legislating that merchants must accept the new CBDC next to the existing private payment rails. Making acceptance mandatory is a dangerous approach if it displaces the competition and the solution is not a well-designed, privacy-preserving CBDC. Only then the customers can decide on the payment method they like to use. That will drive competition and prevent oligopolistic actions from the large incumbents of the payments space.

Disbursing government funds (like social security, children's allowances, ...) via CBDC may be another good way to get the ball rolling with regard to user sign-ups.

15.9.6 Ensure Users Have, and Recognize, Significant Benefits over Existing Solutions

This may include education and sponsored trials to bring the solution close to the citizens and to get them to try it. Using it and experiencing the USPs firsthand may go a long way in driving adoption. If the citizens are afraid of "Big Brother's Digital Dollar" and there are no hard facts to dispel the attacks as lies, then citizens will not even trial the solution and the outlook for a successful deployment are bleak.

15.9.7 Ensure the Role for the Financial Sector with Some New Upsides

Make sure the commercial banks are involved in the process, as the consensus seems to converge on a two-tier model where the commercial banks do the onboarding with KYC, AML, and CFT and that they have an opportunity to add value-added services on top of the basic CBDC features to compensate for eventual losses in their traditional deposit business. Do not expect to only rely on existing financial intermediaries and expect to progress on the financial inclusion side.

15.9.8 Define a Step-by-Step Roll-out Plan with Optional Accelerators

The roll-out plan should be a step-by-step model, where during a pilot more and more users are being onboarded while the system is being tested and the fit of the features is validated through real productive usage. This allows for early insights and quick adjustments if unforeseen challenges turn up. The Chinese are doing this well and successfully with the e-CNY, even though maybe the adoption of e-CNY is slower than the PBOC had wished for at the moment.

As the existing projects have clearly demonstrated that fast adoption is not a given, incentive programs should be planned, and even giving interest on CDBC deposits should not be excluded as a possibility to enhance take up.

15.9.9 Have a high-Quality Support Structure with Call Centers Available to Support

With better response times than what we all have come to expect from current call centers with 20 minutes waits and bad service a common occurrence, it is very important for a new CBDC to have multi-channel support (phone, email, chat…) that is highly skilled and readily available when something goes wrong. This can provide a lot of comfort in the early days and should be worth its investment in gold. Also important here is to make sure that law enforcement is ready and prepared to act swiftly in the new situation.

15.9.10 Marketing and Education Plans for Users and Merchants

Marketing has to start long before the first pilots go live. As surveys have shown, it is not unusual for more than 50% of all citizens to be unaware of CBDC efforts in European countries.

Therefore, the marketing must start as soon as the decision for a CBDC is taken and it should start with general education. Information should be disseminated across all channels, from road shows, brochures, internet, and special events like giveaways and lotteries.

If the CBDC design is bad or unspecified, the American equivalent of "Big Brother's Digital Dollar" criticism may take over the airwaves and that could spell the end of any adoption hopes in the near term. A successful project will know how to preempt that with the right design and the necessary commitments to make such attempts look foolish. If the project offers real privacy, make that clear to the privacy activists and civil liberties unions and enroll them in the communications effort from the start to preferably avoid a highly visible "Big Brother's Digital Dollar" communications disaster as in the United States.

Education should start across the geographic roll-out area as soon the solution is launched, maybe even in the pre-launch period with some "free" money for participants, and further incentives for them in a train the trainer model. Think about pre-launch communities that could be a fertile spreading ground, like universities and high schools.

The marketing and education efforts must continue without interruption and across the spectrum until the desired adoption numbers are reached.

For example, in fall 2020, the PBOC launched a lottery giveaway in Shenzhen, where they distributed rCBDC red packets worth 10 million yuan to residents. Giving gifts of cash in small red envelopes known as "red packets" is common in China. Residents had to register online and were randomly awarded 200 yuan each. To claim their prize, recipients had to sign up for the rCBDC digital wallet app, and during the one-week trial, they were able to spend their funds at over 3,000 local shops that were accepting the rCBDC. The outcome of the trial revealed that 1.9 million residents applied, and 8.8 million yuan were awarded in more than 62,000 transactions, demonstrating a high adoption rate and success as a new payment method. Similar lottery-style tests were conducted in other Chinese cities, like Shanghai (350′000 red packages of 55 yuan) and Beijing.

15.9.11 Monitor Adoption

It is important to monitor adoption from day 1 with anonymized and aggregate data regarding user conversions to rCBDC, rCBDC transaction volumes, rCBDC transaction value, and results from customized surveys on subjects like user demographics. Go back to point 10 (Marketing) and make the necessary incremental messaging, incentive and product adjustments (see e-CNY approach) if adoption is not satisfactory.

During the 6-month pilot of the Uruguayan e-Peso in late 2017, data indicated that the main use case was person-to-person transactions between users. Additionally, the data revealed that users were interested in more cost-effective digital money options. The study's findings [108] provided valuable insights into specific market segments that the central bank of Uruguay could have focused on to increase adoption rates in the case of a roll-out.

In conclusion: Be aggressive and do not fall for the fallacy of believing that a central bank must already plan measures that will keep adoption under control and prevent disintermediation of private payment solutions before it is even launched. No rCBDC has so far come anywhere near an uptake that would hurt banks or payment providers, not even in the most successful example of China. Too much success is not a problem likely to become reality. It is nevertheless great to see that fast adoption of payment solutions is possible if things are done correctly, as recently demonstrated by the success implementation of the fast payment solution PIX in Brazil.

Make sure the solution is fit for purpose, easy to use, and is adding significant value. You must avoid the reputation of mass surveillance tool. Analyze the needs, plan well, communicate in abundance, involve all the stakeholders from the start, execute accordingly, monitor the evolution, and adjust the efforts based on a continuous feedback loop. This hopefully will get you to a successful launch and into a continuously strong uptake by users.

16

Architecting a Wholesale CBDC

Wholesale CBDCs (abbreviated wCBDC) are designed for use by a select number of important financial institutions (with most central banks providing access to a number of financial institutions ranging from 10 to 5000 depending on the country), which are allowed to keep a central bank reserve account at the central bank, used for interbank payments and settlements.

16.1 Objectives of a Wholesale CBDC

Annually, large multinational companies transfer over US$23 trillion across countries, which is equivalent to around 25% of global GDP [63]. However, the wholesale cross-border payment processes they currently rely on are suboptimal in terms of cost, speed, and transparency. These processes result in transaction costs/payment fees exceeding US$120 billion per year [63]. Additionally, hidden costs, from liquidity being trapped and settlements being delayed on average by 2–3 days, need to be absorbed as well.

The challenges faced by large corporates in cross-border transactions stem from gaps in the existing correspondent infrastructure setup and inconsistencies in legal, regulatory, and operational frameworks across multiple jurisdictions. These pain points can be summarized as follows :

L. V. Schumacher, *Decoding Digital Assets*, https://doi.org/10.1007/978-3-031-54601-3_16

1. Correspondent banking system:
   The details of the correspondent banking system were introduced in Sect. 15.4.17. The lack of interoperability among payment infrastructures in different countries necessitates the use of correspondent banking for cross-border payments. This involves sequential processing across multiple intermediaries, each with their own operating hours, messaging standards, and pre-funding requirements and hence payment processing becomes uncertain, lacks real-time transparency, and sometimes balances get trapped in nostro/vostro accounts. On top, settlement and credit risks with several counterparties are introduced into the process.
2. Legal, regulatory, and operational consistency:
   Varied legal and regulatory requirements related to AML and CFT, as well as differing operational windows of domestic payment infrastructures, add to transaction costs and time delays. These lacks of consistency across jurisdictions create the large complexity in cross-border transactions.

Overall, these challenges in the correspondent infrastructure setup and legal, regulatory, and operational frameworks contribute to the suboptimal cost, speed, and transparency in cross-border payment processes for corporates, leading to inefficiencies and hidden costs. Addressing these issues would require coordinated efforts among stakeholders, including financial institutions, regulators, and technology providers, to streamline processes, enhance transparency, and improve cross-border payment experiences for corporates.

In this environment, central banks are investigating wholesale Central Bank Digital Currency (wCBDC) solutions for several reasons:

1. **Improving payment systems:**
   Wholesale CBDC solutions can potentially enhance the efficiency, security, and resilience of payment systems used by financial institutions. By leveraging blockchain or Distributed Ledger Technology (DLT), wholesale CBDCs could enable faster, cheaper, and more transparent interbank transactions, reducing settlement risks and costs associated with traditional payment systems.
2. **Exploring new monetary policy tools:**
   Wholesale CBDCs could provide central banks with new monetary policy tools. For example, central banks could use wCBDCs to implement more precise and effective monetary policies, such as real-time adjustments to interest rates or targeted liquidity management, to influence the money supply and promote financial stability. This could be achieved through

programmable features of wCBDCs and direct connectivity to financial institutions.

(a) Smart contracts: wCBDCs could be designed using smart contracts, which are self-executing computer programs that run on a blockchain or distributed ledger technology. Smart contracts can be programmed to automatically trigger certain actions or conditions when predefined criteria are met. For example, a smart contract embedded in a wCBDC could be designed to adjust interest rates or liquidity levels based on specific macroeconomic indicators, such as inflation, GDP growth, or unemployment rates. This could allow central banks to implement monetary policy in real-time, as the smart contract would automatically execute the desired actions when the predefined criteria are satisfied.
(b) Dynamic interest rates: wCBDCs could be designed to have adjustable interest rates that can be changed in real-time by the central bank. For example, the central bank could set different interest rates for different financial institutions or transaction types, and these rates could be updated dynamically based on changing market conditions. This would allow the central bank to fine-tune monetary policy by adjusting interest rates on a case-by-case basis, depending on the specific needs of the financial system.
(c) Real-time liquidity management: wCBDCs could enable real-time liquidity management by providing direct connectivity between financial institutions and the central bank. Financial institutions could hold wCBDCs as reserves and use them for interbank transactions, with the central bank monitoring and managing the liquidity levels in real-time. The central bank could adjust the liquidity levels of wCBDCs through open market operations, such as buying or selling wCBDCs, to manage the overall liquidity in the financial system and influence interest rates.

3. **Mitigating risks of private digital currencies:**
The rise of private digital currencies, such as cryptocurrencies or stablecoins, has raised concerns about financial stability, consumer protection, and monetary sovereignty. Wholesale CBDCs could be seen as a way for central banks to maintain control over the money supply and payment system, and mitigate the risks associated with private digital currencies by offering a safe and regulated alternative for financial institutions to settle transactions in a similar way that commercial banks settle transactions between themselves with the central bank reserves as the common trusted asset.

4. **Keeping up with technological advancements:**
   Central banks are also motivated to investigate wholesale CBDC solutions to stay abreast of technological advancements in the financial industry. Blockchain and DLT have the potential to disrupt traditional financial systems, and central banks want to understand the implications and possibilities of these technologies to ensure that they can effectively regulate and oversee the evolving landscape of digital currencies.

16.2 Operating Model for a Wholesale CBDC

A wholesale central bank digital currency (wCBDC) is a digital currency that is issued and backed by a central bank and is intended for use by financial institutions and market infrastructures. The operating model for wCBDC operations will depend on the specific design and objectives of the central bank, but here are some potential operating models:

1. **Direct issuance by the central bank:**
   In this model, the central bank would issue wCBDC directly to financial institutions and market infrastructures. The central bank would maintain the ledger of all transactions and would be responsible for the overall management and security of the currency.
2. **Intermediated issuance:**
   In this model, the central bank would issue wCBDC to a designated intermediary, such as a clearinghouse or commercial bank, who would then distribute the currency to financial institutions and market infrastructures. The intermediary would be responsible for managing the ledger and ensuring compliance with regulatory requirements.
3. **Hybrid model:**
   This model would combine elements of both direct and intermediated issuance. For example, the central bank could issue wCBDC directly to some financial institutions and market infrastructures while using an intermediary for others.
4. **Distributed Ledger Technology-based model:**
   In this model, the wCBDC would be based on a Distributed Ledger Technology (DLT) platform. The central bank would still be responsible for the overall management and security of the currency, but transactions could be validated and recorded on the DLT platform by a network of nodes, which could include financial institutions and other market players.

In the case of wCBDC and based on all the projects and pilots conducted around the world, we can expect, in contrast to the retail CBDC case, the DLT-based model to be the consensus choice of most central banks, as the DLT can offer some features that have a significant impact in the wholesale world, like atomicity and immediate settlement on a specific date/time. DLT becomes even more the default choice, when cross-border transactions come into play, as it allows to introduce a fair decentralized governance model—the only way to bring some of these parties, for each of whom sovereignty is a key topic, together in a cross-border system.

16.3 Use Cases for a Wholesale CBDC

As seen already in Sect. 13.4, where we listed the use cases that were most prominent in the literature on the CBDC topic, we learnt that cross-border usage was by far the most prominently mentioned feature in wholesale CBDCs.

But unfortunately, no cross-border functionality can be exploited, before the basic functionalities of a wCBDC have been deployed domestically. Therefore, let us start with the domestic side of things.

In developed economies, interbank payment systems for domestic transactions are generally effective, with real-time gross settlement (RTGS) systems in place. RTGS systems enable immediate and individual settlement of interbank transfers throughout the processing day. Transactions are settled in real-time, without any waiting period, and on a one-to-one basis, making them final and irrevocable. Additionally, many countries have Instant Payments Services that offer near-real-time retail funds transfers, allowing immediate clearing between payment service providers.

While wholesale Central Bank Digital Currencies (wCBDCs) for domestic use are discussed, they may not provide significant additional functionality for economies already equipped with well-functioning commercial banking sectors and interbank payment systems like RTGS. Banks can efficiently transact with each other using reserves held at the central bank, similar to the way they would with wCBDCs. Therefore, issuing a wholesale CBDC for domestic payments only may not offer substantial benefits but could introduce new risks. Therefore, only countries without a solid RTGS system are likely to consider adopting wholesale CBDCs for domestic purposes only.

The base functionalities that need to be covered in any wCBDC system, no matter if the final target is cross-border functionality or not, are the following:

a. Minting:	Conversion from Reserves to wCBDC
b. Issuing:	Sending wCBDC to Commercial Banks
c. Burning:	Redemption of wCBDC back to Reserves
d. Transferring:	Sending wCBDC from Bank A to Bank B
e. DvP:	Delivery versus Payment
f. PvP:	Payment versus Payment

The Swiss project Helvetia is a good example of the functionality that such a domestic wCBDC system could bring to market. Although the Swiss have the most advanced RTGS system of the western world, called SIC which also integrates the settlement of securities, the Swiss National Bank is conducting leading research into wCBDC topic.

Project Helvetia

Project Helvetia is a collaborative initiative involving the Bank for International Settlements (BIS) Innovation Hub, the Swiss National Bank (SNB), and financial market infrastructure operator SIX. It aims to explore the potential of wholesale central bank digital currencies using Distributed Ledger Technology.

The project sought to demonstrate the feasibility and legal robustness of two alternative approaches to wholesale CBDC. The first approach involved using a centralized ledger maintained by the central bank, while the second approach utilized a non-centralized DLT system. The goal was to assess both options in a near-live setup and evaluate their practicality for wholesale transactions.

Project Helvetia recognized the potential of wholesale CBDCs to enhance financial systems, particularly in cross-border payments and remittances. By leveraging this technology, the project aimed to make existing financial processes faster, more cost-effective, and more secure.

The resulting reports provided insights into the progress and findings of Project Helvetia's Phase II. They detailed the technical aspects, legal considerations, and operational requirements of implementing a wholesale CBDC. The project highlighted the importance of collaboration between central banks, financial institutions, and technology providers to ensure the successful development and implementation of wholesale CBDCs.

Overall, Project Helvetia served as an important initiative in exploring the potential benefits and challenges associated with wholesale CBDCs, contributing to the ongoing research and development efforts in this field.

Cross-border transactions, involving the transfer of assets or currencies between financial institutions in different countries, are extensive and valued in the trillions of dollars daily. SWIFT facilitated nearly 7 billion cross-border payment messages in 2019, and FX turnover was US$ 6.6 trillion per day in April 2019. It is such an issue that the G20 [124] has made enhancing cross-border payments a priority.

Cross-border settlement, more specifically, is the exchange of domestic assets or currencies between foreign financial institutions situated in different jurisdictions. These settlements depend either on international arrangements, like Continuous Linked Settlement (CLS) for settling FX transactions and International Central Securities Depositories (ICSDs) for handling cross-border securities transactions, or on intermediary networks leveraging domestic arrangements, such as correspondent banking.

Despite the vast amounts of cross-border transactions, efficient international arrangements only cover a limited assortment of currencies, assets, and participants. Consequently, cross-border settlements often involve more risks than domestic ones and are typically costly, slow, and opaque.

Use cases like Delivery versus Payment (DvP) and Payment versus Payment (PvP) reduce settlement risk and foster global financial stability. The security provided by central bank money supports crucially important settlement with a common, unique settlement asset as we saw before in this book in the chapter on tokenized deposits. Yet, only a few international arrangements settle in central bank money, an area that could be expanded. Furthermore, reducing intermediaries that link investors and issuers across borders could help investors better understand their rights and claims relative to the ultimate issuer.

Wholesale CBDCs (wCBDCs) can improve cross-border settlement in significant ways. Central banks could launch wCBDCs on separate domestic platforms with interconnections between them. Alternatively, several wCBDCs could be pooled in a "corridor network" where central banks agree on common governance for the network.

16.4 Features of a Wholesale CBDC

The key features necessary for a wholesale CBDC built on the features outlined in Sect. 12.7. We will not spend any further time on the 5 features listed below as they have been covered in detail before and no new wholesale-specific elements need to be added:

16.4.1 Extensibility

See Sect. 12.7.7 for a refresher if needed.

16.4.2 Interoperability

See Sect. 12.7.8 for a refresher if needed.

16.4.3 Fungibility

See Sect. 12.7.10 for a refresher if needed.

16.4.4 Resilience

See Sect. 12.7.11 for a refresher if needed.

16.4.5 Efficiency

See Sect. 12.7.12 for a refresher if needed.

In the case of a wholesale CBDC, the following features need to be specified further for a wholesale solution design and deployment.

16.4.6 Security

As a wCBDC will be handling many high value transactions, it is important that the infrastructure supporting the wCBDC system must be resistant to tampering. This involves measures like secure code practices, intrusion detection systems, and ongoing security testing and monitoring. The wCBDC infrastructure must be robust against cyberattacks. This involves both technological measures and a culture of security, including regular employee training.

As the system is most likely a permissioned DLT or any other system where the participants are limited and where unauthorized access must be prevented, robust authentication mechanisms need to be in place for the wholesale solution. These might include digital certificates, multi-factor authentication (MFA), or even biometric verification in some cases.

wCBDC transactions need to be secure, preventing unauthorized transactions while enabling traceability and audibility. Encryption, digital signatures, and other cryptographic measures are needed to ensure this.

16.4.7 Availability 24/7/365

A wCBDC should extend the availability of the system from currently 5 days a week, during business hours to a system that is available around the clock. Therefore, a wCBDC system must operate with high availability in excess of 99.95% and low downtime. This requires a highly resilient infrastructure to mitigate the risks of system failures and their associated impacts.

16.4.8 Settlement Time/Transaction Times

Settlement is also a critical issue for wCBDC systems, but rather than instant settlement in the wCBDC space, immediate settlement at a predetermined date is the key functionality. This includes immediately now (= instant) as an option.

16.4.9 Settlement Finality/Consensus Mechanism

Settlement finality is critical in wholesale CBDCs because it ensures that once a transaction is completed, it cannot be reversed or modified, providing certainty and reducing risk for participants. In a wholesale CBDC system, financial institutions may use CBDCs for large-value or time-critical transactions, such as interbank payments or securities settlement. As these transactions often involve significant amounts of money, any uncertainty or delay in settlement increases risk, can cause financial instability, and disrupt the entire payment system.

16.4.10 Privacy/Confidentiality of Transactions

In wCBDC, hard privacy from all third parties is not as important as in the rCBDC case as personal freedoms and mass surveillance are not a topic here.

Although transparency is crucial for auditing and regulatory purposes, ensuring privacy of the transaction details from third parties is essential for the parties involved in the transaction.

Privacy in this case corresponds more to confidentiality from all other participants not involved in the deal. This is absolutely crucial. While the central bank may be allowed to see all transactions, other connected banks can under no circumstances see transactions of other participants, where they were not a party to the transaction as this could give away critically important information on positions and strategies of competitors. So here, more specifically confidential transactions are the feature that needs to be implemented. This may be achieved through techniques such as zero-knowledge proofs or other privacy-enhancing technologies (PET).

If the tokens carry the transaction history as we have already seen in Sect. 12.7.10, this again may impact the fungibility in addition to the confidentiality.

16.4.11 Atomicity

Simultaneous settlement (or atomic swaps) of all assets involved in a transaction, whereby assets are linked to ensure the transfer of any asset only occurs if all the other assets are simultaneously transferred (e.g. to achieve delivery versus payment in a securities transaction or payment versus payment in a foreign exchange transaction). Either all parts of the transaction get executed together, or none is. This is a great new functionality that is missing today and that can have a significant impact on the conduct of business in financial services. This atomicity increases transparency and speed, in a setup where today many different legs need to be completed in different systems and there is no bird's eye view on the total progress and status. DLTs will make a major difference in this aspect.

16.4.12 Performance/Transaction Processing

Transaction processing is essential in wholesale CBDCs as it determines the speed, scalability, and overall efficiency of the payment system. In a wholesale CBDC system, financial institutions may use CBDCs for large-value or time-critical transactions, such as interbank payments or securities settlement. These transactions require high-speed processing to ensure that the transfer of ownership of assets and the transfer of value are completed quickly and accurately. Speed and throughput requirements are nevertheless significantly lower than in a retail CBDC system, as the number of participants is much lower, and the patience of the users is higher. Near real-time transactions processed within a few seconds (1–5) may be totally fine for transactions that used to take 1–2 days to settle in the past, while in rCBDC systems the bar has moved to milli- and nanoseconds.

Efficient transaction processing is also critical to achieving real-time gross settlement, which is a vital feature of wholesale CBDCs. RTGS ensures that transactions are processed and settled in real-time, eliminating credit and liquidity risks and reducing settlement timeframes. The baseline for a wCBDC is the current performance of systems for domestic transaction (which in many countries is already good) and for cross-border transactions (where the current setup leaves a lot of room for improvement.

16.4.13 Programmability

Programmable wholesale CBDCs will most likely utilize smart contracts as a key new feature. They can automate compliance checks, significantly reducing the need for manual oversight and potential errors. Transactions can also be executed with greater efficiency and speed. Risks in financial transactions can be minimized, such as counterparty risk, through mechanisms like atomic swaps. Programmability allows for complex transaction structures that can be executed based on certain conditions. This could be particularly beneficial for automated payments. It also ensures greater transparency and provides a robust audit trail, which is crucial for audits and dispute resolution. Furthermore, programmability can enhance interoperability between different financial systems, paving the way for a more integrated global financial system.

However, such an implementation is not without its challenges. There is a high level of technical complexity involved, which could introduce new types of technical bugs or vulnerabilities. Greater transparency might also raise privacy concerns, requiring a balance to be struck. Smart contracts, despite their power, have been known to be exploited by hackers, as they often contain security vulnerabilities. Secure and bug-free programming is not an ability most humans were born with. Therefore, implementing programmability and smart contracts into wCBDCs needs to be without universal access to the programming and managed carefully to minimize risks and ensure regulatory compliance.

16.4.14 Sovereignty

Sovereignty in the context of wholesale CBDCs involves multiple dimensions, including monetary policy sovereignty, data sovereignty, and technological sovereignty as we have already detailed in Sect. 12.7.6.

One aspect that we need to mention here is a peculiarity that affects cross-border wholesale CBDC. Such a system can in our opinion best be realized by a decentralized consortium DLT where the different partners all keep a part of their sovereignty on a system level, which until today has not been possible with the traditional client server architectures, where only one party can be the owner and administrator of the system.

16.4.15 Reporting

Reporting in a wholesale CBDC system involves collecting, aggregating, and analyzing data on transactions, liquidity, and risk management, and making this information available to regulatory authorities and market participants. This allows them to monitor the performance and stability of the payment system and to take corrective action if necessary.

Effective reporting is also crucial for financial institutions to manage their own risks effectively, as they need to monitor their own liquidity and exposure to other participants in the system. By having access to real-time and accurate data, financial institutions can make informed decisions and manage their risk effectively while also meeting all relevant legal and regulatory reporting requirements, including those specified in anti-money laundering (AML), sanctions, and combating the financing of terrorism (CFT) rules.

16.4.16 Integration into Central Banks and Commercial Banks

Wholesale CBDCs are typically issued and managed by the central bank, which acts as the trusted and central authority in the payment system. Therefore, the wCBDC system needs to be integrated into the RTGS systems and the accounting systems of the central bank. The central bank is responsible for ensuring the stability and integrity of the payment system, including setting the rules and standards for participation, monitoring the system's performance, and providing liquidity support if necessary.

Commercial banks, on the other hand, can use wholesale CBDCs to facilitate large-value or time-critical transactions, such as interbank payments or securities settlement. To participate in the CBDC system, commercial banks need to comply with the central bank's rules and standards, such as meeting minimum capital requirements, maintaining appropriate risk management practices, and reporting data on transactions and liquidity. The commercial bank systems will usually be integrated to the wCBDC via an API using EBICS (Electronic Banking Internet Communication Standard), SEPA (Single Euro Payments Area), or similar standards, and this is often based on ISO 20022 messages.

16.4.17 KYC/AML

The KYC (Know Your Customer) requirements for a wholesale CBDC (wCBDC) are most likely the same as for the reserve accounts at the central bank. Hence the connection and setup can happen quickly and easily if the participants do not change.

For new joiners, the process will likely be the same as the one set up for connections to the RTGS system for central bank reserve accounts.

The wCBDC system may also include mechanisms for detecting and preventing illicit activity, such as money laundering, avoidance of sanctions, or terrorist financing. These mechanisms could include transaction monitoring and reporting requirements, as well as sanctions screening and other risk management tools, where extensibility and interoperability play an important role. In most cases we would expect these checks to be conducted via connected systems instead of being functionality built into the wCBDC solution.

16.5 Domestic Use of a Wholesale CBDC

The wholesale CBDC concept has been in existence for several decades through central bank's RTGS systems, allowing commercial banks to settle such transactions digitally using central bank money. These current wholesale systems usually operate on centralized databases maintained by the central bank.

The future iterations, which we call wholesale CBDC, may utilize Distributed Ledger Technology (DLT) as a non-centralized ledger system. An example of a domestic wholesale CBDC project is Project Helvetia, which we have seen in Sect. 16.3.

Many central banks recognize the potential of wholesale CBDCs to enhance the speed, cost-effectiveness, and security of existing financial systems. Nevertheless, in developed countries, the RTGS systems in place are usually well developed and highly performant for executing domestic interbank transactions and there will be limited benefits in deploying a domestic wCBDC. In emerging markets and developing economies, significant benefits may already be reaped in the domestic payments area.

In developed countries, the really valuable benefits of wCBDC will mostly be reaped from improvements in cross-border transactions, where the complexity is high, many steps are required per transaction, many organizations are involved, settlement is slow and costs are high. Hence when it comes to cross-border payments and remittances, leveraging wholesale CBDCs can massively streamline processes, reduce expenses, and bolster the reliability of these transactions in significant ways for both advanced and emerging economies.

We will look at this cross-border opportunity in the next chapter.

16.6 Cross-Border Use of a Wholesale CBDC

The traditional model of cross-border payments through correspondent banks is inefficient, costly, and carries settlement risks as we have seen. Settlement in central bank money, the safest settlement asset, is limited to interbank domestic payments on access-controlled central bank real-time gross settlement systems, with the exception of Continuous Linked Settlement (CLS) for FX transactions, which supports only a limited number of currencies.

According to the Bank of England website, cross-border payments are forecast to grow from $150 trillion in 2017 to over $250 trillion by 2027, due to

1. expanding manufacturing supply chains across borders,
2. cross-border asset management and global investment flows, and
3. international trade and e-commerce

The correspondent banking model itself has costs of nearly $120 billion for $23.5 trillion in cross-border transactions [126]. The model presents even more challenges for emerging market and developing economies (EMDEs), leaving many without sufficient or affordable access to the global financial system. Moreover, FX settlement risk has increased due to a declining share of global settlements using PvP mechanisms, and existing arrangements such as CLS do not support many EMDE currencies.

The following graph shows the BIS survey results collected from central banks around the globe on the cross-border frictions that a wCBDC could fix, grouped by advanced economies (AE) and by emerging market and developing economies (EMDE) (Graph 16.1).

Cross-border use of wholesale CBDCs (wCBDCs) offers one of the highest rewards in the CBDC space, but it is not a low hanging fruit. It is much rather a high hanging tough nut. It is important for several reasons:

1. **Efficiency/Long transaction chains:**
   Currently, cross-border payments can be slow, costly, and subject to multiple intermediaries with different compliance jurisdictions. wCBDCs have the potential to significantly reduce transaction times and costs by allowing direct peer-to-peer transfers between financial institutions, bypassing intermediaries such as correspondent banks.
2. **Liquidity management/Funding costs:**
   Financial institutions often need to hold multiple currencies to manage their liquidity needs. By using wCBDCs, they could potentially reduce their reliance on foreign exchange transactions, which can be costly and time-consuming.
3. **Risk management incl. FX costs:**
   Cross-border transactions are subject to a range of risks, such as exchange rate fluctuations, settlement risk, and counterparty risk. wCBDCs have

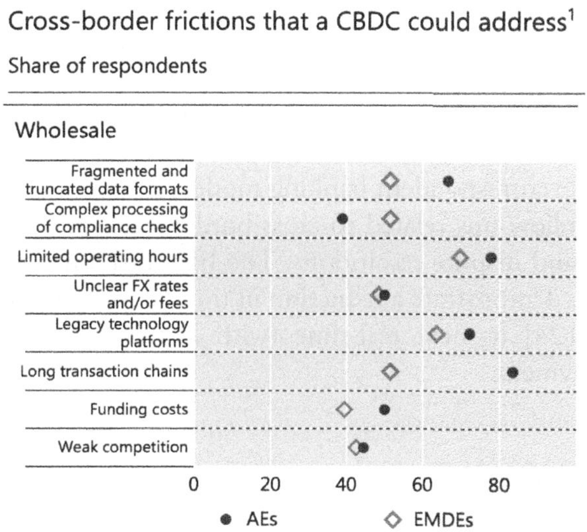

Graph 16.1 Cross-border frictions that wCBDC could address (*Source* BIS)

the potential to mitigate some of these risks by offering real-time settlement, reducing counterparty risk, and providing greater transparency and traceability in cross-border transactions.

4. **International trade:**

   Cross-border payments are a critical component of international trade, and wCBDCs have the potential to facilitate more efficient and secure trade transactions. By reducing transaction times and costs, wCBDCs could help to promote greater cross-border trade and investment, particularly in emerging markets.

5. **Complexity and speed:**

   Correspondent banking is typically illustrated as a chain that extends from the payer, through intermediary banks, to the payee. The length of this chain can vary depending on the location of the payer and payee, as well as the correspondent banking relationships that exist between them. A longer chain would involve more intermediaries, thereby lengthening the overall transaction time.

Efforts have been made to improve the speed of cross-border payments, such as SWIFT gpi. This service allows messages to be sent and received in under five minutes, and 92% of payments clear within 24 hours. However, the BIS IthanonLionrock to mBridge [124] project revealed that participant banks experience delays of up to half a day or more at each intermediary correspondent bank for an average cross-border transaction. Manual processing, compliance checks, and differences in time zones and operating hours for local settlement networks can cause further delays, resulting in settlement times that can last from 3 to 5 days. This number was derived in the report by adding (1/2–1 days × 2–3 intermediary banks + 1–2 days from time difference delays) for a total of 3–5 days.

Moreover, the correspondent banking model can also cause uncontrollable delays due to follow-ups related to cross-border sanctions, frequent internal investigations, and dispute resolutions. The IthanonLionrock 2 (IL2) prototype was able to demonstrate a reduction in transaction times from an average of 3–5 days [124] to near real-time (with less than 10 seconds latency) cross-border payment.

16.7 Architectures for Wholesale CBDC

Now let us look at how domestic use and cross-border use reflect themselves in the possible architectures for wholesale CBDC systems, based on what we saw in Sects. 16.5 and 16.6.

16.7.1 Domestic Model

A domestic wCBDC model can be realized in different ways and with different architectures:

Centralized Architecture: In a centralized architecture, the central bank would issue and manage the wCBDC. It would keep the record of all the transactions, effectively acting as the sole ledger keeper. This represents the existing RTGS systems of today and is hence not adding any new features. Therefore, we can move on to the next model.

Decentralized Architecture: A decentralized architecture could leverage Distributed Ledger Technology, like blockchain. This means that transaction verification and the maintaining of the ledger could be distributed across different nodes (participating financial institutions). In this scenario, the central bank might still have ultimate control over the issuance of the wCBDC, but the transaction verification could be more decentralized. Here new features come into play as illustrated in the previous paragraphs. Project Helvetia, which we have seen in Sect. 16.3, gives an idea on how this could look like. Such a decentralized setup is by far the most prominent model used in the majority of wholesale CBDC projects.

Hybrid Architecture: A hybrid architecture would be a mix of centralized and decentralized elements. For example, the central bank could control issuance and maintain a master ledger, but transaction verification could be delegated to approved entities (e.g. commercial banks) that maintain their own copies of the ledger. Here also new features may come into play as illustrated in the previous paragraphs.

16.7.2 Multi-CBDC Models

16.7.2.1 Compatible wCBDC Systems

The compatibility of payment systems through common technical and legal standards can reduce frictions and barriers to cross-border payments, but achieving compatibility can take time. In designing an multi-CBDC

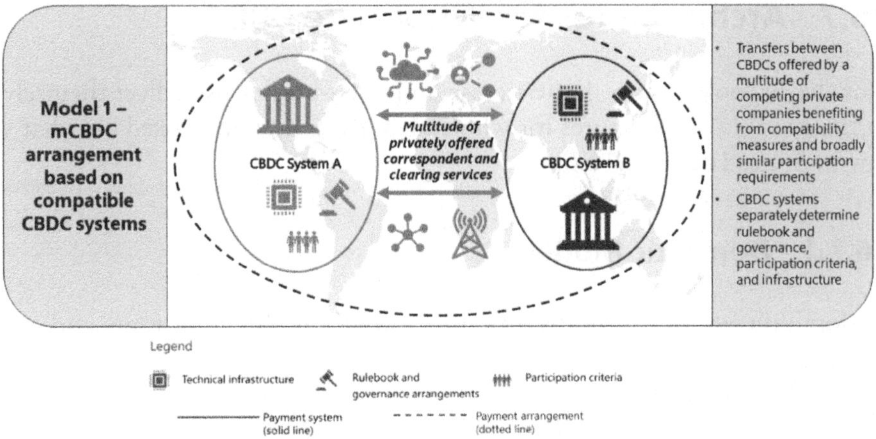

Graph 16.2 Compatible wCBDC systems (*Source* BIS [126])

(mCBDC) system, common technical and legal standards can reduce operational burdens and simplify KYC and transaction monitoring processes.

An mCBDC system could benefit from a clean slate, with international standards in mind, and encourage a diversity of private participants. But incumbent banks with large networks and foreign exchange operations may still have an advantage. Central banks have tools to influence payment arrangements, provide safety features and efficiency through interlinking their system with others and a common clearing mechanism (Graph 16.2).

16.7.2.2 Interlinked CBDC Systems

Linking payment systems requires compatibility measures and can be done through a shared technical interface or a common clearing mechanism. The former involves contractual agreements between systems, while the latter links systems through designated settlement accounts, which can be distributed or centralized.

For CBDCs, central banks could offer foreign exchange or allow other central banks to hold their CBDC, acting as correspondents for their distributors or end-users. A more centralized approach could use a trusted intermediary as a clearing mechanism (Graph 16.3).

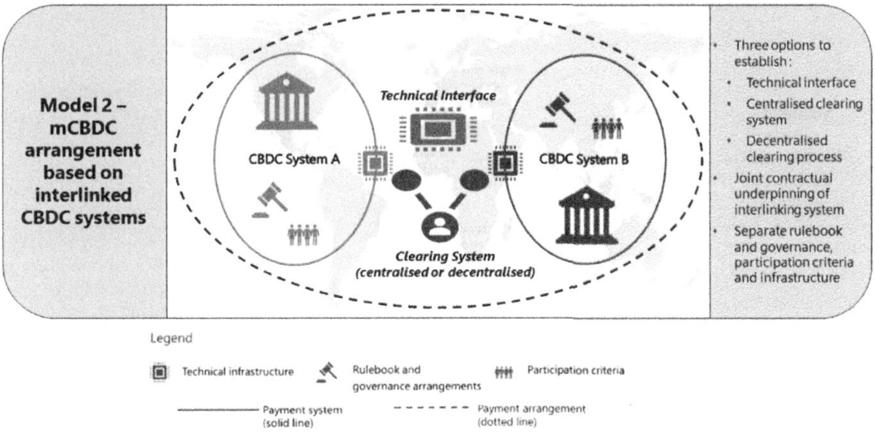

Graph 16.3 Interlinked CBDC systems (*Source* BIS [126])

16.7.2.3 Single mCBDC Multi-currency System

Multi-currency cross-border payment systems using *w*CBDCs have the potential for increased operational functionality and efficiency. *They* also raise governance and control challenges. These systems could vary in design, with multiple systems for different use cases, and could potentially exploit economies of scale in development and maintenance.

However, central banks would need to work through the wider policy implications of issuing a wCBDC, such as the impact on monetary policy, financial stability, and payments policy. The development of a new system and collaboration with the private sector would also take time and consideration of various factors, as seen in the example of CLS settling foreign exchange transactions. The use of CBDCs in a tokenized form could theoretically enable different and more integrated models for settling transactions on a single distributed ledger (Graph 16.4).

The chart below by the BIS [125] shows the improvements that can be expected for each of the six key identified frictions for each of the three models that we just reviewed (Table 16.1).

The idea of the single mCBDC multi-currency system displayed in Model 3 has been trialed with Project mBridge [126], started by the BIS Innovation Hub Hong Kong Centre, the Hong Kong Monetary Authority, the Bank of Thailand, the Digital Currency Institute of the People's Bank of China, and the Central Bank of the United Arab Emirates.

The platform's functional scope included key requirements such as CBDC operations, foreign exchange (FX) execution models, accessibility, liquidity

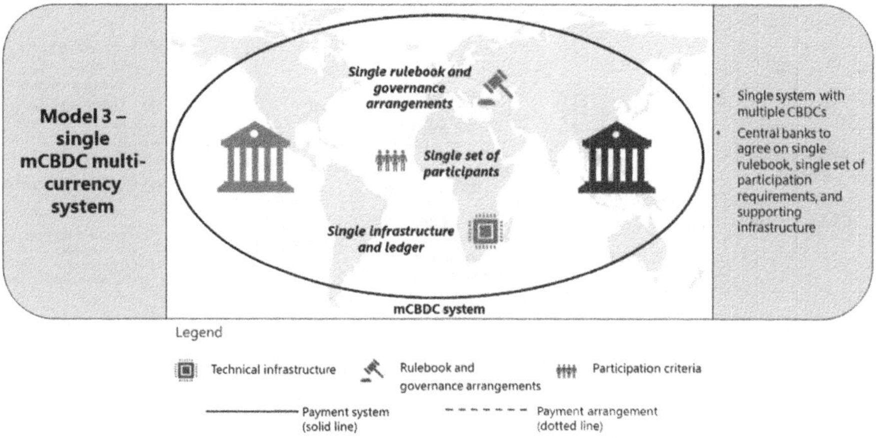

Graph 16.4 mCBDC system (*Source* BIS [126])

management, and regulatory compliance. International trade was picked as mBridge's first business use case.

In terms of CBDC operations, the platform enabled central bank participants to issue and redeem their wCBDC, while commercial bank participants can initiate peer-to-peer wCBDC push payments. Additionally, payment versus payment (PvP) transactions can be achieved.

Regarding FX execution models, the platform automatically matched PvP transactions with the best available FX Board Rate, ensuring execution at the agreed rate. It also facilitated direct FX quotations through a Request for Quote (RFQ) mechanism, allowing execution of FX transactions at the agreed rate. Furthermore, the platform can incorporate FX rates agreed upon outside the platform, ensuring execution at the agreed rate.

In terms of accessibility, the platform provided the capability for banks, exchanges, corporates, and other participants to run their own nodes on the ledger or interact with them through application programming interfaces (APIs).

Liquidity management was another important aspect, as the platform allowed banks to queue transactions when there is insufficient liquidity, deferring execution until enough liquidity becomes available. It also initiated netting of queued transactions periodically at the individual central bank level using an automated Liquidity Saving Mechanism (LSM).

In terms of regulatory compliance, the platform offered features for central banks to monitor transactions executed in their wCBDC in real-time. They could also set currency threshold limits for end-of-day balances and automatically reduce the balance of commercial banks at a specified rate, if their

Table 16.1 Potential improvements of different mCBDC arrangements to frictions in correspondent bank arrangements for cross-border payments

Potential improvements by model			
Frictions cross-border payments	**Model 1–mCBDC arrangement based on compatible CBDC systems**	**Model 2–mCBDC arrangement based on interlinked CBDC systems**	**Model 3–single mCBDC multi-currency system**
Legacy technology platforms	Compatible systems allow for efficiency gains in existing banking relations	A common clearing mechanism could reduce the number of relationships and provide economies of scale	A single system does not require such relations (however, a single system may add to operational costs)
Limited operating hours	CBDCs can be open 24/7, eliminating any mismatch of operating hours		
Fragmented and truncated data formats	Compatible message standards allow payments to flow without data loss or manual intervention	The message standard (eg ISO 20022) adopted by the interlinkage would act to harmonise standards across systems	Single message standard across the system eliminates mismatches
Unclear FX rates and unclear incoming fees	Compatibility requirements for wallet providers could enable users to calculate fees and rates prior to a payment	Common calculation of rates and fees for transfers using any interlinkage would aid transparency	A single system would likely be designed to include options for FX conversion
Long transaction chains	CBDCs could settle instantly, reducing the need for status updates		
Complex processing of compliance checks	Compatible compliance regimes reduce uncertainty and costs	Interlinking systems do not impact multiple or conflicting compliance requirements	Single set of access requirements means compliance could be equivalent across the system

Source BIS [126]

holdings exceed the threshold, thereby ensuring compliance with jurisdiction-specific regulations. Moreover, commercial banks could extract transaction information for compliance reporting, surveillance, and analysis purposes.

The involved central banks constructed this platform, the mBridge Ledger, rooted in a novel blockchain technology, and designed to facilitate real-time, peer-to-peer, cross-border payments, and foreign exchange transactions using CBDCs. Furthermore, it was engineered to ensure adherence to policy and legal requirements specific to different jurisdictions, as well as conforming to various regulatory and governance standards.

By providing a shared platform on which participants can conduct peer-to-peer payments directly in the safety of the wCBDCs of multiple jurisdictions, mBridge looked at the potential to alleviate many of the challenges in international payments, extend PvP protection to currencies beyond those covered by existing systems, and support the use of local currencies in cross-border settlement. The system also implemented privacy controls, options to do manual and automatic issuance/redemption, as well as simple one-currency push payments and dual-currency FX PvP transactions.

The mBridge pilot conducted a large-scale, six-week pilot settling real-value transactions in CBDC from four participating jurisdictions directly on the mBridge ledger. It represented the largest cross-border CBDC pilot to date, with over US$12 million of CBDCs issued onto the platform, over US$22 million of payments and FX PvP instantly settled across borders, and the greatest number of direct pilot participants. The pilot included 20 of the region's largest commercial banks settling real value on behalf of their corporate clients, primarily focusing on settlement for international trade as well as between interbank groups.

The pilot's success demonstrated the platform's ability to improve cross-border payment speed and efficiency and reduce settlement risks. This pilot was an important step that allowed the participants to see how things could work in the future. One of the key elements for the future is developing these initial steps into a product, where the architecture really allows for a decentralized governance and ownership—that will be a critical element that will determine the future potential of this initiative on the way to improve the future of cross-border transactions.

The next step *currently planned* in Project mBridge is to continue development in 2023 and 2024 *until* a Minimum Viable Product (MVP) *is ready.*

17

Conclusion

As we reach the conclusion of our journey through the history of money, the existing digital payment landscape, and the promising future of digital currencies, we've extensively studied the dynamics of cryptocurrencies, stablecoins, and Central Bank Digital Currencies (CBDCs). We've acknowledged that while cryptocurrencies have the potential to serve as store of value, their high volatility hinders their functionality as an efficient means of payment. This hurdle, coupled with the limited acceptance in the traditional world, means that cryptocurrencies are not able to serve as a primary means of payment today.

Stablecoins, another form of digital currency, continue to grapple with their own set of challenges. Although designed to combat the volatility inherent in cryptocurrencies, stablecoins still suffer from fluctuations of varying degrees depending on the type of stablecoin they are. Moreover, their acceptance as a legitimate form of payment is currently mostly confined to the crypto-world, which hampers their broader utility. This may change if ways can be found to put them to use outside the crypto-world as they offer some interesting characteristics. However, another exciting prospect in this realm is the deposit token, a category of stablecoin proposed by the incumbent banks under prevailing regulation. Given that bank deposits form the most significant proportion of money in circulation today, deposit tokens could potentially revolutionize the financial landscape, especially if a common settlement asset like a CBDC is deployed. It will also be interesting to watch the evolution of stablecoins, driven by innovative non-banks, versus the evolution of deposit tokens, driven by regulated, usually conservative banks.

L. V. Schumacher, *Decoding Digital Assets*, https://doi.org/10.1007/978-3-031-54601-3_17

The concept of CBDCs, particularly, offers immense potential, both in terms of monetary policy and practical utility. Central banks worldwide are increasingly viewing CBDCs as a potentially stabilizing element for their respective digital payment systems. When examining wholesale CBDCs, we observe significant opportunities in terms of atomic settlements, immediate settlements at specified moments, and cross-border wholesale payments. However, these potential benefits come hand in hand with substantial challenges. Legal and regulatory complexities need to be addressed effectively for these advantages to be fully realized. While technological capabilities continue to advance, the ultimate success will hinge on the adept navigation of the legal and regulatory landscape.

Turning our attention to retail CBDCs, we see a different spectrum of possibilities. Retail CBDCs could turn our world into a dystopian '1984' as imagined by George Orwell or revolutionize the financial landscape for the better by introducing improved privacy measures, instantaneous settlements, and the intriguing concept of programmable money. A simple payment authorization instead of a complicated personal multi-factor authentication, with the potential for one-click transactions, is another promising possibility. Furthermore, retail CBDCs could pave the way for innovative business models through the deployment of micropayments and significantly impact the international remittance business by facilitating efficient cross-border payments.

However, with these promising opportunities come substantial risks. Critical issues such as privacy breaches, security threats, mass surveillance, and potential misuse of programmable money warrant careful attention. We also want to remind of the words of the cybersecurity guru Bruce Schneier [168] here: "*Data is a toxic asset. We need to start thinking about it as such and treat it as we would any other source of toxicity. To do anything else is to risk our security and privacy.*" CBDC transaction data together with health data has the highest level of toxicity as we have seen. Credit card data is not far behind and definitely commercially exploited much more today. The challenge for CBDCs lies in leveraging these potential benefits while effectively mitigating the accompanying risks.

Reflecting on our journey and the evolution of money, it is apparent that the declining usage of physical cash has been a major driver propelling these developments. As we move toward an increasingly digital era, it's crucial to focus on establishing the digital counterpart to cash. It's not just about creating another iteration of the current digital payment systems like Visa, Mastercard, or PayPal; what's required is a reliable, efficient, and widely accepted digital form of cash. With existing retail CBDC launches and pilots attracting underwhelming user interest, to put it mildly, it is already time to consider more cash-like, privacy-focused CBDC solutions if successful adoption is the goal.

Central banks, consequently, have a significant task at hand. They must strive to provide a digital form of cash that not only satisfies user needs but also earns societal trust and leaves nobody behind. Policymakers, who will play a decisive role in this evolution, often lack familiarity with the technological and cryptographic nuances. Central banks for the first time in their lives need to account for the desires of the individual consumers in a product design. This is a complex journey that demands deep understanding and thoughtful decision-making, against the interest of powerful lobbies.

With 130 central banks conducting CBDC projects and pilots in July 2023 according to the Atlantic Council CBDC tracker website [166] and the BIS forecasting the circulation of 15 retail and 9 wholesale CBDCs by 2028, it is pretty clear that CBDCs will be part of our lives within a decade.

These future CBDCs could manifest in two starkly different ways. One path could lead us toward a dystopian future, with implications of mass surveillance and diminished personal freedom reminiscent of '1984' as mentioned before. The other path could guide us toward a future characterized by enhanced privacy, greater financial inclusion, and lower transaction fees.

As such, it's imperative for citizens to understand the differences between CBDC designs, to remain vigilant, informed, and vocal in influencing these designs and their consequences, with the goal to shape the digital monetary future that best serves society. We give credit to the American presidential candidates and politicians, we have encountered in the book, for taking a position against the wrong type of CBDC this early in the process, even though many of their positions may be too absolute and ignoring the good options available to us. The latest American initiatives that differentiate between mass surveillance tools and privacy-preserving digital cash give us hope that the right solutions may have a chance. In addition, the BIS just published a report on a project called Tourbillon that moves the needle further toward possible privacy. We count on the fact that politicians and citizens in more countries will take interest, invest the time to understand, and stand up for the right type of CBDC.

As we have seen in this book, CBDCs come in all shapes and flavors, and picking the right one is critical for the future most of us wish to see. I sincerely hope this book will contribute to that goal and outcome. I thank you for your time and interest.

Table 17.1 Comparison of DLT-based deposits, Stablecoins, Cryptocurrencies & CBDCs

	Cryptocurrencies	DLT-based deposits	Stablecoins	CBCDs
Issuer	Decentralized miners	Commercial banks (centralized)	Non-bank private companies (centralized)	Central banks (centralized)
Examples	• Bitcoin • Ethereum • Zcash • Monero	• SGD deposit tokens by MAS/JPM • Blockchain deposit accounts on JPM Coin private blockchain	• USDC by Circle/Coinbase • USDT by Tether • PYUSD by Paxos/PayPal	• Jamaica JamDex, Bahamian SandDollar • Chinese Digital Yuan, Nigerian eNaira (pilots) • Digital Euro (ongoing investigation)
Adoption & Use	• The value of all existing cryptocurrency is around $804 billion • Bitcoin: 250,000 transactions and 1,000,000 active addresses per day	• JPM Coin, live with material transaction volumes • Deposit token projects like DK, SBA generally still in concept phases	• 1st major stablecoin issued in 2014 • US$131 billion market capitalization (as of April 2023)	• Over 130 central banks investigating CBDCs • Live projects listed above (Bahamas, Jamaica & Nigeria) with low volumes and little uptake so far
Use cases	• Store of value • Speculation	• B2B transactions • Cash management	• Onramp from fiat to crypto • Settlement of crypto-asset trades • Payments	• Retail payments • Institutional payments & settlements for banks and PSPs
Backing assets	None	Claim on the issuer, like regular bank deposits	1:1 assets held by issuer to meet redemptions, typically as HQLA	Claim on the central bank

	Cryptocurrencies	DLT-based deposits	Stablecoins	CBCDs
Regulatory frameworks	No regulatory framework in most markets, although regulatory frameworks are emerging (like MICA in EU)	Subject to similar supervision and oversight as other regulated bank deposits by national regulators	No regulatory framework in most markets, although regulatory frameworks are emerging (like MICA in EU)	Secured and governed directly by national central banks and regulators
Risk management	No unified risk management framework	• Mandatory minimum liquidity, regulatory capital and risk management by jurisdiction • Banks' internal risk management practices	• No unified risk management framework • Issuers´ internal risk management practices	No risk to be managed, because backed by the central bank
Emergency protections	• No traditional protections • Decentralized model • Independent from governments and central banks	• Strength of existing bank balance sheet • Contingency funding sources at central bank • Resolution and recovery planning to overcome financial distress	• Liquidation of reserve assets • Resolution under traditional bankruptcy laws	• No liquidation risk, because backed by the central bank • CBDC should have an emergency shutdown provision in case of cyber-hack

Source Author adapted from Oliver Wyman, Onyx/JP Morgan [60]

17.1 Summary Chart

Comparison of Cryptocurrencies, DLT-based deposits, stablecoins, and CBDCs (Table 17.1).

17.2 Key Items to Remember

- The technology is available to provide any level of real/hard privacy that is desired in a CBDC solution. The decision which type of privacy to adopt is exclusively a policy decision.
- Privacy and Security are not in contradiction. More privacy also means more security.
- Real privacy does not come at the expense of usability. Real spender privacy is implementable in the most user-friendly way of all, as one-click transaction, where no identification is needed.
- Real privacy is always cryptographically enforced and cannot be reverted. Any other "privacy" is trust based, where you must trust one or more third parties to do the right thing. Hence, just call it trust.
- Privacy that can be removed by third parties (without consent) is NO privacy at all!
- Privacy must be maintained across the entire CBDC ecosystem before privacy can be genuinely claimed.
- Anonymity means without any name. It exists both ways or one-way, and can never be reverted nor can transactions be linked together.
- Pseudonymity may be uncovered with sufficient efforts in linking data together.
- Anonymity= Pseudonymity + Unlinkability
- Fully offline solutions can never be 100% secure (as per CAP theorem). One can only mitigate (not remove) the vulnerabilities.
- Quantum computing really affects only asymmetric key cryptography, by solving the factorization and discrete logarithm problems. On Q-day, encrypted data is affected into the past, while signatures are only affected going into the future.

17.3 rCBDC Key Features: Opportunities and Risks

Below you will find my personal classification of those features I consider unique sales propositions (USP) for a CBDC over current digital payment solutions, as pure opportunity without downside and those that have unique value but do not come without risk:

Privacy as in one-sided anonymity	– USP –	Opportunity
Fast settlement/transaction times	– USP –	Opportunity
High performance/scalability	– USP –	Opportunity
Easy accessibility	– USP –	Opportunity
Micropayments	– USP –	Opportunity
Cross-border	– USP –	Opportunity
Programmability of money	– USP –	Opportunity & Risk
Offline payment (2-sided)	– USP –	Opportunity & High Risk

* * *

If you enjoyed the reading and found value in this book, please leave a positive review on the platform where you made your purchase. Reviews genuinely aid authors in gaining more exposure for their work. Should you wish to connect further, you can find me and reach out to me on:

My website and blog: http://www.digitalekho.com/,
LinkedIn: https://www.linkedin.com/in/leonschumacher/
Twitter: @CIOekho

I will provide regular insights and opinions on these platforms and would love to connect with you. I'm eager to hear your thoughts, assist you anyway I can, and delve deeper into discussions about future designs of money.

Thank you for taking interest and letting me share my insights through this book. I sincerely hope it provided you with intriguing and valuable perspectives. Help us shape the right money for the future!

Addendum

A. Suppliers with Traction in the Market

By traction, we mean that these suppliers either have participated in CBDC pilots or have been endorsed in white papers by central banks.

A.1 rCBDC Suppliers

Bitt

Bitt Inc. is a Barbados based software company that has successfully launched a CBDC in Nigeria and in the Easter Caribbean Currency Union.

https://www.bitt.com/

eCurrency Mint

eCurrency Mint is an Irish software company that has delivered the CBDC solution for the JAM-DEX solution in Jamaica.

https://www.ecurrency.net/

Giesecke+Devrient

Giesecke+Devrient (G+D) is a German company, which has created a subsidiary called G+D advance 52 GmbH and launched a CBDC product called Filia. G+D has been testing a card-based CBDC platform in Ghana that is supposed to allow for multiple consecutive offline transactions.

https://www.gi-de.com/en/

L. V. Schumacher, *Decoding Digital Assets*, https://doi.org/10.1007/978-3-031-54601-3

NZIA

NZIA Limited was created from the initial efforts of IBM in the Bahamas. NZIA Limited brings together the collective know-how and expertise of IBM, a leader in enterprise blockchain, along with Zynesis Pte. Ltd., a Singapore-based software development company specializing in blockchain solutions. They introduced the first CBDC on the planet based on the NZAI Coretx DLT.

https://nzia.io

R3 Corda

R3 is a DLT infrastructure provider. Corda is their product. They have seen initial success and have been involved in several wholesale and retail projects (like the Swedish eKrona)

https://r3.com/

Ripple

Ripple is a real-time gross settlement system, currency exchange, and remittance network that is open to financial institutions worldwide and was created by Ripple Labs Inc., a US-based technology company.

www.ripple.com

Soramitsu

Soramitsu is a Japanese software company that has developed a CBDC solution based on Hyperledger Iroha. They have implemented a CBDC-like solution in Cambodia and did a project with the central bank of Laos.

https://www.soramitsu.co.jp/

Taler Systems

Taler Systems is a Luxembourgish software company that comes from developing payment solutions with privacy for the internet. This solution was then adapted together with Swiss National Bank to fit retail CBDC requirements. Their specialty is one-sided privacy (spender anonymous, recipient transparent) that offers the best trade-off between privacy and prevention of illegal activities, and microtransaction with a bearer instrument.

https://www.taler-systems.com

Summary

See Table A.1.

Table A.1 2023 rCBDC supplies

	Bitt	eCurrency Mint	G+D	NZIA	R3 Corda	Ripple	Soramitsu	Taler Systems
DLT or DB	**DLT**	**DB**	**DLT or DB**	**DLT**	**DLT**	**DLT**	**DLT**	**DLT or DB**
DLT back-ends currently supported	**Hyperledger Fabric & any in theory**	**No**	–	**No**	**Corda**	**Private XRP ledger**	**Hyperledger Iroha**	**ETH, BTC & any in theory**
Database back-end supported	**No**	**Yes**	**Yes**	**No**	**No**	**No**	**No**	**Yes**
Programmable Payments	**Yes**	**Yes**	**Yes**	**Yes**	**Yes**	**Yes**	**Yes**	**Yes**
Programmable Money					**Yes**	**Yes**	**Yes**	**Yes**
Offline payments	**No**	**No**	**Yes**	**No**	**With partner**	**No**	**No**	**Yes**
Mobile Wallet support	**Yes**	**Yes**	**Yes**	**Yes**	**Yes**	**Yes**	**Yes**	**Yes**
Central Bank Endorse-ments (Paper, PoC, Pilot or Live)	**Eastern Caribbean, Nigeria**	**Jamaica**	**Ghana, Thailand, Eswatini, Brazil**	**Bahamas**	**Sweden+wholesale projects**	**Palau, Bhutan, Colombia, Montenegro, Georgia**	**Cambodia, Laos**	**Switzerland, Austria**
Guaranteed hard/real privacy	**No**	**No**	**No**	**No**	**No**	**No**	**No**	**Yes—Spender**

(continued)

Table A.1 (continued)

	Bitt	eCurrency Mint	G+D	NZIA	R3 Corda	Ripple	Soramitsu	Taler Systems
Privacy approach	**Data-split**	**Adaptable**	**Pseudonym**	**-**	**Pseudonym**	**Pseudonym**	**Pseudonym**	**Spender (one-sided) anonymity**
Privacy in ecosystem	**Trust based**	**Trust based**	**Trust based**	**Trust based**	**Trust based**	**Trust based**	**Trust based**	**Math based**

A.2 wCBDC Suppliers

Consensys

ConsenSys [106] is a private blockchain software technology company based in New York City.

In 2020, ConsenSys acquired banking blockchain platform Quorum from JPMorgan Chase & Co. Investors in ConsenSys include Animoca Brands, Coinbase Ventures, HSBC, ParaFi Capital, Microsoft, SoftBank, Temasek, and others. It is the Quorum blockchain that is the software solution that is most often a candidate for wCBDC solutions.

https://consensys.io/

Hyperledger

Hyperledger, a comprehensive project encompassing open-source blockchains and associated tools, was initiated by the Linux Foundation in December 2015. Leading tech companies such as IBM, Intel, and SAP Ariba have contributed toward the collective development of blockchain-powered distributed ledgers under this project. In October 2021, it underwent a rebranding and is now known as the Hyperledger Foundation.

There are different Hyperledger blockchains, including Besu, Fabric, and Iroha that have been used in CBDC related projects.

https://www.hyperledger.org/

Partior

Partior is a payment platform that operates across borders and is headquartered in Singapore. Partior was created as a result of the collaboration known as Project Ubin, and serves as an open industry platform for banks globally to facilitate real-time multi-currency payments across borders.

Partior labels itself "*An open industry platform, developed to transform and accelerate interbank value movements in a digital era.*" The platform is supported by major financial institutions such as DBS Bank, J.P. Morgan, and Temasek and has already been launched, causing a significant impact in the finance industry.

https://www.partior.com/

R3 Corda

R3 is a New York-based DLT infrastructure provider with a product called Corda. The Corda Blockchain aims to revolutionize the way businesses conduct transactions with its innovative smart contract technology.

As a permissioned peer-to-peer (P2P) distributed ledger technology (DLT) platform, Corda connects networks, enabling the building of applications that drive digital transformation in sectors including retail finance, corporate finance, capital markets and exchanges, investments, insurance, and non-financial infrastructure.

https://r3.com/

Ripple

Ripple is a real-time gross settlement system, currency exchange, and remittance network that is open to financial institutions worldwide and was created by Ripple Labs Inc., a US-based technology company.

www.ripple.com

Summary

See Table A.2.

Table A.2 2023 wCBDC supplies

	Consensys	Hyperledger	Partior	R3 Corda	Ripple
DLT or DB	**DLT**	**DLT**	**DLT**	**DLT**	**DLT**
DLTs back-end supported	**Consensus Quorum, Hyperledger Besu**	**Hyperledger Besu, Hyperledger Fabric Hyperledger Iroha**	**Ethereum**	**Corda**	**Private XRP ledger**
Programmable Payments	**Yes**	**Yes**	**Yes**	**Yes**	**Yes**
Programmable Money	**Yes**	**Yes**	**Yes**	**Yes**	**Yes**
Endorsements (Paper, PoC, Pilot or Live)	**Australia, Hong-Kong, South Africa…**	**Cambodia,**	**Singapore,**	**Sweden, Switzerland, France…**	**Palau, Bhutan, Colombia, Montenegro**

Source Author

Glossary

51% attack An attack on a cryptocurrency blockchain by a group of miners who control more than 50% of the network's mining hash rate.

Algorithmic stablecoin A stablecoin that is uncollateralized and aims to maintain a stable value through the use of algorithms and smart contracts to dynamically match the supply of the stablecoin with user demand.

AnaCredit ECB System. Name stands for "Analytical Credit Datasets." AnaCredit aims to establish a dataset containing detailed information on individual bank loans in the euro area, harmonized across all member states.

Asset A resource controlled by an enterprise as a result of past events, and from which future economic benefits are expected to flow to the enterprise.

Authentication (aka Identification) A process or activity to verify the identity of a user, process, or system.

Automated Clearing House (ACH) A network operated by the National Automated Clearing House Association (Nacha) to aggregate US transactions for processing bank-to-bank money transfers.

Bancor Global currency proposed in 1944 in Bretton Woods by John Maynard Keynes only be used for wholesale trade settlement, not for individual trading or holding.

Bank transfers Direct transfers of funds from one bank account to another.

Belgian-Luxembourg Economic Union (UEBL) Currency union from 1922 and replaced by the introduction of the euro.

Bitcoin mining The process that puts new Bitcoins into circulation and verifies then adds transactions to the blockchain. This happens by solving complex computational problems.

L. V. Schumacher, *Decoding Digital Assets*, https://doi.org/10.1007/978-3-031-54601-3

Blind signature Digital signature that allows a signer to create a signature without learning the content of the message that they signed.

Block explorer A block explorer is an online tool that enables you to search for real-time and historical information about a blockchain, including data related to blocks, transactions, addresses, and more.

Bretton Woods The term "Bretton Woods" typically refers to the Bretton Woods Conference of July 1944 and the resulting international financial system established after World War II. It created the IMF, the World Bank and a system of fixed exchange rates where countries would peg their currencies to gold, but only the US dollar was directly convertible to gold at a rate of $35 per ounce.

Cash Banknotes and coins

Central bank Financial institution that is responsible for managing a country's monetary policy, currency supply, and interest rates.

Central bank money (aka central bank reserves) Reserves for select financial market participants maintained by the central bank, used mainly for interbank transactions and for settling large-value transactions between financial institutions.

Central Bank Digital Currencies (CBDC) An additional digital form of central bank money next to coins, banknotes, and reserves, issued and backed by a central bank, and intended to be used as a means of payment and a form of legal tender.

CFA franc Common name for two-related currencies of the same value, the West African CFA franc and the Central African CFA franc. CFA stands for "*Communauté Financière Africaine*" (African Financial Community).

CIA Triad A common model that forms the basis for the development of security systems based on Confidentiality, Integrity, and Availability.

Clearing The process of transmitting, reconciling, and, in some cases, confirming transactions prior to settlement, potentially including the netting of transactions and the establishment of final positions for settlement.

Clearing House Inter-Payments System (CHIPS) Privately operated and managed system that facilitates dollar-denominated domestic and international funds transfers.

Credit cards Payment cards that can be used online or at a point of sale (PoS) terminal and that have a certain amount of credit to be used and paid back later. Credit cards are also a digital means of payment today.

Cross-border payments Transactions between different countries and requiring coordination among banking systems on both sides of the border to bridge national boundaries and exchange rates.

Crypto-collateralized stablecoin Stablecoin which is backed by collateral in other cryptocurrencies.

Cryptocurrencies Digital or virtual currencies that use cryptography for security and are often decentralized.

Crypto primitives (cryptographic primitive) A crypto primitive is a low-level cryptographic algorithm that serves as a basic building block for constructing cryptographic protocols, systems, and applications. Cryptographic primitives are designed to accomplish specific security tasks, and they are rigorously analyzed and tested for their security properties.

Cipher Algorithm for performing encryption or decryption using a secret key

Ciphertext An encrypted message

Commercial bank Money (aka private money) Money created by commercial banks when receiving cash in deposit and reusing it by granting loans.

Confidentiality An example of trust-based privacy, where a small group of people or companies know the information (e.g. your payment details), but promise not to share it with others (i.e. to keep it for themselves or confidential).

Counterparty risk The probability that the other party in an investment, credit, or trading transaction may not fulfill its part of the deal and may default on the contractual obligations.

Current assets Assets that can be easily converted into cash and cash equivalents. They can also be called liquid assets.

Data Minimization A principle which states that only the minimum necessary information should be collected and held for a specific purpose.

Decentralized financial applications (DeFi) Decentralized finance is an emerging financial technology based on secure distributed ledgers (or blockchains) similar to those used by cryptocurrencies.

Decryption The process of turning ciphertext back into plaintext.

Debit cards Payment cards that can be used online or at a point of sale (PoS) terminal and that are connected to a bank account.

Deferred net settlement (DNS) Netting and settlement take place after a specified period. Incoming and outgoing payments offset each other. Payments are settled periodically in batches.

Digital certificate (aka public key certificate) Digital file used to cryptographically link ownership of a public key to the entity that owns it. Digital certificates are for sharing public keys to be used for encryption and authentication.

Digital money (aka electronic money) Money that is stored, exchanged, and transacted electronically, such as cryptocurrencies, mobile wallets, or bank transfers.

Digital payments Refer to electronic transactions made through digital channels, such as computers, mobile devices, or the internet, to pay for goods and services.

Digital payment token Type of digital asset that is used as a medium of exchange for making payments in digital transactions and typically stored in digital wallets

Digital signature A digital equivalent to a handwritten signature on paper. A digital or cryptographic signature should be unforgeable and additionally protect the integrity of the message and ensure it was not altered.

Digital wallets Software applications that enable users to send, receive, and manage their digital assets electronically. They come in all forms or fashion, some can handle many different tokens and payment methods, others can't.

Eastern Caribbean Currency Union (ECCU) Currency union which groups 8 Caribbean countries that use a common currency, the Eastern Caribbean dollar.

Electronic Banking Internet Communication Standard (EBICS) A widely recognized and adopted standard for electronic banking communication in Europe, primarily in Germany, Switzerland, and France. EBICS supports various types of transactions, including domestic and cross-border payments, direct debits, standing orders, and liquidity management.

Elliptic Curve Digital Signature Algorithm (ECDSA) A digital signature scheme which is US government standard, and an update of the earlier DSA algorithm, adapted to use elliptic curves.

Electronic Funds Transfer (EFT) First digital system introduced in the 1960s to transfer funds between banks electronically, with access limited to large corporations and financial institutions.

Enron The Enron scandal involved the US energy company Enron using accounting loopholes to hide debt and inflate profits. When the deceit was exposed in 2001, Enron declared bankruptcy, leading to a $74 billion loss for shareholders. The scandal prompted regulatory reforms, including the Sarbanes–Oxley Act.

E-money Means electronic money, digital currency or digital cash, and it is a type of currency that is electronically exchanged and transacted.

Encryption The process of disguising or encoding a message in a way that keeps its content confidential.

Exchange rate fluctuations A natural outcome of floating exchange rates, which is the norm for most major economies. Numerous factors influence exchange rates, including a country's economic performance, the outlook for inflation, interest rate differentials, capital flows, and so on.

Federal Deposit Insurance Corporation (FDIC) An independent agency created by Congress to maintain stability and public confidence in the US financial system. To accomplish this mission, the FDIC insures deposits; examines and supervises financial institutions for safety, soundness, and consumer protection; makes large and complex financial institutions resolvable; and manages receiverships. As of the end of 2022, the FDIC had just over $128 billion in its Deposit Insurance Fund, backing more than $10 trillion in insured deposits. The Deposit Insurance Fund is funded two ways: through premiums charged to the insured banks, and through interest earned on funds invested in US government securities. Similar schemes exist in other countries as well.

FedNow A new RTGS system, currently being rolled out by the US Federal Reserve, to provide instant, round-the-clock settlement of payments, complementing the Fedwire system.

Fedwire This is the US Federal Reserve's system for domestic and international funds transfer, handling both messaging and settlement functions. It is a real-time, gross settlement (RTGS) system.

Fiat-collateralized stablecoin A stablecoin using fiat currencies like USD, EUR, GBP as collateral.

Fiat money (aka central bank money) Money that is not backed by a commodity but has value because of government decree or regulation. Most of the modern-day currencies, such as the US dollar, Euro, or Japanese yen, are fiat money aka central bank money.

Fixed assets Assets that cannot be easily and readily converted into cash and cash equivalents. Fixed assets are illiquid assets.

Fractional banking (Fractional reserve banking) Fractional banking is a system in which banks hold only a fraction of deposits as reserves. The rest is loaned out or invested. This creates money and expands the money supply, while still allowing for customer withdrawals.

Hash function Function that takes an arbitrary block of data and returns a fixed-size bit string, the cryptographic hash value, such that any (accidental or intentional) change to the data will (with very high probability) change the hash value.

Hash Value A hash value is a fixed-size bit string is returned by a cryptographic function, the hash function, for any given data block. Any change to the data will alter the hash value. The ideal cryptographic hash function is easy to compute, hiding to recreate the original message, preventing a change to the message without changing the hash, and collision-free, i.e. impossible to find two different messages with the same hash.

High-quality liquid assets (HQLAs) Assets are considered to be HQLAs if they can be easily and immediately converted into cash at little or no loss of value.

Homomorphic encryption A cryptographic technique that allows data to be encrypted in such a way that it can be processed by a third party without needing to be decrypted first.

Key agreement protocols Cryptographic methods used to securely establish and exchange cryptographic keys between parties over an untrusted network. These keys can then be used for encrypting and decrypting messages or data. One of the most famous key agreement protocols is the Diffie-Hellman key exchange.

IP Address An IP address, which stands for "Internet Protocol address," is a unique numerical label assigned to each device connected to a computer network that uses the Internet Protocol for communication. An IP address serves two main functions: host or network interface identification and location addressing. Examples: in IPv4 192.168.0.1. and in IPv6: 1200:0000:AB00:1234:0000:2552:7777:1313.

IMEI number IMEI stands for "International Mobile Equipment Identity." It is a unique 15-digit number assigned to every mobile device, such as smartphones and tablets, to identify them on a cellular network. The IMEI number is used by cellular networks to recognize valid devices and, thus, can be used for stopping a stolen phone from accessing that network. You can find your IMEi number on most phones by dialing *#06#.

Latin Monetary Union (LMU) Currency union established in 1865 by France, Belgium, Italy, and Switzerland

Legal tender A form of payment that is recognized by law as acceptable for the payment of debts and obligations.

Liability Refers to an obligation that a person or organization owes to another party.

Liquidity coverage ratio (LCR) The requirement whereby banks must hold an amount of high-quality liquid assets that's enough to fund cash outflows for 30 days.

M_0 (also called base money) The narrowest measure of the money supply including only physical currency in circulation and reserves held by commercial banks at the central bank.

M_1 A broader measure than M_0 including all the components of M_0 plus checking account deposits held by individuals and businesses at commercial banks.

M_2 The broadest measure of the money supply including all the components of M_1 plus savings accounts, money market accounts, and other time deposits held by individuals and businesses at commercial banks.

Message A sequence of bits. Examples include digital representations of texts, payment transactions, or medical images.

Mobile payments Payments made using a mobile device or smartphone application.

Money laundering The process of disguising the proceeds of illegal activities as legitimate funds.

Multi-signature Digital signature that requires that multiple signers jointly create one signature.

Narrow banks Financial institutions that cover 100% of liabilities with central bank reserves and do not lend to the private sector, instead focusing solely on facilitating payments. This compares to most of our commercial banks today, which are in the business of fractional reserve banking.

Non-fungible tokens (NFTs) A type of digital asset that represent unique items, such as digital art, collectibles, and virtual real estate, on a blockchain.

Nostro/Vostro accounts Accounts that correspondent banks hold with each other in different currencies. Nostro comes from the Latin word for "ours," as in "our money that is on deposit at your bank." Vostro comes from the Latin word for "yours," as in "your money that is on deposit at our bank."

Other-asset-collateralized stablecoins Stablecoins collateralized with commodities such as gold or silver or by bonds and shares.

Permissioned DLT (Distributed Ledger Technology) A type of decentralized system where access to the network and its functionalities is restricted to a select group of participants who have been granted permission by a central authority.

Permissionless DLT (Distributed Ledger Technology) A type of decentralized system where anyone can participate without requiring permission or authorization from a central authority.

Post-quantum cryptography The study of cryptographic algorithms that do not rely on strong assumptions that could be broken by the appearance of a quantum computer and the subsequent use of a quantum algorithm.

Private money (aka Commercial bank Money) Money created by commercial banks when receiving cash in deposit and reusing it by granting loans.

Q-Day The day on which a quantum computer, able to crack the currently used crypto primitives becomes available.

Quantum cryptography The development of cryptographic algorithms that only run on quantum computers.

Quantum-proof Secured against the consequences of a quantum computer becoming available.

Quantum-ready Upgradeable to quantum-proof, by updating crypto primitives in use for example, once a quantum computer becomes available.

Utility tokens A type of crypto-asset token that is designed to provide access to a specific product or service within a blockchain ecosystem.

Real-time gross settlement (RTGS) A system where each payment is settled on a gross basis individually or on a net basis as a batch. If the payer has insufficient funds, the payment is either rejected or queued.

Retail CBDC (abbreviated rCBDC) CBDC designed for use by the general public and intended to be a digital equivalent of physical currency.

Retail payments The everyday transactions that most people engage in, such as buying food at a restaurant with a credit card, making grocery purchases with cash at a supermarket, or using online payment service providers like PayPal for online shopping.

Ring-signatures Digital signatures that allow multiple signers to sign for a group without revealing which group members participated in the signing.

Security tokens A type of cryptocurrency token that represent ownership in an asset, such as a company's stock, real estate, or commodities. These tokens are designed to comply with securities laws and regulations.

Seigniorage The difference between the cost of producing currency (paper money and coins) and its face value.

Settlement: The discharge of an obligation in accordance with the terms of the underlying contract.

Settlement account An account containing money and/or assets that is held with a central bank, central securities depository, central counterparty, or any other institution acting as a settlement agent, which is used to settle transactions between participants or members of a commercial settlement system.

Settlement asset An asset used for the discharge of obligations as specified by the rules, regulations, or customary practice for a financial market infrastructure.

Settlement finality Settlement finality is defined as the point when the irrevocable and unconditional transfer of an asset occurs. Final settlement is a legally defined moment.

Settlement risk The risk that one party in a financial transaction will not be able to hold their end of the deal by failing to deliver the cash or the security required to complete the transaction. Settlement risk may also occur when there is a lag in payment from one party, usually due to time zones. Settlement risk is different from counter party risk.

Single Euro Payments Area (SEPA) An initiative that harmonizes electronic payments in euros across Europe. It establishes common standards and formats for euro-denominated payments within the participating countries. SEPA focuses on credit transfers and direct debits in euros within the SEPA zone.

Signature (physical) Scribble appended to a message to assert the origin or approval of the message by the signer.

Society for Worldwide Interbank Financial Telecommunications (SWIFT) A consortium of member financial institutions operating a global messaging system for the actual settlement of payments both locally and internationally.

Stablecoin A type of digital asset or cryptocurrency is designed to maintain a stable value relative to a traditional currency, commodity, or other asset.

SWIFT Customer Security Program (SWIFT CSP) Program introducing the SWIFT Customer Security Controls Framework (CSCF) with about 30 specific controls, some advisory and some mandatory, with the goal of adopting stronger security standards and improving response times to address potential threats as reaction to the central bank of Bangladesh hack.

TARGET2 (Trans-European Automated Real-time Gross Settlement Express Transfer System 2) Second version of a real-time gross settlement (RTGS) system that is owned and operated by the Eurosystem, which consists of the European Central Bank (ECB) and the national central banks (NCBs) of those European Union (EU) member states which have adopted the euro as their currency. The shift from national real-time gross settlement systems to TARGET in 1999, followed by the upgrade to TARGET2 in 2007, marked the creation of the first integrated market infrastructure for large-value wholesale payments across Europe.

Threat model A structured representation of all the information that affects the security of an application.

TIPS (TARGET Instant Payment Settlement) It is a pan-European instant payment settlement service that facilitates real-time, round-the-clock, and irrevocable money transfers in euro.

Tokenization The process of representing claims in a digital form that allows them to be transacted on programmable platforms.

Tokenized deposits (sometimes also referred to as deposit tokens) A novel financial product that offers investors greater flexibility and allows traditional bank deposits or savings accounts to be converted into digital assets represented by tokens.

Transitivity The ability to immediately re-spend funds that are received offline, without connecting to the outside world. Transitivity implies that each transaction is fully settled in real-time, transferring the funds from sender to recipient instantly and the recipient can right away re-spend them.

Troika A term used to refer to the single decision group created by three entities, the European Commission(EC), the European Central Bank (ECB), and the International Monetary Fund (IMF).

Unit-based solutions A unit-based solution on the blockchain, based on UTXO, refers to a system where transactions are represented as inputs and outputs. Ownership of funds is proven by the possession of unspent outputs (UTXOs), and spending involves consuming one or more UTXOs and producing new ones, ensuring that each unit (or UTXO) is only spent once.

Unlinkability It means that different interactions of the same user with the system should not be linkable to each other.

Vostro accounts See Nostro/Vostro accounts

Waterfall A waterfall is a method for facilitating the use of a digital euro by automatically converting the amount of digital euro that exceeds a defined holding threshold into private money in a linked liquidity source chosen by the end user, such as a commercial bank account.

Wholesale payments Payments executed behind the scenes and serving as the underlying infrastructure of the financial system, facilitating the transfer and settlement of funds between financial institutions.

Wholesale CBDC (abbreviated wCBDC) A CBDC designed for use by a select number of important financial institutions, which are allowed to keep an account at the central bank and are used to facilitate interbank payments and settlements.

World Bank Not a central bank but an international financial institution founded to promote economic development and reduce poverty around the world based in Washington D.C.

Zero-knowledge proof Proof that allows a prover to demonstrate to a verifier the veracity of a claim without revealing any additional information, other than the claim and that it must be true.

References

1. The book of crypto, Henri Arslanian. Edition 1, ISBN 978-3 030-97951-5, 2022.
2. Cashless, Richard Turrin, Authority Publishing, ISBN 978-1949642720, 2021.
3. IMF Working Paper WP/23/37: Crypto Assets and CBDCs in Latin America and the Caribbean Opportunities and Risks Appendino, M., O. Bespalova, R. Bhattacharya, JF. Clevy, N. Geng, T. Komatsuzaki, J. Lesniak, W. Lian, S. Marcelino, M. Villafuerte, Y. Yakhshilikov.
4. BIS, 2021 BIS Central Bank Survey on CBDCs and Digital Assets.
5. PriceWaterhouseCoopers, Global CBDC Index 2021/2022.
6. CBDCtracker, www.cbdctracker.org.
7. Swiss National Bank, Working Paper "How to Issue a CBDC David Chaum, Christian Grothoff and Thomas Moser, March 2021.
8. Bank of England and HM Treasury, The Digital Pound: a new form of money for households and businesses, Consultation Paper, February 2023.
9. CoinTelegraph 12.1.2023, Gareth Jenkinson, Nigeria Revisits Its Payments Landscape Amid Sluggish eNaira Adoption.
10. Techmonitor, 30.3.2022, Greg Noone, How e-Naira Is Turning cbdc Theory into Reality, https://techmonitor.ai/policy/digital-economy/how-enaira-is-turning-cbdc-theory-into-reality.
11. 3rd Global Cryptoasset Benchmarking Study, Cambridge Center for Alternative Finance, 2020.
12. The Libra white paper; LIBRA Association, June 2019, https://www.docdroid.net/kudDQUQ/librawhitepaper-en-us-pdf.

L. V. Schumacher, *Decoding Digital Assets*, https://doi.org/10.1007/978-3-031-54601-3

13. ECB, April 2021: Eurosystem Report on the Public Consultation on a Digital Euro.
14. Deutsche Bundesbank, Monthly Report October 2021: What Do Households in Germany Think About the Digital Euro? First Results from Surveys and Interviews.
15. The Technology of Retail Central Bank Digital Currency, BIS Quarterly Review, March 2020, Raphael Auer & Rainer Boehme.
16. https://www.zippia.com/advice/money-laundering-statistics/.
17. Federal Reserve Board: The Federal Reserve Payments Study 2016.
18. Congress.gov, S.4313—Defending Americans from Authoritarian Digital Currencies, Act117th Congress (2021–2022), Sen. Tom Cotton.
19. ECB/Eurosystem, July 2022, The Case for a Digital Euro: Key Objectives and Design Considerations.
20. ECB/Eurosystem, 16 Jan 2023, Digital Euro—Stocktake.
21. Sveriges Riksbank, The Riksbank's e-krona Project, Report 1, September 2017, https://www.riksbank.se/en-gb/payments--cash/e-krona/e-krona-reports/e-krona-project-report-1/.
22. Sveriges Riksbank, The Riksbank's e-krona Project, Report 2, October 2018, https://www.riksbank.se/en-gb/payments--cash/e-krona/e-krona-reports/e-krona-project-report-2/.
23. The Tribune, www.tribune242.com, Smartphone Penetration Hits 98% of Bahamians, March 29, 2022.
24. Western Standard, www.westernstandard.news. Feds Could Freeze Accounts with as Little as a $20 Donation to the Freedom Convoy, Feb 23, 2022—Updated May 3, 2022.
25. "Europe and IMF Agree €110 Billion Financing Plan with Greece". IMF Survey online, 2 May 2010, Retrieved 28 June 2015.
26. Why a Digital Euro should be Online-First and Bearer-Based, Christian Grothoff & Florian Dold, March 26, 2021.
27. Brewer's Conjecture and the Feasibility of Consistent, Available, Partition-Tolerant Web Services, Seth Gilbert & Nancy Lynch, SIGACT News, 33(2):51–59, June 2002.
28. Coindesk.com: Circle to Cover Any Shortfall in USDC Reserves, Sparking Stablecoin Rally, Danny Nelson, March 11th, 2023.
29. Coindesk.com, The World Could Be Facing a Dark Future Thanks to CBDCs, by Gneet Kaur, March 23RD, 2023.
30. https://www.bloomberg.com/news/articles/2023-02-21/nigeria-seeks-new-tech-partners-to-revamp-enaira-central-bank-digital-currency?leadSource=uverify%20wall.
31. Federal Reserve Bank of San Francisco, Findings from the Diary of Consumer Payment Choice, May 2022.
32. FDIC, National Survey of Unbanked and Underbanked Households, 2021.
33. https://emmer.house.gov/2022/1/emmer-introduces-legislation-to-prevent-unilateral-fed-control-of-a-u-s-digital-currency.

34. https://www.cruz.senate.gov/newsroom/press-releases/sen-cruz-introduces-legislation-prohibiting-unilateral-fed-control-of-a-us-digital-currency.
35. https://theconservativetreehouse.com/blog/2023/03/11/kristi-noem-sends-warning-about-state-level-effort-to-redefine-currency-same-legislation-currently-hitting-20-states/.
36. https://www.flgov.com/2023/03/20/governor-ron-desantis-announces-legislation-to-protect-floridians-from-a-federally-controlled-central-bank-digital-currency-and-surveillance-state/.
37. Statista, https://www.statista.com/statistics/201182/forecast-of-smartphone-users-inthe-us/.
38. Federal Reserve Bank of Kansas City, What Consumer Surveys Say about the Design of a U.S. CBDC for Retail Payments, Franklin Noll, March 29, 2023.
39. Statista, https://www.statista.com/statistics/209117/us-internet-penetration/.
40. Gjefle, Erin, Zach Herring, Cris Kubli, Brennan O'Rear, and Georgia Rakusen. "Centering Users in the Design of Digital Currency." Maiden Labs, supported by MIT Digital Currency Initiative, December 2021.
41. Kantar Public. "Study on New Digital Payment Methods." Commissioned by the European Central Bank, March 2022.
42. OMFIF (Official Money and Financial Institutions Forum), "Digital Currencies: A Question of Trust." 2020.
43. EDPD, Letter on Digital Euro, 18 June 2021 REF: OUT2021-0105.
44. Wired, The Full Story of the Stunning RSA Hack Can Finally Be Told, Andy Greenberg, May 28, 2021.
45. DMR, AliPay Statistics & User count (2023), October 19, 2022, https://expandedramblings.com/index.php/AliPay-statistics/.
46. M. Dorjmyagmar, M. Kim, and H. Kim. Security Analysis of Samsungknox. 19th International Conference on Advanced Communication Technology (ICACT), pages 550–553, 2017.
47. R. Guanciale, H. Nemati, C. Baumann, and M. Dam. Cache Storage Channels: Alias-Driven Attacks and Verified Countermeasures. In 2016 IEEE Symposium on Security and Privacy (SP), pages 38–55, May 2016.
48. Moritz Lipp, Daniel Gruss, Raphael Spreitzer, Clémentine Maurice, and Stefan Mangard. Armageddon: Cache Attacks on Mobile Devices. In Proceedings of the 25th USENIX Conference on Security Symposium, SEC'16, page 549–564, USA, 2016. USENIX Association.
49. Aravind Machiry, Eric Gustafson, Chad Spensky, Christopher Salls, Nick Stephens, Ruoyu Wang, Antonio Bianchi, Yung Ryn Choe, Christopher Kruegel, and Giovanni Vigna. Boomerang: Exploiting the Semantic Gap in Trusted Execution Environments. In NDSS, 2017.
50. Adrian Tang, Simha Sethumadhavan, and Salvatore Stolfo. Clkscrew: Exposing the Perils of Security-Oblivious Energy Management. In Proceedings of the 26th USENIX Conference on Security Symposium, SEC'17, page 1057–1074, USA, 2017. USENIX Association.

51. Ning Zhang, Kun Sun, Deborah Shands, Wenjing Lou, and Y Thomas Hou. Truspy: Cache Side-Channel Information Leakage from the Secure World on Arm Devices. IACR Cryptol. ePrint Arch., 2016:980, 2016.
52. Dan Goodin. Intel SGX Is Vulnerable to an Unfixable Flaw That Can Steal Crypto Keys and More. Technical report, ARS Technica, 2020.
53. Alexander Nilsson, Pegah Nikbakht Bideh, and Joakim Brorsson. A Survey of Published Attacks on Intel SGX, https://arxiv.org/pdf/2006.13598v1.pdf, 2006.
54. Ravie Lakshmanan. Intel CPUs Vulnerable to New 'SGAxe' and 'Crosstalk' Side-Channel Attacks, https://thehackernews.com/2020/06/intel-sgaxe-crosstalk-attacks.html, June 2020.
55. Security Research Labs. New Sim Attacks De-mystified, Protection Tools Now Available, https://srlabs.de/bites/sim_attacks_demystified/, 2019.
56. Peter Buttler. Wib Vulnerability: Sim-Card That Allows Hackers to Takeover Phones, https://readwrite.com/2020/01/06/wib-vulnerability-sim-card-that-allows-hackers-to-takeover-phones/, January 2020.
57. Mengyuan Li, Yinqian Zhang, Zhiqiang Lin, and Yan Solihin. Exploiting Unprotected I/O Operations Inamd's Secure Encrypted Virtualization. In USENIX Security Symposium, 2019.
58. Computers & Security 129 (2023) A Survey on the (In)Security of Trusted Execution Environments, Antonio Muñoz, Ruben Ríos, Rodrigo Román, Javier López.
59. Oliver Wyman, Onyx by JP Morgan, DEPOSIT TOKENS, A Foundation for Stable Digital Money.
60. Jonas Gross, CBDC Academy: Technical Solutions and Their Implications on the Use Cases, August 2021. https://si.linkedin.com/posts/grossjonas_cbdc-technologies-and-use-cases-activity-6977873599168684033-oHSC.
61. IMF "Cyber Risk for the Financial Sector: A Framework for Quantitative Assessment," Antoine Bouveret, IMF Working Paper WP/18/143, June 2018.
62. Oliver Wyman, Unlocking $120 Billion Value in Cross-Border Payments, Jason Ekberg, Tek Yew Chia, Michael Ho, and Laura Liu.
63. https://www.finextra.com/newsarticle/42117/bank-of-england-begins-building-britcoin-team?mc_cid=8662fc617f&mc_eid=7796050ba3.
64. https://www.imf.org/en/Publications/fandd/issues/2022/09/kiff-taking-digital-currencies-offline.
65. Fox News, Tulsi Gabbard's Warning: If This Happens, We No Longer Have Freedom, https://www.youtube.com/watch?v=_DYQWx94ZBg, April 11, 2023.
66. OENB, Svetlana Abramova, Rainer Böhm, Helmut Elsinger, Helmut Stix, Martin Summer, Working Paper 241, What Can CBDC Designers Learn from Asking Potential Users? 2022.
67. https://www.reuters.com/article/us-cyber-heist-federal-special-report-idUSKCN1011AJ.

68. Board of Governors of the Federal Reserve System, Money and Payments: The U.S. Dollar in the Age of Digital Transformation, January 2022.
69. Board of Governors of the Federal Reserve System, Findings from the Federal Reserve Payments Study, December 2021.
70. Bank of England, The Digital Pound: Technology Working Paper, February 2023.
71. Sveriges Riksbank, The Riksbank's e-krona Project, Pilot Phase 1, April 2021, https://www.riksbank.se/en-gb/payments--cash/e-krona/e-krona-reports/e-krona-pilot-phase-1-report-3/.
72. Sveriges Riksbank, The Riksbank's e-krona Project, Pilot Phase 2, April 2022, https://www.riksbank.se/en-gb/payments--cash/e-krona/e-krona-reports/e-krona-pilot-phase-2/.
73. Tax Justice Network/PSI/Global Alliance for Tax Justice, The State of Tax Justice 2021, November 2021.
74. Money Under 30, Kevin Mercante, The Future of Cash-Will It Disappear or Become Obsolete? June 1, 2022.
75. Tipalti, Comparing the Top Global Payment Methods.
76. PriceWaterhouseCoopers, Global CBDC Index, 1st edition, 2021.
77. BIS, Auer & Boehme, The Technology of Retail Central Bank Digital Currency, BIS Quarterly Review, March 2020.
78. BIS, L. Gambacorta, Central Bank Digital Currencies: Motives, Architectures and the International Dimension, 18th Annual NBP-SNB Joint Seminar "Digital Finance", 16 November 2022.
79. Atlantic Council, Econographics, Ananya Kumar, A Report Card on China's Central Bank Digital Currency: The e-CNY.
80. Federal Deposit Insurance Corporation (FDIC), 2015 FDIC National Survey of Unbanked and Underbanked Households.
81. Satoshi Nakamoto, Bitcoin Whitepaper, 2008, https://bitcoin.org/en/bitcoin-paper.
82. OECD, Privacy Guidelines (in Effect): Recommendation of the Council Concerning Guidelines Governing the Protection of Privacy and Transborder Flows of Personal Data.
83. EU GDPR: Regulation (EU) 2016/679 of the European Parliament and of the Council of 27 April 2016 on the protection of natural persons with regard to the processing of personal data and on the free movement of such data, and repealing Directive 95/46/EC (General Data Protection Regulation).
84. California Consumer Privacy Act (CCPA): California Law TITLE 1.81.5. California Consumer Privacy Act of 2018 [1798.100—1798.199.100].
85. Soundtrack from Musical Cabaret with the name MONEY, Fred Ebb & John Kander, https://www.stlyrics.com/lyrics/cabaret/money.htm.
86. Bank of Canada: Briefing on Digital Currencies, Grahame Johnson, Lukasz Pomorski, Senate of Canada, Ottawa, Ontario, April 2, 2014.
87. The White House, Joe Biden, Executive Order on Ensuring Responsible Development of Digital Assets, EO14067, March 9, 2022.

88. Atlantic Council, Report: Missing Key: The Challenge of Cybersecurity and Central Bank Digital Currency, Giulia Fanti, Kari Kostiainen, William Howlett, Josh Lipsky, Ole Moehr, John Paul Schnapper-Casteras, and Josephine Wolff, June 15, 2022.
89. G+D, CBDCs: 12 Aspects of a Successful Adoption, Roman Hartinger, March 2023.
90. IberPay Trialed Digital Euro with Blockchain Tokens, Account-Based CBDC Coexisting, July 22, 2021, by Ledger Insights.
91. LinkedIn, Public-Permissioned Blockchains as Common-Pool Resources, by Jesus Ruiz, February 13, 2020.
92. The Cost of Cash in the United States, The Institute for Business in the Global Context at Tuft's University, September 2013, by Bhaskar Chakravorti, Benjamin Mazzotta.
93. SNB, Bank Notes and Coins, Costs https://www.snb.ch/en/iabout/cash/cash_lifecycle/id/cash_lifecycle_costs.
94. Board of Governors of the Federal Reserve System, How Much Does It Cost to Produce Currency and Coin? https://www.federalreserve.gov/faqs/currency_12771.htm.
95. The Visual Capitalist, How Many U.S. Dollar Bills Are There in Circulation? April 17, 2018, by Jeff Desjardins.
96. Payment Versus Trading Stablecoins, Gordon Liao, 25 Mar 2023.
97. Investopia, Liquidity Coverage Ratio, https://www.investopedia.com/terms/l/liquidity-coverage-ratio.asp.
98. Arvix:2304.14717, FaulTPM: Exposing AMD fTPMs' Deepest Secrets by H.N. Jacob, C. Werling, R.Buhren, JP. Seifert, May 2, 2023.
99. The 'Payto' URI Scheme for Payments, https://datatracker.ietf.org/doc/html/rfc8905.
100. 2014 California Proposition 47, Wikipedia, https://en.wikipedia.org/wiki/2014_California_Proposition_47.
101. ABC News, April 12, 2023, https://abcnews.go.com/Business/foods-closes-flagship-san-francisco-store-employee-safety/story?id=98524964%C2%A0.
102. ConsenSys, Wikipedia, https://en.wikipedia.org/wiki/ConsenSys.
103. Bitcoin and Cryptocurrency Technologies. Princeton University Press, by A. Narayanan, J. Bonneau, E. Felten, A. Miller and S. Goldfeder, 2016.
104. Board of Governors of the Federal Reserve System, The Stable in Stablecoins, December 16, 2022 by Garth Baughman, Francesca Carapella, Jacob Gerszten, and David Mills.
105. ECB/Eurosystem, Progress on the Investigation Phase of a Digital Euro—Third Report.
106. Sveriges Riksbank, E-krona Report, E-krona Pilot, Phase 3, April 2023, https://www.riksbank.se/en-gb/payments--cash/e-krona/e-krona-reports/e-krona-pilot-phase-3/.
107. Cizmic Consulting, Strategies for Achieving High CBDC Adoption, February 2021 https://cizmicconsulting.com/insights/cbdc-adoption-considerations/.

108. Federal Reserve Bank of Kansas City, kcFED Payments System Research Briefing. What Consumer Surveys Say about the Design of a U.S. CBDC for Retail Payments, March 29, 2023 by Franklin Noll.
109. DCI, MIT Media Lab, Maiden: CBDC: Expanding Financial Inclusion or Deepening the Divide? January 2023 by Narula, Swartz, Frizzo-Barker.
110. BIS (Bank of International Settlement) (2022), Annual Economic Report 2022, III. The Future Monetary System.
111. Digital Euro: Opportunities and Risks, CFS-IMFS Special Lecture Goethe University 11.07.2022 by Joachim Nagel.
112. Banca d'Italia, The Role of TIPS for the Future Payments Landscape, November 2020, by Ignazio Visco.
113. BIS Speech: Innovation and the Future of the Monetary System, 22 February 2023, by Mr Agustín Carstens.
114. Bloomberg Report: De-Dollarization Is Happening at a 'Stunning' Pace, Jen Says, by Stephen Jen and Joana Freire of asset management firm Eurizon SLJ Capital.
115. Swift, SWIFT Customer Security Controls Framework, https://www.swift.com/myswift/customer-security-programme-csp/security-controls.
116. https://googleprojectzero.blogspot.com/2017/07/trust-issues-exploiting-trustzone-tees.html.
117. BIS Bulletin 73: Stablecoins Versus Tokenized Deposits: Implications for the Singleness of Money, by Rodney Garratt and Hyun Song Shin https://www.bis.org/publ/bisbull73.htm.
118. Google, https://developers.google.com/search/blog/2014/08/https-as-ranking-signal.
119. NIST Computer Security Resource Center, https://csrc.nist.gov/projects/cryptographic-module-validation-program/certificate/3672.
120. CNN Accusations Against Huawei, https://edition.cnn.com/2019/01/29/tech/us-indictment-huawei-takeaways/index.html#:~:text=In%20indictments%20released%20late%20Monday%2C%20US%20prosecutors%20accuse,scheme%20to%20pay%20employees%20to%20steal%20trade%20secrets.
121. Intel PTT Vulnerability, https://www.intel.com/content/www/us/en/support/articles/000030081/software/chipset-software.html.
122. Coindesk: Crypto Security Firm Unciphered Claims Ability to Physically Hack Trezor T Wallet, Margaux Nijkerk, May 24, 2023.
123. BIS-IH IthanonLionrock to mBridge, Building a Multi CBDC Platform for International Payments, September 2021.
124. CPMI, BISIH, IMF and the WB, Joint Report to the G20, Central Bank Digital Currencies for Cross-Border Payments, July 2021, https://www.bis.org/publ/othp38.pdf.
125. BIS-IH, Project mBridge: Connecting Economies Through CBDC, October 2022.
126. Eurosystem: Digital Euro—Prototype Summary and Lessons Learned, 2023.

127. ECCB Blog, The ECCB's Digital Currency (DCash) Is a Critical Step in the Buildout of a Digital Economy in the ECCU, March 1, 2021, T. Antoine, Governor EC, https://eccb-centralbank.org/blog/view/the-eccbas-digital-currency-dcash-is-a-critical-step-in-the-buildout-of-a-digital-economy-in-the-eccu.
128. https://www.linkedin.com/pulse/public-permissioned-blockchains-common-pool-resources-jesus-ruiz/.
129. McKinsey, Global Payments 2021: Transformation Amid Turbulent Undercurrents, October 7, 2021, https://www.mckinsey.com/industries/financial-services/our-insights/global-payments-2021-transformation-amid-turbulent-undercurrents.
130. Tech Target, What Is the CIA Triad (Confidentiality, Integrity and Availability)? Wesley Chan, February 2023, https://www.techtarget.com/whatis/definition/Confidentiality-integrity-and-availability-CIA.
131. David Chaum, eCash, https://de.wikipedia.org/wiki/ECash.
132. EDPB, 1.2 Billion Euro Fine for Facebook as a Result of EDPB Binding Decision, May 22, 2023, https://edpb.europa.eu/news/news/2023/12-billion-euro-fine-facebook-result-edpb-binding-decision_en.
133. Federal Reserve Bank of St. Louis, Functions of Money—The Economic Lowdown Podcast Series, https://www.stlouisfed.org/education/economic-lowdown-podcast-series/episode-9-functions-of-money.
134. Wikipedia, Bank Note Reporter, https://en.wikipedia.org/wiki/Bank_note_reporter.
135. Digital Currency Initiative, MIT Media Lab, Maiden, CBDC: Expanding Financial Inclusion or Deepening the Divide? Jan 2023.
136. Tether, Tether's Latest Q1 2023 Assurance Report, May 10, 2023, https://tether.to/en/tethers-latest-q1-2023-assurance-report-shows-reserves-surplus-at-all-time-high-of-244b-up-148b-in-net-profit-new-categories-for-additional-transparency-reveals-bitcoin-and-gold-allocations/.
137. BIS, Bulletin #73, Stablecoins Versus Tokenised Deposits: Implications for the Singleness of Money, https://www.bis.org/publ/bisbull73.pdf.
138. Die Deutsche Kreditwirtschaft, Working Paper on Commercial Bank Money Token, Version 1.5, March 6th, 2023.
139. The Regulated Liability Network, Whitepaper, November 15, 2022, https://regulatedliabilitynetwork.org/wp-content/uploads/2022/11/The-Regulated-Liability-Network-Whitepaper.pdf.
140. Monetary Authority of Singapore, Project Guardian, https://www.mas.gov.sg/schemes-and-initiatives/project-guardian.
141. Swiss Banking Association, The Deposit Token, White Paper, March 2023, https://www.swissbanking.ch/_Resources/Persistent/9/4/1/1/941178de59b98030206fc15ac8c99012f65df30b/SBA_The_Deposit_Token_EN_2023.pdf.
142. Bitcoin.com, News, Industry Execs Claim Freshly Minted 'Virgin Bitcoins' Fetch 20% Premium, Jamie Redman, https://news.bitcoin.com/industry-execs-freshly-minted-virgin-bitcoins/.

143. Bloomberg.com, Nigeria Seeks New Tech Partners to Revamp Enaira Central Bank Digital Currency, Anthony Osae-Brown, February 21, 2023, https://www.bloomberg.com/news/articles/2023-02-21/nigeria-seeks-new-tech-partners-to-revamp-enaira-central-bank-digital-currency.
144. Sverige's Riksbank, E-krona Pilot Phase 3, https://www.riksbank.se/en-gb/payments--cash/e-krona/e-krona-reports/e-krona-pilot-phase-3/.
145. Yahoo Finance, the Block, 'Digital Dollar' Proposal Stripped from Latest Congressional Coronavirus Stimulus Bill, Michael McSweeney, March 24, 2020, https://finance.yahoo.com/news/digital-dollar-proposal-stripped-latest-141213745.html.
146. The Digital Dollar Project, https://digitaldollarproject.org/about/.
147. Federal Reserve Bank of Boston, Project Hamilton Phase 1 Executive Summary, https://www.bostonfed.org/publications/one-time-pubs/project-hamilton-phase-1-executive-summary.aspx.
148. Robert F. Kennedy Jr. on Twitter, https://twitter.com/robertkennedyjr/status/1643658603885101073.
149. ECB-Eurosystem, Report on a Digital Euro, October 2, 2020, https://www.ecb.europa.eu/euro/html/digitaleuro-report.en.html.
150. ECB-Eurosystem, ECB Publishes Progress Report on Digital Euro and Study on Possible Features of a Digital Wallet, April 24, 2023, https://www.ecb.europa.eu/press/pr/date/2023/html/ecb.pr230424_1~395626f0d9.en.html.
151. Oracle, Oracle TimesTen Scaleout Sets New Performance Standard for In-Memory Databases, Jul 25, 2018, https://www.oracle.com/corporate/pressrelease/oracle-timesten-scaleout-performance-072518.html.
152. GNU Taler, www.taler.net.
153. Bloomberg.com, Google and Mastercard Cut a Secret Ad Deal to Track Retail Sales, Marc Bergen, Jennifer Suraine, https://www.bloomberg.com/news/articles/2018-08-30/google-and-mastercard-cut-a-secret-ad-deal-to-track-retail-sales#xj4y7vzkg.
154. Coindesk.com, Ethereum, https://www.coindesk.com/learn/top-questions-about-proof-of-stake-and-staking-answered/.
155. LedgerAcademy, TPS, https://www.ledger.com/academy/glossary/transactions-per-second-tps.
156. Phemex, What Is Transactions Per Second? https://phemex.com/blogs/what-is-transactions-per-second-tps.
157. The Atlantic Council, A Report Card on China's Central Bank Digital Currency: the e-CNY, By Ananya Kumar, https://www.atlanticcouncil.org/blogs/econographics/a-report-card-on-chinas-central-bank-digital-currency-the-e-cny/.
158. SWIFT, Swift Traffic Highlights, https://www.swift.com/about-us/swift-traffic-highlights.
159. https://buybitcoinworldwide.com/bitcoin-uptime/.
160. BIS Innovation Hub Project Polaris, A Handbook for Offline Payments with CBDC, May 2023.

161. ACMQueue, Volume 20, Issue 4, Mapping the Privacy Landscape for Central Bank Digital Currencies, Raphael Auer, Rainer Böhme, Jeremy Clark, Didem Demirag. September 20, 2022.
162. Jamaica Observer, Taking Digital Currencies Offline, https://www.jamaicaobserver.com/business/taking-digital-currencies-offline/.
163. https://shop.ledger.com/pages/ledger-nano-x.
164. IMF, Behind the Scenes of Central Bank Digital Currency: Emerging Trends, Insights, and Policy Lessons, Soderberg et al. 09 Feb 2022.
165. https://www.atlanticcouncil.org/cbdctracker/.
166. Libra, Whitepaper, An introduction to Libra, 2019, https://sls.gmu.edu/pfrt/wp-content/uploads/sites/54/2020/02/LibraWhitePaper_en_US-Rev0723.pdf.
167. Schneier, Bruce. 2016. "Data Is a Toxic Asset, so Why Not Throw It Out?" https://www.schneier.com/essays/archives/2016/03/data_is_a_toxic_asse.html.
168. Agustin Carstens, speech on October 19th 2020 on "Cross-Border Payment—A Vision for the Future", https://meetings.imf.org/en/2020/Annual/Schedule/2020/10/19/imf-cross-border-payments-a-vision-for-the-future at 00:24:30.
169. ECB, Occasional Paper Series: Central Bank Digital Currency: Functional Scope, Pricing and Controls, Bindseil, Panetta & Terol, https://www.ecb.europa.eu/pub/pdf/scpops/ecb.op286~9d472374ea.en.pdf.
170. Kantar Public, Study on Digital Wallet Features, Commissioned by the European Central Bank, March 2023, https://www.ecb.europa.eu/press/pr/date/2023/html/ecb.pr230424_1_annex~93abdb80da.en.pdf.
171. Cato Institute, Policy Analysis, Central Bank Digital Currency: Assessing the Risks and Dispelling the Myths, Nicholas Anthony and Norbert Michel, April 4, 2023 https://www.cato.org/sites/cato.org/files/2023-03/policy-analysis-941-updated.pdf.
172. Financial Times, Quantum Computing Could Break the Internet, https://ig.ft.com/quantum-computing/.
173. https://en.wikipedia.org/wiki/Grover%27s_algorithm.
174. Josyula R. Rao and Pankaj Rohatgi, "Can Pseudonymity Really Guarantee Privacy?" 9th USENIX Security Symposium Paper, 2000, https://www.usenix.org/events/sec2000/full_papers/rao/rao_html.
175. Cookie Banners and Privacy Policies: Measuring the Impact of the GDPR on the Web Michael Kretschmer, Jan Pennekamp and Klaus Wehrle, RWTH Aachen University, Germany.
176. Kerckhoff's Principle, Wikipedia, https://en.wikipedia.org/wiki/Kerckhoffs%27s_principle.
177. Cryptoticker: Ledger Faces Backlash and Delays Key-Recovery Service…Till When? https://cryptoticker.io/en/ledger-faces-backlash-and-delays-key-recovery-service-till-when/.
178. Cryptopolitan, Damilola Lawrence, Crypto Wallet Maker Ledger Launches Controversial Recovery Service Amid Backlash, May 16, 2023, https://www.cryptopolitan.com/ledger-launches-recovery-service-amid-backlash/.

179. www.anastasis.lu.
180. https://en.wikipedia.org/wiki/Evaluation_Assurance_Level.
181. https://en.wikipedia.org/wiki/FIPS_140-2.
182. BIS Papers No 136, Making Headway—Results of the 2022 BIS Survey on Central Bank Digital Currencies and Crypto by Anneke Kosse and Ilaria Mattei.
183. Ron DeSantis, Big Brother Digital Dollar Initiative, https://www.flgov.com/2023/03/20/governor-ron-desantis-announces-legislation-to-protect-floridians-from-a-federally-controlled-central-bank-digital-currency-and-surveillance-state/.
184. The Sun (Nigeria) CBN Upgrades eNaira App with NFC Chip, Widens Sensitization, https://sunnewsonline.com/cbn-upgrades-enaira-app-with-nfc-chip-widens-sensitisation-2/.
185. Qi Gong, Governor of PBOC Speaking at MAS https://www.linkedin.com/feed/update/urn:li:activity:7087362968971079680/.
186. ECB/Eurosystem: Progress on the Investigation Phase of a Digital Euro—Fourth Report, https://www.ecb.europa.eu/paym/digital_euro/investigation/governance/shared/files/ecb.degov230713-fourth-progress-report-digital-euro-investigation-phase.en.pdf.
187. Cato Institute's 2023 CBDC National Survey, May 31, 2023, Survey Reports, Emily Ekins & Jordan Gygi, https://www.cato.org/survey-reports/poll-only-16-americans-support-government-issuing-central-bank-digital-currency.
188. New Inception Attack Leaks Sensitive Data from All AMD Zen CPUs, Bill Toulas, August 8, 2023, https://www.bleepingcomputer.com/news/security/new-inception-attack-leaks-sensitive-data-from-all-amd-zen-cpus/.
189. Daniel Moghimi, https://downfall.page.
190. CBDC Anti-Surveillance State Act, Tom Emmer, US Congress H.R. 5403, https://docs.house.gov/meetings/BA/BA00/20230920/116343/BILLS-118-HR5403-E000294-Amdt-12.pdf.
191. ECash Act, Stephen Lynch, US Congress H.R.5410, https://www.congress.gov/bill/118th-congress/house-bill/5410/text.
192. Senate Enrolled Act No. 468, Indiana Uniform Commercial Code Amendments, https://trackbill.com/bill/indiana-senate-bill-468-uniform-commercial-code-amendments/2321755/.
193. Citi GPS: Global Perspectives & Solutions, Future of Cross-Border Payments, September 2023.
194. American Cryptology During the Cold War, 1945–1989 Book III: Retrenchment and Reform, 1972–1980 by NSA, 1998, https://archive.org/details/cold_war_iii-nsa/cold_war_iii-ISCAP/page/n239/mode/2up.
195. Digital Euro—Privacy Options, Presentation by Eurogroup, https://www.ecb.europa.eu/paym/digital_euro/investigation/governance/shared/files/ecb.degov220404_privacy.es.pdf.

196. The cr.yp.to Blog, Daniel J. Bernstein, 2022.08.05: NSA, NIST, and Post-quantum Cryptography: Announcing My Second Lawsuit Against the U.S. Government, https://blog.cr.yp.to/20220805-nsa.html.
197. The cr.yp.to blog, Daniel J. Bernstein, 2023.10.03: The Inability to Count Correctly: Debunking NIST's Calculation of the Kyber-512 Security Level, https://blog.cr.yp.to/20231003-countcorrectly.html.
198. FSI Insights on Policy Implementation, No 4, Central Bank Digital Currencies: A New Tool in the Financial Inclusion Toolkit? Elements of Decentralisation: DLT and Token-Based Access Graph 9, p. 18.
199. BIS Papers No 136 A Growing Number of Central Banks Are Considering a Public-Private Partnership for a Potential Retail CBDC, Graph 10, p. 12.
200. 201. BIS Papers No 136, Making Headway—Results of the 2022 BIS Survey on Central Bank Digital Currencies and Crypto, Central Bank Involvement in CBDC Work Advances Further, Graph 2, p. 5.
201. BIS Annual Economic Report 2021, Table III.1, p. 76.
202. BIS Papers No 136 Central Bank Involvement in CBDC Work Advances Further, Graph 2, p. 5.
203. FSI Insights on Policy Implementation, No 4, Central Bank Digital Currencies: A New Tool in the Financial Inclusion Toolkit? CBDC Account/Wallet Tiers, Table 1, p. 21.
204. 205. Prodan, Silvana et al. "Exploring Consumer Sentiment on Central Bank Digital Currencies: A Twitter Analysis from 2021 to 2023." Proceedings of the International Conference on Business Excellence 17 (2023): 1085–1102.
205. BIS Annual Economic Report 2021, Table III.2, p. 82.
206. Exhibit from "On the Cusp of the Next Payments Era: Future Opportunities for Banks", September 2023, McKinsey & Company, www.mckinsey.com. Copyright (c) 2023 McKinsey & Company. All rights reserved. Reprinted by permission.

Index

L. V. Schumacher, *Decoding Digital Assets*, https://doi.org/10.1007/978-3-031-54601-3

J

K

L

M

N

O

GPSR Compliance

The European Union's (EU) General Product Safety Regulation (GPSR) is a set of rules that requires consumer products to be safe and our obligations to ensure this.

If you have any concerns about our products, you can contact us on ProductSafety@springernature.com

In case Publisher is established outside the EU, the EU authorized representative is:

Springer Nature Customer Service Center GmbH
Europaplatz 3
69115 Heidelberg, Germany

The manufacturer's authorised representative in the EU is Springer Nature Customer Service Centre GmbH, Europaplatz 3, 69115 Heidelberg, Germany. If you have any concerns regarding our products, please contact ProductSafety@springernature.com

Printed and bound by CPI Group (UK) Ltd, Croydon, CR0 4YY
28/09/2026
02224060-0015